WINGS *of*
COURAGE

OSPREY
PUBLISHING

WINGS *of* COURAGE

TALES FROM AMERICA'S ELITE FIGHTER
GROUPS OF WORLD WAR II

Editor
TONY HOLMES

First published in Great Britain in 2010 by Osprey Publishing,
Midland House, West Way, Botley, Oxford, OX2 0PH, UK
44-02 23rd Street, Suite 219, Long Island City, NY 11101, USA

E-mail: info@ospreypublishing.com

Material in this volume has previously been published as *354th Fighter Group*; *332nd Fighter Group*; *475th
Fighter Group*; and *Very Long Range P-51 Mustang Units.*

Every attempt has been made by the Publisher to secure the appropriate permissions for material
reproduced in this book. If there has been any oversight we will be happy to rectify the situation and
written submission should be made to the Publishers.

A CIP catalog record for this book is available from the British Library

Print ISBN: 978 1 84908 219 8

Page layout by: Myriam Bell Designs, France
Index by Fineline Editorial Services
Typeset in Myriad Pro and Perpetua
Originated by PDQ Media, Bungay, UK
Printed in China through Worldprint Ltd

10 11 12 13 14 10 9 8 7 6 5 4 3 2 1

Cover image by Gareth Hector, © Osprey Publishing.

For a catalog of all books published by Osprey Publishing please contact:

NORTH AMERICA
Osprey Direct, c/o Random House Distribution Center, 400 Hahn Road,
Westminster, MD 21157
E-mail: uscustomerservice@ospreypublishing.com

ALL OTHER REGIONS
Osprey Direct, The Book Service Ltd, Distribution Center, Colchester Road, Frating Green,
Colchester, Essex, CO7 7DW
E-mail: customerservice@ospreypublishing.com

Osprey Publishing is supporting the Woodland Trust, the UK's leading woodland conservation
charity, by funding the dedication of trees.

www.ospreypublishing.com

CONTENTS

Part Three
475TH FIGHTER GROUP: THE PACIFIC ELITE
John Stanaway

Part Four
15TH, 21ST AND 506TH FIGHTER GROUPS: THE TOKYO CLUB
Carl Molesworth

INTRODUCTION

In June 1932, the United States Army Air Corps (USAAC) could boast just four fighter squadrons. By VJ-Day, the United States Army Air Force (USAAF) could field 67 frontline fighter groups, each of which consisted of three fighter squadrons. The expansion of US airpower, fueled by global conflict, had been dramatic. Yet the fruits of America's war industry would have been useless had it not been for the highly skilled aviators strapped into the cockpits of Warhawks, Lightnings, Thunderbolts and Mustangs and sent aloft to combat the enemy in Western Europe, North Africa, the Mediterranean, the China/Burma/India theater and the Pacific.

USAAF pilots during World War II were intelligent young men in their late teens or early twenties, drawn to flying from all walks of life. They were the cream of their generation, as admission standards for pilot cadets were much more restrictive than for any other branch of the armed forces. Indeed, studies done in late 1942 had shown that for the USAAF to graduate 50,000 pilots annually, some 500,000 applicants would be needed to qualify for the 100,000 student places in the training program. The washout figure ran at 50 percent throughout the war, despite the desperate need for pilots for much of the conflict.

All of the pilots whose exploits fill the pages of this volume went through a similar training regime prior to reaching the frontline and taking the fight to the Luftwaffe, Regia Aeronautica, Japanese Army Air Force or the Imperial Japanese Naval Air Force. Aviation Cadets would undertake Primary training, Basic training and Advanced training at civilian- and military-run schools scattered across America's southern states. By the end of his course, which lasted six to eight months, the graduating cadet would boast around 200 flying hours in his logbook, as well as a similar total for ground-school instruction.

With his training completed, the tyro aviator was awarded his silver pilot's wings of the USAAF and given the rank of flight officer, or commissioned as a second lieutenant. Transition flying then followed, where the pilot learned to fly the type of aircraft he would be taking into combat. This lasted five weeks, and in that time pilots could expect to fly ten hours in a frontline type. Aerial gunnery was also introduced at this point. At the conclusion of transition training, pilots reported to unit training groups, where they were welded into fighting teams ready for service overseas. This tried and tested system duly produced 35,000 day-fighter crews between December 1942 and August 1945.

In the early war years the hastily trained cadet became a full-fledged fighter pilot in inferior types such as the P-39 Airacobra and early versions of the P-40 Warhawk. Attrition was very high, as they were thrown into action against better-trained and more combat-experienced enemy pilots flying vastly superior fighters. Forced to hold the line against great odds, the survivors of the dark days of World War II gained valuable experience that shaped them into the highly effective squadron and group leaders that headed the expanded USAAF in 1944–45.

By then considerably improved fighter types such as the P-38J/L Lightning, P-47D Thunderbolt and the P-51B/D Mustang were coming on line. Better-trained pilots were also emerging from the USAAF's flight schools, and once in the frontline they were given superior machinery to fly and effective leadership from combat veterans. This combination soon proved irresistible on all war fronts, as USAAF fighter groups inflicted telling losses on an enemy that could not offer its attrition replacements such extended training and a seemingly endless supply of advanced piston-engined aircraft.

The fighter groups featured in this book saw action in all the key combat theaters to which the USAAF was committed in World War II. As is to be expected, the principal American fighter types – the Warhawk, Lightning, Thunderbolt and Mustang – are the key players in this story. The exploits of a number of high-scoring aces are also included, two of whom, Maj Tommy McGuire of the 475th FG and Lt Col Jim Howard of the 354th FG, were awarded the Medal of Honor (America's highest combat decoration).

Each of the units profiled has its own distinctive claim to fame. The 354th FG was known at the "Pioneer Mustang Group" after it gave the Merlin-engined P-51 its combat debut in the European Theater of Operations in late 1943. By war's end 44 of its pilots had "made ace" and the group had been credited with downing 637 enemy aircraft.

The 332nd FG was the USAAF's one and only African-American fighter group. Part of the Tuskegee Experiment, it had been formed in 1942 by the USAAF in an attempt to prove that African-Americans were not capable of flying combat aircraft. The exploits of the unit quickly exploded this myth. Flying the Warhawk, Thunderbolt and Mustang from bases in North Africa and Italy, the 332nd claimed 111 aerial and 150 strafing victories. Both feared and respected by the enemy, the group never lost a bomber under escort to enemy attack – a feat unmatched by any other USAAF fighter group in World War II.

Formed with the best available fighter pilots in the Southwest Pacific, the Lightning-equipped 475th FG was the fastest-scoring group in-theater from the time it entered combat in August 1943 until VJ-Day. Fighting over Oro Bay, Rabaul, Hollandia, the Philippines and Luzon, the 475th produced some of the USAAF's leading aces as it totalled 552 aerial victories against the Japanese.

Finally, the exploits of the three USAAF Very Long Range P-51 units, which were involved in some of the very last aerial engagements of World War II, round out the book.

Dubbed the "Tokyo Club" by their pilots, the 15th, 21st and 506th FGs flew 1,300-mile round trips over the vast Pacific escorting B-29 Superfortresses as they attacked the Japanese home islands. Based on the tiny island of Iwo Jima, and braving extreme weather fronts, their job was to protect the "heavies" from Japanese fighters as they targeted Tokyo and other key cities between March and August 1945.

This volume offers a rare glimpse into the world of the USAAF fighter pilot in action against a determined enemy across the globe.

Tony Holmes

Part One
354TH **FIGHTER GROUP**

The Mustang Pioneers

GENESIS

The 354th Fighter Group (FG) was one of a number of new groups that were formed to reinforce the US Army Air Force, and enable it to fight in a myriad of combat theaters during the early days of World War II. The 354th was formed at Hamilton Field, California, on November 15, 1942. Its initial commander was Maj Kenneth Martin, a softly spoken pilot from Missouri, whose intensity saw that the group got off to a good start, which in turn held it in good stead when it came time for the unit to enter combat. The squadrons of the 354th were the 353rd, 355th and 356th FSs.

Martin selected his new squadron commanders carefully. The 356th FS was headed by Capt Charles Johnson, who had already seen combat in the Philippines and during the defense of Port Moresby in New Guinea, where he had been wounded in action. His unit was duly nicknamed the "Red Ass" squadron, and its insignia took the form of a bucking red donkey. This sobriquet would later prove most apt, for pilots in the European Theater of Operations (ETO) routinely suffered from "red asses" following hours sat on rock-hard parachute packs (enhanced by a deflated rubber liferaft) whilst performing long-range escort missions in their P-51s!

The 355th FS was headed by Capt George Bickell, who had ventured to the Pacific in June 1942 and had flown a Curtiss P-40 off the US Navy aircraft carrier USS *Saratoga* when his 73rd FS was assigned to the island of Midway to compensate for the loss of the fighters in the battle that had taken place there a few days earlier. Having seen the destruction at Midway and Pearl Harbor at first hand, Bickell was champing at the bit to see combat action. His 355th FS became the "Pugnacious Pups," as depicted by the invulnerable bulldog on its insignia. Finally, the CO of the 353rd FS was Maj Owen Seaman, whose squadron adopted the nickname the "Flying Cobras," depicted by a coiled, ready-to-strike Asian reptile. Little did the initial members of the squadron imagine how lethal their unit would become.

On January 18, 1943, the newly formed 354th FG found itself on its way to Tonopah, Nevada. It had been thought that the new base would be complete by the time the group arrived, but all that was present were the windswept runways. Tents were soon erected and new pilots began to turn up, most of whom were fresh out of flying school at Luke Field, Arizona, where they had graduated on North American AT-6 Texan advanced trainers.

The 354th FG's initial equipment consisted of the Bell P-39N Airacobra, which was a "hot ship" for green pilots fresh out of training school. Possessing a top speed of over 330mph, and blessed with a high degree of maneuverability, the Bell fighter's primary oddity was the fact that the engine was mounted to the rear of the pilot, with the propeller shaft passing forward under the cockpit. The fighter had been bought by the Army Air Force without the supercharger recommended by the manufacturer, resulting in the P-39's performance drastically tailing off at ceilings in excess of 12,000ft. This in turn made the aircraft unsuitable for air-to-air combat, hence its allocation to newly formed Stateside fighter groups such as the 354th FG.

Aside from its poor altitude performance, the P-39 had also developed a reputation for being tricky to handle in the air. Indeed, if not flown with due care whilst maneuvering hard (during a dogfight, for example), it had a way of putting a pilot into a flat spin from which most did not recover. Unfortunately this was the fate that befell one of the 354th's young pilots during the group's first days of training. This problem also cost the outfit one of its original squadron COs when, on February 6, 1943, Capt Charles Johnson took off in a newly delivered P-39 and got himself into a flat spin from which he did not recover. He was replaced as CO of the 356th FS by Capt Richard Neece.

Maj Kenneth Martin almost fell victim to the P-39's spinning characteristics as well, although he was skilled enough to discover a technique for recovering the aircraft. Having taken the Airacobra up to 19,000ft to perform some aggressive maneuvering, he blacked out when his oxygen system failed. When he regained consciousness at 5,000ft, Martin found himself in a flat spin. Struggling to recover, he tried various methods with no result until he shoved the stick fully forward and kicked hard opposite rudder. The aircraft pulled out of its dive.

In late February 1943 the 353rd and 356th FSs, along with Group Headquarters, moved to Santa Rosa, California – the 355th FS went to Hayward, California. Training continued, with some air-to-air gunnery sorties being flown against tow targets during the period. However, there was so much rain and fog in Santa Rosa that training was hampered.

Capt Neece departed the 356th FS in May 1943, and he was replaced by Maj James H. Howard, a former US Navy fighter pilot who had resigned his commission in June 1941 in order to fly with the American Volunteer Group (AVG). Howard was a veteran of extensive combat against the Japanese over China and Burma, and had been credited with 2.333 aerial victories and four strafing kills flying P-40C/Es. His pilots found him to be quite a taskmaster, but they were truly inspired by his teaching, as recounted here by future ace Richard E. Turner in his autobiography, *Mustang Pilot*:

The assumption of command by Howard gave the squadron a tremendous boost. The enthusiasm and eagerness kindled under Johnson burned brightly again, for here was a commander whose skill was legendary, and whose superior leadership was soon amply demonstrated. Howard initiated a program of training in mutual support tactics as practiced and proven in combat by the Flying Tigers in China. His insistence upon perfection resulted in an aggressive, well-tempered fighting squadron, finely tuned to the anticipated conditions of actual combat.

The 353rd FS moved to Portland, Oregon, in May 1943, and it was followed there by the 355th FS the following month. June also brought a movement by the 356th FS, which now found itself based in Salem, Oregon. From this time forward the pilots of the 354th FG filled their time with formation flying, and learning gunnery, dive-bombing, skip-bombing and strafing tactics. Men were lost in flying accidents during this period, but with the torrid pace of their training such fatalities were inevitable. Pilots were not only becoming honed for the job that lay ahead, they were also building up flying time which would stand them in good stead during the many combat missions that would follow.

By September the group was beginning to undergo inspections to determine its degree of readiness, and in early October orders were received at group HQ instructing the 354th to head for Camp Kilmer, in New Jersey. Trains were duly boarded by group personnel on the 6th, bound for the east coast. The journey to England had begun at last.

MUSTANGS!

On the morning of October 21, 1943, the men of the 354th FG departed the USA aboard the British army transport HMS *Athlone Castle*. Later that day the vessel joined a convoy for the trip to England. The journey was memorable only for its inconveniences and boredom, with lots of gambling and poor food being the memories of note for most of the pilots during the 12-day passage. And following the ship's arrival at Liverpool, disembarkation was delayed for three days due to heavy fog.

Early on November 4 the men boarded a train for Greenham Common, in Berkshire. There they viewed hardstands, taxiways and two 6,000ft runways, but no aircraft. On the way over there had been much speculation as to what aircraft the men would fly on their arrival. Most felt that in view of what was already being utilized, they would probably be outfitted with Republic P-47 Thunderbolts. Others felt that they might get Lockheed P-38 Lightnings. Summing up the feeling of most pilots in the 354th at this stage in the war, Richard Turner remembers that, "our eagerness to get a piece of the action was such by now that we would have been happy to take our old beat-up P-39s into the middle of hell!"

Unbeknown to the men of the 354th, their dilemma was being solved during their voyage at the very highest levels of the Army Air Force. A new version of the North

American P-51 Mustang had just entered production, and the initial aircraft were destined for England. The new P-51B was fitted with the Packard-built Rolls-Royce Merlin 61 engine, which was not a "gas guzzler" and provided the aircraft with a very long range. Not only that, it was fitted with a two-stage, high-altitude supercharger which gave it the capability to fly as far as any American heavy bomber then in service, and to engage the Luftwaffe's best fighters at the higher ceilings favored by the enemy.

The shortcomings of the P-51A with its original Allison engine had relegated the aircraft to low-altitude tactical work, and it was already being utilized by two tactical reconnaissance units in the Eighth Air Force. For this reason new Mustangs destined for England were intended for the Ninth Tactical Air Force. However, when Gen H. H. "Hap" Arnold, Chief of the Army Air Forces, was told of the capabilities of the new P-51B by the commander of VIII Fighter Command, Maj Gen William Kepner, he decided that this was the aircraft needed by the Eighth Air Force for use as a long-range escort for his beleaguered bombers.

Gen Ira Eaker then worked out a plan whereby the Merlin Mustangs would be assigned to the Ninth Air Force for administration, but operationally they would be assigned to his Eighth Air Force. Thus, the 354th was the first unit in England to operate the P-51B, and it would remain under Eighth Air Force control operationally until its transfer to the Ninth Air Force became a tactical necessity following the D-Day landings.

Gen Elwood "Pete" Quesada, who had been appointed Commander of IX Fighter Command, immediately turned his attention to the arrival and equipment of the 354th FG. There was one firm commitment that had to be determined. Quesada asked Lt Col Martin how long it would take him to have his unit ready for ops. Martin replied, "Two weeks." The 354th would have only until December 1, 1943 to attain combat readiness.

When this was announced to the pilots of the 354th they were ecstatic. Here was a brand-new fighter that could do 440mph at 30,000ft, could maneuver with anything in the air and had the range to go anywhere the bombers could go. Transition began immediately, but the only aircraft the group had to start out on were a handful of old P-51As loaned from the tactical reconnaissance units. Finally, on November 11, five new aircraft were received, and two days later the group moved to Boxted, on the Suffolk–Essex border. Here, the men found a typical British base with runways, taxiways, hardstands and a hangar. Engineering and operations buildings, as well as mess and housing units, took the form of Nissen huts. The 354th would stay here until April 17, 1944.

The new Mustangs came in slowly and the pilots and groundcrews busied themselves getting the aircraft checked out, and working on any problems that arose. The few technical hitches that were found in the P-51B had to be eradicated before the aircraft could be declared combat-ready. There were no technical manuals available at the time, so things had to be worked out by trial and error. One immediate problem centered on the fact that the nuts and bolts within the Merlin engine were metric, which meant that the wrenches and sockets brought over from America by the groundcrews did not fit! Tools were quickly sourced from the RAF.

Only 24 combat-ready P-51Bs had arrived by the last day of November, when Gen Lewis Brereton, Commander of the Ninth Air Force, visited Boxted. On his departure it was announced that the 354th FG would fly its first mission the following day.

INTO THE ARENA

The initial missions of the 354th FG were led by Lt Col Donald Blakeslee, a veteran combat pilot and ace from the 4th FG. He had started out with the Royal Canadian Air Force (RCAF), and then transferred to the Royal Air Force (RAF) before joining one of the American "Eagle" squadrons prior to their induction into the USAAF in September 1942. Mission No 1 was flown on December 1, 1943.

Blakeslee's briefing covered the vital points to be instilled in the pilots before they ventured over enemy territory for the first time. Also discussed were some of the basic rules relating to air-to-air combat should the Luftwaffe be encountered. One of those most emphasized by Blakeslee was the head-on pass. The veteran Spitfire and Thunderbolt pilot told the novices that never under any conditions did an American pilot break during the closure between the two aircraft. One of the listeners asked the question, "What do you do if the enemy pilot doesn't break?" Blakeslee replied curtly, "Son, you will just have earned your flight pay the hard way."

Shortly thereafter 24 Mustangs, led by Blakeslee, with Lt Col Martin on his wing, took off. As they climbed to altitude through heavy cloud the airplanes headed for Belgium and the Pas-de-Calais area in France. After only an hour and twenty minutes aloft, the Mustangs were back on the ground. Only one thing marred the first mission – some flak holes suffered by one of the P-51s.

Mission No 2 did not take place until December 5, when 36 Mustangs (along with 34 P-38s and no fewer than 266 P-47s) flew their first bomber support mission escorting 452 B-17s and 96 B-24s to the Amiens area of France. Weather prevented the bulk of the bombers from reaching their target, and there were no casualties amongst the 354th FG. Mission No 3 (on December 11) saw 44 P-51s winging their way over Germany for the first time, escorting 583 bombers to Emden. All went well until Lt Norman Hall of the 353rd FS was spotted spiraling down into the undercast during the return leg. No word from him was ever heard.

On December 13 the "Pioneer Mustang Group," as the 354th now called itself, sortied 41 P-51Bs to the German port of Kiel to "ride herd" on 710 "Big Friends." As the group headed home Lt Glenn T. Eagleston, who was flying mutual support with Lt Wallace Emmer, sighted a Messerschmitt Bf 110 about 3,000ft below and off to starboard. Eagleston peeled off and made four passes at the twin-engined fighter. His first pass was from 90 degrees, closing to dead astern. No results were observed, and the enemy fighter went into a tight 360-degree turn slightly down as the rear gunner returned the P-51 pilot's fire. The second pass silenced the gunner as strikes were made on the fuselage. Pass number three set the right engine on fire with parts flying off. On the final pass from dead astern Eagleston's guns jammed – a common problem with the B-model Mustang. The Bf 110 was last seen in a shallow glide with the engine still burning as it entered the undercast. Eagleston had to settle for a "probably destroyed." There was one loss on the mission, when Lt Buford Eaves failed to return. He was later reported as a prisoner of war (PoW).

Lt Col Blakeslee was leading the group again on December 16, with 39 Mustangs helping to provide penetration support for 631 bombers attacking the German city of Bremen. This time the 354th scored its first confirmed victory when Lt Charles F. Gumm sighted Bf 109s queuing up to the rear of some Fortresses. He later reported:

> Lt Talbot and I climbed after them, and when within 400 yards range two of the enemy aircraft saw us and broke left and straight down. We closed on the other two and I dropped back a little to cover Lt Talbot's tail, but the enemy saw him and broke left and down. By then I was almost in a position to fire on my '109, which was still flying straight for the bombers. Lt Talbot pulled up and to the right to cover my tail while I closed to about 100 yards and fired a two-second burst, noticing no effects. I then closed to about 59 yards and fired a three-second burst, noticing a thin trail of smoke coming from the right side of the engine. I fired again at very close range and was showered with smoke and oil and pieces which I pulled up through and glanced back to see the fighter going down to the left with a large plume of smoke coming from the right side of the engine. Then I looked for Lt Talbot again, and saw him chasing an Fw 190, with another '190 closing on him. I went down after the latter fighter and they both broke straight down and away, so we went back to the bombers.

Lt Col Martin led the next mission to be flown by the 354th FG, on December 20, which saw the group head for Bremen and Wilhelmshaven once again. This time the fighter force ran into heavy opposition as the Luftwaffe sortied all manner of aircraft in an attempt to repel the 546-strong bomber force. Maj Jim Howard spotted three Bf 109s off to one side of the formation, making passes at the bombers. One attacked from the port side and then pulled up under a B-17, presenting Howard with the opportunity to close in on the German fighter from about four o'clock. Whilst still out of range he fired a burst to scare his opponent, and then closed on him as the Bf 109 pilot tried to position himself for another attack.

Shoving the throttle fully forward, Howard rapidly closed from dead astern, and a two-second burst from his four .50cal Brownings struck the Messerschmitt, which began to emit heavy black smoke. Lt H. B. Smith, Howard's wingman, reported seeing pieces fly off the Bf 109 before it exploded and fell away in an uncontrollable vertical dive.

Three other Bf 109s were destroyed during the course of the mission, including one claimed by Lt Col Blakeslee. However, the 354th had in turn lost three pilots, including the CO of the 353rd FS, Maj Owen Seaman. A veteran of combat in the Pacific, Seaman had been forced to ditch his Mustang in the North Sea after it had suffered engine failure. He was never seen again after his fighter hit the water. Capt Robert Priser, an ex-RCAF and RAF pilot, replaced Seaman as CO of the 353rd FS.

The next action of note for the group took place on a mission to Ludwigshafen on December 30, when scattered enemy opposition was encountered. The interception of these fighters did not go as well as planned, however, and the Mustang pilots were only able claim a single Dornier Do 217 destroyed – the credit for the bomber's destruction was shared between four pilots. In return two pilots were lost when Lt Hays Appell of the 356th FS and Lt Bill Turner of the 355th collided over Germany. Parachutes were sighted coming from both aircraft and the pilots were duly taken prisoner.

The 354th closed the year by escorting bombers returning from targets in France on the 31st. Upon arriving over enemy territory, the P-51 pilots spotted a straggling B-17 that was coming under attack from three Bf 109s. The group's leading flight quickly closed on the enemy and two fighters were downed, with Lt Col Martin sharing in one of the victories.

THE MUSTANGS GALLOP

There were important changes made in the high command of the Eighth Air Force in early January 1944, and these drastically altered the role of the escorting fighter groups. With the invasion of France an objective for the new year, it was mandatory that the Allies gain air superiority before the assault on "Fortress Europe" could be successfully consummated. When Gen Dwight Eisenhower was chosen to head up the supreme command overseeing the invasion forces, he picked his own commanders, including those of the USAAF in England. Gen Jimmy Doolittle was chosen to take command of the Eighth Air Force, replacing Gen Ira Eaker.

When Gen Doolittle took over the Eighth Air Force, the primary objective of the fighters became that of engaging the Luftwaffe and destroying it, rather than staying exclusively with the bombers to ensure their protection. This meant that VIII Fighter Command, still headed by Gen William Kepner, was able to despatch fighters out in front of the bomber stream as a blocking force. A fighter group could also pursue the enemy away from the bomber stream if its leader believed they could be successful, and it would not result in the bombers suffering excessive losses.

The 354th FG was now up to full strength, as it was fully equipped with new aircraft and the pilots to fly them. Bad weather held up operations for the first few days of the month until January 4, when Maj Bickell led 42 Mustangs to Kiel in support of 569 bombers. High winds over the North Sea prevented the 354th's timely rendezvous with the bombers, and the fighters joined them late after they had already fought off numerous enemy attacks. The Luftwaffe was finally engaged near Cuxhaven, some 65 miles southwest of the target, and one German fighter was downed. However, the 354th also suffered a loss when Lt John Nall was last seen chasing a Junkers Ju 88 down through the undercast.

The group enjoyed far more success 24 hours later, when Maj Howard led 41 P-51s back to Kiel. As the 245-strong bomber stream (protected by 111 fighters) neared the target, the weather cleared, and the crews could see for miles over a landscape covered with snow. German fighters remained conspicuous by their absence until the first of the bombers turned for home. Suddenly, a formation of some 45–50 twin-engined Bf 110s and Do 217s appeared.

One of the first Mustang pilots to effect an interception was Lt Warren S. "Red" Emerson of the 355th FS, who had become separated from his flight. Attacking alone, he did not hesitate to close on six rocket-firing Bf 110s. Emerson opened fire from about 200 yards and attained good strikes on one of the Messerschmitts, shattering the canopy and causing one of its engines to smoke heavily. The fighter went down in an ever-steepening dive, allowing Emerson to claim it as probably destroyed.

He then climbed back up to 25,000ft and began to close on another four Bf 110s. Going in with guns blazing, Emerson destroyed one of the enemy aircraft and sent the others scattering. About three minutes later he was engaged with another three enemy fighters, and this time his Mustang was hit by a shell which badly damaged the aircraft, severing its hydraulic lines. Emerson was also struck by a shell fragment which deeply gashed his neck and cut through his parachute harness. Just when it appeared as if the Mustang pilot would be shot down, he was rescued by Lt Wallace Emmer of the 353rd FS. Although out of ammunition, the latter pilot attacked the enemy aircraft and succeeded in scattering them. The 356th FS's Lt Richard E. Turner was also in the thick of things that day, as his combat report reveals:

I was flying Starstud Green No 1, with Lt Stolzle as No 2, Lt Goodnight No 3 and Lt Miller No 4. We were despatched to cover a middle box of bombers with Starstud Blue Flight. Upon turning to starboard, we contacted a Dornier 217 [almost certainly a Bf 110 – Editor] lining up to the rear of the bomber formation. I tried to come on line astern but overshot the turn, and Lt Goodnight, with his wingman, closed on the Do 217. I pulled up and called Lt Stolzle, telling him to drop belly tanks, after which I spotted a Do 217 trying to sneak in on the bombers, so I closed in from above and fired at approximately 300 yards, observing strikes on both sides of the fuselage. I continued to close fast and continued firing in bursts of varying lengths. One engine caught fire and started trailing black smoke, and then I observed the right engine blow up in a large flash of flame. The Do 217, out of control, floundered down in a slow spiral. I claim it destroyed.

I then pulled up and took a quick burst at another Do 217, passing overhead, but observed no strikes. I then turned on another which might have been the same as the above and followed it down in a twisting turning dive from almost dead astern. I observed strikes but no results. I pulled up in a climbing turn and saw another Do 217 and started after it. At this time I saw tracers fly over my right wing. I looked back and found an Me 110 on my tail instead of Lt Stolzle. I pulled my stick back as far as I could and shot up, stalling out over the Me 110, who in turn shot under me while trying to pull up. Instead, he pushed his nose down and my plane fell through in a stall loop by itself and came out behind the '110's tail. I was very close, and fired at zero degrees deflection and saw strikes around the cockpit. Its right engine also caught fire. After I ceased firing I saw the canopy fly off and a round object came into view, which I assumed was the pilot bailing out. I almost collided at this point so I pulled up and away.

I then saw a single-engined plane some 5,000ft above me, and I climbed after it to join formation, for I was almost out of ammunition – my right guns were by then the only ones still functioning. Coming up under the single-engined plane, I observed it to be blue-gray instead of dark brown, so I closed to identify it from beneath and behind. I saw the crosses on the fuselage – an Me 109. I tried to line up astern for a shot, but had to be content with 15 degrees deflection to the left with only 20 or 30 rounds coming out, which expended my supply of ammunition. I was glad to see the '109 split-ess down and away, so I climbed out hunting for a '51 to come home with.

Lt Col Martin was also involved in the big shootout, and on his third interception of the day he reported:

Another Me 110 came into view and I closed to 200 yards, firing at the fuselage and right engine, which burst into flames. Lt Lane closed in and also fired, causing further damage. The rear gunner appeared dead and the pilot bailed out. The fighter was seen to crash by Lts Welden and Lane.

Future 5.25-kill ace Lt Tommy "Gnomee" Miller from Turner's flight also shot up two of the Bf 110s, severely damaging them. He was credited with a probable victory for the first fighter and a definite kill for the second one. His post-mission report stated:

I was Starstud Green No 4. Lt Goodnight, my element leader, made a steep right turn, coming in behind a Do 217. I dropped back to cover him and a '110 came up behind Goodnight. I closed to 300 yards dead astern on this E/A [enemy aircraft] and fired a one-second burst. I observed strikes on its belly between the engines. The E/A rolled over and started down, but before reaching the vertical he righted himself and I observed one 'chute open. The E/A then started a steep diving turn and I did not see him recover.

As I pulled up from the first encounter, I saw another '110 600 yards ahead and to the right. I closed to 400 yards and fired three short bursts – I observed no hits. On the fourth burst the left engine threw out an intense cloud of white smoke and large pieces flew off. The E/A then did a half-roll and started down with his left engine out. I closed to 150 yards and got in two more bursts. As he hung there upside-down, I observed strikes on the right engine, and a number of pieces were falling off. I then saw strikes on his elevator and a large section of that flew off too. As I pulled up over him, he was floating along upside-down with both engines on fire.

When the final tally was counted for the day, the 354th "Pioneer Mustang Group" had chalked up 14 confirmed victories without loss, an outstanding accomplishment for a group on only its 12th mission. The next meeting with the Luftwaffe took place on January 11, when Maj Howard led the group to Halberstadt (where a plant producing parts for the Ju 88 was sited) and Oschersleben (home of a large Fw 190 factory). VIII Fighter Command felt sure that these raids would provoke a response from the Luftwaffe, and indeed they did. Maj Howard reported:

Our group was assigned to the first boxes of bombers to provide target support. When we rendezvoused with the bombers from the rear, being unable to determine where the first box was, I despatched two squadrons to cover the rear boxes. At this time I received a call from Goldsmith 12, who stated that the forward boxes were being attacked. Starstud squadron was sent to the forward box, arriving at 1130hrs. I later discovered that this was where all the activity was centered, but at the time was unable to do anything about it, except use what we had to best advantage. The bombers passed over the targets and bombed, by which time it was 1150hrs.

We then met our first E/A. Flights of Starstud were despatched to deal with various attacking E/A and I also began attacking with my flight. On the first encounter, which tuned into a melee, my flight lost me.

When I regained bomber altitude, I discovered that I was alone and in the vicinity of Goldsmith 12 and Goldsmith 15. It was here that I spent approximately a half-hour chasing and scaring away attacking enemy aircraft from 20,000 down to 15,000ft. There was one box of B-17s in particular that seemed to be under pressed attack by single-engined and twin-engined aircraft. There were twenty-odd bombers in a very compact formation. The attacking E/A were working individually. I could see from my position that each box was being harassed by attackers, but the majority of them were out of range for me. I had to choose the most opportune target and dive on him before he was able to get within range of the bombers. I had five combat encounters within this period of half an hour.

Each time I would climb back up to bomber level, only to find another E/A tooling up for an attack. I was quite busy in a constant merry-go-round of climbing and diving on attackers, sometimes not firing my guns but presenting a good enough bluff for them to break off and dive away. For the first encounters and combat, all four guns fired. On the third I had two guns and on the fourth and fifth encounter only one gun. When I got down to one gun I was still engaged in this dive, attack and climb game for another two or three attacks. The E/A seemed reluctant to stay and fight, and would dive out.

The reason for no other friendly aircraft being in the vicinity, or with me, was that the Starstud squadron had been sent off to deal with attackers, and the remaining two squadrons were engaged covering the boxes in the rear. I would say that there were about 100-plus engaging enemy aircraft throughout all the boxes during this period. It's hard to estimate the number of enemy aircraft present during the major portion of this running fight, but all the boxes I could see had some activity around them.

We were supposed to be with the bombers for an hour, and had already gone over that time. Had the relieving force of friendly fighters arrived and made rendezvous on time, it would have been possible to bag many more. But, using what we had on hand to a good advantage, I believe we came out on top with a very impressionable score.

On his return from the mission Maj Howard modestly claimed two fighters destroyed, two probably destroyed and two damaged as his score for the day. Leading the 353rd FS on the 11th was future 15-kill ace Lt Jack T. Bradley, who recounted his day's activities as follows:

I was leading the squadron formation. We rendezvoused with the bombers at about 1115hrs at 23,000ft near Minden. The group leader despatched our squadron to cover the last three boxes into the target area. I assigned "Blue Flight" to the right of the boxes, "White Flight" to the left and "Red Flight," of which I was the leader, to the rear – all members of "Green Flight" had previously aborted. We effected target cover uneventfully until about 1145hrs. At this time "Blue Leader" called "bandit at the rear of bomber formation." I observed an Me 110 out of range but closing on our "Big Friends" from astern.

As my flight was in better position for attack than the other two, I peeled off to intercept the Me 110. As the flight dived towards the E/A, he broke down and to port. I fired a short burst from 45 degrees deflection at 400 yards, closing to 230 yards at approximately 15 degrees with only two guns in operation – one gun had jammed almost immediately. I thought that I had hit him, but the range was too great for me to positively claim that I had damaged him. When last seen, the E/A was in a steep dive, doing approximately 500mph indicated. I observed an explosion on the side of a hill directly in the line of flight of the E/A shortly thereafter.

My flight rejoined the bombers on the starboard side of the formation. At about 1210hrs I saw two Fw 190s about 3,000ft above and approximately half a mile to starboard. I dived to the right to get directly beneath them and started to climb with everything forward. I later learned that at this point my second element left formation to engage an Me 110. The Fw 190s were in trail about 100 yards apart at about 23,000ft.

I closed fast to about 100 yards on the rear E/A, opening fire with about 15 degrees deflection. The E/A seemed to shudder momentarily and immediately burst into flames – I believe he exploded as I passed him, as some force jarred my aircraft rather violently.

By now in range of the lead E/A, I held my fire until I was just 50 yards astern, pulling slightly to one side for small deflection. I fired a short burst and the E/A caught fire. As the pilot attempted to split-ess, I caught him with a second burst while he was on his back, nose down. I broke left to clear my tail and was rejoined by my wingman, who had been on my tail. The E/A was last seen engulfed in flame in a vertical dive. I signaled my wingman into mutual support, and we continued to provide target cover.

The 355th FS was also very busy, as future 13-kill ace Lt Robert Stephens reported:

I saw a straggler being attacked by three Me 410s. Picking out one of the '410s as my target, I worked in behind him. He saw me and started a steep spiral down. Following him, I gave him a few short bursts. Observing no strikes, I pulled off him at 12,000ft. I circled around once more and saw that the same '410 was climbing back up toward the box of bombers. I waited for him and got behind him, this time unnoticed. With only one gun firing, I shot several long bursts before I saw strikes on his left engine nacelle. Then the engine blew up and the plane caught fire. I closed in, still firing, and observed more strikes all over the fuselage. Pulling up so as to avoid running into him, I rolled left to see the entire '410 engulfed in flames.

On their return to Boxted the pilots were exuberant. Most of them had fired their guns in anger, and even though a number of pilots had failed to down an aircraft, many had at least damaged one. The overall confirmed score did not come through for some days, but when it was finalized the total was 16 destroyed, 7 probably destroyed and 19 damaged!

However, the biggest story of January 11, 1944 did not break until the men of the 401st Bombardment Group (BG) found out who their "saviour" was that day – Maj Jim Howard was traced through the "buzz letters" on his aircraft. A few days later things were spelled out more clearly when a letter arrived for Maj Howard from Col Harold W. Bowman, CO of the 401st BG. In his letter he stated:

> Your unprecedented action in flying your P-51 alone and unaided into a swarm of German fighter planes, estimated between 30 and 40, in an effort to protect our Fortresses in the target area is a feat deserving of the highest commendation and praise. The fact that the odds were overwhelmingly against you, and that you had no hope of receiving assistance in your unusual struggle, did not deter you in your determination to engage the enemy.
>
> The magnificent fight which you put up in the ensuing struggle was one which has elicited the praise and admiration of every one of the Fortress fliers who witnessed your actions. Members of this Group, returning from the operation, were lavish in their descriptions of the way you shot down enemy planes and, in particular, spoke in glowing terms of the attempts you made to protect the Combat Wing against attacks.

The men of the Fortresses would confirm at least six victories for Howard, but the modest flier did not choose to do so. Regardless, the crews of the 401st recommended Maj Jim Howard for the Medal of Honor, which he received a few weeks later. Embarrassed with all the laudatory action by the bomber men, and the press when interviewed regarding his action, Howard would only say, "I seen my duty and I done it." Maj Jim Howard was the sole American fighter pilot flying in northwestern Europe to be awarded his nation's highest honor. There was no immediate repeat of the 354th's great success as bad weather came in and kept the P-51s on the ground for the next few days.

One of the biggest problems that the Mustang pilots were encountering during this period was the jamming of their fighters' machine guns. It was found that this was due to the fact that the guns were canted at an angle. When the aircraft was being maneuvered violently while in combat, the ammunition did not feed cleanly into the guns. This was finally rectified when one of the maintenance men obtained some electric ammunition feed motors that were being used on Martin B-26 bombers to feed ammunition from the boxes to the aircraft's guns. These also seemed to work fine in the P-51, so all the Boxted fighters were quickly modified.

The 354th did not go back out until January 14, when Maj Bickell led 43 Mustangs (out of a force of 645 fighters, escorting 552 bombers) to the Pas-de-Calais area of France. Only one victory was scored, and the group also lost a pilot to causes unknown. Bad weather then moved in once more, and the group enjoyed a seven-day vacation from operations.

The 354th sortied again on January 21, when all three squadrons escorted bombers returning to targets along the French coast – no German aircraft were encountered by the group. Three days later, newly promoted Col Martin led the group to Frankfurt, and although limited action was seen, a skirmish with four Fw 190s near Brussels cost the 353rd FS its commander, Capt Robert Priser. He had served with the RAF before joining the 354th, and he, along with Capt Joseph Giltner who was on a temporary assignment to the group from the 357th FG, was downed by the Focke-Wulf fighters. Young Texan Capt Jack T. Bradley (one of the original members of the group) became the new CO of the 353rd FS.

Maj Howard led 40 Mustangs to Frankfurt on January 29, where they sighted a number of Luftwaffe fighters in the air but were unable to close with most of them. On the way home the enemy was engaged in the vicinity of Kirchberg, and four Fw 190s were shot down and two probably destroyed without loss.

The following day Maj Howard led the group to Brunswick and once again, soon after leaving the target, large numbers of twin-engined fighters turned up and were engaged. Howard went after one of the Bf 110s, which he later described as, "a nightfighter version with radar antenna on the nose." The Mustang pilot opened fire and his opposite number made a violent diving turn to the right. He entered the undercast before Howard could close any further.

The major then sighted a straggling B-17 with a Bf 110 closing on its rear. As the enemy aircraft started firing at the bomber, the P-51 pilot closed to within range and opened up with his four "fifties." Firing commenced at about 300 yards, and continued until Howard had to pull up to avoid a collision. The Bf 110 rolled to the left and headed down for the clouds. A fire started near the fuselage, and before the fighter had reached the undercast flames could be seen pouring out from one of its engines.

Newly promoted Capt Richard Turner also observed a straggler being harassed, although this time the bomber's tormentors took the form of four Bf 109s. He immediately led his flight down to attack the Messerschmitts, and three of them broke for the clouds. The fourth fighter continued with his attack, however, as Turner recounted:

I dropped 30 degrees of flaps to keep from overrunning. I opened fire at about 200 yards at zero degrees deflection. I saw that my fire was going underneath the '109, so I raised the pip, whereupon the fighter exploded. The Me 109 broke up immediately in front of me, so I flew through it. I turned into the sun and picked up my flight.

Altogether, five enemy fighters fell to the guns of the 354th that day for no losses. The new year had started well for the group, January seeing the "Pioneer Mustang Group" credited with 42 official victories for the loss of just three pilots. And not only did Maj Jim Howard win the Medal of Honor, he also became the first P-51 ace, and the first ace of the group, when he scored his fifth victory on January 30.

MISFORTUNE AND "BIG WEEK"

The 354th FG continued to fly bomber escort missions in February, Col Ken Martin leading 50 Mustangs to Wilhelmshaven on the 3rd, although the group saw little action. Nonetheless, the P-51 flown by Lt Richard Klien was lost when its engine froze up due to a leaking oil line. The pilot was forced to bail out over the North Sea, some 14 miles east of Southwold in Suffolk. The water was bitterly cold at this time of year, and he was given little chance of survival. However, Klien was lucky, for he was picked up by a German naval vessel and made a PoW.

Subsequent missions on February 4, 5 and 6 saw no aerial action, but this all changed on the 8th. Word had come down from Eighth Air Force Headquarters to the effect that fighter escorts returning from missions where the bombers were not being harassed could "hit the deck" and strafe opportunist targets. Maj Howard had led 41 Mustangs to Frankfurt that day, and after clearing the target area, he had given his pilots permission to get strafing. The men shot up locomotives, airfields and any other targets of interest they could locate. However, flak around most German airfields was very intense, and four pilots were lost. A disturbed Col Martin declared a halt to the strafing action until further notice.

One of the most frustrating, and potentially deadly, threats that the group had had to face from the beginning of its operations in the ETO was attacks made on its aircraft by P-47s and, at times, P-38s. Unfortunately, the silhouette of the P-51 closely resembled that of the Bf 109, and although Mustangs had visited all VIII Fighter Command bases so that pilots could view the aircraft close-up, the attacks continued. And just such an incident during the 354th's mission to Brunswick on February 10 almost cost them one of their most outstanding pilots.

Some 30 Bf 109s and around 50 twin-engined fighters had come up to oppose the bombers, resulting in numerous engagements taking place during the course of the mission. Col Martin was credited with a Bf 109 and an "Me 210" (actually a Bf 110), and altogether the 354th downed eight fighters for the loss of a single P-51. Upon returning to Boxted, the pilots reported that whilst trying to deal with Luftwaffe attacks, they had encountered considerable trouble from numerous P-47s – and there were plenty of them in the skies over Germany on this day, with 357 Thunderbolts from eight groups having sortied to Brunswick!

For example, Lt Glenn Eagleston and Lt Edward Regis had joined in a combat between some P-47s and Bf 109s, with Eagleston quickly latching onto one of the Messerschmitts. Having damaged his prey, the Mustang pilot was on the point of finishing off the fighter when his P-51B was attacked by a Thunderbolt.

In the ensuing melee, Lt Regis managed to down a second Bf 109, but Eagleston's victim escaped when his aircraft was badly damaged by one of the P-47s. The future ace's Mustang had sustained a bad hit in its oil system, and began to hemorrhage precious lubrication fluid as it headed back across the English Channel. Fortunately for Eagleston, he was able to make landfall and bail out just miles from Boxted at Ardleigh. Descending by parachute during a heavy snowfall, Eagleston landed amongst a group of Home Guard men, who duly drove him back to his base.

The next day, February 11, the 354th notched up its 25th mission when Col Martin led 38 Mustangs that were tasked with escorting 223 B-17s sent to hit targets in Frankfurt, Ludwigshafen and Saarbrücken. This date was doubly significant, for it also saw the Eighth Air Force's first permanently assigned Mustang group, the 357th FG, complete a "milk run" to France. The group was led by none other than Maj Jim Howard. A number of senior pilots from the 357th had previously completed missions with the 354th as part of the group's introduction to the ETO.

Although the 357th had seen nothing but scattered flak over occupied France on the 11th, to the northeast the 354th had run into a large formation of twin-engined fighters just as the bombers had approached Frankfurt. Now very much combat veterans, the Mustang pilots acquitted themselves well with claims for 11 enemy aircraft destroyed – Lt Charles Gumm top scored by downing an Me 410 and a Ju 88, leaving him just one victory short of ace status. However, there were two more losses, with one of them being none other than group CO, Col Ken Martin. Here, he recounts his mid-air collision:

The Germans were attempting to keep us from getting to our rendezvous with the bombers – first they hit us from above when we passed the French coast on the way in, then again when we were close to the bombers. Their radar could always put them on top of us. Usually they went for the bombers, but on this occasion they had realized that they needed to stop us before they could get to the bombers or they would be vulnerable from the rear while making their attack. On the second attack my wingman was shot down, and I was able to get the '109 that got him [giving Martin his all-important fifth kill – Editor].

Finishing a quick 360-degree turn after shooting down the '109, I saw another '109 approximately a mile away, so I headed my plane toward him. He was in a slight turn and saw me coming toward him, so he wheeled around and headed for me. We were both firing in a head-on run. Due to our past gun trouble, I looked at mine to see if they were firing, as I did not seem to be hitting the target. However, they were firing, as were the guns on the Me 109. I guess my aim was poor, and so was his. Anyway, the last thing I remembered was seeing the cross on the side of the '109 on my right at the same level, about 10ft out, just as we hit.

Miraculously, both Col Martin and his Luftwaffe opponent survived the collision, and wound up in the same hospital. Martin ended the war a PoW, and he was never credited with the destruction of this final Bf 109. The following day Gen Pete Quesada visited Boxted and pinned silver leaves on Maj Jim Howard, promoting him to lieutenant colonel and giving him command of the 354th FG. Capt Richard Turner duly filled the vacant CO's position within the 356th FS, although he was more than a little surprised when he was told that he was to replace Jim Howard as the unit's commanding officer:

The men in the squadron had expected a major or lieutenant colonel to be transferred in to assume the CO position Jim had vacated. To the surprise of us all, it was I who was promoted to the job of squadron commander. I was only a captain, and a newly promoted one at that, and the inherent responsibilities of the new job made me unsure of my own qualifications for the position. I even went so far as to suggest to Howard that I would just as soon remain with the squadron as a flight commander. Howard made it very clear that he, "didn't give a damn what I'd just as soon do," pointing out that it was his responsibility to assign positions in the best interest of the squadron, not the individual. It was the only time I was ever reprimanded and commended at the same time.

Throughout February the Eighth Air Force had been waiting for a few days of good weather to commence Operation *Argument*, which was a series of missions targeting German factories involved in the production of aircraft for the Luftwaffe. It was hoped that these missions would also spur the Luftwaffe into action, thus giving the pilots of VIII Fighter Command a chance to inflict critical losses on Germany's fighter force.

Finally, on February 19, several days of good weather were forecast, and orders were hastily sent out to bases across East Anglia and southeast England for the mobilization of virtually all USAAF fighters and bombers in the area. The following day saw the beginning of what was to become known as "Big Week."

On February 20, deputy group CO Lt Col Bickell led 54 P-51s that had been given the job of providing close support to 417 B-17s from the 1st Bomb Division heading for targets in Leipzig. No fewer than 835 USAAF fighters sortied on this day (including 19 from the 357th FG), setting a record for VIII Fighter Command which lasted until February 25, when 899 were put up! The vast majority of these machines were P-47s, 660-plus being drawn from 11 groups, including two from the Ninth Air Force. The 354th arrived early at the pre-briefed rendezvous point, and immediately sighted a formation of bombers coming under attack from 50-plus German fighters. The P-51 pilots sprung into action in defense of the B-17s, and a massive fighter battle ensued. Capt Jack Bradley remembers:

We had rendezvoused [R/V] with the bombers of the 1st Task Force about 30 minutes early south of Hannover. The group leader assigned our squadron to the middle box of bombers. The first box was under attack when we made our R/V, and I called this information to my group leader. I assigned half my squadron to the right of the bomber formation and I lead the other eight in support of the left side. About 20 minutes after the R/V, "Blue Flight" attacked four Me 109s coming in at eight o'clock to the bomber formation. At 1300hrs I saw a B-17 straggler from the first bomber box being stalked by a '109. I gave my flight instructions to drop belly tanks and attack the E/A. As I closed into range, "Blue Flight" cut me off and shot the E/A down. I saw the E/A in flames and out of control.

I assembled the flight and rejoined the bomber formation at 1320hrs. I saw another '109 preparing to attack a second B-17 that was aborting. I opened fire on the E/A before he could fire on the aborting "Fort." The '109 split-essed and dived down. I dived with him and fired a short burst, which was not effective. I closed to 350 yards and fired about a four-second burst. I saw strikes beginning on the right wing and fuselage, and the E/A went into a vertical dive from about 10,000ft. I started to pick up my wingman and tried to watch the E/A hit the ground. However, I lost sight of him for a few seconds and after completing the turn, I saw an explosion on the ground with white smoke and flame coming up.

The group was credited with 14 confirmed victories and no losses. Lt Col Howard led the 354th the following day when the group escorted B-17s from the 3rd Bomb Division that had been sent to attack targets in Brunswick. Once again the Luftwaffe rose in a fury, with over 200 fighters converging on the bomber stream. Large dogfights filled the sky, and pilots from the 354th claimed a further ten aircraft destroyed.

One of the victorious Mustang pilots was Lt Albert Redfern of the 356th FS who, along with his element leader, ended up in a turning fight with an Fw 190. Redfern stated that he and the Focke-Wulf pilot continued to turn into each other for a full ten minutes before the American began to drop his flaps – first to ten degrees and finally to 20, when he was finally able to pull his nose through to take a shot. The German pilot began to drop full flaps too when he saw what was happening, but it was too late. As he hung momentarily, after dropping his flaps, he was hit by Redfern and went down in an uncontrollable spin. When Redfern came out of the spin, he found a further two Fw 190s on his tail, but he was saved by his element leader, Lt V. E. Chambers, who chased them away.

Squadronmate Lt Frank O'Connor also "bagged" an Fw 190 after following it through a series of barrel rolls. He finally caught the German pilot with a solid burst of fire, which sent him down in flames – O'Connor was also credited with damaging a second Fw 190 and probably destroying an "Me 210" (almost certainly an Me 410).

On February 22 the 354th FG went to Aschersleben and Halberstadt, with Lt Col Bickell leading the group. Nearing Germany, the Mustangs were intercepted by a host of Luftwaffe fighters before some of them had even rendezvoused with the B-17s. Perhaps the most colorful combat of the day was flown by Capt Robert J. Brooks of the 356th FS, who was fortunate to return home. His post-mission statement read:

I was leading Starstud Squadron. We had just rendezvoused with the 2nd Combat Wing south of the target. After about five minutes of escort, a flight of 16-plus unidentified aircraft appeared at 11 o'clock high to the bombers. My flight climbed from 23,000ft toward the bogies. I identified the aircraft as Me 110s and dropped tanks. The '110s had a high cover of Me 109s. I lined up on the lead Me 110 at about a 20- to 30-degree deflection from the right beam and fired a short burst. I turned right and observed strikes in the center of the fuselage. I claim this '110 as damaged.

We then pulled up to meet the attack of the high cover '109s. As we pulled toward the rear of the bomber box about four '109s came down and we engaged them. I maneuvered in order to intercept one of the E/A, which was then at about 21,000ft. I lined him up and got in a 20-degree deflection shot from high, right astern. I fired a short burst and saw strikes along the right wing and the cockpit area. This E/A seemed to be hit hard by the fire, for he flicked to the left as I hit him and went straight down. I claim this '109 as damaged.

As we were climbing back up to bomber level, I saw two '110s attacking a straggling "Fort." We closed in for the attack, but the '17 was using very violent evasive tactics and we had trouble lining them up. I fired a short burst, allowing insufficient deflection, but then dropped 20 degrees of flaps and fired about four short bursts from high astern. I got hits along the right wing. As my fire hit the E/A, he straightened out and I moved in close, firing from about ten degrees deflection. These hits were in his engine, and caused large quantities of black smoke. The E/A then slowly rolled over onto its back and spiraled down, and it appeared to be out of control. I claim this Me 110 as probably destroyed.

As we climbed back up to the bombers I spotted a lone '109 at approximately 23,000ft, tooling up for an attack on the box. I closed in from the right and pulled up astern and a little below. I fired a long burst, observing strikes on the wings and tail surfaces. I continued to fire short bursts and the '109 then exploded along the wing roots while pouring a trail of black smoke. The E/A flipped over into a tight spin and did not pull out. I claim this Me 109 as destroyed.

We regained bomber altitude, 23,000ft, and spotted three bandits at three o'clock to the bombers. We turned into the attack as they started down. They saw our flight and positioned themselves for an attack on us. I turned cross-sun while watching them, and identified them as '109s. They closed on us from astern and above. Waiting until the E/A were within firing range, I then called a break. The flight split up. I checked my tail, saw it was clear and pulled up in a tight spiral for an attack.

I saw two aircraft coming down on me, head-on, from 20,000ft. The lead ship was a '109, and I presumed the second one to be a wingman. The '109 was in my sights and I fired at almost point-blank range. The '109 was not firing at me. I saw his yellow spinner and continued to fire, observing strikes on his ship. I thought we were going to collide, but at the last minute he lifted one wing to break, and by so doing hit my left wing, shearing off a 3ft section of the tip. I maneuvered to avoid a spin and saw the second aircraft, which was a P-51, on the '109's tail, pouring hits into the already-smoking E/A from slightly above. The P-51 was flown by Lt Welden, my wingman. The entire flight joined up and we started for home. I claim this '109 as destroyed, shared with Lt Welden.

A most remarkable day for Capt Brooks! Overall, the 354th had added a further 13 victories to its ever-increasing tally for the loss of one pilot, Lt Wah Kau Kong of the 353rd FS. Wah, who prided himself in being the only Chinese fighter pilot in the ETO at that time (Lt Frank S. Fong of the 359th FG arrived in the UK soon after Wah's death), had just shared in the destruction of an Me 410 with Capt Jack Bradley when his Mustang was hit hard by cannon fire from a Bf 110. P-51B-1 43-12393 *Chinaman's Chance* exploded in mid-air.

An escort mission to Schweinfurt on the 24th saw very little activity for the 354th, with the only victory being an "Me 210" (Me 410) shared by Capt Robert Stephens and an unknown P-38 pilot. Perhaps the most significant event of the day was the combat debut of the Ninth Air Force's 363rd FG, which became only the third P-51B-equipped outfit to be declared operational in the ETO.

Lt Col Howard led the group to Nuremburg on the 25th, and future 6.25-kill ace Lt Robert Welden of the 356th FS once again found himself in the thick of things, sharing a Bf 109 with three other pilots, an Fw 190 with Lt Tommy Miller and claiming a Bf 109 downed all by himself. Aces Capt Robert Stephens and Lt Charles Gumm also scored on this mission, increasing their tallies to 6.5 and six kills respectively. Overall, a total of seven victories were chalked up by the group.

The week of February 21–25, which became known as "Big Week," had seen the Eighth Air Force drop over 10,000 tons of bombs on the German aircraft industry for the loss of 132 bombers and 29 fighters. USAAF bomber gunners and fighter pilots had claimed 204 Luftwaffe aircraft destroyed during this period, and while this figure may have been overstated, the Germans had lost air superiority over their homeland. More significantly, the Luftwaffe had suffered the loss of many experienced fighter leaders and veteran pilots, who would prove to be irreplaceable.

It was thought at the time that the raids had also damaged the German aircraft industry to the point that it would never recover. Unfortunately this did not prove to be true, for so much of the production process had by then already been dispersed and moved underground. Indeed, as 1944 progressed the production of fighter aircraft in particular increased. Eventually this provided the Luftwaffe's fighter force with a surplus of aircraft and no experienced pilots to fly them.

Capt Jack Bradley led the 354th to Brunswick on February 29 for the group's last sortie of an eventful month, although it proved to be little more than a "milk run." However, on the way home South Carolinian Lt James Lane suffered an overheated engine and was forced to belly-land his P-51, thus joining the ranks of the PoWs. A member of the 356th FS, Lane's loss was felt particularly hard by his CO, Richard Turner:

> Jim Lane was the first pilot I lost as CO. It was a hard blow for me for Jim had been an old classmate of mine in 42-I. During assembly on the runway at take-off, Lane had parked too long downwind with his engine running, thus depriving his radiator of sufficient air cooling, and popped his coolant overflow valve. It was standard procedure to abort the mission and let an alternate take your place when this happened, but Lane had been grounded for some time by the flight surgeon and had only recently regained flying status. He had been impatiently looking forward to this mission, feeling behind the rest of us in opportunities for kills.
>
> Ignoring the rule of aborting, he deliberately took off in his regular position. Below 20,000ft his engine operated normally, but once the group got to rendezvous altitude at 25,000ft, the loss of coolant caught up with him, overheating the engine and causing it to fail. By the time anyone was aware of his trouble there was nothing we could do to help him as he deadsticked his Mustang down to inevitable capture. It was a tragic and unnecessary loss, for we encountered no opposition on the mission. It was, however, a sad lesson to the squadron on the high cost of negligence.

February had seen the 354th FG make excellent progress, flying a dozen escort missions and scoring a confirmed 63.5 kills for the loss of 12 pilots. Tragedy struck the group on the first day of March, however, when the 355th's Lt Charles Gumm met his fate in a desperate attempt to save others. Ironically, having scored the 354th's first victory, and duly becoming one of its early aces whilst completing more than a dozen missions deep into enemy territory, Gumm was to lose his life on a routine training flight when his assigned P-51B suffered engine trouble.

He could have easily bailed out, but instead he made an attempt to bring his ailing Mustang back to Boxted. Gumm was within visual distance of his base when his engine finally quit, just as he was approaching the village of Nayland on the Suffolk–Essex border. The ace continued to fight the controls of the rapidly descending Mustang in an effort to clear the rooftops of a small row of houses that lay directly in his path. He succeeded in guiding the fighter away from the village, whereupon he attempted to land in a nearby field, but one wing hit a tree and the P-51 smacked into the ground, killing Charles Gumm. He had saved the villagers at the cost of his own life.

"BIG B"

Right from the start of the Eighth Air Force's daylight bombing campaign in August 1942, aircrewmen had always wondered when they would get to strike at the capital of the Third Reich, Berlin. Bomber crews had quickly realized that it would be a disaster for them to attempt such a mission unescorted, but with the arrival of the P-51B in the ETO, as well as the delivery of improved versions of the P-47D, they could now go all the way.

Berlin at last became a target on March 3, when a number of bomb groups briefed for an attack on the capital. The 354th, meanwhile, was tasked with providing the escort for bombers striking at Oranienburg, only a few miles north of Berlin. Lt Col Bickell led the mission, which encountered terrible weather. The Mustangs climbed to 42,000ft, where they lost contact with the bombers – most of the "heavies" had been recalled, leaving a mere handful that never received the word to return. No opposition was seen over the target area.

On the way out of the target area the P-51s encountered about 20 German fighters in the vicinity of Ludwigslust, and a series of dogfights took place. Capt Richard Turner was leading the 356th FS when he sighted some 15 Bf 109s coming down on him. His combat report stated:

> I called Starstud ships to drop tanks and break, which we did. After breaking, my engine quit and I discovered I had not switched tanks. I lost about 5,000ft in starting my engine, and became separated from my flight. The '109s were on my tail, closing fast. I chopped the throttle and lowered flaps, skidding to the right, which allowed the first E/A to overshoot. I then proceeded to close on him and I opened fire at very close range. I observed strikes at the wing roots and around the canopy. I broke away, fearing the E/A behind me. As I did so, I saw the '109 that I had just fired on smoking and the pilot bailing out. The 'chute opened and the aircraft continued to fall through the overcast.
>
> I turned with the second '109, who was trying to pick up deflection on me. At this point another Starstud ship came down and drove off the E/A, the '109 split-essing and diving away out of sight.

Lt Mark Tyner picked up the only other victory of the day. The following day, Berlin was once again the target for most of the bombers, but the dreadful weather continued. Many aircraft received recalls, and only a handful made it as far as the German capital. The 354th succeeded in reaching the target however, led there by Lt Col Howard, although once over Berlin they met with little opposition. Indeed, only one victory was claimed when aces Lts Bob Shoup and Frank O'Connor of the 356th FS shared in the destruction of a Bf 109. Two pilots did not return from the mission, one ditching his Mustang in the North Sea 25 miles east of Lowestoft, on the Suffolk coast.

There was no activity on March 5, but clear weather the following day brought about the first real mission to Berlin, which was in turn the cause of one of the biggest aerial battles of the entire war. The Luftwaffe put up literally every fighter it had in response to the 730-strong bomber stream sortied by the Eighth Air Force. Escorting the B-17s and B-24s were 801 fighters, including 100 P-51Bs from the 4th, 354th and 357th FGs. Despite the massive fighter presence, no fewer than 69 bombers and 11 fighters were lost. The Luftwaffe paid a high price for this success, however, with USAAF fighter pilots alone being credited with 81 aircraft destroyed, in addition to the numerous claims made by bomber gunners.

The 354th did not encounter any of the big gaggles of fighters that the 4th, 56th and 357th FGs engaged, although its pilots did see significant action, downing seven aircraft. Future 14.5-kill ace Lt Lowell "Brue" Brueland of the 355th FS recalled:

Our flight saw about six Ju 88s above and just ahead of us – between us and the bombers. We went after them and tried to head them off, but they had the advantage of altitude. I managed to tag onto the last one, opened fire and kept on scoring hits. His engine then started smoking. I kept firing and the engine burst into flames, sending him down out of control. As I pulled up on another '88, I looked back and saw the first one explode. I fired on the one ahead of me and his engine started to smoke.

Lt Billie Harris, my wingman, who was coming up under me yelled, "Let me have him." I pulled up and let him have it. He got hits all over it. The '88 smoked like hell and went into a dive, and I saw the pilot pull up the canopy and jump out.

Lt Col Bickell, who led the 354th on the mission, had this to report:

An Me 109 came down for a tail pass at the "Forts." I came down from 23,000ft, blacked out, and came to at 13,000ft. I started back up and got on the tail of the '109 and started firing. He bailed out. We saw about 50-plus Me 109s and Fw 190s but they would not engage.

There was no action the following day, but on March 8 the 354th returned to Berlin. Once more the bombers were out in great numbers, with 623 of them being escorted by

891 fighters, 174 of which were P-51s (from the 4th, 352nd, 354th, 355th, 357th and 363rd FGs). For the Luftwaffe it was another day of frustration, for as hard as its units fought, they again suffered heavy losses. The escorts were credited with the destruction of 79 enemy aircraft, while the bomber gunners again entered high claims.

The 354th's contribution to this impressive tally were the two kills claimed by Lt Frank O'Connor, which took his score to 7.5 victories. Having managed to chase down an Fw 190 and a Bf 109 some 50 miles southwest of Berlin, he duly made short work of both fighters. O'Connor's P-51 had, however, been struck by two .50cal "slugs" fired from one of the bombers when he got too close during the interception!

These bloody aerial clashes over Berlin finally paid off for the Eighth Air Force on March 9 when 526 bombers, escorted by 808 fighters, had free rein over the German capital. To the amazement of all involved the Luftwaffe remained absent from the skies, leaving the B-17s of the 1st and 3rd Bomb Divisions to accurately hit their targets while their escorts roamed all over the city at will. This mission was certainly proof positive that Allied airpower had achieved air superiority over Europe. This was the goal of the current air offensive, for the impending invasion of France would have been doomed to failure had this not been accomplished.

The "Pioneer Mustang Group" was idle for about a week following this hectic sequence of long-distance raids. It next sortied into Germany on March 16, when 740 bombers struck the Messerschmitt factories in the Augsburg area. Appearing in strength once more, the Luftwaffe hit the bomber stream hard, with rocket-firing Bf 110s proving to be amongst the most formidable foes.

The most successful pilot of the day for the 354th was Californian Lt Bill Simmons of the 355th FS. Forced to abort the mission just short of the target due to a rough-running engine, he turned back in the company of his wingman. Within seconds of dropping his auxiliary tanks, Simmons discovered that his engine was no longer playing up, and the two Mustangs turned back to take part in the mission. Whilst looking for other P-51s to formate with, they sighted a number of enemy aircraft and dived down on them. Both men overshot the German fighters due to the speed of their dive, but when they pulled up they found themselves behind two Fw 190s that were getting ready to attack the bombers. Simmons moved in on one of them and opened fire. Good strikes were observed and then he sighted the canopy sliding back. Simmons recalled:

I didn't watch the pilot bail out because the other joker was still up above. My wingman told me later he saw the pilot bail out. I zoomed back up and there he was as big as life, just sitting there. I closed this time to a very close range. When I fired, the plane literally started to come apart. The strikes were all grouped on the empennage and canopy. This new ammo is the real thing (armor-piercing incendiary). The Jerry fell off into a glide, getting steeper all the time. I believe the pilot was dead.

I started back up and noticed a plane leveled off 1,000 to 2,000ft above the cloud deck. My first thought was that the second '190 had somehow survived, so I went down to finish him. It turned out to be an Me 109. I closed to zero deflection and moved in. The first burst tore pieces off the plane, and I saw strikes all over the canopy and fuselage. The canopy flew off, almost hitting me. It looked like the pilot was starting to get out when my next burst hit all over the canopy, where pieces were still coming off when I passed over him and to the side. I could see the pilot slumped over on one side of the cockpit. My wingman, Lt William Y. Anderson, did a great job of covering my tail throughout the engagement.

The 353rd FS's Capt Don Beerbower also claimed a Bf 109 during the course of the mission to raise his score to nine, and thus become the top ace of the 354th FG. Overall, the group chalked up an even dozen for the day (for the loss of TSgt Donald Dempsey of the 356th FS, one of five flying technical sergeants assigned to the group in March 1944), and then picked up another six victories when a return visit was made to Augsburg 48 hours later. Capt Beerbower claimed yet another Bf 109 on this occasion, as did squadronmate 1Lt Eagleston, whose score now stood at eight.

Following an uneventful mission to Frankfurt on March 20, the 354th escorted bombers bound for Brunswick and the city's Messerschmitt factories three days later. The trip turned out to be more of a fighter sweep than anything else, and a number of Bf 109s appeared. In the ensuing battles the Mustang pilots claimed five destroyed, but at a cost of three of their own. There was no further scoring during the month. March had seen an additional 31 victories added to the group's scoreboard, pushing the overall total of enemy aircraft destroyed in the air to date to over 150.

The 354th had not had it all its own way, however, with an escort mission to Schweinfurt on the 24th adding a further three casualties to the growing list of pilots that had either been killed, posted missing in action or were PoWs. Two of the pilots had collided whilst avoiding flak over the Dutch coast and one had been lost to unknown causes. Lt Col Bickell then led a mission on March 26 that would provide a taste of what lay ahead for the group – the Mustangs went to Creil, in France, to dive-bomb a large marshaling yard. Some pilots enthusiastically embraced this type of mission, eagerly dropping their two 500lb bombs, while others stated that this was not their "cup of tea."

An escort mission to an airfield near Biarritz in France the following day wrapped up an historic month for the 354th. The group had overflown Berlin not once but several times during March 1944, and had played an important role in proving that the USAAF had wrested air supremacy from the Luftwaffe.

COMMAND CHANGES AND OUTDOOR LIFE

On April 1, 1944 the 354th FG was part of a 475-strong fighter escort sortied in support of 440 bombers that had been sent to attack a chemical plant in Ludwigshafen. All 245 B-17s of the 3rd Bomb Division were recalled, however, after encountering thick cloud over France, and the 195 B-24s of the 2nd Bomb Division that supposedly released their ordnance over the target did so 100 miles south of Ludwigshafen due to pathfinder force equipment failure, and resulting navigational errors! This resulted in cities in France and neutral Switzerland being bombed, and the latter country was subsequently paid $1,000,000 by the US government as part of a formal apology.

Few enemy fighters were encountered due to the bombers being way off course, although one flight from the 353rd FS got mixed up with a group of Bf 109s. Several fights took place and two enemy fighters were downed. With more bad weather moving in over the next few days, canceling virtually all missions, the most important item of discussion at Boxted was the group's impending move to the Advanced Landing Ground (ALG) at Lashenden, in Kent, which was sited between the county town of Maidstone and Ashford. There were to be no more paved runways, Nissen huts and heated structures. Instead, all personnel were to move into tents, all supply and messing was to be carried out in field conditions and the aircraft were to operate off steel matting. Preparations for the invasion were certainly underway.

On April 5 the Mustangs sortied to France to attack enemy airfields. Bombs were dropped, installations were strafed at Orleans and Bourges and six aircraft were deemed to have been destroyed on the ground for the loss of a single P-51 and its pilot to flak. Leading the 356th FS on this mission was Capt Turner, who recounted in his autobiography:

We took off on a fighter sweep of Luftwaffe airfields in Châteauroux, Conches, Chartres and Bourges. At a point central to the targets the group separated, and I led my squadron to hit Bourges. Twenty miles from the target I instructed "Green Flight" to fly over Bourges at 10,000ft as top cover, and deployed "Red" and "Blue" flights on courses at deck level so they could hit from three different directions at one-minute intervals. I hit the field first with "Red Flight," and caught a landing Me 410, hitting him on the landing roll and causing him to burst into flames, leaving a trail of debris down the runway. Banking round after my first pass, I dived on an Me 110 being serviced on a hardstand, starting a raging fire beneath him as my incendiaries, and those of my wingman, ignited the gasoline spilling from his tanks.

Pulling up again, I rolled over and down on another twin-engined aircraft poised at the edge of the field with props revving for take-off. The burst from my "fifties" chewed into him at perfect range, and he blew up. Calling the squadron, I told everyone to climb back up to 15,000ft and rendezvous ten miles northwest of Bourges.

Following this mission we were all convinced of one thing – that it was a lot more difficult to attack German aircraft on the ground than in a nice uncomplicated air fight.

A few days later the group realized that command changes were in the offing when the 355th's CO, Lt Col Bickell, was appointed Deputy Group Commander. Capt Robert Stephens took over the reins of the unit. The following day "Big Jim" Howard pinned on the eagles of a full colonel.

Col Howard led the group accompanying 664 bombers that were sent to attack Brunswick on April 8. The mixed force of B-17s and B-24s from three bomb divisions was attacked by 60-plus Fw 190s and more than 15 Bf 109s in the vicinity of Wittingen, and Maj Jack Bradley later reported:

They pounced from above like rain. I saw six of them below me and dove down at full throttle, pouring lead at them as I plunged through their formation. One "firecrackered" in mid-air, the pilot floating down in a 'chute.

Bradley got another almost immediately, and pulled in on a third that seemingly never saw the Mustang on his tail. Capt Don Beerbower also claimed three that day, destroying two Fw 190s and a Bf 109. Overall, the 353rd FS was credited with a dozen enemy fighters shot down. Col Howard went down on an Fw 190, and as he attacked, another Focke-Wulf fighter tried to come up under him and his wingman. Lt Robert Shoup saw this and dropped down on its tail. The future 5.5-kill ace was spotted, however, for the Fw 190 broke for the deck. Shoup managed to stay with him, scoring as they rushed earthward. At about 5,000ft the Fw 190 went into a spin, which continued until it crashed.

When the day's total was added up, the 354th had scored a confirmed 20 victories, with several more probables and damaged. Four pilots did not return from the air battle, one of them as a result of a mid-air collision with a Bf 109. Howard led the group again the next day, this time to help bring home B-17s and B-24s from Marienberg and Gdynia, where they had bombed aircraft factories. The 354th picked up the "heavies" as they headed west, and encountered a number of attacking enemy fighters en route.

Lt Shoup and his flight ran into ten Fw 190s that were determined to get to the B-17s, and they dispersed them. Shoup downed one and then sighted a straggling bomber under attack, but it was too late to save it. As he dived down to drive an Fw 190 off, four men bailed out of the Flying Fortress. The now-defenseless B-17 dropped lower and lower until a series of telling bursts from the Focke-Wulf fighter caused the bomber to veer off to the left, wing over and crash. Shoup was by now rapidly closing on the tail of the victorious Fw 190, and when he overran the German fighter he found himself looking down into its cockpit. His opponent was frantically searching the sky to the left and right of him for the P-51, which he knew was behind him somewhere, but the Fw 190 pilot apparently never saw Shoup directly above him!

The Mustang ace throttled back, moved in behind the Fw 190's tail and fired a long burst, no deflection needed. The enemy aircraft bounced off the ground a couple of times and then cartwheeled across a field and burst into flames. Shoup was the highest scorer of the day with two kills, whilst eight other pilots from the 354th claimed singles.

On April 10 the 354th flew two missions in a day for the first time, the second of these seeing the group escort Martin B-26 medium bombers to their targets, which was also another first. In the morning, the group had sent bomb-toting Mustangs to attack a marshaling yard in the Belgian town of Hasselt. The group returned to Belgium that afternoon when the Ninth Air Force B-26s headed for the railyards at Namur. A Luftwaffe force of some 20 fighters attempted to attack the bombers from the rear, but the 354th intervened and downed five of them. The 356th's Lt Robert Goodnight was the most successful pilot of the day, claiming an Fw 190 and a Bf 109 to take his score to 7.25 kills.

The 354th flew its longest escort mission to date on April 11 when it escorted 341 B-17s of the 1st Bomb Division to Sorau and Cottbus airfields, just east of the Polish border. The round trip was almost 1,300 miles in length, meaning that the P-51 pilots faced more than five hours in the cockpit. No opposition was encountered over the targets, but on the way home three Bf 109s made a fleeting pass at the bombers near Wittenberg. Capt Turner chased after them and promptly shot down two of the Messerschmitts as they prepared to land at their airfield. He and his flight then proceeded to strafe the base, destroying three Henschel Hs 129s on the ground. In return, two P-51s were destroyed, with the loss of both pilots. One fell to flak and the other had had his Mustang so badly shot up by enemy fighters that he could not make it all the way home.

The following day Col Howard led the group to Leipzig, but the mission was ruined by very bad weather, which prevented a proper rendezvous. Lts Robert Meserve and Pat Moran shared an Fw 190 for the 354th's only claim of the day.

April 13 was a very active day for the 354th. Lt Col Bickell was to have led the Mustangs to Schweinfurt, but engine trouble turned him back and Capt Maurice Long of the 355th FS took over. Shortly after the group had rendezvoused with 172 B-17s from the 1st Bomb Division, the Luftwaffe arrived in force. Lt William Y. Anderson was flying wing to Lt Glenn Eagleston as part of the 353rd FS's "Red Flight," and recalled the action:

Following rendezvous, the lead box of bombers was tapped by 40 Fw 190s, which came in high and head-on. Lt Eagleston fired at one and I saw a strike on the wing root of an Fw 190. I also fired, but saw no strikes as my aircraft had an oil leak and my windscreen was completely covered. The Fw 190s which we met head-on returned fire but did not hit us. They were firing 20mm stuff, and it exploded over and around us. Lt Eagleston and I then orbited to the right, and we had made about a 180-degree turn when Lt Eagleston went down on two Fw 190s which were at three o'clock to us. He was drawing in to fire while I covered, and two Fw 190s came in on his tail. I called "break" so he had to break off the attack.

We then returned to the bombers and saw about 25-plus fighters come through the second box and start in on the third box when we met them head-on and broke up their attack. All of them went down except two, which started climbing. After climbing for about three minutes, Lt Eagleston caught up with the second Fw 190 of the two-ship formation and fired. I saw strikes on the canopy, engine and wings. The Fw 190 then bunted and Lt Eagleston followed and fired again. The canopy came off and all kinds of debris flew out of the cockpit, followed by the pilot, who bailed out.

The other Fw 190, meanwhile, was still circling and watching us beaver his buddy, and trying to get into a position to tap us, but before he had a chance we were back up again and cutting inside of him. Lt Eagleston's blower was out so he couldn't quite reach a firing position, so I opened up wide and got on the Fw 190's tail. He must have been watching Lt Eagleston, for I don't believe he saw me until I cut across the circle we were making and I fired from about 45 to 50 degrees deflection. I saw strikes on the engine and canopy, and the Fw 190 flipped over in a steep spiral. I followed him down and kept firing, but saw no strikes. He was smoking badly so I just followed, and at 4,000ft he started spinning violently. I began to pull out in order to keep from going in with him, leveling out at 2,000ft. I went into a climbing turn and saw wreckage of an enemy aircraft in a small wooded area below.

The two Mustang pilots headed for home at low level, managing to set fire to an Me 410 that they found on an airfield along the way. A total of 13 victories had been scored, with Capts Charles Lasko and Frank O'Connor and Lt Mailon Gillis all getting doubles. Two pilots were lost in the air battles. The group was not surprised to get an announcement at this time that Col Jim Howard was being moved up to Ninth Air Force Headquarters effective from April 11. Also as expected, Lt Col Bickell, known to his men as "Uncle" George, was appointed the new commander of the 354th FG.

A costly fighter sweep was flown on April 15, with 616 aircraft from 16 groups being given the job of strafing airfields in central and western Germany – the 354th FG was slated to hit Rostock. Winds aloft were gusting at up to 100 miles per hour over the North Sea, and numerous groups aborted as their fighters became scattered all over the sky.

Very little damage was done by those aircraft that made it to Germany, and no fewer than 19 fighters were lost due to the weather. Three of those belonged to the 354th FG, the trio of pilots being listed as missing in action.

This would prove to be the last mission flown by the 354th FG from Boxted, as with bad weather continuing to put operations on hold, the group instead devoted its full attention to moving its aircraft and equipment to its new home at Lashenden. The "Pioneer Mustang Group" had flown some 55 missions from Boxted, and 47 P-51s had been recorded as missing in action, compared with claims of 169 enemy aircraft shot down.

By mid-April the ground echelon had already moved to Lashenden, setting up tents and putting necessary outdoor furnishings in place, and on the 17th IX Fighter Command decreed that it was time to fly the Mustangs in. One squadron had left by mid-afternoon, and as it had made the trip successfully, so a second squadron was despatched. However, the weather had by now taken a turn for the worse, and the pilots could not find their new field. Running low on fuel, they were forced to land wherever they could when they discovered that Boxted was "socked in." Late that afternoon the third squadron took off and was able to arrive safely.

The 354th's first two missions from its new base befitted its surroundings, as they were of a tactical nature – one dive-bombing in Belgium and the other a fighter sweep over Germany. Both saw no aerial action.

The primary discussion within the 354th was now concerning its new base. With no frills and comforts, some of the men said it was more like a "boy scout camp." However, there were added attractions, for a bus ran right by the base en route to Maidstone, which the men immediately took a liking to. All personnel, officers and enlisted men alike, were quartered in six-man tents, and had to endure cold showers and outdoor latrines. The runway and "hardstands" consisted of heavy-gauge chicken wire, fastened down to mats. All in all things were not too bad until it rained, then the mud became a big problem. Richard Turner remembers:

> On the 17th we had flown our planes to the new airstrip, and a "strip" it was! Its surface was made of the new metal interlocking strips which were laid down over quickly compacted earth. These strips were fine for normal operations, but were deadly when wet. If you applied too much power suddenly on the wet metal during taxiing and take-off, the torque force of the prop could neatly swing you 90 degrees away from your intended path. We also exchanged our comfortable huts for foxholes until tents were set up. More than ever now it was evident that we were being groomed for things to come, for the long-awaited Invasion, we hoped.

Bomber escort duties were resumed on April 24 with a trip to Munich, the Luftwaffe being met on two occasions and the 354th returning home with four victories and no losses. Soon after arriving at Lashenden, the 354th welcomed newly promoted Lt Col Charles Teschner as its new Deputy Group Commander. He had transferred in from the P-47-equipped 362nd FG (where he had led the 378th FS), based just a few miles away at Headcorn ALG. Teschner's initiation into the 354th came when he was elected to lead the group on an escort mission to Mannheim on the 25th. Upon its return, the 354th strafed an airfield and claimed 17 aircraft destroyed. Only one enemy fighter was shot down, however, and two of their own pilots were lost on the mission. One of those missing was six-kill ace Lt William Simmons of the 355th FS, whose P-51B was struck by flak near Ansbach, in Germany. Although he was seen to bail out, word reached the group that Simmons' body had been found near the wreckage of his fighter.

Recently promoted Maj Richard Turner led the group to Brunswick on the 26th, and the mission would prove costly for the 354th. High winds aloft and ten-tenths undercast below made navigation difficult, and the bombers were never found. Lt Edward Regis was lost to flak and Lt Franklin Hendrickson was forced back due to a bad engine, with Lt Joseph Lilly sent along as his escort. Neither pilot returned that day, but Hendrickson made it back months later and Lilly became a PoW.

Two more pilots almost did not make it home. Lts Mailon Gillis and Leonard Jackson had become lost, and when Maj Turner returned to base and learned that they were missing, he had his fighter hastily refueled and took off to search for them. Although he experienced some difficulty himself, he finally contacted the men over the radio as they flew over the Brest Peninsula, heading for Spain! He succeeded in turning them round and guiding them back to Gosport, on the Hampshire coast, where they landed after having been in the air for eight and a half hours. Realizing that time was of the essence, and having taken off in search of his lost squadronmates before being given formal approval for the sortie, Turner was initially reprimanded by IX Fighter Command HQ:

> Under the circumstances I would have been happy in view of the results to take a bust in rank. Later the reprimand was reversed, and instead they awarded me a cluster to my Distinguished Flying Cross for my action in this affair.

Two dive-bombing missions were flown on April 27, and 48 hours later Col Howard returned to lead the group on an escort mission to Berlin. A formation of 30 Bf 109s was initially encountered, followed by 60 Fw 190s. Capt Glenn Eagleston quickly became involved in a skirmish when the Messerschmitts arrived on the scene and broke into two sections. Capt Don Beerbower and his flight engaged one section while Eagleston and his wingman, along with the remnants of their flight, took on a gaggle of about 11 aircraft. Eagleston reported:

The E/A, which were still together, broke into us while we were still in formation, and I fired a one-second burst at 90 degrees and saw damaging strikes on one '109. After a few more turns I was in position to fire at the last E/A and did so, firing a two-second burst from 20 degrees, scoring many hits. The E/A started smoking badly, and then broke up and into me. The E/A did a complete loop and I fired at the top of it, scoring a few more strikes, after which he straightened out and jettisoned his canopy. I thought he was going to bail out, so I pulled out to one side. Instead, he headed for the clouds, attempting to get away. I followed him down and fired another burst, scoring a few strikes. By this time we were down to around 1,000ft, and the pilot bailed out, striking the tail surfaces as he went. His 'chute failed to open.

Six fighters fell to the guns of the 354th, but the group lost three pilots in return. While engaged with the Luftwaffe, the Mustang pilots noted that the German fighters made repeated overhead attacks at the bombers, before zooming back up to altitude and then renewing their offensive. This new tactic seemed to work quite well at the expense of the bombers, 63 of which were lost to all causes during the mission – 13 USAAF fighters were also destroyed.

An uneventful escort mission to Lyon, in France, on April 30 wrapped up yet another memorable month for the 354th FG. Its pilots had continued to score heavily, with their tally of kills now exceeding 250, for the loss of 56 pilots. The 354th had also changed bases in what was its first step to becoming more of a tactical fighter group in preparation for the invasion of continental Europe, and an eventual move there.

PREPARING FOR INVASION

May brought about more tactical missions aimed at airfields, bridges and troop installations in the occupied countries of Europe. On the first two days of the month four dive-bombing missions – two in Belgium, one in Holland and one in France – were flown. The first escort mission did not come until the 4th, when Lt Col Bickell led the Mustangs to Berlin once again. No opposition was encountered over the target, so a fighter sweep was made on the return flight, and only a solitary Fw 190 was attacked and shot down by Capt Frank O'Connor. This proved to be "Pinky" O'Connor's final victory, taking his tally to 10.75 kills, and making him the 356th FS's then ranking ace. Indeed, his tally would only eventually be bettered – by 0.25 of a kill – by longtime squadron CO, Richard Turner.

A further two missions were flown to Berlin on May 7 and 8. The earlier one was largely uneventful, with no hits and no losses as far as the Luftwaffe was concerned. Some opposition was encountered the following day, however, and Capt Eagleston experienced a combat which was a real heartbreaker for an escort pilot. He reported:

Capt Jack Bradley ordered me to accompany an aborting B-17 back out when we were in the Berlin area. Time was 1100hrs. I escorted the "Big Friend" until 1200hrs, and we were in the Nienburg area when four Me 109s came in at six o'clock, 3,000ft above us. I climbed up to engage and instructed my wingman, Lt Charles W. Koenig, to stay low with the bomber. I engaged the last E/A, which broke into me and split for the deck. I was attempting to head off the other three E/A when 12 Fw 190s made a head-on pass at the bomber, scoring many strikes. We attempted to ward off this attack too, but it was hopeless. Seven 'chutes were seen to leave the bomber. The gaggle broke to the right with the exception of one, which made a turn to the left. When we made our attack from astern, this E/A turned onto Lt Koenig's tail. I called a "break right" to him and he did so. His break took him beneath the clouds and we became separated.

I attacked the gaggle from astern, firing two-second bursts, and seeing strikes on the last '190. The major part of the strikes were on the right side of the fuselage and cockpit. A minor explosion took place and several pieces flew off. I fired a one-second burst, scoring strikes on the left wing, About 1½ft of wingtip disintegrated and the E/A rolled to the left, smoking badly. I followed it down and fired another short burst, scoring a few more strikes. The E/A went straight into the ground and crashed.

I pulled out at 2,000ft and climbed back up to 12,000ft, attempting to attack the gaggle again. The Fw 190s broke in several directions and were coming at me from all angles, so I dove to the deck, flew for about ten minutes, regained altitude and went home.

Three Bf 109s were downed by the Mustangs during the mission, which cost the 354th one pilot. A short escort trip over Belgium on May 9 saw a few enemy fighters engaged in the target area, but it was not until the P-51s turned for home that they met four Fw 190s and downed two of them.

Capt Maurice Long led the group to Saarbrücken on the 11th, where the presence of the bombers provoked the Luftwaffe into action. More than 50 Bf 109s and Fw 190s formed up and began following the bombers. The P-51s climbed up to the German fighters' altitude and combat ensued until the majority of them had been broken up and chased off in all directions.

Lt Robert Welden was leading his flight when, 11 minutes off target, nine Fw 190s and 14 Bf 109s were seen flying a course parallel to, and some 3,000ft above, the box of bombers he was escorting. The Fw 190s came almost abreast of the B-17s before turning to make a broadside attack on the bombers. They then dived, came within 1,000 yards of the bombers and pulled up. Welden radioed the flight behind him to tell them that he was engaging the Fw 190s, and that they should in turn take on the Bf 109s. Welden stated:

I did a 180-degree turn with my flight and came in behind the '190s, but due to their superior speed at the time, I had to open fire at approximately 900 yards in an attempt to scare them off the "Forts." The last three E/A did break down, but six continued the attack.

As I closed on the last E/A's tail and fired a burst, the gaggle broke left and down. I observed no strikes at the time. I closed to 300 yards in a tight turn to the left and fired a short burst, getting strikes on its left wing and tail. The '190 reversed his turn and I gave him another squirt, seeing more hits on the cowling and canopy. The E/A began to smoke a great deal and pieces flew off. At 100 yards, going straight down, I fired about a two-second burst into the E/A's fuselage, getting many strikes – I watched the E/A go down in an uncontrolled dive and crash into the ground.

Totals for the day were 11 confirmed victories for the loss of one Mustang. Veteran 355th FS pilot Lt Clayton Gross was the top scorer with two Bf 109s destroyed. The 354th traveled to Leipzig the following day, and ran into small numbers of fighters but no big gaggles. Six aircraft were nevertheless shot down, with Capt Jack Bradley scoring victories ten and 11. The 356th FS suffered the loss of 5.5-kill ace Lt Bob Shoup on this mission (his 60th), however, and he sat out the rest of the conflict as a PoW.

Lt Col Bickell led the group on May 13 on what was the P-51's longest escort mission to date, when total of 289 B-17s of the 1st Bomb Division went after an oil refinery at Politz, near the port of Stettin on the Baltic Sea coast – the total round trip was over 1,400 miles. Just before rendezvousing with the bombers, the 354th spotted 50-plus Bf 109s heading away from the bomber stream. Bickell knew better than to fall into their trap, and instead stayed with the "Big Friends."

Minutes later the bombers were attacked by 75 single-engined fighters north of Denham. The 354th engaged just as another 30 German fighters joined in the fight near Lübeck. During a series of swirling dogfights, the Mustang pilots were successful in downing ten enemy fighters for the loss of just one of their own. The top scorer was the 353rd's Lt Carl Frantz, whose haul of three Bf 109s (and a fourth damaged) boosted his overall tally to ten, while Lt Col Bickell and Capts Emmer and Brueland all claimed doubles. "Brue" Brueland also had to make a rescue. Squadronmate Lt Clayton Gross had been viciously attacked by two red-nosed P-47s, leaving his P-51B badly damaged. Brueland heard his call for help and finally found him, whereupon he flew close escort for the irate Mustang pilot all the way back to Lashenden.

The following day saw another advance in preparations for the group's eventual transfer to the Continent. The now-familiar six-man tents were struck and all personnel had to move into two-man pup tents. Excess clothing and personal effects were also boxed up to be sent home, and officers' "pinks and greens" (dress uniforms) were stuffed into B-44 bags that were duly placed in storage for an indefinite period. Following two days of bad weather, the group took to the air again, but nothing of great consequence occurred. A fighter sweep and several bomber escorts proved uneventful, and Richard Turner was just one of many pilots in the 354th becoming increasingly frustrated by the Luftwaffe's growing absence in the skies over Germany;

> The month of May was a busy month, but a lean one for me. The group destroyed 75 more German planes, but most of them were bagged in five or six missions, which made the remainder tail-weary experiences, for the most part, with little enemy action to liven them up. This, of course, was ideal for bombers, but for us fighters it meant hour upon hour of routine patrol, unable to move in the cramped cockpit. I seldom ever got a glimpse of the enemy. It seems I either missed the missions where a fight developed, or I was on the wrong side of the bomber stream to be part of a big engagement.

The Eighth Air Force struck out after enemy oil targets once more on May 28, with the 354th taking the bombers to Magdeburg. A gaggle of over 60 Bf 109s and Fw 190s were met on the way in and sharp action ensued, one pilot scoring a "draughty" victory without his canopy! Capt James W. Edwards stated that he was leading a flight from the 356th FS when Nos 3 and 4 dropped down to attack a Bf 109 while he and his wingman stayed above as top cover. Then Edwards and his wingman went down. As he recalled:

> My No 2 and I went down too fast and hit compressibility. The dive started at 25,000ft and I pulled out at about 500–700ft, losing my canopy in the pull-out. After I regained control I was alone, so I started climbing. At 4,000ft I was jumped by two Fw 190s. I saw them coming and fired two short bursts in their general direction to shake them up a bit. I dropped 20 degrees of flaps and started turning, losing altitude at the same time.
>
> At 500ft I had no trouble turning inside of them despite my canopy having gone, damaging my flaps as it tore loose. We made about two more turns at 500ft, and I was about to get deflection on them when the leader snapped and spun. He hit the ground and flames spread for 200 yards from where he had hit. The remaining Fw 190 dived for the deck, and I didn't chase him as I knew I could not catch him with the added drag.

The group scored a total of ten victories for the day, with Maj Jack Bradley picking up another two. Two pilots, including 8.5-victory ace Lt Don McDowell of the 353rd FS, were lost. Another three uneventful escort missions were flown to round off the month. However, new and exciting things had come to pass, with the arrival of the first P-51Ds for the 354th. The new model sported a "bubble" canopy, which greatly improved visibility. Armament had also been increased to six .50cal Brownings (three in each wing), with booster motors to help eliminate the gun jams that had plagued the P-51B/C.

D-DAY AND A MOVE TO FRANCE

Bad weather caused a slow start to operations in June, but it did not diminish the tension and excitement of the group's wait for D-Day. All airfields, bridges and rail checkpoints had been bombed over and over again to impede any moves that the Germans might make to oppose the operation. The 354th did not fly on the first two days of the month, but June 3 saw the Mustangs bombing rail targets between Soissons and Laon. One aircraft was lost when Lt John H. Arnold was forced to bail out in the target area.

Capt Robert Stephens led the 355th FS on a dive-bombing mission against a rail junction at Bourges on June 4, and as the Mustangs came off the target they spied a Focke-Wulf Fw 56 trainer doing aerobatics. Apparently, its pilot had made an aircraft recognition mistake which would prove fatal – those were not Messerschmitts he was showing off for! Capt Stephens gave him a short burst, which took his landing gear off, and then Lts William King and Huston O'Hair attacked the little aircraft and turned it into a fireball. The most fortunate thing that happened to the P-51 pilots during this whole one-sided episode was that they narrowly avoided colliding with each other whilst trying to shoot the Fw 56 down.

The men of the 354th had known something was afoot in respect to the invasion of France since their departure from the permanent comfort of the "real" fighter base at Boxted, for the tents and steel matting runway and taxiways of the ALG at Lashenden. As summer approached, the moment of invasion grew ever nearer, and the pilots of the "Pioneer Mustang Group" clearly sensed this. Richard Turner described this period in his autobiography:

> Since the 25th of May the group had been informed officially that it was now on a six-hour alert status, and had been assigned two officers from General Patton's Third Army to stay with us and set up ground liaison procedures. There were a rash of secret staff meetings and numerous assignments of enlisted men to special transportation waterproofing schools, all of which clearly indicated that something special was in the breeze. Our flying hadn't changed much, except that more dive-bombing, fighter sweeps and strafing missions were being thrown in with our normal escort duties, and this stepped up the pace of operations somewhat.

It didn't take much brainpower to guess that the invasion of the Continent was imminent. The clincher came when we discovered a small detail of cameramen among us who had been assigned to cover our first day activities on "D-Day."

D-Day for the 354th began when the pilots were called in for a briefing on the night of June 5. Col Bickell (he had been promoted in late May) informed them that this would be a night mission, which would be quite dangerous, but that this was the big event. The pilots then moved to their aircraft and were airborne by 2057hrs. They rendezvoused with C-47s and gliders over Portland Bill and headed for France. The Mustangs continued to orbit over the 15-mile stream of aircraft until their charges descended to land on "Utah" Beach. Weather conditions on return were so bad that most of the Mustangs were forced to land at Stoney Cross, in the New Forest, as this airfield was equipped for night landings. The pilots duly laid down wherever they could find a space and got a little sleep, before being woken up at 0530hrs the next morning. Take-off was at 0700hrs for another trip escorting more C-47s to "Utah" Beach. This time the group returned to Lashenden.

The 354th saw little action again (other than some squadron-strength missions) until June 12, when the entire group flew a dive-bombing mission with 500lb bombs against rail installations around Laval and Le Mans. The most notable event of the mission occurred when, en route to the target, and carrying two 500lb bombs, Capt Wallace Emmer engaged and destroyed an Fw 190 down on the deck. Having quickly despatched the fighter for his ninth kill, he then bombed the target. June 13 saw more dive-bombing, along with the strafing of targets of opportunity during the flight home. One of the targets that was well worked over was a large convoy of enemy trucks caught on roads around St Lô. The devastation was overwhelming, although the 356th FS suffered the loss of Lt W. R. Perkins when his Mustang hit a tree during a strafing pass and was destroyed.

The aerial action picked up on the afternoon mission of June 14, when the group escorted Douglas A-20s and Martin B-26s to bomb tactical targets near Caen. Ten Bf 109s were spotted intercepting a formation of B-26s, so the Mustangs went to work. Five of the Messerschmitt fighters were downed, with Capt Don Beerbower being credited with one destroyed and one shared to raise his score to 14.5 victories.

On the morning of June 15 the first detachment of the air echelon departed for France, en route to A-2 (Criqueville) airstrip sited on the Normandy coast. These men had the chore of setting up the field before the P-51s came over. The 354th had been officially informed on June 13 that it was to move to France in order to give close support to the army's advance. "Thus our work with the Eighth Air Force came to its conclusion. We continued our operations under the control of XIX Tactical Air Command of Brigadier General Otto P. Weyland" – this was how Richard Turner described the group's final break from its "surrogate" command.

Around this time the men of the 354th began to take note of strange noises at night which they at first thought might be German bombers. However, no bombs fell, but red lights moved across the sky heading west. They soon discovered that these were V1 rockets, one of Hitler's new, so-called secret weapons. The rockets actually consisted of a ramjet engine with short stubby wings, carrying a high-explosive warhead. They flew at nearly 400mph and were unguided except for being fired in the general direction of southeast England. Most were aimed at London, having been launched from what looked like ski jumps. The pilots soon picked up on Lt "Willie Y" Anderson's nickname for them – "Doodlebugs."

The group was back out dive-bombing and strafing on June 16 and 17, and on the latter date the 353rd had just finished working over a road junction near Caumont when "Willie Y" chased after a V1. He duly shot the pilotless flying bomb down, and on returning to base wanted to know, "How many doodlebugs make an ace?"

Other pilots also scored kills on their way back home, although their opponents were manned Fw 190s from 10./JG 2. Four Focke-Wulf fighters were destroyed near Vire, with Maj Jack Bradley's shared claim pushing his score up to 14. Three P-51s had been lost during the course of the day, however, one machine being downed by the explosion of its own bomb, which killed pilot Lt A. J. Diziere. The remaining two men, Lts T. L. Donohoo and J. Rody, were both captured.

The following day Maj Turner also shot down a "Doodlebug" and caused a second to crash after flipping it over with his wingtip. This was how he described the mission in *Mustang Pilot*:

In the early morning of the 18th of June, we ran a dive-bombing mission into France which was completed within two hours. On the return trip to base I hovered my flight in a loose orbit at 6,000ft between Calais and Dover. With plenty of fuel and ammunition left, I was tempted to subtract a few buzz bombs from the many the Germans were sending over to terrorize London. They traveled at an altitude of between 2,000 and 3,000ft, and usually cruised at speeds of between 300 and 500mph. I felt that if we could pick them up over the Channel and dive on them, we stood an excellent chance of knocking them down since they were unable to evade us in any way.

I sighted one below and dived on it, pulling out behind it, but slightly out of range. I tried to close the distance, but the missile was just a little too fast. I chased the infernal machine for ten minutes, alternatively diving to gain speed, and pulling up to lob long-range bursts at it. Eventually one of my bullets must have scored a chance hit in the engine, for suddenly it emitted a long streamer of yellow flame and lost speed quickly. In a curving dive, it plunged into a vacant field below, where it exploded harmlessly. Encouraged by my success, I proceeded back to the Channel area to pick up another.

I began to wonder how I was going to get the next V1, because most of my ammo was expended, and my gun barrels had burnt out.

Soon I saw another one and made a very steep dive to gain extra overtaking speed. This bomb must have been moving more slowly than the first one, for I almost overran it as I pulled out of my dive. As I flew alongside the little monster, I had a new idea. I knew they were controlled by a gyro guidance "brain," and perhaps this mechanism could be upset without gunfire. I carefully edged close to it and placed my wingtip about a foot under its tiny fin. Rolling my plane suddenly neatly flipped the V1 upside-down, and it promptly spun into the shallows of the Channel near the English shore, where it blew a useless hole in the water. Jubilant with my success, I rushed back to Maidstone and hastened to tell the other pilots of the new pastime that I had discovered.

Following days of strafing and dive-bombing, a real change came about on June 20 when the 354th was called on to resume escorting the bombers for the Eighth Air Force. Capt Stephens led the men to Magdeburg, but the trip turned out to be uneventful, much to the chagrin of the pilots.

Things picked up a bit on the 21st when Capt Emerson led the mission to Genshagen, near Berlin. Just after rendezvousing with B-24s of the 2nd Bomb Division, Capt Max Lamb of the 356th FS (who was leading a flight flying at about 23,000ft) sighted Me 410s queuing up to attack the bombers. As they made their move to come in from four o'clock, Lamb dived down with his Mustangs from astern. They in turn were spotted by the Messerschmitts, which broke in all directions. Lamb slotted in behind one of the Me 410s diving for the deck, fired a couple of bursts and set its right engine on fire. His pursuit of the bomber-destroyer continued down to about 4,000ft, from which height the Me 410 pilot attempted a split-ess and clipped the treetops, cartwheeled into the ground and exploded.

Within seconds of Lamb starting his climb back up to the bomber stream, he had spied another Me 410 flying along in a straight line at just 100ft above the ground. Seemingly oblivious to the presence of the Mustang, the Messerschmitt flew on as Lamb "parked on its six o'clock" and opened fire. Good strikes were seen, and the right engine stopped and began to emit volumes of black smoke. A few more bursts caused the Me 410 to pull up and then turn over on its back, before crashing into the ground. Four of the twin-engined fighters were destroyed for the loss of 2Lt R. K. Porter, who was shot down and killed over the target area in his P-51B.

The 354th flew its last sorties from Lashenden on June 22, these being individual squadron missions where pilots were primarily tasked with hitting targets of opportunity. The only unit to engage the Luftwaffe during the course of the day was the 353rd FS, which had dropped bombs on tank cars and goods wagons. On its return leg home the squadron was attacked from below by three Bf 109Gs, and two of the Messerschmitts were quickly destroyed, one falling to future 14-kill ace 1Lt Ken Dahlberg (this was his first victory) and the second being shared by Capt Eagleston (taking his tally to 14.5) and Lt Charles Koenig (whose score now stood at 2.5 out of an eventual 6.5 kills). The German pilots had, however, shot down and killed 2Lt C. H. Stewart in their initial pass.

Late that afternoon two squadrons departed Lashenden for A-2, with the third unit following the next morning. Missions from the new strip began immediately, and its closeness to the frontline allowed the 354th to fly six to eight missions a day, including sweeps, ground support sorties and even top cover missions for P-47s bombing and strafing.

Nine missions were flown on June 23 – mostly patrols, with little occurring. The group lost Lt P. E. Moran, however. Three days later flak again took its toll on the 354th when two fighters were shot down, 2Lt J. D. Carpenter and Flt Off D. L. Richards both being killed, as was Lt W. J. Walbrecker, who hit a pole whilst strafing on the same day. The group encountered the Luftwaffe once again on June 28, when two flights from the 356th FS on an assault-area patrol of the beachhead spotted a lone Bf 109 being chased by five Spitfires. When the fighter entered the squadron's patrol area, Maj Turner led his flight into the fray:

Excitement raced through me now as I gauged the distance between the Spits and the '109. If he turned back to Le Havre, which was out of my patrol area, I'd have to let the Spits have him. But if he came on to the Caen area he'd be entering my territory, and the Spits would have to take pot luck. Any German fighter in my patrol area was fair game, and I wasn't planning to waste time being polite to our allies. As it turned out, I was downright rude. The '109 pilot saw us coming, and turned south toward Caen. Forgetting the Spitfires and everything else but my prey, I whipped over in a steep right turn and latched onto the tail of the '109, sandwiching myself between him and the Spits. Naturally, my flights followed, and the Spitfires had to pull up and abandon the chase or get run over by a herd of P-51s.

Turner despatched the lone fighter with two bursts of fire from close range. The pilot bailed out and the Bf 109 crashed just 20 miles from A-2, so Turner and his crew chief, SSgt Cliff "Tommy" Thompson, drove over in a jeep to inspect the downed fighter, which was more or less intact:

From the wing root to the nose of the plane, we counted around 200 .50cal holes. No wonder the pilot had bailed out so quickly! I knew that I had scored a number of hits, but I had no idea that the fire had been so concentrated. It gave me a new and added respect for the destructive powers of my guns.

It was the turn of the 353rd FS to encounter enemy aircraft the following day, when Fw 190s flown by pilots that seemed quite experienced were intercepted during an afternoon patrol near Berriere. Four of the Focke-Wulf fighters were downed, all of which fell to current or future Mustang aces, namely 1Lts Carl Bickel, Ken Dahlberg and Robert Reynolds. The latter pilot also shared in the destruction of a second Fw 190 with Capt Wallace Emmer, whose score now stood at 10.5 kills.

Further patrols were flown on the last day of the month, and once again a flight of Mustangs from the 356th FS sighted an engagement between some Spitfires and Bf 109s. This time, however, the fight was taking place at 30,000ft over the French town of Vire. Led by Maj Turner, the squadron climbed for a solid 15 minutes to join the fray – the Mustangs had only just departed A-2 when the melee was spotted. The four Spitfires turned north and the four Bf 109s continued south, seemingly oblivious to the P-51s climbing hard beneath them. Turner opened fire once he was within range, and the German fighters immediately attempted to turn into the US fighters. The 356th pilots easily countered this maneuver by turning even harder, and three of the Bf 109s dived away, leaving the fighter that Turner had "winged" lagging behind. The major soon finished this machine off, taking his tally to ten kills in the process, and the Mustangs continued to chase the three remaining Bf 109s as they dived headlong for the ground. Finally overtaking them, Lt Welden later reported:

> I closed to about 200 yards, fired and saw large pieces coming off the left wing. I moved over to the right wing root and fired a short burst, which resulted in coolant and black smoke streaming back. I closed to 100 yards dead astern, fired a long burst, and the E/A's whole left stabilizer came off – the plane went into a loose, uncontrolled, oscillating spin.

Welden had just scored his final combat kill, taking his overall tally to 6.25. The remaining two Bf 109s were despatched by 2Lt W. K. Pendergrass and 1Lt R. T. Stolzle.

PATROLS AND MORE PATROLS

With Allied forces doing their best to break out of Normandy, the men of the 354th thought that there would be much more action for them to come in July. However, the entire month was spent flying boring fighter sweeps and patrols over the beaches. With the Luftwaffe all but wiped out in France, the patrolling fighters rarely encountered any enemy opposition in the air. And with the job of providing long-range fighter escort for heavy bombers now exclusively within the Eighth Air Force's remit, the 354th found itself with little to do but strafe ground targets.

Undoubtedly the most extraordinary event of the month took place, appropriately, on July 4, when Gen Elwood "Pete" Quesada arrived at A-2 along with the Supreme Commander of Allied Armies in the ETO, Gen Dwight Eisenhower. This was not an inspection trip, however, for the group's 355th FS happened to be flying just the aircraft they were looking for.

Several weeks earlier, a team from the group's servicing squadron had removed the fuselage tank from behind the pilot's seat of war-weary P-51B-5 43-68777 and installed a second seat in its place – the quartet of wing guns had also been deleted. This allowed the aircraft to be used either as a "hack," an instructional aircraft or just the thing to take crew chiefs for rides! Maj Turner remembers the July 4 flight well:

They would fly a personal reconnaissance of the St Lô area in the twin-seated Mustang. Colonel Bickell informed me that he had chosen my squadron to provide the other three aircraft and pilots for protective escort to the two generals during their flight over the area. I was extremely proud to have my squadron chosen to accompany such important personnel, though I must admit, the grave responsibility made me a little nervous.

I selected the pilots from my senior flight commanders. General Quesada would lead the flight, with a flight commander who had flown over 50 missions on his wing, and I would lead the second element with another flight commander on my wing. The three accompanying pilots would have a cumulative experience of some 175 missions and 40 aerial victories. The plan was to carry out the flight under the guise of a routine patrol, and to have nothing said over the R/T that would give the slightest indication that this was a special flight, or that important personnel were involved. If anything happened to that old war-weary P-51 and its important passengers, Allied troops would be dealt a crippling psychological blow. Needless to say, I slept fitfully that night.

The next morning as I looked over the twin-seater, I couldn't help but wonder if General Eisenhower would know when he climbed into the back seat that he would virtually be trapped there until landing, when the crew chief could unfasten the closures. It would have been a near impossibility to get out of that rear seat in the air. I myself wouldn't have ridden in the back seat of that monster for all the tea in China.

At briefing my pilots and I were introduced to General Eisenhower who shook each of us by the hand, saying that he understood that he was to be flying with the finest fighter pilots in the ETO. It was deeply gratifying to be so addressed by the Supreme Commander of the Allied Forces. The general seemed genuinely interested in us, and in our opinions. He was a man of authority and determination, whose manner impressed all those who saw him.

As we went out to our planes, I watched General Eisenhower climb with some difficulty through the small opening behind the cockpit into the cramped bucket seat. There wasn't enough room for both him and a parachute, so the general flew without one. I watched his face as the crew chief buttoned down the Zeus fasteners on the Plexiglas window with a screwdriver, and if he had any misgivings about his helplessness, he showed no concern.

Gen Quesada fired up the engine, taxied out and away they went. Col Bickell then hastened to get all flyable Mustangs in the air to protect them. In about an hour the P-51B landed on the steel mat runway and the mission was over. Maj Turner, who had had to abort early on in the mission when the new P-51D that he was flying suffered an engine instrument failure, was on hand when Gen Eisenhower returned to A-2:

As I arrived the general was being helped out of his cubbyhole with a wide grin on his face. He was so pleased with the mission that he could hardly wait to get back to his planning staff and start the gears grinding. This was the first time in history that a ground general had personally reconnoitered the terrain of a planned battle operation from a fighter in the presence of the enemy.

Although he had clearly enjoyed his one-off Mustang mission, Gen Eisenhower did not enjoy the next day when he was admonished for the impromptu act by his boss, Gen George C. Marshall (Chairman of the Combined Chiefs of Staff Committee), in the Pentagon in Washington, DC. To make matters worse, Marshall only found out about the flight when he read the daily newspapers on July 5! Regardless of Gen Marshall's disapproval, the 354th was proud of their aircraft's employment, and named the P-51B *THE STARS LOOK DOWN*.

The next aerial action for the group came on July 7 during a fighter sweep led by Capt Don Beerbower. The Mustangs ran into some 30 Fw 190s in the vicinity of Perdreauville, and although the German fighters were not eager for combat (they broke for the deck in all directions), the P-51s set off after them in hot pursuit. The 353rd FS managed to shoot down four Fw 190s, veteran pilot Capt Felix Rogers claiming two of these to push his tally to six kills, thus giving him ace status. "Buzz" Beerbower also claimed a Focke-Wulf, taking his score to 15.5 destroyed. This would prove to be his last victory.

Following this brief flurry of fighter activity, the doldrums returned to the 354th FG, the group flying eight or nine missions per day. Virtually all sorties were performed by two flights of eight aircraft, and with an early sunrise during the summer months, most days saw the first patrol airborne by 0530hrs. These patrols and sweeps would continue throughout the day until as late as 2215hrs.

Thanks to such a hectic mission schedule, by the end of July many of the original cadre of pilots who had arrived in the ETO with the 354th back in November 1943 were now becoming tour-expired. The Eighth Air Force had defined the length of combat tours for its fighter pilots long ago, but no attempt had been made to introduce such a policy within the Ninth Air Force. Therefore, those pilots in the 354th that had been in combat since December 1943 had now flown close to 130 sorties. Some returned to the group after leave in the United States, but most became instructors for the rest of the war.

There was no further aerial action for the 354th until July 17. On this date Capt Virgil Dietrich was leading the 355th FS on a patrol when 20-plus Fw 190s were encountered in the St Lô area. Dietrich claimed one fighter destroyed and Capt Lowell Brueland bagged a second, taking his tally to 8.5 kills. The 354th suffered the loss of Lt Thomas Cannon during the engagement, his P-51 last being seen in the combat area.

Later that day a patrol from the 353rd FS caught six Fw 190s in the same area, and the Mustang pilots managed to break them up and shoot down a single fighter. After departing the combat area, Lt Harvey Chapman found himself flying headlong into a formation of some 40-plus Fw 190s. He broke into the formation with his guns blazing, before immediately split-essing for the deck and effecting his escape.

The third encounter of July 17 came when Maj Robert Stephens of the 355th FS led a sweep to the Paris area. Approximately 50 Fw 190s and Bf 109s were sighted above the Mustangs, who at once started climbing up to engage them. In a reversal of recent encounters, some of these Luftwaffe pilots proved to be quite aggressive, and a series of dogfights took place. The 355th managed to down three Fw 190s, one of which became Maj Stephens' tenth victory. Two Mustangs failed to return from the battle, however.

Following this day of action, German fighters were encountered only fleetingly during the next week. For example, a group fighter sweep on July 18 intercepted just two enemy aircraft near Amiens, with one falling to the 354th and the other to P-47s patrolling in the same area. A squadron sweep by the 356th FS turned up eight Bf 109s in the Le Mans area, but only one Messerschmitt was shot down.

Capt Wallace Emmer led the 353rd on yet another fighter sweep on the afternoon of July 26, ground controllers vectoring the aircraft to the St Lô area once again. Allied air-search radar had detected more than 40 Bf 109s that were preparing to attack ground forces. The Mustangs pilots wasted no time in downing nine of the Messerschmitts, Capt Emmer himself being credited with two destroyed and one shared (with Lt Carl Bickell). Lt Clifford Dean was the other high scorer with two Bf 109s. Late that afternoon Capt Warren Emerson was leading the 355th on an escort mission for B-26s when their unit intercepted 20 Bf 109s and 20 Fw 190s, split into two formations. The squadron destroyed five, including an Fw 190 claimed by Emerson, for the loss of one Mustang.

Capt Lowell Brueland and seven other 355th FS Mustangs were on a patrol southeast of St Lô on the afternoon of July 28 when a large formation of Bf 109s was sighted. Three Fw 190s then also appeared on the scene. The encounter as reported by Brueland stated:

As we went in for the attack I noticed three Fw 190s. Following them, I attacked one, which pulled up through a thin layer of clouds at about 8,000ft when I hit him. He pulled into a tight turn and I hit him again. This time he bailed out, and I saw his 'chute open.

Numbers three and four men in my flight followed the other Fw 190s. I found three more Me 109s flying through the clouds at about 5,000ft. Covered by my numbers three and four men from "White Flight," we followed the Messerschmitts southeast for several minutes before we caught one of them in the open. I hit him and he broke down, and as I hit him again in his dive, he bailed out. I didn't see his 'chute open, the plane going straight in.

We then pulled back up and found four more Me 109s flying southeast, 3,000 to 4,000ft above and ahead of us. As the clouds thinned out we pulled up behind them. I took the one on the left and my number two man took the one on the right. My target was hit on the first burst, and he pulled straight up and bailed out. His 'chute opened. The remaining three broke down, with my two and three men behind them. Number two shot one of them down, and as I circled the area to get the two boys back in formation, 25 to 30 Fw 190s flew directly over us at 7,000ft (I was at 4,000ft). Just as they passed, I noticed an Fw 190 coming up at me from directly below and behind. I broke into it, and as we circled, another came down from above. I pulled straight up into him and fired head-on. I hit him and both Fw 190s headed for the deck. I did not follow for I was short on gas and ammunition.

This triple haul (and one damaged) ran Brueland's score up to 11.5 confirmed. The last encounter for the month took place on July 30 when Lt Col Teschner led the group on a patrol that was designed to give coverage to B-26s supporting the breakthrough at St Lô. The 356th's Maj Richard Turner sighted a flight of three bogies trailing two flights of P-51s, so he went down to investigate. They turned out to be Bf 109s, which split as soon as they were discovered. Turner sent one element after the two that broke in one direction while he took the other. After a long chase with his Mustang at full power, the major finally succeeded in hitting the Bf 109 in the cockpit with "one lonely strike." This seemed to slow the Messerschmitt down, the pilot choosing to end the series of turns that he had been making in favor of a last-ditch dive for freedom. "I was pleased at this for I knew I could overtake him in a dive," Turner later recounted.

Sensing his 11th kill, the ace inched his P-51D ever-closer to the Bf 109, firing intermittently. Seeing a scattering of strikes, which slowed his victim down even further, Turner hit him with a solid burst just before the Messerschmitt reached a bank of cloud. The German fighter began to stream coolant and pieces flew off. A fire erupted and the canopy came off, nearly hitting the Mustang. Then the pilot bailed out, his 'chute opening up as the P-51 flew past the burning Bf 109. Resuming his patrol, Maj Turner had just claimed his 11th, and last, aerial victory.

Although the 354th FG had scored just 36 victories for the month of July, the group total had now exceeded the 400 mark.

COVERING PATTON'S ARMY

As mentioned earlier, the 354th FG had been assigned to the new XIX Tactical Air Command, under the command of Brig Gen Otto P. Weyland, in June. This change had had little impact on the group's day-to-day routine until the arrival of Gen George Patton's Third Army in Normandy in August 1944. And it was during this month that the new American force started its drive through France, making full use of its armored columns. From then on the 354th FG would work very closely with the Third Army until VE-Day, quickly gaining the utmost respect from Patton and his men.

The first mission flown by the group in August, on the 1st, saw the 353rd FS supporting B-26s which had been sent to bomb bridges and rail installations. Four Bf 109s were intercepted as they came down in a line-astern attack on the B-26s, but not before a single Marauder had been lost. Three of the Messerschmitts were destroyed, one of which fell to Lt "Willie Y" Anderson to give him ace status. But the next few days saw no further action, and the Mustang pilots were becoming restless. Even the presence of Patton's army advancing eastward did not spur the Luftwaffe into any great action.

On August 7, Maj Turner was leading his 356th FS in a fighter sweep east of Chartres when a crashed Bf 109 was spotted in a field. The major went down to take a closer look, and discovered a whole squadron of well-camouflaged Messerschmitt fighters. Several strafing runs were made, and by the time the Mustangs had departed 13 enemy aircraft were either in flames or in ruins. Maj Turner destroyed three of the Bf 109s and Capt Verlin Chambers two.

Tempering this success was the loss of three Mustangs, with ace Lt Tommy Miller and two newer pilots, Lts Harbers and Charles Simonson, going down. Miller and Harbers fell victim to a flak gun sited in a church steeple, while Simonson was hit during a strafing pass on the Bf 109s. The latter pilot had bailed out over a battalion of US tanks, and he soon returned to the group, while Tommy Miller ended up a PoW. Harbers was killed.

The 353rd also saw combat that same day, when a fighter sweep led by Capt Emmer ran into a dozen Bf 109s flying in pairs in the Laval–Alençon area. The P-51s quickly sorted them out, downing six, with Capt Emmer getting his 14th and last victory and Lt "Willie Y" Anderson claiming his final two kills to take his tally to seven. Two men were lost, however, namely Lts Edwin Pinkerton and Loyd Overfield. The latter pilot had claimed three Bf 109s to "make ace," before in turn being shot down – he would return to the group five days later, and eventually finish his tour with 11 kills.

The 354th had never suffered the loss of five pilots in one day, and this was hard to take. August 7 had been bad enough, but things got even worse on the 9th. The group's ranking ace with 15.5 kills, Capt Don Beerbower, had been acting as squadron commander of the 353rd FS in the absence of Maj Jack Bradley, who had been on leave in the United States since June 30. Recently promoted to major, Beerbower was leading the unit on a morning armed reconnaissance sweep between Épernay and Reims when he sighted an airfield about three miles north of the latter town. He dropped down to investigate.

On his first pass he came under fire from heavy flak, but this did not prevent him from spotting some 30 Ju 88s scattered around the airfield perimeter. Beerbower informed his pilots that he was going to make east to west passes against the flak guns while they strafed the Ju 88s from north to south. The CO knocked out two gun emplacements in addition to destroying one of the Ju 88s on his pass, while his squadron left seven bombers in flames.

Making one more pass while his Mustangs cleared the airfield, Beerbower now became the sole target for all the remaining flak sites. His veteran P-51B suffered multiple hits, and he was seen to pull up, jettison his canopy and go over the side. Some of his pilots speculated that the ace must have struck the empennage as he bailed out, for although he reached the ground alive, Maj D. M. "Buzz" Beerbower died in captivity later that day. He was just 17 days short of reaching his 23rd birthday.

The whole group was in shock over the demise of its top ace, and an outstanding leader. None took the loss harder than his squadronmate, Capt Wallace Emmer. Ironically, Emmer was now called upon to take temporary command of the 353rd. In the late afternoon he took to the skies as part of a group-strength armed reconnaissance mission (led by Capt Chambers of the 356th FS) to the Rouen area.

All seemed to be going well until the Mustangs came under fire whilst cruising at 11,000ft north of Reims. One of the shells hit Emmer's P-51D and exploded, causing the Mustang to burst into flames. The aircraft soon lost height and began to shed parts, and Emmer was last seen huddled down in the cockpit prior to jettisoning the canopy and going over the side. He survived the jump but was very badly burned, and after spending months in various German hospitals, Capt Wallace Emmer died in a PoW camp on February 15, 1945 from an attack of myocarditis (inflammation of the heart muscle), caused by an infection that he had contracted due to his weakened physical state. Following the shock of losing two squadron commanders in one day, the 353rd FS welcomed seven-kill ace Capt Felix "Mike" Rogers as the new squadron CO – he had served with the unit since June 1943.

During this period the group began packing up and preparing for its impending move to Gael, on the Brest Peninsula. This base was located on a high plateau, and was coded A-31. Richard Turner was one of the first pilots to visit the new airfield:

We moved our base of operations once again during the 11th through the 13th of August, from the A-2 beach strip to a field near Monfort. The new airfield was about 25 miles west of Rennes at the root of the Brest Peninsula, and we were curious to see it since the base had been recently held by the Luftwaffe before Patton's rapid advance had forced them to flee.

It was interestingly situated with pockets of German resistance all around it, bypassed by the fast-moving Third Army. To the west of us a large fortification was still manned by a diehard German regiment. There was a pocket of Germans still offering resistance to the south, at Saint Nazaire, and another around Falaise in the rear. All this gave the new base an unexpected atmosphere of tension. But when we arrived we found the landing strip was in good shape, although the buildings were severely damaged. Group Command promptly appropriated the buildings for its own use, and the squadrons set up bivouac areas in tents again as before.

The group did not conduct its first mission from the new field until August 14, the 354th in the meantime flying routine patrols, a few escort missions for light and medium bombers and ground attack sorties for Patton's army.

The Mustangs were back in action on the 16th. That afternoon, the 356th was returning from a patrol when 70 Fw 190s, loaded with bombs, were sighted flying at 2,000ft. Although drastically outnumbered, the eight P-51s dove down and broke up the formations, forcing the Fw 190s to jettison their bombs. Some of the German fighter-bombers broke and ran while others stayed to fight, allowing Lts Keith Aldrich and Walter Williams to down two of them. Two Mustangs were lost to the enemy in return.

That same afternoon Lt Charles Koenig was leading a patrol of 353rd FS Mustangs that spotted about 20 Fw 190s forming up in elements of two above a hole in the overcast at 11,000ft near Maintenon. The two flights of P-51s had just climbed to 14,000ft in order to attack the Focke-Wulf fighters from above when another 60-plus Fw 190s joined the fray from out of the clouds below. Lt Kenny Dahlberg later reported:

I felt sure that I had bought it that day. There were eight of us against 80 of them. Everywhere you looked there was a Mustang mixing it with three or four Jerries. The first one I got was on the tail end of a flight of four. I poured lead into him, getting hits around the canopy area. The plane went down smoking and out of control.

I tagged onto a second, gave him a few bursts and the damn thing blew up, splashing me with oil. At the same time I noticed my oil line had been hit. I wheeled around and dropped, hoping to make it back to my own lines. Looming smack in front of me was a lone Fw 190. That's when I found my gunsight was out, so I used tracers from 60 degrees and closed to 30 degrees. My bullets hit and he blew up.

> I noticed tracers coming over both my wings. I checked my tail and saw four Fw 190s converging on me for the kill. I saw a nice black cloud and I ducked into it.

Dahlberg did not make it back to his base that day. After losing most of its oil, the engine in his fighter heated up and he was forced to bail out. He was assisted in evading the Germans by a French couple who hid him until he could be helped through the lines to join advancing American troops.

Despite having been shot down, Dahlberg's triple haul had taken his tally to exactly five kills. He was joined in "acedom" by Lt Charles Koenig, whose pair of Fw 190s destroyed (plus a probable and a damaged) had boosted his final tally to 6.5 victories. Yet despite the creation of two new aces, perhaps the most outstanding performer of the August 16 clash was Lt John E. Bakalar, who accounted for three fighters in his first-ever combat sortie! He would not score again.

Other pilots to taste success in this engagement included Lt Charles E. Brown, who bagged two before he was forced to bail out (he also returned to the 354th a few days later), and Lt Woodfin Marcellus Sullivan, whose two Fw 190s took his final wartime tally to four destroyed and one damaged. Sullivan was lucky to return to base, for he got so low during one of his combats that he severely damaged his Mustang's wing when he hit a tree!

The following day (August 17) Capt Warren Emerson led eight P-51s from the 355th FS on a morning escort for a squadron of P-47s bombing targets in the Dreux area. Upon rendezvousing with the Thunderbolts, Emerson spied two Fw 190s preparing to attack from above. He chased the two German fighters through scattered cloud from 3,000 to 4,000ft, before hitting the trailing aircraft with a solid burst of fire as it made its way into the overcast. Although one of the pilots in the flight saw the aircraft go into a spin and crash, "Red" Emerson failed to get this kill officially confirmed. He emerged from the clouds to find himself right behind a second Fw 190, and several bursts of fire knocked pieces off the airplane and the pilot bailed out. There was no doubt about this one being confirmed.

As Patton's Third Army broke out and rolled on toward Paris, the 354th found itself flying continuous patrols to protect its flanks. Capt Verlin Chandler led the 356th FS on a fighter sweep in the Paris area on August 18, and during the course of the mission the squadron enjoyed great success. Chandler later reported:

> We circled the Beauvais airfield looking for aircraft. Hellum Red Three called in some aircraft parked towards the edge of a forest on the side of the airfield. We made three passes at them. I opened fire from about 400 yards, and fired up to about 100 yards. When I left, the plane I had fired at was burning. I claim this Me 109 as destroyed [before leaving, the formation had claimed seven Bf 109s destroyed – Editor].

About 80 miles east of Épernay I was looking over a suspicious landing field when I noticed eight aircraft taxi out and start to take off. I waited until six planes were airborne before I called "Hellum Flight" and started down after them. No 8 wasn't airborne so I skipped him and started firing at No 7, who was just getting his wheels up. I fired from about 300 yards from dead astern up to 50 yards and then I had to pull up to avoid a collision. When I rolled over and looked down, the plane had crashed and was burning on the edge of the field that he had just taken off from. I claim this Me 109 as destroyed.

I then saw another Me 109 on the tail of a P-51, so I called the pilot and told him to keep turning while I made a pass at the '109. I fired from about 200 yards, with about 30 degrees of deflection. I saw a number of strikes. The Me 109 rolled over and the canopy fell away, but the pilot did not bail out. The '109 crash-landed in a field. The pilot got out and ran into a forest. I strafed the plane and set it on fire. I claim this '109 as destroyed.

Aside from Verlin Chandler's two Bf 109s shot down, Lt Frederick Warner was also credited with two Messerschmitt fighters destroyed, while three others were shared amongst the rest of the flights.

On August 24 Gen Hoyt Vandenberg, Commander of the Ninth Air Force, paid his first visit to the 354th. During his time at A-31, Vandenberg presented the group with its first Distinguished Unit Citation (sometimes called a Presidential Citation) for outstanding performance of duty in action against the enemy from November 4, 1943 through May 15, 1944. Decorations were also awarded to many of the pilots who had distinguished themselves flying with the first Mustang fighter group in the ETO.

The day after Gen Vandenberg's visit, Allied troops arrived in Paris. While celebrations took place on the streets of the city, for the 354th it was business as usual, and on this occasion the group went after the Luftwaffe on its remaining airfields north of the city. Badly aggrieved by the fall of the French capital, the enemy chose to rise to the challenge thrown down by the group, and thus allow the 354th FG to achieve its greatest single-day victory tally of the entire war.

It all started on the first fighter sweep of the day, led off from A-31 at 0810hrs by Maj Robert Stephens. The 16 Mustangs of the 355th FS were heading for Beauvais and Épernay when, just north of Reims, they were attacked by a mixed force of 20 Bf 109s and Fw 190s. Maj Stephens quickly downed two Focke-Wulf fighters, boosting his overall tally to 13. Nearby, Lt Bill Davis had gone into a Lufbery with an Fw 190, and after a few turns he pulled his nose through, fired and the enemy pilot jettisoned his canopy and bailed out. Davis then gave chase to a second Bf 109 and had seen his rounds strike home when he ran out of ammunition! Capt Maurice Long had to finish the fighter off.

By then the latter pilot had already downed an Fw 190 in the initial attack and shot another off the tail of a Mustang, before completing the job on Davis's Bf 109. Long's haul of 2.5 kills gave him an overall tally of 5.25, allowing him to join the ranks of the 354th's fighter elite – these were also his last claims of the war. A total of nine enemy fighters had been destroyed during the clash, and the only Mustang that failed to return from the sweep was downed by flak encountered on the way home.

The second successful mission of the day involved Maj Richard Turner, his 356th FS and a German airfield near Beauvais. A fuel truck and at least seven Fw 190s parked in a large hangar were spotted off to one side of the field, and on its first low pass the squadron took out the tanker. The hangar duly caught fire thanks to the blazing truck, and the blaze quickly spread to the Fw 190s. A further three aircraft were also destroyed by the strafers, and other hangars and installations were left in flames.

The 355th FS undertook its second mission of the day at 1704hrs when Capt Warren Emerson led a dozen Mustangs on a fighter sweep of the Reims area. Here, they encountered 15 Fw 190s. The aircraft had just begun to split off into individual dogfights when two more groups of about 30 Bf 109s and Fw 190s joined in the battle.

At this point Capt Emerson had to break off his first combat with a Focke-Wulf in order to meet the onslaught of the newcomers, quickly latching onto the tail of an Fw 190 and shooting it down. He then switched his attention to another Fw 190 that was chasing a P-51, and as the German pilot pulled up into a steep climbing turn, Emerson hit his canopy area with a few shots and the aircraft caught fire. The Mustang pilot pulled up above the Fw 190, stalled out and came back down so close to the Focke-Wulf that he dented his wingtip!

Emerson then went after a third Fw 190, but as he dived toward his foe he saw tracers off his wing. Immediately breaking off his attack, he turned and saw aircraft wreckage in the air and a parachute blossoming above it. Emerson quickly realized that his wingman, Lt McClure, who had been with him through all of his earlier combats, had been shot down. Fortunately McClure evaded capture and returned to A-31 about two weeks later.

Joining up with two other Mustangs, Emerson climbed back into the fight. The three P-51s were then attacked by two Bf 109s, and he maneuvered himself around one of the Messerschmitts and saw good hits that set its drop tank on fire. The pilot bailed out, giving Emerson a score of three victories for the day (and his last of the war), thus making him an ace with six kills.

Lt William King also scored three times in the ruckus, all of his kills being Fw 190s. The first was sent down in an inverted spin, the second was abandoned by its pilot after King had hit the fighter with just a handful of rounds, and the third tried to shake the Mustang pilot off, but to no avail. Like Emerson, King's three kills were his last claims of the conflict, and they boosted his tally to 5.5 victories.

Capt Virgil Dietrich, who had been leading a flight when "Red" Emerson initially engaged the first enemy formation, had sighted the additional Luftwaffe fighter force as they entered the fray and duly attacked them. He swiftly maneuvered onto the tail of an Fw 190 and, after firing a series of short bursts, the pilot bailed out. Dietrich (who finished his tour with four kills) then chased another all the way to Calais, but could not shoot it down.

Lt Robert Foye was also leading a flight that got caught up with a formation of Fw 190s, and he destroyed one in the initial attack. Returning home with his wingman, Foye heard a call from Emerson and went back to investigate. As he approached, an Fw 190 turned in front of him, so he fired and the enemy fighter went straight in. Foye then latched onto the tail of a third Fw 190, and it was only after he had completed a few turns with the German aircraft that he discovered he was out of ammunition, so he broke off the combat and returned home.

Three pilots besides Lt McClure did not return from the battle, Lt Norman Mayse last being seen in combat with an enemy aircraft, Lt George Hoehn bailing out but evading capture and Lt Harold Gray (who was Lt Foye's wingman) being shot down and killed after the initial engagement.

The last big fight of the day occurred later that afternoon when the 356th FS ventured out on yet another fighter sweep. A large formation of enemy fighters was discovered west of Reims, and the Mustang pilots attacked. Lt Bart Tenore describes the action:

I was leading "Green Flight" when our squadron bounced a large formation of Me 109s and Fw 190s, which passed under us at about 3,000ft. "White Leader" led his flight to the left, attacking a group of '190s, and I split-essed onto about 15 Me 109s. The E/A headed for the deck, and only one of them attempted to turn into us. He made a half-hearted head-on pass but did not open fire, instead rejoining the formation, which flew line abreast down a valley. I opened fire on the first '109 on the right-hand side of the formation and got hits on the fuselage and radiator coolers. He crashed in a wood. I then took on the next ship in the formation and fired dead astern on him. He was flying above the treetops, and as I followed him over a small knoll, I saw him hit the ground and explode.

I then moved into position behind a third '109 and got some hits. He crashed in front of me and I had to pull up to avoid hitting the debris. As I was attacking the third ship, I was flying line abreast with another '109, which Lt McIntire said flew into the ground right next to me. We tailed the last '109 for a long time, and I registered a few hits with the one gun I had left firing. When my ammo ran out, Lt McIntire moved into position to fire, but the '109 outclimbed us as McIntire scored some hits with his last remaining gun.

This massacre resulted in a dozen confirmed victories for the men of the 356th. Besides Lt Tenore's three (of an eventual score of four, one probable and 1.5 damaged during his ETO tour), Lt Francis McIntire was credited with three (of an eventual score of 4.5 and

0.5 damaged during his ETO tour) and Lts Clyde D. Sharman and Robert Lester got doubles. The total score for the day was 24 destroyed in the air for the 355th FS, and 12 in the air and ten on the ground for the 356th FS.

For the rest of the month squadron-strength fighter sweeps continued to be flown, but the only one that encountered any kind of opposition from the Luftwaffe came on August 28. Maj Stephens was leading a patrol in the vicinity of Châlons, Reims and Soissons when his Mustangs were bounced by some 50 Fw 190s and Bf 109s over Épernay. Stephens duly destroyed a Messerschmitt in a climbing Lufbery for his 13th and last kill of the war. His combat report stated:

> The Jerry had made the mistake of trying to turn with our Lufbery. In doing this he lost
> his speed advantage and couldn't get away. I got on his tail and had him in my sights when
> he half-rolled. I rolled after him. Then, before I fired a shot, he bailed out.

Elsewhere, Capt Lendon Buer, leading Blue Flight, had attacked six Bf 109s that were diving on "White Flight," which broke on Buer's call. He took the tail-end Bf 109 and went into a climbing turn after it. A rolling fight ensued until the enemy aircraft suffered a number of telling strikes and dived into a forest.

After a slow start, August 1944 had become a very productive month for the 354th FG. The group's pilots had scored 72 aerial victories and claimed the destruction of 38 aircraft on the ground, but this success had come at a high price. No fewer than 18 pilots had been shot down, although the good news was that seven of them had returned to the group before the end of the month.

STALEMATE

By September the bulk of the German Army in the west had moved back behind the Moselle River and established a series of defensive positions around the fort city of Metz. The Luftwaffe had also pulled its fighter units back to airfields in the Third Reich in order to defend both industrial targets and cities alike against near-daily heavy bomber raids. In the wake of these tactical withdrawals, the only German stronghold remaining in the west was the Brest Peninsula.

The 354th FG was now kept busy flying continual fighter sweeps over this area, seeking out pockets of enemy resistance on the ground and very occasionally encountering the Luftwaffe in the air, which was usually conspicuous by its absence. The first part of the month was marred by rain, but once the weather improved numerous dive-bombing missions were flown against the besieged garrison at Brest. Another thing that hindered the group when it came to engaging the Luftwaffe was the sheer distance that now separated its base from the aerial action that was routinely taking place over the frontline. However, the 354th FG would soon experience yet another move, taking it far closer to the German border.

There was one bright spot early in the month, which occurred during an armed reconnaissance mission on September 10 flown by Lts Carl Bickel and Harold Price. The pair had attempted to strafe a train near Saarbrücken, which had beaten into a nearby tunnel. As they pulled up, Bickel sighted an He 111 bomber flying west at 1,000ft. The Mustang pilot easily caught the Heinkel and set it on fire with two long bursts, but before he could finish it off he was driven away by heavy flak. Price then sighted Bickel's wounded prey moments later, and he duly finished it off with two long bursts. Despite having only "winged" the He 111, Carl Bickel was duly credited with a full kill, taking his overall tally to 5.5, and thus giving him ace status. This would be his final claim of the war.

The big day of the month came 48 hours later when Capt Charles Brown led a sweep over Koblenz and nearby Limburg airfield. At the latter site, two flights from the 353rd FS strafed Ju 88s and Fw 190s parked on the edge of the field, destroying eight of them.

The Mustangs then climbed to about 9,000ft and headed for Frankfurt. En route, they sighted about 40 Fw 190s flying some 2,000ft below them. Above the Focke-Wulf fighters were a further 30 Bf 109s with drop tanks. While the bulk of the P-51s dived down and attacked the Fw 190s, Capt Brown and his flight immediately began climbing after the Bf 109s. He was not able to down any of them in the subsequent whirl of combat, however, although he did succeed in breaking up the formation and keeping them away from the other Mustangs. Brown also radioed in flights from the 355th FS, which then joined in the air battle.

2Lt Bruce Carr had set fire to two Ju 88s during the strafing run on the airfield and had followed his flight up to 9,000ft when the Fw 190s were sighted. He later reported:

My flight was closest to them so I made a bounce on the rear of the enemy formation. At this point Lt John E. Miller left my flight and was not seen after that. The Fw 190 that I picked out broke in a sharp climbing turn to the left. I fired a 30-degree deflection shot from 150 to 100 yards. I got many strikes on the left wing and around the engine. This ship seemed to explode and became enveloped in flames. The pilot immediately bailed out.

I then saw a lone Fw 190 on the deck trying to get away from the fight. I dived after him and fired a short burst at about 30 degrees deflection from about 250 yards. I saw a few strikes and he started a turn to the left. I closed to about 150 yards, fired again and got strikes on his engine and around the cockpit. As I fired he snapped to the left on his back and flew into a hill.

I then climbed back up to about 6,000ft, where I saw an Fw 190 diving for the deck 80 degrees off the direction I was flying in. I turned right and fired a very short burst at 80 degrees deflection from 300 yards. I saw hits all around the cockpit. The E/A steepened its dive, rolled over on its back and went in. The pilot did not get out.

I climbed back up to about 10,000ft and ran into about 30-plus Me 109s. There were too many for me, and I saw a P-51 below me smoking. I was afraid they would bounce him so I went down and gave him cover. After we had gotten away from the E/A I flew up close to the smoking P-51. It was Lt Robert Reynolds, and he told me over the R/T that he had destroyed three Fw 190s. I gave him cover until his engine caught fire due to a lack of coolant. He bailed out at 5,000ft.

Abandoning his P-51B northeast of Luxembourg, the 20-year-old ace (his triple haul had boosted his tally to seven kills) descended safely to become a PoW. Bruce Carr, meanwhile, returned home alone, having taken his own score to 4.5 kills.

Another 353rd pilot to enjoy a successful day was Lt Dahlberg, who had previously claimed a three-kill haul on August 16 to "make ace." On September 12 he went one better, as he stated in his combat report:

On my strafing run I was going so fast I couldn't aim. When we reformed at 7,000ft we sighted 40 Fw 190s and took off after them.

Dahlberg quickly downed his first two Focke-Wulf fighters with accurate strikes on their respective cockpit areas. He continued:

> They both blew up with the first burst. As I pulled up from the second one, I got on the tail of another Fw 190. As we started to climb up I cut his right wing off with my bullets. He bailed out. I looked around and saw an Fw 190 riddling a P-51, who in turn was shooting at another '190. I dropped down to give a hand, got some hits around the canopy and the Jerry went flying into the ground.

When the fight was over Dahlberg had scored four times, Carr and Lts Omer Culbertson and Robert Reynolds had achieved the "hat trick" with three apiece while Capt Virgil Dietrich and Lt Melvin Thayer were credited with doubles. In all, some 22 Fw 190s had been downed for the loss of two Mustangs.

The next big event of the month was the move to ALG A-66 at Orconte, on the Marne River. Aircraft were parked on grass, and the runway consisted of heavy sheets of tarpaper applied directly onto the grass. Upon arrival, personnel from the group joined in a mad scramble for lumber to build what they could to improve their tent quarters.

The only other aerial action for the month took place on September 26 when Lts Ira Bunting and Clifford Dean shared in the destruction of a Bf 109 while on a sweep in the Wesel area. Later that day Lt Francis McIntire was leading an aerial patrol in the Arnhem area when he was vectored to Düsseldorf. On arrival, he found a number of Bf 109s engaged in combat with P-38s. Two of the Messerschmitts broke away from the fight following the appearance of the P-51s and attempted to flee, but Lts McIntire and Harriman Thompson chased them down. Thompson quickly overhauled his target, gave it a blast and the Bf 109 went straight in. He then caught up to the second Bf 109, opened fire but overran the fighter. Trailing Thompson, McIntire came in for his shot and saw strikes on the Bf 109, although the German fighter continued on its way. Finally, Thompson pulled in behind the Messerschmitt for a second time and finished it off. On the return journey home, McIntire spotted a lone Bf 109 on the deck and downed it at minimum gun range.

The last combat of the month took place on the 28th. Lt Robert L. Young of the 356th FS had been participating in a sweep over Germany when his element leader's P-51 developed engine trouble and he escorted him home. Along the way, a lone Fw 190 was sighted flying some 6,000ft below them, so Young dived after it and shot the fighter down – the P-51 pilot later remarked in his combat report that his German counterpart had probably never even seen his attacker.

October was plagued with more bad weather, although the group attacked a number of rail targets, both through dive-bombing and strafing. It also flew a few escort missions for B-26s, although the vast majority of the missions performed were armed reconnaissance sweeps, attacking targets of opportunity. And the latter were now becoming scarce too, with the enemy building up its defenses for the impending fight for the German homeland.

It was not until the end of the month that the 354th once again met the Luftwaffe in the skies, and a spectacular air battle ensued. Capt Glenn Eagleston was leading the group on a bombing mission, targeting German airfields, when the Mustangs met a large force of Bf 109s. Eagleston reported:

The group was proceeding on course at 1130hrs when "Ripsaw" [ground control] informed me of a large number of bogies at twelve o'clock to the group, east of Durlach. I sighted the bogies at 1140hrs, nine o'clock to our group, and going in the opposite direction some 2,000ft above us. The bogies made a wide diving turn and came in on us at six o'clock from slightly above. When definite recognition as enemy Me 109s had been made, I waited until the enemy gaggle had almost set itself for a bounce and then called a group turn of 180 degrees to the left to meet the attack head-on. I ordered the group to jettison bombs and proceeded to attack. E/A formation was very well spread out and semi-line abreast in flights of four and eight. Estimated strength, 60-plus.

I encountered a single Me 109 at about 10,000ft and tacked on to him, but I had trouble catching this E/A so I fired a short burst at 45 degrees without observing strikes. I then fired a one-second burst at 30 degrees and observed strikes on the fuselage and left wing root, and the E/A started smoking. After this I pulled up astern, zero degrees and fired a two-second burst from 100 yards. The E/A started to burn and the pilot bailed out.

Observing a flight of four Me 109s at 11,000ft, I bounced these E/A and fired a one-second burst at the No 4 man, observing a few strikes on his fuselage. The E/A broke into me and started a climbing turn. This pilot was particularly aggressive, and showed no desire to run. I was also amazed at the performance of the E/A, which showed climbing and turning ability far above any Me 109 that I had ever encountered. I rat-raced this E/A for about five minutes without getting into a shooting position. Finally, this E/A pulled straight up and I closed to 100 yards and fired a two-second burst into him, scoring many strikes on the fuselage. The E/A started to smoke badly and pieces came off. It fell into a slow spin and burst into flames. I observed this aircraft crash and explode. The pilot did not get out.

By this time the E/A were split up and coming in from all directions so that it was very necessary to keep looking around. My wingman, Lt Frederick I. Couch, had been unable to release his bombs, yet in spite of this he had stayed in an excellent covering position through severe and violent maneuvering, making it possible for me to concentrate on my targets. I observed a single Me 109 at about 10,000ft, slightly above and climbing, going in the opposite direction. I pulled up underneath him with the E/A almost in a loop and fired a two-second burst from about 100 yards at almost a 90-degree deflection, scoring many strikes directly under the cockpit. The E/A started to burn and fell off in a spin. The pilot bailed out and his E/A crashed and exploded.

The enemy pilots varied from aggressive to very aggressive, and appeared to be highly experienced. Instead of operating in their usual gaggle formation, they tried at all times to stay in four- and eight-ship flights.

Eagleston had been accurate in his description of the opposition, for the 354th had encountered the Stab. (Headquarters flight), as well as II., III. and IV. Gruppen of JG 53. The air battle lasted about 35 minutes, and the results were amazingly close to what was claimed. The Mustang pilots were credited with 21 kills, which was exactly the number of Bf 109s that JG 53 admitted losing! Ten pilots were killed and four wounded, and included amongst the former was IV./JG 53's Gruppenkommandeur, Hauptmann Morr. A staffel commander was also killed during the engagement. The pilots of JG 53 claimed eight P-51s destroyed, compared with four actually lost by the group. High scorers for the day were Capt Eagleston with three (taking his tally to 15.5 kills), Capt Harry Fisk with three (boosting his score to exactly five, these being his last claims for the war) and Lts Bruce Carr and Philip Cohen with two each. For Carr, his tally had now exceeded the magical five-kill mark, and many more victories were yet to come!

Despite only 34 missions being flown during the month of October, the group had lost ten pilots. And the 354th got the new month off to a shaky start when, on November 5, deputy group leader Lt Col Jack Bradley lost control of his aircraft and crashed on take-off. Fortunately, he was not injured, and the balance of the group continued on their mission attacking airfields.

One site that was hit was Schwäbisch Hall, which was battered with 500lb bombs and then strafed – at least six aircraft were set on fire. Lt Hayden Holton of the 353rd FS participated in this attack, dropping his ordnance directly onto a hardstanding in front of a hangar packed with aircraft. The P-51s then continued over to Crailsheim airfield, and as they approached the target a train appeared on the edge of the field and Holton blasted it, sending steam shooting high into the air. The 353rd then proceeded to attack the field, destroying several Me 163s and Bf 110s.

The 355th and 356th FSs, meanwhile, had hit Sachsenheim as well as Crailsheim, and upon returning to A-66, the group was credited with having destroyed 28 enemy aircraft on the ground, including ten jets. However, this did not compensate for the one loss of the day, 10.75-kill ace Maj Frank O'Connor. His Mustang had been squarely hit by flak, forcing the CO of the 356th FS to pull up in a zoom climb from low level and bail out. Upon landing, O'Connor only survived the attentions of an angry civilian mob through the timely intervention of a Luftwaffe sergeant from the base that he had just attacked! He was duly packed off to become a PoW. With the loss of Maj O'Connor, Capt Earl Depner took over the reins of the 356th FS.

The rainy weather that had stalled American attacks on the German lines also caused problems for the 354th. When Patton's Third Army began its offensive on the Saar River the dam on the Marne River overflowed, which in turn caused the group's airfield to become flooded. Nearly all the 354th's buildings, as well as the tent living areas, were largely inundated, yet with ground installations literally floating around A-66, the pilots continued their attacks on German airfields.

The group received what many considered to be the worst blow in its short history on November 13. The men were told that they would be giving up their P-51 Mustangs for Republic P-47 Thunderbolts! They could not believe it, but it was true. The P-47s were due to arrive shortly so that pilots and groundcrews could familiarize themselves with the big radial-engined fighter. And to make matters worse, the unit was forced to vacate a soggy A-66 for nearby A-65 (Perthes), a defunct German installation with terrible conditions, on the 14th. Once at the latter site the men performed their tasks as best they could, while trying to dry their things out.

Some good news was announced the following day, however. The 354th would be moving to A-98 at Rosières-en-Haye, about six miles north of Toul, and some ten miles northwest of Nancy. The depressing event of the day was the arrival of the first Thunderbolts for the pilots to begin their orientation on.

The only aerial combat for the month occurred on the 17th while seeking out a rail junction to bomb. The pilots dropped their ordnance on a double rail line between Achern and Spenweiler, severing the tracks. Bf 109s then attacked the P-51s as they were pulling out of their dives, and Lt Clifford Davis claimed one of them shot down in flames. Later in the day Lt Richard Poole Jr and Maj Marshall Cloak were attacked by a swarm of enemy fighters, and the former downed one Bf 109 before he was shot down and Cloak claimed two.

Dive-bombing missions continued despite terrible weather, and several aircraft were lost not only to German flak but to the rain and wind which made flying a real hazard. The aircraft began their move to Rosières-en-Haye on November 25, the new camp taking shape rapidly, with living quarters mounted on planking and rigged for cold, winter weather.

On the afternoon of November 26, four Thunderbolts from the 356th FS took to the sky to perform the first P-47 mission flown by the 354th FG. Bad weather kept the group grounded for the rest of the month. The group had flown just 34 missions during November and destroyed about 50 enemy aircraft on the ground. Only two confirmed aerial victories were added to the scoreboard, while a further 12 pilots had been lost to flak and weather.

THUNDERBOLT BLUES

While the conversion to P-47s certainly had a poor effect on the morale of the men of the 354th, it did not affect their devotion to duty and their determination to see the job through to the end of the conflict in Europe. The group's reequipment with the rugged Thunderbolt signaled an end to armed reconnaissance missions where pilots went looking for trouble in the air. The 354th's primary duty now was dive-bombing, strafing and supporting troops on the ground.

By the first week of December the 355th FS had also finished its conversion onto the P-47 and had started flying combat missions, but the 353rd FS was still very much in a transitionary phase, and was therefore still conducting sorties with its last remaining P-51s. It was whilst flying one of these final dive-bombing missions with the Mustang that on December 1 the unit engaged a gaggle of 30 Bf 109s. The German pilots dropped their belly tanks and prepared to scrap with the 353rd, and in the dogfight that ensued three Messerschmitts were downed – two of them by the unit's pilot of the moment, Capt Ken Dahlberg. In return, the 353rd lost a single Mustang to flak.

Practically all the missions flown for the next few days involved dive-bombing and armed reconnaissance, as the 354th sought suitable ground targets to attack. On December 16 the group made further use of a weapon it had initially employed with devastating effect during the attacks on German strongholds on the Brest Peninsula in September – napalm. A refined petroleum jelly that was pumped into standard underwing drop tanks, napalm exploded when it hit the ground, showering the enemy with a wave of scorching heat and flames. While there was some opposition to its use on humanitarian grounds, napalm proved to be a hugely effective way of neutralizing isolated pockets of resistance which had been bypassed by the Allied advance.

The entire complexion of the frontline over which the 354th FG had been flying on a near-daily basis changed drastically on December 16 following the launching of Field Marshal Karl Gerd von Rundstedt's surprise Panzer offensive. Masked by bad weather, which kept virtually all Allied aircraft on the ground, German forces broke through poorly defended American lines and pushed forward to form a pocket into Allied territory, where they were finally halted during the legendary battle of the Bulge. However, both during and immediately after the offensive, the 354th had a full-time job assisting the hard-pressed GIs on the ground by flying numerous bombing and strafing sorties.

Despite all this flying, the men of the 354th soon began to wonder if they would ever score another aerial victory. Finally, on December 17, 353rd FS Operations Officer and five-kill ace, Maj James Dalglish, spotted an Me 410 taking off from an enemy airfield. A diving attack put him on the tail of the twin-engined aircraft, which he shot down. This was Dalglish's first kill since commencing his second tour with the 354th FG in mid-October, having previously served with the 355th FS until declared tour-expired at the end of June. This lone Me 410 was also the first aerial victory scored by the 354th with the P-47.

The following day the 355th FS flew a mission in heavy fog, but the weather made the target impossible to locate. The Thunderbolt pilots did spot a dozen Fw 190s dive-bombing US troops east of Düren, however, and three German fighters were downed for the loss of two P-47s. Marginally better weather conditions on the 19th allowed Capt Kenn Dahlberg to lead four flights from the 353rd FS on a dive-bombing mission against the HQ of the 116th Panzer Division southwest of Prüm:

> Twelve of us started out, but we got jumped by more than 40 Messerschmitts and had to drop our bombs in order to fight. I'd like to say right now that the Luftwaffe was successful, because it prevented us from carrying out our bombing mission. You can't maneuver a fighter if you're carrying bombs, so we had to dump them or get shot down. Four of our fighters never got into the scrap because our formation was broken up by the intense German flak. Eight of us who did get into the fight knocked down nine Germans.

Just prior to being bounced by the Bf 109s, Dahlberg had led his charges down through the mist-shrouded hills of the Schnee Eifel, where he was amazed to discover the roads below him jammed solid with German vehicles of all shapes and sizes. He was just about to attack when the Messerschmitts appeared. These Luftwaffe pilots proved to be both experienced and aggressive, and the Americans had to fight hard to survive. Of the nine victories claimed (four by Dahlberg), only six were confirmed, half of these falling to the flight leader. The 353rd FS suffered the loss of three pilots in the engagement.

At this time practically all the missions being flown by the 354th were in support of embattled American troops in the vicinity of the Belgian town of Bastogne. After a week of terrible weather, consisting of snow, freezing rain and fog, things finally started to improve, and the group escorted a huge formation of C-47s which managed to drop much-needed supplies to the men of the 101st Airborne Division and others who were surrounded at Bastogne. The improving weather also allowed the 354th FG to give better support to the troops on the ground.

On the morning of the 24th the 353rd discovered a number of enemy goods cars near the German border town of Trier, and whilst in the process of attacking them 16 Fw 190s intervened. The Thunderbolts tore into them instead, and succeeded in driving them off. Lt Orin Rawlings was able to down one of the German fighters as they fled.

The ring around Bastogne was finally broken on December 26, and during one of the numerous support missions flown that day, Maj James Dalglish and his flight surprised 20 Fw 190s strafing American troops. They immediately intercepted and broke them up, claiming four of the enemy fighters. As December came to a close the 354th tallied up the many missions flown – there were 113 of them. Only 16 aerial victories had been scored for the loss of ten of their own, but the pilots had gone all-out to support the ground forces, and had seen the German offensive stopped.

On January 1, 1945 the Luftwaffe flew massive low-altitude attacks against Allied airfields in Belgium, Holland and northern France. Considerable damage was done and many Allied aircraft were destroyed, but the Luftwaffe suffered massive losses in return – losses from which it would never recover. Indeed, 300 aircraft and 233 pilots had been lost in the worst single-day defeat the Luftwaffe had ever known.

The 354th continued constant attacks against the enemy during the first days of 1945. However, there was great opposition from flak on these sorties, and on the 2nd six missions were flown and four pilots were lost to ground fire. The good weather did not last, and for several days the 354th was grounded. Snow and overcast skies dominated the entire area, and nothing was seen of the Luftwaffe following its New Year's Day disaster.

As the month came to a close the Germans had been thrown back, and they were now doing their utmost to delay the advance of American troops into the Fatherland. The 354th continued to fly ground support and suffer losses to flak, but the destruction of enemy equipment and personnel on the roads was impressive. The group managed to fly 79 missions during the month despite being grounded for a total of 17 days. There were no aerial victories, and nine pilots had been lost.

During February there were more ground support missions accompanied by more bad weather, although the temperatures at last began to slowly climb. With spring not too far away, the 354th eagerly awaited the final Allied breakthrough into Germany, which would hopefully end the war in Europe. With thoughts of victory in mind, the group received tremendous news on February 8. It was informed that within a week the 354th would be issued with Mustangs once again.

As part of the struggle to gain ground in Germany, napalm began to be used more frequently by the 354th in an effort to break up some of the more stubborn resistance along the frontline. Some small villages were incinerated to dislodge the enemy, and it was on just such a mission on February 14 that the 353rd FS's Capt Ken Dahlberg was hit by flak and forced to bail out. He had evaded capture once before (in August 1944), but this time the 14-victory ace did not make it back to base, and instead he sat out the rest of the conflict as a PoW.

Ironically, Dahlberg missed the arrival of the first contingent of Mustangs, which came in that afternoon! There was much jubilation in camp that night, for the 354th FG had once again become the "Pioneer Mustang Group."

"DEUTSCHLAND KAPUT"

Once the Mustangs arrived at Rosières-en-Haye, the 354th wasted no time in getting them into action. Its squadrons simply parked the unloved P-47s in a quiet corner of the airfield and continued with their missions. From that day on the group was concerned with practically nothing but fighter sweeps and fighter patrols. The first P-51 mission was flown on February 16, 1945, and success came early. The 356th FS, led by Capt Loyd Brandt, had just strafed some locomotives when ground control vectored them onto a gaggle of bogies that had been detected. In the brief combat that ensued three Bf 109s were destroyed, with one losing its tail in a dive and the pilot bailing out of a second fighter before he was even shot at!

The 353rd FS enjoyed its first success with its new mounts on the 22nd when a flight was attacked by three Bf 109s while on a fighter sweep. All of the Messerschmitt fighters fell to the guns of the P-51 pilots. The final days of the month were marred by bad weather, but the group did encounter a few of the Luftwaffe's Me 262 jet fighters. Several were damaged but none were destroyed, and ever-eager for success, the 354th pilots looked forward to their next encounter with the German jets. March 1, 1945 saw Col George Bickell depart on leave, and Lt Col Jack Bradley step up to command the group in its final two months of war.

The pilots of the 354th did not have to wait long for another meeting with the Me 262. On the morning of March 2 Capt Bruno Peters of the 355th FS had led a fighter sweep to Fulda and then south to Kassel, where they encountered two Me 262 fighter-bombers of I./KG(J) 54. Diving from 12,000ft through haze and overcast, Peters caught the first at 1,500ft, while Flt Off Ralph Delgado pursued the second, scoring hits on the jet which caused the pilot to bail out. Apparently, no one saw Peters' victim go in, so it was classified as "destroyed unconfirmed." However, I./KG(J) 54 recorded the loss of Feldwebels Heinrich Griem and Gunther Borlitz, both of whom bailed out.

Later in the day the 353rd FS was flying a sweep when Lt Cary Salter radioed in that he had spotted a locomotive stopped at a water tank. Capt Theodore Sedvert led the flight down in a dive from 10,000ft, but as he dropped through the haze, he spied an Me 262 cruising along. Sedvert pulled behind the jet and hit it with a three-second burst. The fuselage and cockpit took heavy hits, and the pilot started to bail out, his flying overalls visibly in tatters. Seeing that he was too low to take to his parachute, he instead attempted a crash-landing but the jet exploded on impact.

A week passed before any further aerial successes were recorded. While on patrol around noon on March 9, 353rd ace Lt Bruce Carr caught a careless Fw 190D flying along by itself northwest of Frankfurt and quickly disposed of it. This took Carr's tally to 7.5 kills. With American troops now across the Rhine River and continuing to advance, there was high hope that the war would soon be over, but in the meantime, the 354th continued to strike at the enemy whenever possible. All squadrons flew escort missions for medium bombers on March 13, and all successfully shot down German aircraft. A total of four victories were scored, with the 355th FS's Maj Lowell Brueland increasing his score to 12.5 (his final wartime tally).

On the morning of March 15, P-51s from the 353rd spotted a bevy of Fw 190s about to bounce a lone P-38. Climbing to head off the attack, the Mustang pilots destroyed two enemy fighters, one of which fell to the guns of Maj Glenn Eagleston – the group's leading ace, his score now stood at 17.5. Later the same day the 356th FS downed two Fw 190s near Fulda.

Twenty-four hours later, Bruce Carr was leading the 353rd FS on a sweep northwest of Limburg when his flight intercepted some 30 Bf 109s. Engaging the German pilots at 16,000ft, Carr's flight became embroiled in a big dogfight that saw the 353rd claim nine Bf 109s destroyed, with Lt Ivan Hasek seeking credit for 4.5 victories. The Victories Credits Board did not go along with either Hasek or Carr, however, for the former was credited with only two kills while none of Carr's three claims were confirmed.

The 353rd again encountered a formation of fighters on March 21 while on a sweep west of Darmstadt. Fifteen Fw 190s carrying drop tanks were met, and the tanks were discarded immediately. These pilots were not aggressive, however, and broke for the deck as quickly as possible. The 353rd claimed to have destroyed six fighters but only three were confirmed, two going to future ace Lt Franklin Rose (these were his second and third victories).

The classic engagement of the day occurred later, when Capt Sedvert observed an Me 262 at only 500ft flying over Osthofen. He dived on the jet just as it dropped a bomb on the town, and good strikes were seen on the fuselage, slowing its speed considerably as it crossed the Rhine River. Sedvert then pulled up astern of his target, only to find that he was out of ammunition. He then drew up alongside the jet and became furious when the German pilot thumbed his nose at him. Sedvert rolled back his canopy and emptied his .45cal pistol in the direction of his foe with no result. He continued to follow the Me 262 all the way to Wiesental, where he watched it belly in.

The 353rd was back in the thick of things the following day when the group flew a record 19 missions. Fifteen Fw 190s attacked the squadron from above and behind, northeast of Mannheim, and nine German fighters were downed, with Lts Franklin Rose and Calvin Walker getting doubles. Rose had taken his tally of kills from one to five in just 23 hours, and these were to be his last victories of the war.

While the US First Army was already across the Rhine, Gen Patton's Third Army was struggling to get into Germany. However, on the night of March 22 a crossing was at last made, and in an effort to consolidate this breakthrough, the 354th was up before dawn. The group would fly a total of 23 missions that day.

All of the squadrons saw action on the 23rd, and all of them claimed aerial victories. Top scorer for the day was 5.5-kill ace Maj George Max Lamb, who claimed three kills but was only awarded credit for two. He was leading a flight from the 356th FS northeast of Hanau when ground control vectored him after ten Fw 190Ds. Just as the P-51s caught up with the bogies they split-essed, although Lamb latched onto the tail of one of the fighters and scored a series of hits. However, just as he was about to shoot the Focke-Wulf down he had to break off the engagement and go after another Fw 190 that was on his wingman's tail. The latter pilot subsequently saw his leader's first targeted Fw 190 go in. Lamb reported:

I had been firing at an E/A on the deck and saw my wingman in trouble. Just as the E/A was doing a wingover to get on his tail, I called a break and zoomed up. The E/A saw me coming and stall-turned into me. We met almost head-on, and I fired a short burst in front of him. There was an explosion and flames and the '190's empennage came off, part of it hitting my windshield.

My wingman had found another '190 and was having trouble with him. I cut in and closed to about 50–100 yards while in a vertical bank. I fired a short burst after he disappeared under my nose and heard my wingman say, "you got that son-of-a-bitch." I rolled over and saw the E/A go into the ground.

New group CO Lt Col Jack Bradley was also involved in one of the missions that day, during which he scored his 15th and final victory (a Bf 109) of the war. In all the 354th claimed 17 kills on March 23.

The following day the Allies carried out Operation *Varsity* – the airborne jump across the Rhine by the US 17th Airborne Division and the British 6th Airborne Division. All Ninth Air Force fighters were up to provide fighter cover for the mission, including the 354th. Nearly 1,000 USAAF and RAF fighters escorted the procession of C-46s, C-47s and gliders into Germany.

The following day the group flew 21 missions covering the bridgeheads that the ground troops had established, and it was whilst overflying the Mainz–Worms area that the 353rd, led by Maj Glenn Eagleston, intercepted two Bf 109s. Both fighters were destroyed, with Eagleston notching up yet another victory to take his final wartime tally to 18.5. This impressive total made him the Ninth Air Force's ranking ace.

Despite only one other aerial victory being scored before the end of the month, the group nevertheless continued to inflict considerable damage on rail targets, rolling stock and airfield installations on a daily basis. Low-level losses continued to remain high, however, with a number of pilots being shot down by flak during these sorties. Indeed, four men were lost during a dive-bombing mission on the very last day of the month.

During March the group was officially credited with shooting down 45 enemy aircraft, plus the destruction of numerous aircraft on the ground. Flying 242 missions in the month, the 354th also destroyed a record number of ground targets. Eleven pilots were recorded as missing in action from these operations.

April found the Allied armies advancing in all sectors against a crippled German army that was forbidden to surrender. Even though desperately short of ammunition, fuel and manpower, the Wehrmacht struggled on. The Luftwaffe, meanwhile, still possessed thousands of aircraft but had no fuel to get them airborne, nor trained pilots to man them. Fighter sweeps and area cover patrols were the order of the day for the 354th, with the Mustang pilots seeking out anything they could attack in the air or on the ground. On April 1 the only thing sighted aloft was a lone Ju 188 in the Kassel–Erfurt area, and its destruction was shared by Lts Bruce Carr and Fred Canada of the 353rd FS.

The following day Lts Andy Ritchey and Cary Salter, also from the 353rd FS, flew a memorable weather reconnaissance mission. The flight, led by Lt Ritchey, was just passing over the airfield at Erfurt when two Fw 190s were seen coming in to land. The Mustangs dived from 12,000ft, firing as they closed, and only one of the German pilots was seen to bail out before both Fw 190s hit the ground just seconds later.

Ritchey and Salter then flew west over Gotha, where they shot down another Fw 190 that they found alone at 3,000ft. Immediately after this encounter the pilots sighted over 90 Bf 109s and Fw 190s flying west in waves of eight at 3,000ft. Most were carrying belly tanks, and they were undoubtedly en route to attack Allied troops on the Rhine. Undaunted by the sheer number of German fighters, Ritchey and Salter set about spoiling the formation, downing a Bf 109 and an Fw 190 in the process, as well as damaging a third aircraft. Andrew Ritchey was subsequently credited with three fighters destroyed, and he would "make ace" 18 days later.

That afternoon Lt Bruce Carr was leading two flights of Mustangs in the vicinity of Schweinfurt when another large gaggle of Luftwaffe fighters was observed flying at 12,000ft. The ace wasted no time in wading into the enemy aircraft, and the Mustangs entered the fray with their guns blazing. By the end of the fracas some 15 German fighters had been destroyed, and Lt Carr had downed three Fw 190s and two Bf 109s. The only 354th FG pilot officially recognized as being an "ace in a day," Carr was also the last pilot in the ETO to achieve this outstanding feat. He stated after the mission:

> It was really a piece of cake. They were in two circles when we hit them, and they seemed to sit there while I fired away. Of course there were times during the combat that I had enemy aircraft on my tail while I was attacking, but fortunately they were poor shots.

Aside from Bruce Carr's five-kill haul, his squadronmate Lt Henry Rudolph claimed two Fw 190s destroyed to "make ace." The 353rd and 355th FSs again encountered German fighters on April 4, although only on a small scale. The former unit scored two victories while the 355th notched up another four kills.

It was the 356th FS's turn to engage the enemy on the 10th, when the unit intercepted a gaggle of about 25 Bf 109s in the Mülhausen area. The P-51 pilots had to climb to catch them, and once they had been spotted by the Germans, the enemy fighters continued to climb in an attempt to escape, rather than diving for the deck. Nine were downed, with the honors going to Lt Robert Biglow who claimed three.

The following day Capt Earl Bushwood was leading the 356th FS on an evening patrol when he was vectored onto a formation of over 30 Bf 109s, along with a few Fw 190s. Carrying belly tanks, these aircraft were heading west toward the Allied frontline. Bushwood related:

We were at 10,000ft when we bounced them. I met them head-on – at my level was one flight of three and another of four. They were flying in our type of formation. Above us at about 1,000ft were two more flights, and above them were three more. I flew head-on through one of the flights and called the squadron to engage. My Blue and Green flights were slightly above and behind. I called them down to help.

I took my wingman and started an attack on the flight of three. They started climbing away. One of them was lagging a little and I caught him at 10,000ft. I fired a short burst which didn't do much. I pulled a little more lead, got good strikes and then closed in and shot his tail and lower fuselage off. He spun in, and the pilot did not get out.

While I was attacking, two E/A pulled in behind me. My wingman, Lt Gear, drove them off after destroying the lead ship. I then started attacking the other two. I pulled deflection on the rear one and immediately got strikes in the engine and wing roots. He was smoking and streaming white coolant. I closed very rapidly, as his engine seemed to stop, and I overran him. This put him on my tail, but I put down my flaps and pulled in really tight, and was closing in again when the pilot bailed out.

After scoring his second victory Bushwood was attacked by a Mustang, and another P-51 had to chase him off! Despite this near "own-goal," the 15-minute fight had been most profitable for the 356th, and 17 confirmed victories were recorded. Lt Frank Boron was the top scorer with two and one shared Bf 109s and an Fw 190 destroyed (he finished his tour with four aerial kills).

April 14 was another active day for the group, with the 356th encountering Bf 109s and Fw 190s in the Leipzig area. Capt Richard Asbury and his flight broke up a formation of Bf 109s, which were driven to the deck. Several were downed, including one by Asbury, who also destroyed an Fw 190 that he had bounced whilst it was making passes at an

American armored column. On his second tour in the ETO (he had served for a year with the 363rd FG), Asbury now boasted a tally of 4.5 kills, and he shared in the destruction of an He 111 the following day to give him the all-important half-kill that made him an ace.

Returning to the 14th, there was also jet action during the day when five-kill ace Capt Clayton Gross (on his second ETO tour as well) led a flight of 355th FS P-51s along the Elbe River, south of Berlin. Sighting an Me 262 below him at about 2,000ft, Gross dived after the jet but experienced high-speed compressibility, which he thought would prevent him from firing on the German fighter. However, after fighting with the controls of his Mustang, he was finally able to pull out of his dive just as the Me 262 passed directly in front of him! Gross later recalled:

> The original object of my attention was absolutely dead ahead of me, and I was closing rapidly. My initial burst set its left jetpipe burning, and a fairly large section of his left wingtip flew off, causing me to flinch as it went past me. The speed of my dive caused me to overrun him, and I pulled off to the right and up to lose speed, then rolled back to reposition myself.

Gross then slotted in behind the Me 262 once again, and the German pilot pulled the aircraft into a vertical climb. The Mustang ace followed him, but he soon felt himself being left behind. However, the jet suddenly stalled and began to slide backward, tail first. The pilot ejected.

Later that day nine-kill ace Lt Loyd Overfield was leading a 353rd FS patrol in the Riesa area when an Me 262 was sighted below. Diving down, the P-51 pilot caught the jet, which was traveling throttled back toward a nearby airfield, and blasted it with five bursts. The Me 262 exploded and the pilot bailed out. Twenty minutes later, Overfield scored his 11th and last kill of the war when he downed an He 111 southwest of Dresden.

A lone He 111 also provided Lt Bruce Carr with his last kill of the war the following afternoon, the triple ace spotting the Heinkel bomber as it was coming in to land at Mensdorf airfield. Nicknamed "Peck's Bad Boy," Carr, who had come to the 353rd FS to avoid a court martial for being overly aggressive and insubordinate in the then-defunct 363rd FG, ended up with 15 confirmed victories, three unconfirmed victories, one probably destroyed, two damaged and 11 aircraft destroyed on the ground.

Maj James Dalglish led the 353rd on a mission to the Dresden area on April 16 which resulted in 13 Fw 190s being downed, these aircraft in the main being clearly flown by inexperienced pilots. High scorer was Lt Warren Jolly with three Fw 190s (boosting his final wartime tally to four kills), while Maj James Dalglish and Lts Fred Fehsenfeld and Joseph Sanchez scored doubles. These final two kills took Dalglish's tally to nine and Sanchez's to four (and one unconfirmed destroyed).

Jets were in the news again on April 17. Capt Jack A. Warner of the 356th FS was covering a flight that was strafing in the Karlsbad area when he saw an Me 262 below him at about 1,600ft. He immediately dived on the fighter, and as he approached he noted that the jet was beginning to speed up. However, Warner got within sufficient range to hit the Me 262 in the fuselage, right wing and right jetpipe. After having taken fatal hits the aircraft began to slow, and Warner continued to follow it until it crashed into some trees. Also a two-tour veteran, Jack Warner's success on this day took his final tally to five kills exactly. The 353rd was in action again on April 19 when Fw 190s were encountered in the Weimar area, and six were downed – Lt Kenneth Wise scoring two of the kills. Single victories were also claimed on April 20 and 22.

The 354th took part in some excellent strafing missions against rail targets during this period, as well as attacking enemy aircraft on several of the still-existing, but nearly abandoned, airfields. The last aerial encounters came on April 26, when both the 353rd and 356th FSs met with formations of enemy aircraft. The 356th accounted for six confirmed kills, with Lts Edward Bickford and Walter Crum both being credited with two Fw 190Ds. The 353rd also claimed six confirmed near Charmeng, with Lt John J. Hagen accounting for two Fw 190s and Lt Kenneth Wise one (he also claimed a further two destroyed, although these were never officially credited to him).

The two Fw 190D kills for Edward Bickford and the solitary Focke-Wulf fighter for Kenneth Wise took their tallies to 5.5 and five kills respectively, thus making them the last aces of the 354th FG. Both pilots had only joined the group in December 1944. Fighter sweeps continued to be flown up until May 4, but no further action was seen in the air.

The "Pioneer Mustang Group," although coming into the North European Theater late, had set an unbelievable pace. Following the end of World War II its total official confirmed victory score stood at 637 aerial kills. In actual fact this figure should be higher, as four XIX Tactical Air Command Victories Credits Reports are missing. It is known that an additional 37 victories belonging to the 354th FG were on these reports, which would bring the total up to 674. And although the Ninth Air Force did not credit strafing victories to individual pilots, 354th FG reports give the unit an overall tally of 234 aircraft destroyed on the ground. Finally, the group produced 44 aces.

Ground target totals ran into thousands of locomotives, tanks, armored vehicles and rolling stock destroyed, railroad lines cut, bridges blown up and hundreds of military personnel killed. The 354th FG also achieved three important records for the USAAF: it possessed the top-scoring fighter unit (the 353rd FS), which had more aerial victories than any other Army Air Force fighter squadron in any theater during the war; it was certainly the most outstanding P-51 group of the war; and it can claim the only fighter pilot to be awarded the Medal of Honor in Northern Europe.

Part Two
332ND FIGHTER GROUP

The Tuskegee Airmen

INTRODUCTION

In the late 1930s and early 1940s, America saw itself as a bastion of freedom and equality, especially in light of the horrors that fascism and totalitarianism were visiting upon Asia and Europe at the time. World War II pitted the USA against natural opponents – the militaristic Japanese Empire and despotic Nazi Germany. To most American citizens, the war represented a natural conflict between their virtuous way of life and the immorality of their Axis foes.

To the African-American community, however, the notion that World War II marked the start of a struggle against violence, discrimination and racial inequity was patently absurd. For many of them, this struggle already defined their lives. Prewar America was a divided nation, with blacks and whites living in two parallel societies. In the southeast USA, segregation was a way of life, with blacks attending separate schools, using different restrooms and eating in different restaurants from whites. In most situations, the facilities for blacks were inferior to those for whites. These artificial boundaries were enforced by a social structure that all but endorsed violence against those who would seek to transcend it. In the northeast and west of the USA, these formalized structures did not exist, but discrimination was present in a more random, but equally virulent, form.

In the 1930s, the US Army's treatment of blacks reflected the behavior of society in general. While black Americans had served in combat, and all-black units had distinguished themselves during the American Civil War, the wars against the Plains Indians, the Spanish-American War and World War I, most blacks in uniform were part of "service units," performing menial labor and maintenance roles. Similarly, in the US Navy, the only rate black sailors could hold was mess attendant.

These attitudes permeated the military from the top down, and officials were not hesitant about putting their opinions into print. Chief of the US Army Air Corps, Maj Gen "Hap" Arnold, wrote in 1940 that blacks could be useful as unskilled labor "to perform the duties of post fatigue and as waiters in our messes." Secretary of War Henry Stimson held a similar view, stating that "leadership is not embedded in the Negro race."

Even so, these views did not keep black Americans from aspiring to fly and fight, and in 1939 the door that had been shut began to open. The Civilian Pilot Training Program (CPTP), announced in 1938 by President Franklin D. Roosevelt, mandated that

20,000 college students would be trained to fly each year. This legislation excluded black schools and students. However, in May 1939, as the CPTP was gearing up, barnstormers Chauncey E. Spencer and Dale L. White embarked on a Chicago-to-Washington, DC flight to promote aviation for black Americans. Upon their arrival in the capital, they conducted a meeting with a little-known senator named Harry S. Truman. He listened to Spencer and White's concerns and pledged to help. Truman was especially impressed when he saw Spencer and White's beaten-up biplane, and according to a contemporary account in the *Chicago Defender*, he stated "If you guys had guts enough to fly that thing from Chicago, I got guts enough to do all I can to help you."

A short time later, Congress authorized funds for the extension of the CPTP to several predominantly black universities, and for the training of black students at white colleges. The program was instituted at Howard University, Hampton Institute, North Carolina A&T, West Virginia State and Delaware State. In all, 2,700 black pilots would graduate from the CPTP. At the end of its first year, 91 percent of the black students who enrolled in the course successfully completed the program – the same rate as white students. On October 15, 1939, Tuskegee Institute (a black university in Alabama) was added to the program.

SMALL BEGINNINGS

At that time, Tuskegee was far from an ideal location. The nearest airport, in Montgomery, was 40 miles away, and by February 1940 it was clear something had to be done to rectify the situation. The Institute leased a plot of land and donated $1,000 for materials, and students volunteered their labor to build Airport No 1, which had room for just three Piper Cubs. Still, it solved the problem of the commute, and the students made national news when every member of the first CPTP class passed the Civil Aviation Authority written exams.

The success of Tuskegee Institute's CPTP resulted in the approval of a secondary course of instruction for black students from all over the country, which was conducted at the small airfield at the Alabama Polytechnic Institute in Auburn.

Aviation grew quickly at Tuskegee, and in October the Institute urged its alumni to contribute toward a goal of $200,000 to build a much larger airfield. It also sought donations from charitable organizations. One of these was the Julius Rosenwald Fund, and that group held its annual meeting at Tuskegee in 1941. One of the fund's board members was Eleanor Roosevelt, the wife of the President.

The idea of black aviators intrigued Mrs Roosevelt so much that she asked to be taken for a flight. After resisting the impassioned pleas of her Secret Service bodyguards to remain on the ground, she went up in a Piper Cub with flight instructor C. Alfred

"Chief" Anderson. Shortly after the flight, the fund donated $175,000 to the cause, and Mrs Roosevelt remained a strong backer of the cause of black Americans in aviation for years to come.

Still, the military stuck to its exclusion of black aviators. One flier trying to gain admittance to the Army Air Corps had his application denied, with the stated reason being that "the non-existence of a colored Air Corps unit to which you could be assigned in the event of completion of flying training precludes your training to become a military pilot at this time."

Although virtually all of the military establishment and most of the civilian leadership still fought to keep black Americans in secondary roles, President Roosevelt, enmeshed in an election and eager to court black voters, issued a policy statement on October 9, 1940 that officially mandated that black Americans would serve in numbers proportionate to their representation in the US population in combat and non-combat roles alike. These included aviation roles.

While the Navy all but ignored these policies, the Army took some halting steps, including the promotion of Benjamin O. Davis Snr to brigadier general, making him the first black American to hold flag rank. In December 1940, the Army Air Corps submitted a plan to create an all-black pursuit squadron, and the units required to support it. Still, black aviators had their applications denied by the Army Air Corps for the reason that there were no black units to which they could be assigned. This doubletalk lasted until Howard University CPTB student Yancey Williams sued the Army to force it to admit him as a student pilot. The Army relented, setting its plan for an all-black squadron in motion, and the War Department soon appropriated more than $1 million to build Tuskegee Army Air Field (TAAF).

On July 19, 1941, 11 cadets and one black Army officer were inducted into military aviation training as Class 42-C at Tuskegee. That one officer was Capt Benjamin O. Davis Jnr, the son of Brig Gen Davis Snr. These two men were the only black non-chaplain officers in the entire Army at the time.

The younger Davis was already steeled by years of discrimination – at the US Military Academy at West Point, he had been "silenced" – no one spoke to him outside of official duties during his four years at the academy. His white classmates and superiors issued enough undeserved demerits to Cadet Davis for imaginary infractions to cause his dismissal from the Corps of Cadets, but Commandant of Cadets Lt Col Simon Bolivar Buckner voided half the demerits and Davis graduated.

Since then, Davis had been assigned to a series of four undemanding tours teaching Reserve Officer Training Corps classes at black universities. His daily workload consisted of a single 45-minute lecture to students. The Army had made it painfully clear to Davis that it did not want black officers commanding white men.

Davis applied for flight training and was denied during his final year at West Point, but when the Army initiated its plans for an all-black unit, he was an obvious choice for its commander. The white hierarchy, however, did not abandon its efforts to exclude him. When he took his initial flight physical at Fort Riley, Kansas, "The flight surgeon who gave me the exam did what all flight surgeons were doing when they had black applicants," Davis recalled. "He wrote down that I had epilepsy, and I was not qualified for flying training." The Army Air Force immediately flew Davis to Maxwell Army Air Base in Alabama, where a second physical reversed the findings of the first. With that, Davis was on his way to Tuskegee.

While Davis was a natural choice for CO of the 99th Fighter Squadron (FS), he was not a natural pilot. Indeed, his primary instructor, Tuskegee Director of Instruction Noel Parrish, had to spend extra time with Davis to raise his skills as an aviator to an acceptable level. However, Davis was well equipped with the requisite leadership skills, which he would soon display in combat – both with the Germans and with the hierarchy of the Army.

FLYING TRAINING

Students were given primary instruction in Stearman PT-17s, flying from Moton Field. When they had mastered the biplane, the students traveled 12 miles to the still-under-construction base at TAAF and trained in the Vultee BT-13 – an all-metal fixed-gear monoplane widely known as the "Vibrator." Finally, advanced training was conducted in AT-6 Texans.

Life for the first students at the base was difficult. Living quarters consisted of tents, and the mess hall was a wooden building with a dirt floor. When it rained, the inevitable result was mud inside and out. It was not this way for all personnel on base, however, as white servicemen dined in a mess hall, complete with tablecloths and uniformed black waitresses. Even as the base buildings were completed, segregation remained a way of life.

This was all but guaranteed when Maj James Ellison, the base's first commander and an ardent supporter of the project, was transferred after an incident in the town of Tuskegee in which a black military policeman tried to take custody of a black enlisted man under arrest in the town jail. After the MP and his driver were also arrested, Ellison intervened and succeeded in winning their release.

The white residents of Tuskegee were already furious about the nearby "armed Negroes," and because of this incident Ellison was relieved and replaced by Col Frederick von Kimble. The latter individual promptly had the base's facilities segregated, with signs designating them for either "colored" or "white" use. Davis described the air base as "a prison camp," and other students confessed to being frightened of the prevailing racial climate even while on base.

Von Kimble harbored the belief that blacks had no ability to lead, and was alleged to have told other officers that no black would rise above the rank of captain as long as he was in command. Following an undercover investigation by the War Department into von Kimble's conduct, he was replaced by Davis' former instructor, Col Noel Parrish, on December 26, 1942.

Parrish was the son of a southern minister, and at 33, he looked far younger than his years. But unlike von Kimble and most of the USAAF hierarchy, Parrish was fully committed to the success of the "Tuskegee Experiment." He served to moderate tensions between the town and the base, and while he was unable to completely eradicate segregation on base, he made immense efforts to demonstrate his devotion to his men.

Upon his assumption of command, the men noticed that many of the signs designed to enforce segregation had been removed. Parrish declined to replace them. He joined the black officers' club, arranged morale-building visits from Lena Horne, Joe Louis, Ella Fitzgerald, Louis Armstrong and others, and ran interference for his men with Washington officials who wanted the training program ended. As a result, Parrish was widely respected by his students.

"Parrish is the man who proved that blacks could fly an airplane," Davis said. In those days, "to whites, blacks couldn't do anything very well, except dance and sing. Blacks supposedly couldn't fly airplanes because that was too technical, and Parrish proved they could. He held the future of blacks in the Army Air Corps in his own hot little hands. Anybody, everybody should be extremely grateful to Parrish for his performance of duty. He wasn't doing anybody any favors – he was performing his duty conscientiously in a way that benefited everybody, to include the United States Army Air Force."

CLASS GRADUATION

On March 7, 1942, Class 42-C graduated from flight school at TAAF. Of the original 12 students, five had successfully completed the course – 2Lts Lemuel R. Custis, Charles DeBow, George S. Roberts and Mac Ross, as well as Capt Benjamin O. Davis. These men were the first officers of what would become the 99th FS, and they typified the quality of the officers who would take the squadron to war. Custis had been the first black police officer in the state of Connecticut, DeBow had attended Hampton Institute and "Spanky" Roberts (so dubbed because of his threat to paddle upperclassmen at his fraternity) and Ross had been classmates at West Virginia State College.

As additional classes arrived and graduated, the base received some older P-39s and P-40s for advanced training. The number of men winning their wings crept up slowly, with Charles Dryden, Sidney Brooks and Clarence Jamison graduating in the second class, and Lee Rayford, Bernard Knighten, Sherman White and George Knox receiving their wings in the third class.

For the students who washed out, there were no other aviation roles to fill – they suffered the humiliation of becoming a private in one of Tuskegee's service battalions. "You would start out with a large group, and one by one the fellows would disappear," remembered Samuel Curtis, a member of Class 43-G. "They would go down to the 318th Air Base Squadron, where all the washed-out went to be reassigned – when a fellow was washed out, it was a crushing experience."

Col Parrish, seeing the high washout rate, ordered that Class 42-F should be made up entirely of CPTP graduates, who would be allowed to skip pre-flight and primary training. The graduates of the class included Louis Purnell, Spann Watson, Charles Hall, Willie Ashley, Allen Lane, Graham "Peepsight" Smith, Herbert "Bud" Clark, Paul Mitchell, Faythe McGinnis, Erwin Lawrence, George Bolling and Herbert Carter, along with William "Bill" Campbell and James Wiley, who had been instructors for the previous classes.

Sadly, McGinnis would become the first graduate to die. On the day of his wedding, he volunteered to become the last pilot in an eight-ship formation. The formation went into a loop, and because he had blacked out in the loop or misjudged his altitude, McGinnis flew into the ground.

The students were also plagued by their weary P-40s, which Charles Dryden described as "flying coffins." Mac Ross had to bail out of his P-40 during his first flight in the fighter, the aircraft slamming into a yard behind a shantytown near the base. A short while later, cadet Jerome Edwards was killed when the engine in his Warhawk quit on take-off and the fighter careered into trees.

Tuskegee's fifth class added Walter Lawson, John Rogers, Leon Roberts, Richard C. Davis, Willie Fuller, Cassius Harris and Earl King to the ranks of the 99th. Lawson survived a close call during training when the aircraft he was flying with fellow cadet Richard Dawson crashed while the latter was trying to fly under a bridge. Dawson was killed, but the dazed Lawson was found walking away from the crash, earning him the nickname "Ghost."

With the graduation of Class 42-G in July 1942, the squadron was finally at full strength. Because of Tuskegee's unique role as the USAAF's only air base for black airmen, it could graduate only limited numbers of students. Even so, on May 26, 1942, the 100th FS was activated at TAAF, pointing toward an all-black fighter group, and DeBow and Ross were duly assigned to the new unit. On October 13, the 332nd FG was activated at Tuskegee, consisting of the 100th, 301st and 302nd FSs.

As pilots graduated, they joined an increasing number of personnel stationed at the base. The number of enlisted men trained to service the aircraft and support the units was also steadily increasing, with the 96th Service Group, 83rd Fighter Control Squadron and the 689th Signal Warning Company also sharing the base with the 332nd FG. By mid-1942, almost 220 officers and 3,000 enlisted men were packed into TAAF. As a result, the 100th FS was despatched to Oscoda Army Airfield, in Michigan, where its arrival set a precedent – Oscoda was a white base, meaning that the 100th would be the first unit to desegregate a USAAF facility, albeit temporarily.

Tuskegee would remain in operation throughout the war, graduating 1,030 pilots by the time of its closure in 1949. Many of these men were assigned to the 477th Medium Bombardment Group, which was an all-black B-25 unit that was so badly mishandled by the Army Air Force that it never made it into combat. A further 40 pilots from TAAF were sent to the Pacific, where they flew light aircraft as artillery spotters.

For the rest of the "Tuskegee Airmen," their future was in fighters. In late 1942, the men of the 99th FS occupied themselves by conducting routine training flights, and speculating on why it was taking so long for them to be deployed to a combat theater. For nine long months the unit languished at TAAF, and while the pilots were restless, the time "later paid very great dividends," said Capt Benjamin Davis. During this period of combat inactivity, "we became a squadron. The 99th had a very great advantage from September 1942 until April 15, 1943, when it left Tuskegee. It was an active unit with no personal turbulence. The people got to know each other."

While the squadron was awaiting orders, training took its inevitable toll. Richard C. Davis was killed during a night flight in a P-40 on January 30, 1943, and two months later, on March 24, Earl King was lost when his P-40 dived into Lake Martin, 20 miles north of the base. These pilots were replaced by 2Lts Sam M. Bruce and James L. McCullen.

On April 1, 1943, the 99th received its orders to head overseas. The squadron hurried to prepare for deployment, packing equipment and documents into boxes and personal equipment into trunks. By midnight, the men and their gear were loaded aboard a train for transport to Camp Shanks, New York, which would serve as their port of departure. On April 15 the squadron embarked on the troopship *Mariposa* and slipped through the harbor fog. Through some coincidence, now-Lt Col Davis and his staff found themselves as the senior officers aboard the vessel, putting them in charge of the mixed-race complement of soldiers embarked in *Mariposa*. Lt Col Davis' father had been the first black man in history to command white officers and men of the US Army, and during the 99th's crossing, his son became the second.

"It was apparent, not only to me, but to the people in the 99th, that they held the future of blacks in the Army Air Force in their hands," Davis said later. "This was something that everyone in the 99th understood as early as the autumn of 1942 – that their performance would create the future environment for blacks."

THE FIGHTING 99TH

On April 24, 1943, the *Mariposa* docked in Casablanca, Morocco. "Spratmo" (gossip) aboard ship had suggested that, with the cold-weather clothing that the men had been issued, the 99th FS would be stationed in England. The sight of the brilliant blue skies and the dusty, refugee-filled streets quickly dispelled that notion. Lacking trucks, the men were forced to march with their equipment and gear for three miles in the oppressive midday sun to their bivouac area.

The one man not forced to march was Allen Lane, as he had broken his leg on his wedding day at the end of March. Lane, with his leg in a cast, bounced past his squadronmates aboard a jeep on the dusty road out of town shouting, "Okay, you dummies, on the double!" After setting up camp, Louis Purnell acquired a bottle of Coca-Cola – plentiful in port but rare in the field – to be saved as a prize for the unit's first aerial kill. It was secured in the squadron's safe.

A day later, the unit boarded an ancient train consisting of a locomotive, a coach and a dozen cattle cars for the 150-mile trip across French Morocco to the former Luftwaffe base at Oued Nja, near the town of Fès. The airfield was little more than a meadow ten miles north of the town of Meknès, at the base of the Atlas Mountains, with a large circle bulldozed nearby as a target for dive-bombing practice. Wrecked Bf 109s littered the airfield, and the squadron had to wait a week for its own aircraft to arrive – 27 Curtiss P-40Ls, Merlin-engined variants of the Warhawk that were lightened to improve performance. The P-40L lacked two of the P-40F's six machine guns, as well as about 100lb of armor around the oil cooler, engine and other vulnerable mechanical components.

The squadron used its time at Oued Nja to become familiar with the P-40L, and to study tactics. Pilots were assisted in both by the arrival of three USAAF P-40 veterans of the desert campaign – Col Philip Corcoran and Majs Ralph Keyes and Robert Fackler. Corcoran, who was the real-life model for the character "Flip Corkin" in the popular *Terry and the Pirates* comic strip, was "particularly helpful to the 99th," remembered Charles Dryden. Living with the squadron for a week, he provided advice based on his own combat experiences.

"You P-40 pilots are the most courageous aviators in the war," Dryden recalled Corcoran saying. "The Me 109 and the Fw 190 can outrun, outclimb and outdive the

P-40, so you'll have to stay and fight! But there's one thing you can do – the P-40 can outturn every fighter the Germans have, except one built by the Italians, the Macchi 202, and there aren't many of those in the theater. So if you get jumped, get into a tight turn, reef it in as tight as you can without stalling and just wait him out. If he tries to stay with you, you'll eventually end up on his tail." Corcoran also flew with the squadron and tutored them on dive-bombing – a skill that would prove useful in the coming months.

On one training flight, "Bud" Clark's landing gear failed to lower properly, and, after burning off excess fuel, he coolly set the P-40L down on its belly with minimal damage. His actions earned him the title of "Yank of the Month" from the Army's *Yank* newspaper! Another P-40L was saved by Leon Roberts after he clipped a wire, lopping off the top of the rudder and vertical stabilizer. Roberts nursed the damaged Warhawk back to Oued Nja and put it down safely.

At the end of May 1943, with its training deemed complete, the squadron moved 1,000 miles east to Fardjouna, on Tunisia's Cap Bon Peninsula. "The flying out of Cap Bon could be quite hazardous in that we flew off a dirt strip," Benjamin Davis recalled. "We would take off in a 12-airplane formation. Although we never had a collision, it was a hairy operation, especially if you had to get back into the field soon after take-off in case of an emergency – if there was no crosswind to blow the dust away, the strip would be totally obscured."

Fardjouna also had plenty of German-made diversions for the pilots. Bernard "Jim" Knighten, known to his fellow pilots as "the Eel," got an abandoned *kubelwagen* working, and Gene Carter found a German motorcycle among the piles of destroyed German aircraft littering the field.

THE 33RD FG

The squadron was attached to the 33rd FG under the command of Col William "Spike" Momyer. The group had made an inauspicious start to combat operations at Fardjouna, for when Momyer led its 75 P-40s into the base for the first time, 21 of them crashed on landing. Recovering from this early setback, the 33rd had enjoyed great success on its first day in combat from its new base in January 1943, knocking down eight airplanes. However, it had since been so badly mauled in subsequent battles that it had to stand down to reequip. The 99th FS was assigned in an effort to make good those losses.

Momyer made his antipathy for the squadron known immediately. When Davis and "Spanky" Roberts reported, Momyer did not return their salutes. On June 3 he scheduled a briefing, then moved the time up by an hour without telling the 99th, so the men arrived late. His efforts to embarrass the squadron badly affected its reputation, and only later would the full extent of Momyer's damage be understood.

Twenty-four hours prior to the infamous late briefing, the 99th FS had flown its first combat sorties when William Campbell and Clarence Jamison flew as wingmen to other 33rd FG fighters on an offensive sweep, followed several hours later by a second group operation that involved James Wiley and Charlie Hall. They bombed and strafed the German-held airfield on the island of Pantelleria, 47 miles east of Cap Bon, during the course of both missions. Wiley flew as wingman to Momyer, his P-40L (like all the others involved) carrying 500lb bombs. All four 99th FS pilots dived and dropped their ordnance upon cues given to them by their flight leaders. The next day, the four pilots that had been wingmen on the 2nd led a second bombing strike against the same target.

Attacks on Axis forces on Pantelleria continued, with the 99th rotating its pilots through the missions to give them combat experience. On June 4 Charles Dryden got his chance, his entry into combat having been delayed when wingman Willie Ashley's P-40L experienced a rough-running engine during the squadron's flight from Oued Nja. Dryden and Ashley had been forced to land at the depot at Oujda, where new P-40s were being assembled. Although the depot personnel did not have time to repair the engine problem, they were willing to give the pilots new P-40Ls to replace the "old" ones! The next morning, Dryden's original P-40L, *A TRAIN*, was left behind and replaced by *A TRAIN II*.

On June 4 he found himself over Pantelleria with a 500lb bomb strapped to the belly of his fighter. "Following my leader in a dive, I saw hundreds of red tracers streaking past my cockpit," Dryden remembered. "Concentrating on hitting the target, I didn't have time to get scared. It wasn't until I pulled up from the bomb run that the thought crossed my mind that they were trying to kill me!"

The pilots of the 99th failed to encounter any opposition in the air until June 9, when six P-40Ls piloted by Dryden, Ashley, Sidney Brooks, Lee Rayford, Leon Roberts and Spann Watson provided top cover for a dozen A-20 Havocs attacking Pantelleria. The flight spotted four unidentified aircraft at "five o'clock high," and several minutes later they dived on the formation. Identifying them as Bf 109s, the P-40L pilots turned into the German fighters and a melee ensued that thoroughly tested the flying skills of the men from the 99th FS.

Rayford found two Bf 109s on his tail, and seconds later their bullets stitched across his right wing. However, Spann Watson opened fire on the Germans from long range and convinced them to abandon their attack. Meanwhile, Ashley's excited turn into the enemy induced his P-40L to start spinning uncontrollably. He quickly lost several thousand feet in height directly over Pantelleria.

Corcoran had urged the men never to split up, and with this in mind, Ashley was eager to join up with the only other airplane he could see nearby. However, he soon realized that this fighter was in fact an Fw 190! Ashley opened fire and the Focke-Wulf began to smoke, but persistent ground fire forced the 99th FS pilot to abandon his chase and kept him from confirming that his adversary had indeed crashed.

Meanwhile, Dryden had spotted a formation of 12 Ju 88s above him, and he immediately set off after them. Unfortunately, the unit's P-40Ls were set up for low-level operations, and therefore lacked the essential oxygen system that pilots needed when operating at altitudes in excess of 15,000ft. Dryden, having climbed to 16,000ft, and still out of range of the German bombers, passed out. He came to after his airplane had stalled into a shallow dive and descended several thousand feet.

All six pilots returned safely from the mission, elated at having survived their first brush with their German counterparts. However, their eagerness for a fight would be characterized as "panicky" and "undisciplined" by Momyer in his official report on the engagement to the Army Air Force. He would continue to deliberately minimize and mis-characterize the squadron's achievements in his communiqués to XII Fighter Command HQ throughout his tenure as CO of the 33rd FG.

BASE MOVE

On June 11, 1943, after being pounded by the Allies' Mediterranean air forces, Pantelleria surrendered, thus becoming the first territory ever captured by the use of airpower alone. The 33rd FG moved to El Haouaria a short while later, and the group set its sights on Sicily – the Allies' next major target. Following a short break from the action, on July 2 the squadron was assigned to escort 16 B-25s sent to bomb a German airfield in the Castelvetrano area of Sicily as part of a larger mission that involved 72 fighters and about the same number of Mitchells, Havocs and Marauders.

The lead Mitchell missed the initial point for its run in to the target, forcing the remaining 15 bombers to circle directly overhead the target. Meanwhile, the P-40L pilots could see plumes of dust on the airfield below as German fighters hastily scrambled to meet them. The B-25s dropped their bombs, then started a gentle descending left turn to head back to their bases in Africa.

At that point, having managed to climb above the escorts, the German fighters took full advantage of their superior altitude and made a slashing attack on the 99th FS. The P-40Ls of Sherman White and James McCullen simply disappeared as a result of this pass, having undoubtedly fallen victim to defending fighters. In the blink of an eye, these men had become the first members of the squadron to die in action.

As the bombers continued to make their turn, Charlie "Seabuster" Hall spotted a pair of Fw 190s stalking them. Positioning himself behind the trailing fighter, he fired off a long burst that struck the Focke-Wulf. The latter machine then lurched from a gentle left turn into an abrupt dive, and Hall followed his victim down until he saw it hit the ground in a "big cloud of dust." Moments after losing two pilots to the German fighters, the 99th had scored its first aerial victory. At about the same time that Hall secured this victory,

"Ghost" Lawson also fired at an Fw 190 and claimed it as probably destroyed. He damaged a Bf 109 moments later.

Meanwhile, two Bf 109s had made a head-on pass at the sections led by Dryden and "Bill" Campbell. Dryden called the break, but an apparent radio malfunction kept Campbell from hearing him, so the former threw his P-40L into a turn and fired at the Germans as they climbed away for another attack. Within seconds Dryden was alone, and he searched the sky for a friendly fighter. Eventually, he spotted a P-40L about 500ft below him, flying straight and level.

As he descended to join up, Dryden observed two Bf 109s stalking the American fighter, and he latched onto their tails. He opened fire and damaged the trailing Messerschmitt, but a spurt of tracer flying past Dryden's cockpit snapped his head around. Close behind him was a third enemy fighter. Following Corcoran's directives, Dryden hauled *A TRAIN II* into a tight turn, but instead of getting onto the enemy fighter's tail, the P-40 pilot found that his foe was staying with him in the turn and drawing a bead on him!

"The first time around, I saw the top of his canopy," said Dryden. "The next time around, I saw his nose, and the next time around I saw his belly. At that point I realized it was a Macchi 202!"

Transfixed, Dryden watched as the Macchi C.202's wing-mounted 20mm cannon belched what he thought looked like "dirty gray cotton balls" at his airplane. One shell blew a chunk out of his left wing, and Dryden desperately called for help. "Jim" Knighten heard him and pulled up from the bombers he was escorting and settled into a tight diving turn that placed him behind the Macchi. A burst from Knighten's guns sent the Italian fighter fleeing.

Dryden waved a thank you, and he and Knighten turned back in the direction of North Africa, only to be bounced by two more Bf 109s that attacked from below. The Americans and Germans "scissored" back and forth for about ten minutes, with neither side able to gain an advantage. At one point, Dryden and Knighten thought that they had lost their pursuers, so they dived for the deck, only to spot the two Bf 109s duplicating their maneuver which in turn led them to resume the turning duel. Eventually, even the lone C.202 rejoined the fight, but soon the enemy fighters realized that they were being drawn into Allied territory, and they sped north toward Sicily. Arriving back at Fardjouna, Hall performed a victory roll, and Louis Purnell traveled 15 miles to secure a block of ice to cool the prized bottle of Coca-Cola, which Hall enjoyed in the shade of a grove of olive trees.

Once the Allies had established a beachhead on Sicily on July 10, the squadron flew patrols from Gela to Licata to dissuade the Luftwaffe from harassing the invasion fleet. On the 11th, Dick Bolling's fighter was hit by flak and he bailed out over the Mediterranean. Spending the night bobbing about in his rubber liferaft, he was rescued and returned to the squadron on July 12. Eight days later, the 99th FS relocated to Licata, with its ground echelon and equipment being crammed into 30 C-47s which were in turn escorted by the unit's own P-40Ls. Heartened by the actions of July 2, the 99th FS had no way of knowing that it would not spot another enemy fighter for six months. Instead of flying bomber escort missions, pilots would be assigned "dangerous and dirty" ground support sorties for the rest of 1943.

Because of the segregated nature of the squadron, the 99th's pilots flew more missions – as many as six per day – than their white counterparts. TAAF simply could not graduate pilots quickly enough to offset attrition, which meant that the squadron's first replacements did not arrive until July 23, when Howard Baugh, John Gibson, Ed Toppins and John Morgan landed in North Africa. The pilots' arrival had been further delayed by a mix-up in military transportation that left them stranded in Brazil for three weeks!

Several days later Robert Diez, Elwood "Woody" Driver, Herman "Ace" Lawson, Clinton "Beau" Mills and Henry "Herky" Perry also joined the squadron. Dive-bombing and ground support missions continued unabated until August 11, when a flying accident claimed another pilot. Whilst performing a diving attack on a target, Graham Mitchell developed engine trouble and veered into the path of Sam "Lizard" Bruce's fighter. Bruce pulled up sharply, and while he avoided a collision, his propeller sliced off the tail of Mitchell's P-40L. The latter pilot was killed, but Bruce parachuted to safety.

FIGHTING TO SURVIVE

On September 2, Lt Col Davis was recalled to the USA to take command of the 332nd FG, but instead of going directly to Selfridge Field, he first went to the Pentagon. The efforts of Momyer and others in the Army Air Force to have the 99th sent back to the USA or to some out-of-the-way theater had led to an article in *Time* magazine entitled "Experiment Proved?" It stated that the 99th might be disbanded, based on a report from Momyer claiming that the group did not fight as a team, broke formation when attacked, opted for undefended targets instead of defended briefed targets, avoided bad weather and, in general, performed poorly. "It is my opinion that they are not of the fighting caliber of any squadron in this group," Momyer wrote in his official report. "They have failed to display the aggressiveness and daring for combat that are necessary for a first-class fighting organization. It may be expected that we will get less work and less operational time out of the 99th FS than any squadron in this group."

Momyer's superior, Brig Gen Edwin House, agreed, and the report was endorsed by Maj Gen John Cannon, deputy commanding general of the Allied Tactical Air Force for the Sicilian campaign. Lt Gen Carl "Tooey" Spaatz, deputy commander of the Mediterranean Allied Air Forces, added his opinion that the 99th be reassigned to coastal patrol duty in a location such as the Panama Canal Zone.

"I was absolutely infuriated," said Davis. He was called to testify before a Congressional committee evaluating the squadron's performance, and the viability of the training of black airmen. "I'm sure that all the aces were held by the Army Air Force," Davis explained, "especially with the correspondence going up through channels the way it did, and the statement by Gen House that a Negro didn't possess the physical qualifications that would make him a good fighter pilot."

Davis, accustomed to remaining composed in the face of overt racism, told the committee that the men of the squadron were no different from any other Americans at war in other USAAF squadrons, and their performance paralleled that of other units:

> I recall saying something to the effect that overseas, the reception given to black people on the ground was much more pleasant and more favorable than the reception given to black people on the ground here in the United States. I also stressed the determination of the members of the 99th to demonstrate their abilities and set the stage for the oncoming combat units that were still training in the States.

Davis explained that the 99th had received only 26 pilots since its formation, compared to the 30–35 sent to most other fighter squadrons in the same period. This meant that his pilots flew as many as six sorties per day. Furthermore, the ground attack missions handed down to the squadron meant that it was less likely to encounter enemy aircraft, accounting for its low air-to-air score.

Having heard Davis' argument, "Hap" Arnold said that he would take no action until a study of the performance of all P-40 units in-theater could be completed. Even so, Arnold remained unconvinced that black aviators could perform well in forward combat zones, and he advocated their relocation to a rear defense area. The committee's report, slated to be delivered to President Roosevelt, was revised and edited by Col Emmett O'Donnell.

Bucking the tendencies of his superior officers, O'Donnell included a cover memo which "urgently recommended that this entire subject be reconsidered." He pointed out the absurdity of discrimination during wartime, and he observed that one to four squadrons were but a drop in the overall war effort. Furthermore, "I feel that such a proposal (to disband the 99th) to the President at this time would definitely not be appreciated by him," O'Donnell wrote. "He would probably interpret it as indicating a serious lack of understanding of the broad problems facing the country." Roosevelt never received the report.

When the results of Arnold's study eventually made it to the Pentagon, it proved that the 99th FS was as good as, or better than, other Warhawk units in the Mediterranean. "If that G-3 evaluation had not been made, God knows what would have happened," Davis recalled. He also noted that the report had a secondary effect. "It sent us to the Fifteenth Air Force, and took us out of the nasty, dirty close air support business, and put us into a sort of glamour business – escorting bombers. Sometimes things turn out for the best, and that's exactly what happened."

In Davis' absence, "Spanky" Roberts assumed command of the 99th, with Lemuel Custis as operations officer. The same day that Davis departed for the USA, advance elements of the 99th moved from Licata to the Italian mainland following the Allied landings at Salerno. Upon arriving at their assigned base, the advance party found not a prepared airfield but an active battleground, and they soon came under fire. Their base was still in German hands following a counterattack against the British Army's X Corps, and a second potential field had been repeatedly bombed and strafed by the Luftwaffe. Five days later X Corps repulsed the German attack, and work began on setting up the new field.

The rest of the squadron moved 62 miles from Licata to Termini (a town on the northern coast of Sicily), followed two weeks later by another base change to Barcelona, 70 miles to the east. On September 26 orders reached the squadron instructing Dryden, Rayford, Purnell, "Peepsight" Smith and "Ghost" Lawson to return home so that they could impart their combat knowledge to students at TAAF. Their moment of happiness literally went up in smoke though when Sidney Brooks crashed on take-off in Dryden's *A TRAIN II*. Brooks' own fighter, *El Cid*, had had a rough-running engine when he started it up, so in an effort to take off with the rest of the unit, he jumped into Dryden's fighter.

As Brooks climbed away from the runway, witnesses heard his engine start to splutter. Brooks turned back and executed a neat wheels-up landing, but he failed to drop his belly tank, which sheared off on contact with the ground, then bounced after the Warhawk and exploded against it. Brooks leapt from the cockpit, his flight suit smouldering. As a precaution, he was taken to a British field hospital, and he seemed well enough to make efforts to check himself out that night. However, when his squadronmates came to visit him the next morning, Sidney Brooks was dead, a victim of secondary shock and smoke inhalation.

INTO ITALY

Such was the resistance put up by the Germans at Salerno that the advanced echelon and the rest of the 99th FS did not finally reunite until October 17 at Foggia No 3 airfield. This move coincided with the squadron also receiving a new assignment which saw it leave Momyer's 33rd FG for the 79th FG, led by Col Earl Bates. The latter was thankfully bereft of the biases that had affected the way Momyer dealt with the 99th, and the squadron's combat experience changed considerably.

An indication of Bates' attitude towards the squadron can be gained from the fact that the group's war diaries never once mention the skin color of the men of the 99th FG.

He made sure that the 99th routinely flew missions alongside his other squadrons, and at times had black pilots leading mixed formations that included aircraft from other units in the group.

Combat operations resumed on October 20, when the 99th bombed and strafed shipping targets in the Isernia–Capionne area and hunted for road traffic northwest of Sangro. Two days later the squadron attacked German ammunition dumps in a mission in which two P-40Ls were damaged by flak. Continual beach patrol and armed reconnaissance missions kept the squadron busy, but the Luftwaffe was notable by its absence.

Early November brought a spate of harsh weather, making flying dangerous and life on the ground miserable – the airmen were not immune from the famous Italian mud. Despite the trying conditions, the 99th averaged 48 sorties per day in support of the British crossing of the Sangro River later in the month, and on November 22 James Wiley became the first member of the squadron to completed 50 missions.

Three days prior to Wiley reaching his "half century," the 79th FG had begun a move to Madna, which was a coastal airstrip near Termoli. The pace of operations increased following the base swap, and on November 30 alone, the squadron flew nine missions. During the first week in December, newcomer 2Lt Alva Temple clipped a fence in his P-40L at the end of the still-unfamiliar Madna field on take-off, damaging the Warhawk's landing gear. Instead of turning back, he completed the mission with one wheel partially retracted, then made a crash-landing at Madna that ripped the left wing off his P-40L, *NONA II*.

Despite now flying in a group that genuinely appreciated the 99th FS's efforts in combat, morale was at a low ebb in December 1943 due to a combination of poor weather, dangerous missions made worse by a marginal airfield from which to operate and increasingly combat-weary aircraft. It sank even lower on January 2, 1944 when John Morgan was killed. Morgan's P-40 landed downwind, and he was unable to stop the fighter before it slammed into a ditch at the end of the runway. The rain, mud, lack of aerial opposition, and the gradual understanding that enemies within the USAAF were even more relentless than the Germans in trying to destroy the squadron weighed heavily on the 99th.

On January 15 Lt William Griffin's Warhawk was shot down over enemy territory, and he remained a PoW until May 1945. The next day, the 99th moved from the east coast of the Italian "boot" to Capodichino, near Naples on the west coast, so as to be closer to the coming amphibious assault on Anzio. The latter offensive began in the early hours of January 22, and as the invasion bogged down, the Luftwaffe began to reappear. The opportunity to once again engage German aircraft proved to be a turning point in the 99th FS's war.

AERIAL COMBAT AGAIN

At about 0830hrs on the morning of January 27, a formation of 16 Warhawks led by Lt Clarence Jamison spotted 15 Fw 190s dive-bombing shipping off St Peter's Beach and dived into the enemy formation. According to some 99th FS pilots, aircraft identification proved very simple all through the swirling melee which ensued, because the German fighters were about 80mph faster than their P-40Ls!

As the German Jabos reacted by diving for the deck, eager to escape the beachhead, Jamison and Ashley executed a split-ess and found themselves directly above the German flight leader and his wingman. Jamison opened fire and "hits were registered on the right wing, and chunks flew off," but his four .50cal machine guns then jammed and he was only given credit for an aircraft damaged. Ashley stuck to his quarry and chased him at deck level to within a few miles of Rome, getting so close that he could see the pilot before he opened fire. Bullets peppered the Fw 190 and it burst into flames.

Howard Baugh and wingman Clarence Allen dropped behind another fleeing Fw 190, their fire forcing the fighter-bomber to hit the ground at a shallow angle and crash, giving them each a half-kill. Robert Diez, spotting an unsuspecting Fw 190 flying on a parallel course to him at about 750ft to his left, dropped in behind the Focke-Wulf and opened fire. The Fw 190's cowling flew off and the airplane dived into a yard near a farmhouse. Ed Toppins latched himself onto the tail of yet another Fw 190 and fired a short burst. The airplane bobbed up and then dropped its nose and exploded when it hit the ground.

One Fw 190 pilot who had had enough space between his machine and Leon Roberts' P-40L to pull away and escape instead chose to stay and fight. In a turning engagement that lasted several minutes, Roberts patiently fired and corrected over the course of a sequence of turns before finally hitting the German aircraft, which flipped over onto its back and plummeted to earth.

"Herky" Perry dived on a Focke-Wulf just as it leveled out of a dive and "raked the enemy ship from head to tail at about 300 yards. The airplane seemed to flutter, then fell off on the wing and headed for the ground." Perry's prey was recorded as damaged. Jack Rogers and "Woody" Driver cut off another Rome-bound Fw 190 and holed it with gunfire, losing sight of the fighter as it was smoking and in a steep dive at a height of just 50ft. They were given a share in the probable kill.

The day was not yet done, however, for that afternoon Lemuel Custis led another patrol over Anzio, and inland from the beach he stumbled upon a mixed formation of Fw 190s and Bf 109s. The pilots of these airplanes had more fight in them than the ones encountered that morning, and almost immediately an Fw 190 got on the tail of Lt Erwin Lawrence's P-40L. Lt Wilson "Sloppy" Eagleson spotted Lawrence's evasive maneuvering and cut across the path of the two aircraft, snapping off a 90-degree deflection shot at the Focke-Wulf, which burst into flames and hit the ground.

Lawrence, in turn, found himself set up for a deflection shot on another Fw 190, and Eagleson subsequently reported seeing his squadronmate's Fw 190 "roll over and dive for the ground, smoking excessively." Lawrence was credited with a probable. Custis, meanwhile, spotted an Fw 190 on the deck trying to escape. After chasing it to within seven miles of Rome, he "let loose a burst of fire, and saw tracers hit his fuselage and the airplane crash." Charles Bailey caught another retreating Fw 190 with an outstanding 45-degree deflection shot, causing the pilot to bail out of his stricken machine.

The German fighters extracted some measure of revenge, however, with Allen Lane finding himself the focus of at least four Fw 190s, which riddled his P-40L and forced him to bail out. Sam Bruce was last seen chasing a pair of Fw 190s, but apparently he was set upon by more German fighters and forced to abandon his fighter. Although his parachute deployed, Bruce was found to be dead when he hit the ground.

Rumors quickly circulated about Bruce's cause of death, some stating that he had been deliberately killed by a South African Air Force Spitfire pilot who machine-gunned him in his 'chute because he was black, while others suggested it was more likely that he was mortally wounded by flak or by fire from the enemy aircraft that downed him.

The next day, Charlie Hall's flight spotted a flight of Bf 109s and Fw 190s at 4,000ft approaching Anzio from the north. The Warhawk pilots had a 1,000ft altitude advantage, and they dived on the German fighters, which again turned away. "Six enemy airplanes came down in a string. We intercepted them at 3,000ft and followed them on the deck," Hall told correspondent Art Carter. He closed in to 300 yards before he began firing on one of the Bf 109s. "I gave it two bursts of fire. It flamed and crashed to the ground." Hall then wheeled the P-40L around "and chased an Fw 190 towards Rome," moving to within 200 yards of his target before opening fire.

Meanwhile, C. C. "Curtis" Robinson was diving and firing at another German aircraft when a "brown blur" – Hall's Warhawk – flashed in front of him. Somehow Robinson managed not to hit his flight leader, but he saw Hall "giving it short bursts" until the Fw 190 snapped into a spin and hit the ground.

Lewis Smith had also spotted a target soon after the flight had intercepted the German fighters. "The sky was full of airplanes, but I picked out an Fw 190 and chased him to the outskirts of Rome, firing all the way," he told Carter. When he was in position to fire a 50-degree deflection shot, Smith depressed the trigger. "The (enemy) aircraft veered out of control about 20ft above the ground and burst into flames," Smith reported. "It burned and smoked profusely, and I knew I had got him."

Robert Diez' wingman found an Fw 190 on his tail, so he dragged it across the path of his leader's machine by breaking in front of him. Diez coolly despatched his second enemy fighter in two days. "A portion of the ship's cowling flew off and it went into a steep dive at about 750ft," Diez reported.

Two days of fighting had brought 13 confirmed kills, which dispelled any doubts about the inability of black pilots to perform in aerial combat. "We've been looking forward to this happening, but this is the first time in five months that we have encountered enemy opposition in the air," "Spanky" Roberts told Carter. "We poured hell into them."

INVASION PROTECTION

The resurgence of the Luftwaffe coincided with the difficulties the Allies were having on the ground at Anzio. The squadron's critical ground support responsibilities were supplemented with an increasing number of patrols designed to keep German aircraft from strafing and bombing the troops.

On February 5, a patrol over the beachhead was headed west at about 6,000ft when it spotted at least ten Fw 190s diving toward the beach from a height of 16,000ft, before flattening out on the deck. The P-40s quickly turned into the German aircraft, and Elwood Driver made a diving left turn and pulled up about 300 yards behind an Fw 190. He began firing, "and continued to fire in long bursts, even though my target was pulling away," he reported. "My tracers straddled the cockpit and a sheet of flames burst from the right side. I last saw the airplane burning and headed toward Rome at a height of just 50ft above the ground."

At the same time, Clarence Jamison and George McCrumby were tangling with six Fw 190s when the latter pilot's P-40L was struck by antiaircraft fire. "Something hit underneath my ship," McCrumby told Carter. "Then another burst cracked the side of my cockpit, plunging the airplane into a dive at 4,000ft. I tried to pull out but had no control. The elevators had been knocked out. I had no alternative but to jump."

After sliding the canopy back, McCrumby tried to clamber out the left side of the P-40L, but was thrown back in his seat by the slipstream. "Then I tried the right side and got halfway out when again the slipstream threw me against the fuselage," he said. "I struggled until all but my right foot was free and dangled from the diving airplane until the wind turned the ship around at about 1,000ft and shook me loose. I reached for the ripcord six times before finding it, but my parachute opened immediately, landing me safely in a cow pasture."

Meanwhile, Jamison's aircraft had been riddled by fire from one of the six Fw 190s he and McCrumby had gone after, and whilst trying to escape his Merlin engine overheated and seized up. He crash-landed the Warhawk in a field near the front line and was rescued by US Army Rangers.

Forty-eight hours later, two more Fw 190s were downed, with Leonard Jackson and Clinton Mills each receiving credit for a kill. But the Germans had learned from their experiences with the nimble P-40Ls, opting now to rely on their superior speed in order to avoid engagements. Several of the patrols in February encountered German fighters, but these simply pulled away from Warhawks in the subsequent tail chase that ensued.

Still, the dive-bombing skills that the squadron had honed over the past eight months made them valuable assets, and they were recognized as such by the Luftwaffe, which bombed Capodichino for 30 minutes on the night of March 14. The next day, Mt Vesuvius erupted, spewing ash and rock that inflicted more damage on the Allied air forces in Italy than the Luftwaffe could have ever hoped to have done. Luckily, the 99th FS was little affected by either event.

On March 19 the squadron was tasked with knocking out the "Anzio Express" rail gun that was causing problems by shelling the beaches and airfields. Eight P-40s were sent out to find tunnel openings in which the gun might be hidden, and after dropping four bombs on a suspect tunnel, pilots also strafed the target. One P-40 was damaged by flak, but the "Anzio Express" was permanently silenced.

The squadron also played a part in Operation *Strangle*, which saw Allied aircraft interdicting German transport trains linking the Po Valley and troops holding up the advance from Anzio. During one of these missions, Clarence Allen was shot down north of Rome, and he hid out overnight in a cave. The following morning he discovered that he had been hiding in the middle of a German bivouac area! Eventually, once the German troops had moved out, Allen evaded capture and returned to the 99th FS.

Later in the month, after a successful dive-bombing mission against road traffic, Howard Baugh and Lewis "Smirkin'" Smith spotted a convoy of German trucks and dropped down to strafe it, but they made the mistake of flying parallel to the road instead of at an angle. Smith's aircraft was hit, and Baugh saw him bail out. Smith was not as lucky as Allen – captured almost immediately, he would spend the next 14 months as a PoW.

Despite the lack of recent aerial opposition, the squadron's tally during the Anzio campaign stood at 17, while the total for the three regular squadrons in the 79th FG was 32 (15 for the 85th, two for the 86th and 15 for the 87th). Contrary to the article it published in September 1943, *Time* magazine reported, "The Air Force regards its experiment proven."

On April 2 the 99th FS moved to Cercola airfield, where it was attached to the 324th FG, commanded by Col Leonard Lydon. Other changes included the departure of CO Maj "Spanky" Roberts back to the USA, his place being taken by Capt Erwin Lawrence.

The squadron participated in the battle for Monte Cassino in May, pounding German positions during the push for Rome. By the time Rome fell on June 4, the 99th had flown 500 missions and 3,277 sorties. Following a brief stay at Ciampo airfield, and assignment to the 86th FG, the squadron moved to Ramitelli airfield on June 28, where it joined the three squadrons of the 332nd FG.

AIRACOBRAS AND THUNDERBOLTS

On December 22, 1943, a train left Oscoda Field, Michigan, bound for Fort Patrick Henry, Virginia, carrying the men of the 100th, 301st and 302nd FSs. Having trained at Tuskegee and other bases in the USA, the group was now under the command of Lt Col Benjamin O. Davis. After his combat experiences with the 99th FS, the group was initially a disappointment. He described them as a "gaggle" of pilots who had been "moved around from pillar to post. They'd been to school here and there, but they had not flown enough as a unit."

While the 99th had had nine months to train, the 100th, 301st and 302nd had not enjoyed such a lengthy work-up. Davis blamed the units' early problems on the lack of a cadre of trained pilots and groundcrew who could have imparted their experience and attitudes on the men. They also suffered from a shortage of proper fighter trainers – the worn-out P-40Cs they had flown at Oscoda had directly led to the deaths of two second lieutenants, Wilmeth Sadat-Singh and Jerome Edwards.

Initially under the command of Lt Col Samuel Westbrook, the group was turned over to Col Robert Selway in June 1943, who did his job efficiently. He would subsequently impose segregationist policies on the 477th Medium Bombardment Group that effectively prevented it from succeeding. Much to the joy of the men, Selway was replaced by Lt Col Davis in October 1943, and just before Christmas the group shipped out.

The 332nd's first battle came in Virginia, where the local motion picture theater featured a roped-off area for colored troops. The angered men of the group were ordered confined to quarters by Davis, who then warned the base commander that he would not assume responsibility for the actions of his men if theater segregation was not ended. The ropes came down, but tensions remained high until the group boarded a convoy of troopships on January 2, 1944. During the trip, the group's spirits were lifted by news of the 99th's successes over the Anzio beachhead.

The 332nd's convoy arrived in the Italian port of Taranto 32 days later. "It was a terrible sight because of the bombings," said Samuel Curtis. "Rusting ships were overturned in the harbor. Most of the Italian structures were built out of stone and masonry, and they had been bombed by the Americans first and then, of course, when the Allies took it, the Germans bombed the port too. There was white dusty powder all over everything, and an unpleasant smell that went along with the sights. As the ships pulled up in the dock, we saw these people, these human beings in ragged clothes, with babies. They were going around begging and looking into garbage cans for food. It was a very disturbing sight."

The 100th FS had set up shop in Montecorvino by February 5, and the rumors that they would be equipped with the P-38 or the new P-63 Kingcobra were soon dispelled, as waiting for them at the airfield were war-weary P-39 Airacobras. The squadron, under the command of Robert Tresville, flew its first missions in the P-39 that day. Meanwhile, the 301st (led by Charles DeBow) and the 302nd (with Edward Gleed in command) flew their first missions from Montecorvino two days later.

Flying coastal patrol sorties in second-hand P-39s was not what the group had expected. This assignment required pilots to monitor an area from Cape Palermo and the Gulf of Policastro to the Ponziane Islands. Davis referred to this tasking as "a slap in the face," and flying over the ocean in worn-out fighters was dangerous even when there was no sign of the enemy.

"We went over there and we were really excited," said Samuel Curtis. "We were going into battle and we were going to really show them. Then we had our first casualty." After suffering an engine failure, Clemenceau Givings of the 100th FS bailed out of his P-39 but drowned in Naples Harbor after becoming entangled in his parachute. "I'll never forget the fellow, because he was the life of the squadron," Curtis recalled. "He was a lively kind of guy, and he was the first one lost. One day we came back and they said 'Clem got killed,' and it came as a real shock. It was then we realized we were really in a war zone."

On February 15, the group discovered how unsuited its Airacobras were for combat. Roy Spencer and William Melton of the 302nd FS spotted a Ju 88 flying a reconnaissance mission near Ponsa Point, at the mouth of Naples Harbor. Both men succeeding in damaging the German aircraft, yet the Ju 88 was still able to both climb and accelerate away from its frustrated pursuers.

Six days later, the 100th FS moved to Capodichino airfield, from which the 99th FS was still operating as part of the 79th FG. While the latter unit was engaged in Operation *Strangle*, the 332nd was still assigned to the lowly task of harbor patrol. Bored of these missions, and without Davis' permission, Tresville and Gleed worked out a patrol route that would take them near to the Anzio beachhead, where they hoped to find German fighters.

Davis was furious when he found out and gave Tresville a dressing-down, but Gleed, ever the aggressive go-getter, scheduled another identical mission – 16 fighters took off and headed north toward the beachhead, then turned inland. Gleed had to turn back because of engine trouble with his P-39, but Wendell Pruitt, who was operations officer for the 302nd FS, continued on towards Rome, where fuel started to run low.

The P-39s' straight-line course back to Capodichino took them through the flak corridor between Rome and the beachhead, and Walter Westmoreland's P-39L was shot out from under him. Westmoreland bailed out but broke his leg in the process. As a result of this unapproved mission, an angry Davis relieved Gleed of command of the 302nd and sent him to the 301st. Melvin "Red" Jackson assumed command of the 302nd.

VOLCANIC ERUPTION

On March 15 Mt Vesuvius' eruption layered Capodichino in fine ash, bringing a pause to the aerial action from the base. The lasting effect of this natural disaster was the presence of smoke and ash in the air for several weeks that, according to Walter Palmer of the 100th FS, forced patrols to fly north of the main volcanic plume beyond the harbor, before turning back toward the Anzio beachhead.

These conditions also posed safety hazards in unexpected ways, as 2Lt Virgil Richardson discovered when he landed following a patrol and only then spotted a flock of ash-covered sheep wandering across the runway. Richardson's P-39 hit the animals, causing the nose gear strut to snap. "Then, the gas tank, located directly under my seat, caught fire," Richardson told historian Ben Vinson III. "Let me tell you that there is nothing that can make you move faster than having a live fire under your ass!"

Richardson pulled the handle on the door, which fell off. As he stepped onto the wing of the skidding airplane, it veered to the right, throwing him to the ground. Luckily, he landed on his liferaft, which broke his fall. Even so, his injuries kept him flat on his back for three weeks, followed by a lengthy recuperation at the rest camp in Naples.

Two days after the eruption, the harbor patrols were up and running again. Laurence Wilkins and Weldon K. Groves spotted another Ju 88 making the daily reconnaissance run over the Naples area and, despite holing the aircraft's wing, Wilkins and Groves could only watch as the Junkers used superior speed to escape once again.

By April 15, the headquarters unit of the 332nd FG and the 301st and 302nd FSs had departed Montecorvino and joined the 100th FS at Capodichino. The latter base was far more comfortable, with an electrical generator chief among its amenities. Unfortunately, the airfield was also a magnet for Luftwaffe bombers, which staged a nuisance raid on April 19 that did no harm. Sadly, the same could not be said of the P-39s, for 2Lt Beryl Wyatt of the 100th FS died a few hours later when his misfiring fighter crashed while on a patrol. The following day, group public relations officer Lt Ray Ware informed the pilots that they would soon be converting to the P-47D, much to the glee of the men.

The Luftwaffe returned to Capodichino on the morning of April 21 on yet another nuisance raid. Just as the group was learning to ignore these nocturnal visitations, the base was bombed again on the 24th by between 30 and 40 Ju 88s. The 30-minute attack caused more damage than previous raids, and inspired new enthusiasm for the once-onerous task of foxhole-digging. Later that same day, the group launched a strafing mission, but on take-off the P-39 of 2Lt Edgar Jones of the 100th FS went out of control and the pilot was killed in the ensuing crash. The P-47s could not arrive soon enough.

On April 25 the first six Thunderbolts flew in to Capodichino, these aircraft being hand-me-downs from the 325th FG. The Thunderbolts were distributed evenly between all three squadrons, and their yellow-and-black checkered tails repainted all red – the new group color.

Harbor patrol missions continued to dominate the group's activities, with occasional strafing sorties thrown in. Strafing in the P-39 could be a hazardous undertaking, as the fighter's liquid-cooled Allison engine was vulnerable to even the smallest shell fragment (one hit and the powerplant would lose its vital coolant and seize up in just a matter of minutes), and the Anzio area was teeming with German flak. And just to prove how deadly the guns were, on May 5 1Lt James R. Polkinghorne of the 301st was shot down and killed in his P-39 during a strafing mission.

Capodichino remained a temptation for German raiders into the spring of 1944, and from May 14 onward, the Luftwaffe regularly appeared in the night sky between 0300 and 0400hrs, causing little damage but disturbing the group's sleep. Five days later, the group received an additional ten P-47s and started transition training in earnest. Even these sorties could be hazardous, however, and on May 22 2Lt Henry Pollard (who, in civilian life, had been a well-known saxophone player with the Jimmy Lunceford Orchestra) was killed when his P-47D crashed near Casalnuovo during transition training. Pollard, who had been with the group just three weeks, became the first 302nd FS pilot lost in Italy.

Meanwhile, the Airacobras also continued to exact a toll. On May 24 the 301st lost 1Lt John Henry Prowell Jnr when his P-39L crashed during a convoy protection mission, and nine days later Elmer "Chubby" Taylor's Airacobra caught fire over the harbor. He bailed out, but his parachute failed to open and Taylor plunged to his death.

On May 26 Lt Woodrow Morgan was shot down and captured during a strafing mission in his P-47D. An more ignominious fate befell 2Lt Lloyd S. Hathcock of the 301st, who became disoriented during a flight three days later in P-47D 42-75971. Landing at Rome-Littorio airfield, which was still occupied by the Germans, Hathcock was quickly captured and his Thunderbolt, after having its wingtips and cowling painted yellow (Luftwaffe theater colors), was despatched north to the Rechlin Test Center for evaluation.

In October 1944 the Thunderbolt was transferred to the famous Zirkus Rosarius, whose job it was to familiarize Luftwaffe units with the strengths and weaknesses of enemy fighter types through mock combat with captured aircraft. Hathcock's P-47D was the first of its type to fall into enemy hands with fully functioning water injection, and the aircraft was kept airworthy well into 1945. It was eventually found abandoned, minus its propeller and sitting on its tail, at Göttingen airfield when the base was captured by US troops in the final weeks of the war in Europe.

According to Lt Alexander Jefferson, who met Lloyd Hathcock in a PoW camp after his own P-51 had been shot down by flak in August 1944, "He will never live down the fact that he landed at a German air base due to a navigational error. Their base was 35 miles in one direction and ours 35 miles in the opposite direction. Was he surprised when his groundcrew spoke German and had white faces!"

These events soured the ending of the 332nd's initial period of operations. On May 27, an advance echelon of the 332nd group headquarters moved to Ramitelli. Four days later, the group was detached from the Twelfth Air Force and attached to the Fifteenth Air Force, freeing it from harbor patrols and placing it immediately in the thick of the strategic bombing campaign, which was being waged deep inside German-held territory.

TO WAR IN THE THUNDERBOLT

Col Benjamin Davis wasted little time in getting his newly equipped squadrons into the air. On June 7, 32 P-47s conducted a fighter sweep of the Ferrara–Bologna area, finding little activity other than sporadic flak. During the flight to the target area, 2Lt Carroll N. Langston Jnr's instruments indicated that he was losing oil pressure and he bailed out. A search was launched, but Langston was never recovered. Other pilots reported their oil pressure gauges also mistakenly indicated low pressure, and groundcrews made a concerted effort to repair the gauges, thus solving an innocuous problem that had cost a pilot his life.

The next day, the 332nd launched a 32-airplane escort for 5th Bomb Wing B-17s that were sent to attack targets in the Italian city of Pola (now Pula, in Croatia), the group's first strategic bomber mission escort. Col Davis had vehemently stressed to his pilots at the briefing that the group had to protect the bombers at all costs. He scorned other fighter groups' tactics, stating that "as soon as the bombers reached the target area, they'd peel off and go looking for targets of opportunity. We didn't do that. We went through the target area, and if there were any cripples coming off the target we would assign an element – two fighters – to escort that cripple to a base where he could land safely." The group flew close escort, Davis said, with 12- or 16-airplane squadron formations flying slow turns over the bombers.

While the Pola escort proved uneventful, the mission flown 48 hours later was anything but. At 0700hrs, 39 P-47s of the 301st and 302nd FSs departed Ramitelli (with three aborts) and rendezvoused with the 5th, 49th, 55th, 57th and 304th BWs, which were headed for targets in the Munich area.

As the formation neared Udine, four Bf 109s made a diving attack on a group of Liberators, triggering a swirling dogfight. After the Bf 109s made their firing pass, they turned to the left and Lt Wendell Pruitt latched onto one of them. "As the Jerries passed under me, I rolled over, shoved everything forward, dove and closed on one (a Bf 109G) at 475mph," he reported. "I gave him a short burst of machine-gun fire, and discovering that I was giving him too much lead, I waited as he shallowed out of a turn. Then I gave two long two-second bursts. His left wing erupted in flames." Pruitt's wingman saw the German pilot bail out and the Bf 109 explode when it slammed into the ground.

At about the same time, "Red" Jackson spotted five or six Bf 109s at "11 o'clock high" and closed with them. He fired on one fighter, which started to descend in a spin. Jackson, having lost his flight in his pursuit of the spinning Bf 109, then had another Messerschmitt make a head-on pass at him. He pulled up and the P-47 stalled, allowing the Bf 109 to get on his tail. Meanwhile, Lt Charles Bussey's formation of eight P-47s latched onto the tail of the four remaining Bf 109s, including the one chasing Jackson.

Lt William Green fired on Jackson's pursuer, then Bussey opened up on the same Bf 109, blowing the tail off the German fighter. Bussey's wingman saw the pilot bail out and the aircraft explode in mid-air. Bussey and Green were each given a share in the kill.

Jackson, unaware of the action behind him, used his P-47's injected water boost to scoot into some low clouds in an effort to evade his now-despatched pursuer. As he emerged from the clouds, Jackson saw another Bf 109 at "11 o'clock" and turned into it, eventually getting into a firing position and putting a burst into the fighter's belly. "Metal flew off his left side," Jackson later recalled. "The Nazi pilot bailed out over a German airfield. I hit the deck and came home."

Frederick Funderberg, meanwhile, spotted two Bf 109s 500ft below him at his "nine o'clock." He and his wingman peeled off to engage them and Funderberg fired a quick burst, causing pieces to come off one of the Bf 109s. As his flight passed below the two German fighters and started to pull up for another pass, they came face-to-face with a second pair of Messerschmitts. Funderberg fired off a quick burst and the P-47's eight machine guns tore one of the German fighters apart. Other pilots in Funderberg's flight saw two aircraft splash into the Adriatic, as well as a single parachute, far below them.

Elsewhere, Lt Robert Wiggins spied yet another Bf 109 to his left at about his altitude, so he turned into him and attacked. A full-deflection shot caused pieces of the fighter to fly off, but its pilot put the smoking airplane into a shallow dive to gain speed and climbed away. The day's five kills were not without loss, however, as Cornelius Rogers was killed and the aircraft of Capt Floyd Rayford and Lt William Hunter received flak damage, with Rayford picking up a superficial wound in the process.

Back at Ramitelli, representatives from Republic and senior officers from Fifteenth Air Force HQ were lecturing the pilots not assigned to fly that day about the peculiarities of the P-47. A major stood on a truck telling the assembled pilots, whom he referred to as "boys," that the Thunderbolt should never be slow-rolled below 1,000ft because of its excessive weight.

As if on cue, Lts Wendell Pruitt and Lee Archer, known by the squadron as "the Gruesome Twosome," came screaming across the field on the deck, wingtip-to-wingtip, at the end of the escort mission. They pulled up and threw their P-47s into slow victory rolls. Aghast, the indignant major screamed at the two Thunderbolts, "You can't do that!"

MORE MISSIONS

After a two-day break, the 301st and 302nd FSs put up 30 P-47s to cover the 5th and 55th BWs' raid on Smederevo, in Yugoslavia, on June 11, followed on the 13th by a 32-airplane mission by the same two squadrons escorting the 5th and 49th BWs to the Munich area. On the latter mission, the Luftwaffe once again put in an appearance near Udine, but of the 11 fighters seen, only four pressed home their attacks. One P-47 was damaged, but the bombers were protected.

The Luftwaffe's response was even less enthusiastic during the June 14 mission to Budapest, in Hungary. The 301st and 302nd sent up 29 P-47s to escort the 5th, 49th, 55th and 304th BWs, and although 15 Bf 109s and seven twin-engined fighters were spotted, they made no effort to attack the bombers, or their P-47 escorts.

The long-range missions continued on the 16th, when the 100th, 301st and 302nd FSs covered a maximum-effort bombing raid against targets in the Bratislava area – 40 P-47s escorted the bombers from Banja Luka, in Yugoslavia, to the target. Six days later, the same three squadrons provided escort for another maximum-strength raid to Bucharest-Giurgiu, in Rumania. Both missions passed without incident.

The uneventful trips north came to an end on June 23, much to the group's sorrow. The day's orders called for Capt Robert Tresville to lead 41 P-47s from the 100th, 301st and 302nd FSs on a low-level strafing attack of the strategically placed Airasca-Pinerolo landing ground, which was little more than a mile west of Airasca in the Piedmont region of northwestern Italy. From the start, the mission was beset by problems. Gwynne Peirson's P-47D crashed on take-off, but the pilot survived. Four other P-47s were forced to abort, leaving 36 Thunderbolts in formation to cross the Tyrrhenian Sea at less than 100ft in order to take the airfield, and its occupants, by surprise.

The weather was described as hazy over the water, with a very bright glare from the sun and a cloud base of just 1,000ft. Near Cape Corse, with the pilots finding it very difficult to discern the horizon, 2Lt Sam Jefferson's airplane dropped too low, touched the water and exploded on impact. At almost the same time Earl Sherrard's P-47 pancaked into the water – he scrambled out of his fighter and was later rescued. 2Lt Charles B. Johnson, who was circling Sherrard's machine in order to check that the pilot was still alive, also flew into the water. He was unable to escape from his cockpit before the P-47 sank, however.

A few minutes later, the lead element experienced the effects of the strange weather. Tresville, flying with Dempsey Morgan and Spurgeon Ellington as the second section in his flight, frantically gestured at wingman Willard L. Woods to pull up – the latter was so close to the water that his wing tanks were starting to kick up rooster-tails.

Just after they sighted the coast, according to Woods, Tresville's own P-47 struck the water, which stripped off the drop tanks, ripped off the ailerons and bent the propeller back over the cowling. The Thunderbolt bounced back into the air momentarily, but then slammed back into the water, leaving only its tail visible. Woods later reported that Tresville was looking at a map when he crashed. The group never found the target – radio silence prevented the deputy formation leader from learning of Tresville's crash, and kept him from assuming navigational responsibilities for the attack.

The loss of Tresville, who, like Col Davis, was another rare black West Pointer, was keenly felt by the group. "Tresville was a fantastic guy," said Samuel Curtis. "He was smart, he was bright, he was strong, he was well-coordinated. He would have gone far." Andrew "Jug" Turner assumed command of the 100th FS upon Tresville's death.

On June 23 the group escorted a mission to Sofia, in Bulgaria, and saw no opposition, but two days later it would accomplish one of its more special feats. The 100th, 301st and 302nd FSs were despatched to attack troops in Yugoslavia, sending 20 P-47s out in five flights. One four-ship flight became a two-ship flight when Freddie Hutchins' left drop tank refused to come off, forcing him and his wingman Larry Wilkins to return early to Ramitelli. The other two pilots in the flight, Wendell Pruitt and Gwynne Peirson, continued on, but strong winds forced the fighters off course and they missed the reported location of the troop concentration.

Dejectedly, Pruitt and Peirson set a course for home that carried them over the Italian port city of Trieste. There before them in the harbor, steaming toward the open sea, was what they identified as a German destroyer – a black cross was clearly visible on its funnel. Pruitt and Peirson, flying side by side, opened fire. Pruitt's rounds struck the ship, which in actuality was the German-operated ex-Italian torpedo boat TA-27 (now used as a mine-layer). The vessel soon began to burn, and the smoke attracted the attention of Joseph Elsberry, Joseph Lewis and Charles Dunne, who joined Pruitt and Peirson in their strafing attacks.

On Peirson's second pass, his rounds apparently struck one of the vessel's mines, for it was engulfed by a massive explosion. When the debris cleared, the pilots were rewarded with the sight of the ship rolling over and sinking near Pirano. The group also strafed radar/radio stations around the harbor, shot up trucks and the wharf at Muggio, and sank a sailboat that fired on them off Isola. Peirson landed with several jagged holes in the undersides of his wings, which he suspected were caused by debris thrown into the air by the ship's explosion. He and Pruitt were awarded DFCs for the action.

The day after the group's destroyer-busting mission, 36 Thunderbolts escorted a maximum effort to the Lake Balaton area of Hungary. Two of the flight leaders were forced to abandon their fighters due to mechanical problems with their combat-weary P-47Ds. Lt Andrew Maples bailed out near Termoli, on the outbound leg, and was rescued, but Lt Maurice V. Esters, who took to his parachute near Vetacandrija, was never seen again.

On June 27, a 37-airplane force escorted the 5th and 47th BWs to Budapest, and while there were no combat losses, the Thunderbolts of Larry Wilkins and Washington Ross were damaged in a collision soon after landing. The next day saw an identical number of aircraft escort the 304th BW to the Ferdinand area of northern Italy. On take-off, Lt Edward Laird was killed when his P-47 left the runway and crashed, and Lt Mac Ross survived an emergency landing at Lecce airfield. Lt Alfonso Davis' P-47 had suffered a blown tyre on take-off, and on the way back from the mission, he made a successful forced landing in a field near Otranto. Finally, Lt Floyd Thompson was forced to take to his parachute near Forli, and he was immediately taken prisoner by the Germans.

The last day of June saw the 100th, 301st and 302nd FSs mount an escort mission for five bomb wings sent to attack targets in the Vienna area. Forty-five P-47s took off, and there were just two aborts – a vast improvement from the mechanical woes of the 27th. The mission proceeded without any hitches. Although the group had by now started to receive unpainted "bubbletop" P-47D-30s to complement its older "razorbacks," the June 30 mission would prove to be its final one in the Thunderbolt – the 332nd had begun to receive P-51B/Cs in late June. And like the Thunderbolts before them, these aircraft were also "hand-me-downs" from the 31st and 325th FGs.

In just 30 days of P-47 action, the group had destroyed five airplanes and an enemy vessel. More significantly, its pilots had learned the intricacies of conducting effective close bomber escort missions. The experience would pay dividends, both for the 332nd FG and the bomber crews that it would escort over coming months.

Capt Felix "Mike" Rogers would assume command of the 353rd FS following the loss of two COs in a day, on August 9, 1944. By then a seven-kill ace, Rogers led the unit until he was declared tour-expired on October 1, 1944. He remained in the post-war USAF until retiring with the rank of four-star general in 1978, by which time he had served 36 years in the armed forces. (USAAF)

Newly promoted Capt Don Beerbower poses on the wing of BONNIE "B" in late January 1944. The 354th FG's second-ranking ace with 15.5 kills, Beerbower led the high-scoring 353rd FS from June 30, 1944 until he was shot down by flak during a strafing attack on August 9, 1944. He died of the wounds he had suffered either when his Mustang was hit, or when he reportedly struck the tail of his fighter soon after bailing out. (USAAF)

Photographed in 1944, future six-kill ace Lt Clayton K. Gross' 335th FS P-51B sported its pilot's choice of name, LIVE BAIT, on the traditional port side. Less conventionally, it also bore his long-serving crew chief's wife's name – "Peggy Smith" – on the usually blank starboard side. (Capt Clayton Kelly Gross)

Newly promoted Lt Col Glenn Eagleston (left of the mission board) and group CO Lt Col Jack Bradley (on the right) conduct an open-air briefing at Ober Olm on April 17, 1945. (USAAF)

This 356th FS Thunderbolt has just had the snow shoveled away from its undercarriage in preparation for its next mission. Still grasping his shovel, a weary groundcrewman takes a break after completing the job. (USAAF)

His gaunt face showing the strain, a tired-looking Maj Frank "Pinky" O'Connor enjoys a first post-flight cigarette following yet another armed reconnaissance mission. A veteran of 59 sorties in the ETO by the time he was shot down and captured on November 5, 1944, O'Connor survived Germany's fighters, flak and incensed peasantry to become a career USAF officer. (USAAF)

The 356th FS in particular seems to have made full use of the substantial artistic canvas provided by the Thunderbolt's engine cowlings. This nose art, for Lt John Youngworth's P-47 *BIG ASS BIRD*, was painted by groundcrewman Will Louie. Unsurprisingly, a number of P-47s received this nickname in the various combat theaters in which the fighter saw action. (Will Louie)

The dominance of Allied airpower. Photographed on parade at A-29 airfield in western France, these are the P-51Ds of the 356th FS. (USAAF)

Two flights from the 356th FS return to A-2 in tight formation in late July 1944. The lead aircraft of the lower flight is P-51D *SHORT-FUSE SALLEE*, which was Maj Richard Turner's first "bubble top" Mustang. This was the fighter he used to claim his 11th and last kill on July 30, 1944. Most of these aircraft carry personal markings in the form of nicknames on their noses, and all bar the two olive drab P-51Bs still feature invasion stripes. (USAAF)

Training for the 332nd's enlisted support personnel was carried out at Chanute Field before the men moved to Tuskegee. The number of enlisted men trained to service the aircraft and support the units was steadily increasing, with the 96th Service Group, 83rd Fighter Control Squadron and the 689th Signal Warning Company also sharing the base. By mid-1942, almost 220 officers and 3,000 enlisted men were packed into Tuskegee Army Air Field. (Lt Col Harold C. Hayes Collection)

Cadets learned on an assortment of second-line types, including P-39s and P-40s. These were also the first types many of them would actually fly in combat. (Lt Col Harold C. Hayes Collection)

The most successful fighting outfits within the USAAF in World War II all had one thing in common – a strong, well-respected leader who flew with his pilots on virtually every mission. The 332nd FG was fortunate in having just such a man in Benjamin O. Davis. (Jon Lake Collection)

Capt Wendell O. Pruitt leaves a treasured ring with his crew chief, SSgt Samuel W. Jacobs, prior to taking off. On August 27, 1944, Pruitt destroyed five airplanes in a single day during the 332nd's strafing attacks on Prostejou and Kostoleo. (National Museum of the USAF)

During the return from a mission on November 7, 1944, Fifteenth Air Force photographer Frank Ambrose radioed the fighters escorting these 465th BG Liberators and asked if they wanted to pose for some shots. The result was this photograph of a 100th FS Mustang zooming over the group – something that probably would not have been possible had Col Benjamin O. Davis been leading that day. (Frank Ambrose Photography)

Mac Ross was a member of Tuskegee's first class, but sentimentality did not prevent his classmate Col Davis from relieving him as the 301st FS's operations officer. On July 10, 1944, Ross' Mustang entered a shallow dive and slammed into a hill, killing him. Rumors that the crash was a suicide persist, although the nature of the accident suggests that an oxygen system failure may have claimed his life. (Lt Col Harold C. Hayes Collection)

A striking view of the 100th FS before a mission in November 1944, taken from the top hatch of a 465th BG Liberator. According to the photographer, the bomber crew was unaware of the presence of an all-black unit in-theater until they needed to have the B-24's wheels dug out of the mud and shouted for assistance! (Frank Ambrose Photography)

A 100th FS armorer at Ramitelli reloads the ammunition trays of his P-51B Mustang with .50cal rounds at the height of the airfield strafing campaign in fall 1944. (National Museum of the USAF)

A 100th FS Mustang "rides herd" on a 450th BG Liberator somewhere over the Alps in early 1945. Red-tailed Mustangs were among the favorite sights enjoyed by Fifteenth Air Force bomber crews. (Stanley Purwinis via Tom Purwinis)

Looking the very picture of a fighter pilot, Louis Purnell leaves a briefing at Ramitelli. One of the original members of the 99th, Purnell took advantage of the advance field on the Yugoslavian island of Vis when his engine picked up a chunk of flak during the August 17, 1944 mission to Ploesti. (National Museum of the USAF)

ENTER THE MUSTANG

While the 332nd FG was flying its final missions in the P-39 and mastering the P-47, the 99th FS and its war-weary P-40Ls had moved to a new base at Pignataro on May 10, then transferred across to Ciampino Field and Orbetello for brief stays. On July 3, the squadron finally moved to Ramitelli and officially joined the 332nd FG – a move seen by some in the 99th as a less than positive one. Many pilots in the unit saw the new group as being green and inexperienced, and resented being forced to fly with it. Others viewed it as a step back toward segregation, for instead of flying as a component within a white group, they had again been lumped together in an all-black unit.

Conversely, the men of the 332nd FG feared that the group's leadership roles would be handed over to more experienced pilots from the 99th FS, but this did not come to pass. From an administrative standpoint, this merger created a four-squadron group – a rarity in the USAAF that placed additional pressure on the group commander. To make matters worse, Tuskegee Army Air Field was unable to produce enough pilots for all four squadrons and the then-forming 477th Medium Bombardment Group, meaning that combat tours were far longer than in other groups.

Things were not all bad, however. By July 1944, the 332nd had replaced all of its Thunderbolts with P-51B/C Mustangs, and these aircraft were far better suited to the long-range escort missions that the group was being assigned by the Fifteenth Air Force. The fighter's added range and speed were welcome advantages. Still, the transition from one aircraft to another was not without peril, and Othell Dickson, a standout in training, was killed while performing aerobatics over Ramitelli when his Mustang plunged to earth during an inverted maneuver. Speculation centered on the fuselage fuel tank – when full, it could adversely affect the center of gravity and make recovery from maneuvers like Dickson's impossible.

The arrival of the Mustang coincided with Col Benjamin Davis' difficult decision to relieve Charles DeBow as commander of the 301st and replace him with Lee Rayford, who was a combat veteran from the 99th who had just returned for a second tour. DeBow had failed to meet Davis' expectations for "leadership in the air," the commanding officer stated. Davis also relieved fellow Tuskegee classmate Mac Ross as the squadron's operations officer.

Still, the Mustangs lifted the group's morale, and as a visible sign of confidence, groundcrews applied the group marking of a solid red tail to all of their fighters. "We wanted the American bombers to know we were escorting them," said Herbert Carter. "The red tails would also let the German interceptors know who was escorting the bombers."

On July 4, 1944, the 332nd flew its first mission with the Mustang – a 40-airplane escort of the 5th and 47th BWs. Col Davis led the flight, but turned over command to Lt Claude Govan when his radios malfunctioned. July 5 saw the 100th, 301st and 302nd provide 52 P-51s for an escort mission. All aircraft returned safely, although fuel forced four to land on Corsica. The group sighted two Bf 109s, but the Germans made no attempt to attack the bombers, and they failed to lure the escorting Mustangs away from their charges. On July 6, 37 P-51s escorted the 47th BW to Latisana and Tagliamento Casarsa, and the very next day 47 Mustangs covered a raid on Vienna. All returned safely.

While the junior squadrons of the group were flying missions, the 99th FS received its first P-51B/Cs. On July 8 the old hands worked to master the fighter's intricacies. The rest of the group, meanwhile, was itching to tangle with the Luftwaffe, and on the 8th one of them would. The 100th, 301st and 302nd had sent 46 Mustangs to escort the 304th BW to Münchendorf airfield, and the attack drew 15 to 20 German fighters into the air. Before they could be engaged by the 332nd, however, they were intercepted by a group of P-38s. One Bf 109 made it through the Lightnings and attacked Lt Earl S. Sherrard over the target. Sherrard wrung out his P-51 in an effort to elude the Bf 109, finally shaking him off after a long-running encounter.

Unfortunately, just as the Bf 109 disappeared from sight Sherrard was attacked by the P-38s, and he was forced to repeat his evasive maneuvers. After eluding the Lightnings, Sherrard landed his Mustang at a forward field, pilot and fuel both exhausted. On July 9, 32 P-51s from the 100th, 301st and 302nd FSs escorted the 47th BW to the Concordia Vega oil refineries at Ploesti, in Rumania – it would become a frequent destination for the group. Two Bf 109s and two Fw 190s were spotted, but again they were intercepted by P-51s from another fighter group.

Meanwhile, the 99th FS was struggling to master the Mustang. On July 10, Mac Ross, who had been relieved as group operations officer just a few days earlier, died when the P-51B he was checking out entered a slow, shallow descent and eventually hit the side of a hill. There was little physical evidence to explain the accident – an oxygen system failure seemed to be the likely cause. The next day, during a transition flight in a P-51C, Capt Leon Roberts (the last member of the original 99th FS still with the unit) plunged into the ocean from high altitude. Again, speculation centered on a possible case of hypoxia. At the time of his death, Roberts had flown no fewer than 116 combat sorties.

That same day, the group began a series of missions to soften up southern France. The 100th, 301st and 302nd sent 33 P-51s on an uneventful mission to escort 47th BW "heavies" attacking the submarine pens at Toulon. On July 12, while escorting B-24s of the 49th BW on a mission to destroy railroad marshaling yards in southern France, some 25 German fighters jumped the 332nd over the French coast. After the fray, flight leader Joseph Elsberry claimed three kills and a probable, although for some reason his victories went unconfirmed.

Elsberry's first victim made a pass on the bombers and was turning away when he hit him with a 30-degree deflection shot, resulting in the Fw 190 streaming heavy black smoke and falling off to the left. Next, Elsberry spotted a second Focke-Wulf that turned in front and below him, and he put his Mustang into a 30-degree dive, quickly closing on the hapless fighter. Elsberry started firing and hit the Fw 190's left wing, causing the German fighter to begin to slow-roll. He continued to fire short bursts at his quarry until it slammed into the ground during a split-ess maneuver.

The victorious pilot climbed to reenter the fight, and was rewarded by the sight of a third Fw 190 turning away from him as if to make its escape. Elsberry drew a lead on the German fighter and fired a two-second burst that arced into his target, sending it crashing into the ground, as witnessed by Lts Dunne and Friend. As Elsberry pulled off this target, another Fw 190 shot by in a 45-degree dive, so he flung the Mustang to the right and followed the airplane down. With only his left wing guns firing, Elsberry gave his Mustang *Joedebelle* a bootful of right rudder so as to keep his sights on the fleeing Fw 190 and opened fire, scoring hits across the enemy airplane's left wing root. The Fw 190 started spiraling down, and soon straightened into a dive, but its pilot never recovered and the Focke-Wulf crashed on French soil.

Meanwhile, Harold Sawyer scored a confirmed kill over Nîmes by destroying an Fw 190 after it made an attack on the bomber stream. Six German fighters had dived through the Liberators, then split-essed away, turned left, then split-essed again. Sawyer fired a burst at the trailing aircraft, which never pulled out of its second split-ess and slammed into the ground. Sawyer immediately spotted a second Fw 190 lining up to attack the bombers from about "ten o'clock," and he gunned down this fighter as well, although the latter kill was not confirmed. Lt George Rhodes was shot down during the battle, bailing out near Viterbo, but he was rescued and returned to the squadron.

July 13 brought a return to Italian targets, with the 100th, 301st and 302nd sending 37 P-51s to escort two groups from the 5th BW sent to attack the Pinzano railroad bridge and the Vinzone viaduct. Two days later, the 99th flew with the group's three other squadrons for the first time during a raid on the refineries at Ploesti. The 55th BW had an escort of 61 P-51s, which earned kudos from the bomber crews by chasing off eight Bf 109s that were harassing three straggling "heavies" near Krusevac. Col Davis continued to drill home the message that the group's primary mission was to stay with the bombers, even if it meant "protecting them with your life." While this grated with some of the fighter pilots, none dared disobey the colonel.

MACCHI MENACE

July 16 found 45 Mustangs from the 100th, 301st and 302nd getting a chance to range free on a fighter sweep over Vienna. The group chanced upon a single Macchi C.205 fighter creeping up on a straggling B-24 from the bomber's "five o'clock low" position in a gradual climbing turn.

Although Italy had switched sides in 1943, there were still fascist Italians flying for the *Aviazone Nationale Republicana* (ANR) of Mussolini's rump state, the Italian Socialist Republic. Formation leader Lt Alfonso Davis of the 302nd FS ordered his flight of four Mustangs to intercept the Macchi. As they dived on the fighter, Lt Davis overshot, but his wingman, Lt William "Chubby" Green, turned inside the C.205 and fired a series of bursts that caused the Italian fighter to stream black smoke.

Green followed his foe almost to the deck before the Macchi pilot tried to make a low-altitude turn around a mountain – the disabled fighter caught a wingtip on the mountainside and cartwheeled into a fireball. Meanwhile, Davis had climbed to cover Green, and he spotted a second Macchi about 5,000ft below him. Davis dived on the fighter, catching it in a left turn. A 60-degree deflection shot caused chunks of the fuselage to fly off, before the Macchi fell into a spin to the left and crashed.

The next day, the group returned to southern France, escorting the 306th BW on a bombing mission to the Avignon railroad marshaling yard and railroad bridge. Again, the Mustang pilots found the hunting good, with 19 Bf 109s rising to challenge the formation. Only three chose to attack the bombers, however, running in at the B-24s in a line-astern formation from their "eight o'clock" position. They split-essed away at the sight of the P-51s descending on them, and then made a series of evasive left turns. Three pilots – Luther "Quibbling" Smith, Robert "Dissipatin'" Smith and Larry Wilkins – closed in and methodically despatched their victims, following them all the way down to their final impacts with the ground.

2Lt Maceo Harris was also in the thick of things:

My flight leader and I went down on two bogies, and after they split-essed from me at about 18,000ft, I pulled up all alone in a tight chandelle to the left. I tried to join another ship, but lost him when I peeled off on two more bogies that were after some bombers. The bogies turned steeply to the left, and P-51s were in the vicinity, so I kept on with the bombers because they were hitting the target. Flak was intense over the target, and I kept an eye on the B-24s for enemy fighters that might come in when the bombers left the area.

Upon leaving the target, I joined another P-51 and tried to contact him by radio. My attempt was unsuccessful, so I peeled off alone on three bogies who were approaching a straggling bomber from the rear. They looked like P-51s, and I rocked my wings coming in, but they swung left over France away from the bomber.

I widely circled the B-24 because the top turret gunner was firing at me, but when he stopped firing I came in very close to survey the flak damage. The number two engine was feathered and the number one was smoking moderately.

The B-24's compass was shot out, and while Harris could receive the bomber on radio, it could not receive him. He used hand signals to indicate that the two airplanes would be over Corsica in 40 minutes, and put the B-24 on course. When Harris could not raise "Blacktop" (the control tower on Corsica), he buzzed the airstrip several times to clear the runway. The B-24 made a two-wheel recovery, and Harris landed as well. "The B-24 pilot was Lt Loerb from San Francisco," said Harris. "He is in the 459th BG and his ship is No 129585. He and the co-pilot appreciated my friendly aid, and kissed me after the manner of the French."

1Lt Walter Palmer's day was equally eventful. Taking off through cloud cover, he circled over Ramitelli but failed to spot the rest of his flight, so he decided to catch up with them on his own. Once over southern France, Palmer spotted an airplane heading in the opposite direction, rocking its wings. He rocked his wings in return, but instead of joining up from the side, the aircraft tried to "join up" from behind. Palmer kept his eyes on his new "wingman" and was not entirely surprised when he saw flashes from its guns. He threw his Mustang into a turn and identified the other airplane as a Bf 109. After a series of turns, the German flyer realized that Palmer was getting close to a firing position, so he split-essed for the deck. Palmer wisely set course for home, with a stop in Corsica for fuel.

On July 18, Lee Rayford led 66 Mustangs from all four squadrons to the briefed rendezvous point over southern Germany, but the bombers of the 5th BW, scheduled to strike the Luftwaffe base at Memmingen, in Austria, were nowhere to be found. Rayford decided to orbit in the Udine–Treviso area, which was already known to be a hotbed of Luftwaffe activity, and as the bombers approached, the Mustang pilots spotted a swarm of 30 to 35 Bf 109s to the right of the formation.

The fighters attacked in groups from "three o'clock high" and "five o'clock low," then split-essed away. Twenty-one of the Mustangs rushed to break up the attack, destroying 11 of the German fighters. Once this threat had been dealt with, the formation continued to Austria, but over the target, 30 to 40 enemy airplanes – mainly Bf 109s, Fw 190s and Me 410s – were sighted. Eventually, four Fw 190s swooped in to attack and two were shot down.

The tally for the day was impressive, with Clarence "Lucky" Lester bagging three, Jack Holsclaw two and Lee Archer, Charles Bailey, Walter Palmer, Roger Romine, Edward Toppins and Hugh Warner one apiece. Palmer's victim was a Bf 109, which he hit with several short bursts after it had made a pass at the bombers. "On the second or third burst I noticed his engine smoking heavily, so I broke it off because there were others to shoot down," he later wrote. Palmer closed in on a second Bf 109, but his guns jammed. He considered chopping off the enemy fighter's tail with his propeller, but the Bf 109 headed into a cloudbank shrouding the tops of the Alps, convincing Palmer to break off the pursuit.

Toppins destroyed his opponent by diving at him at a speed so high that when he pulled out, he warped the fuselage of his fighter – the Mustang had to be scrapped after the mission. Two more P-51s were lost in the fray, with Lt Gene Browne surviving to be taken prisoner and Lt Wellington G. Irving being killed. Oscar Hutton was also lost when his Mustang was hit by a drop tank jettisoned by another P-51.

On July 19, 48 aircraft escorted the 49th BW's B-24s during their attack on Munich-Schleissheim airfield. Although four Bf 109s were spotted, they were too distant to be intercepted by the Mustangs. The next day, the group was tasked with escorting the 47th, 55th and 304th BWs to Friedrichshafen, in Germany, followed by a fighter sweep northeast of the target. Once again, the Udine area provided good hunting, with a group of 20 enemy aircraft attacking the bombers from "six o'clock low." Several other groups, consisting of four aircraft each, held formation on either side of the bomber stream, apparently acting as decoys. The attacking fighters were set upon by the 332nd's Joseph Elsberry, Langdon Johnson, Armour McDaniel and Ed Toppins, who each destroyed an aircraft. While the Luftwaffe's interception proved fruitless, a ferocious flak barrage over the target destroyed three B-24s. The 332nd picked up two flak-damaged stragglers around Udine and escorted them to safety.

On July 21 the group sent 60 aircraft north to cover the withdrawal of the 5th BW from the Brux synthetic oil refinery, but weather prevented a rendezvous. The next day, the group provided escort for the 55th BW on yet another mission to Ploesti. Sixty P-51s shepherded the bombers, and while 16 to 20 German aircraft were spotted, they made no effort to attack so were ignored in return. Coming off the target, Jimmy Walker and his flight dropped down to escort a damaged B-24, and were rewarded with a barrage of German flak for their efforts. All five Mustangs received varying degrees of damage, and Walker had to bail out of his crippled P-51C over eastern Serbia. Once on the ground, he ran into anti-communist partisans in the area, and they united Walker with nine other American airmen. His group was eventually rescued by a nighttime pick-up by a US aircraft following 39 days in occupied territory. Walker rejoined the 332nd in September.

INCREASED MISSION RATE

The pace of the escorts picked up as July drew to a close. On the 24th, 35 P-51s covered the 47th BW's B-24s in an attack on Genoa Harbor, and the following day 46 Mustangs watched over the 55th BW during a raid on the Herman Göring Tank Works at Linz, in Austria. On the latter mission, the group's airplanes formed into three groups to cover the beginning, middle and end of the bomber formation. The Luftwaffe threw 40 Bf 109s at the 332nd's last two eight-ship groups, and this tactic resulted in the losses of Starling Penn and Alfred Carroll (both became PoWs). In return Capt Harold Sawyer downed an enemy fighter for his second confirmed kill, and damaged two more.

Due to this operational tempo, mechanical issues began to plague the group – on July 26, 61 Mustangs took off, but 21 returned to base. This high abort rate was due in part to the group's newness to the P-51, but some of it could be explained by the skill level of the groundcrews. While many of the mechanics serving with regular squadrons had had previous mechanical experience in civilian life, this was often not available to black enlisted men. Still, availability rates would gradually rise to equal those of other groups.

The 40 Mustangs that completed the mission to escort the 47th BW to Markendorf airfield in Austria on the 26th found enemy skies filled with German opposition. On the way to the target, the group sighted two groups of six Bf 109s, and another group of Fw 190s was seen near the target, but they remained out of range until the B-24s made their attack. At that point 18 Bf 109s attacked the 332nd, while ten more fighters remained above them as top cover, before finally splitting into two-airplane formations and diving on the bombers.

As usual, the German fighters tried to split-ess their way out of trouble, and as usual, the Mustangs made short work of the fleeing aircraft, with Ed Toppins scoring his fourth kill, William Green bagging one confirmed and one unconfirmed and Freddie Hutchins and Leonard Jackson scoring a single confirmed victory each. Weldon Groves shared a kill with a Mustang from another group, and Roger Romine and Luther Smith claimed unconfirmed victories. The group lost a P-51B to the German fighters during the mission, although its pilot, Lt Charles Jackson, succeeded in evading capture and returned to the group on August 28.

The good hunting continued the next day, when the escorts for a 47th BW raid on the Weiss armament works, near Budapest, were jumped by 25 Fw 190s and Bf 109s north of Lake Balaton. The latter attacked first, followed closely by the Fw 190s. One Mustang was sent down smoking in their initial pass, although the pilot was later safely returned to the squadron, and others were damaged, including Ed Gleed's P-51, which had two guns shot out.

Nevertheless, Gleed tenaciously stuck to the tail of a Bf 109 and began taking aim on it, while at the same time watching a second Bf 109 maneuvering to get onto his tail.

He eventually hit one of the ammunition magazines in his opponent's wing, blowing the latter off and sending the fighter hurtling earthward. At almost the same time, the pursuing Messerschmitt was also shot down. While Gleed and his flight climbed back up to escort the B-24s coming off the target, the bombers were attacked by a dozen Fw 190s, but these were in turn intercepted by the Mustangs and they broke off their attacks. As the German fighters tried to flee, the P-51 pilots gave chase, including Gleed in his two-gunned aircraft.

In the running battle which ensued, Gleed picked out an Fw 190 and followed it all the way down to the deck, before catching the airplane with a fatal burst. He had become separated from his wingman in the process and was now out of ammunition. Adding to his problems, Gleed was attacked by two more Fw 190s, which peppered his already damaged Mustang as he "hedge-hopped" between hills in an effort to shake off his assailants. The chase streaked across a riverbed and between church steeples in a Hungarian town, and when Gleed spotted a valley that led in the general direction of Ramitelli, he pointed the Mustang toward home, firewalled the engine and left the two Fw 190s in his wake. Gleed eventually landed back at his base, where his engine almost immediately quit from fuel starvation.

While Gleed was fighting for his life, the rest of the 332nd FG had been busy too. Alfred Gorham scored a double, and single kills were recorded by Claude Govan, Richard Hall, Leonard Jackson (his third) and Felix Kirkpatrick. This eight-kill haul had been accomplished without sacrificing the protection of the bombers, who once again lost no aircraft to enemy fighters.

Another mission to Ploesti on July 28 as escorts for the 55th BW saw 54 aircraft launch and 14 abort. The group spied seven enemy aircraft in the target area but they were beyond interception range. One Bf 109 was spotted stalking two straggling 332nd P-51s, but the pilot of the Messerschmitt ran for home when the Mustangs broke into it.

After a day off, 43 Mustangs provided escort for the 5th BW's raid on the Tököl armament works in Budapest on the 30th. Prior to the group reaching the rendezvous point, an ANR Reggiane Re.2001 was spotted flying a parallel course to a straggling Mustang flown by 2Lt Carl Johnson. As his squadronmates radioed a warning to Johnson, the Re.2001 made a sharp turn and tried to hit his Mustang with a 90-degree deflection shot. Johnson pulled his P-51 inside the Reggiane and knocked it down with a few well-aimed bursts. Later in the mission, a flight of 332nd aircraft spotted a single Bf 109 and gave chase. However, before they could open fire, a checkertailed Mustang (probably from the 325th FG) swooped in, forcing the red-tailed P-51s to take evasive action, and shot down the Bf 109.

On July 31, it was the 47th BW's turn to hit Ploesti, and 65 Mustangs from the 332nd provided escort. The P-51s arrived at the rendezvous point on time, but had to wait five minutes for the bombers – the mission's only significant problem. One Bf 109 was spotted, but it was too far away to be attacked.

Two days later, 71 group aircraft launched (with 16 aborts) to escort the 5th BW to the Le Pousin oil storage facility and the Portes Lès Valences railroad marshaling yard in southern France. The group heard a report that 50 Bf 109s had been detected gathering around Toulon, but when the formation reached the city, no enemy aircraft were seen. On the way home, Lt Earl Sherrard was badly burned when he crash-landed his damaged Mustang, and he was eventually transferred out of the unit for treatment back in the USA.

The next day, 64 Mustangs were despatched as cover for 5th BW B-17s sent to bomb the Ober Raderach chemical works in Germany. A quartet of Bf 109s was spotted at 28,000ft in the Udine area, but they made no attack on the bombers and failed to lure the escorting fighters away from their charges.

On August 6 the group was tasked with two missions. The first, launched at 0937hrs, saw 64 Mustangs escorting the 55th BW to Avignon in support of the impending landings. No enemy aircraft were sighted. At 1510hrs, Melvin Jackson led eight Mustangs that were tasked with escorting a B-25 that was returning to Italy after being forced to land in Yugoslavia.

Twenty-four hours later, it was back to Germany for the group – 69 Mustangs were launched, with 15 aborts, on an escort mission to the Blechammer oil refineries. The entirety of the German air resistance was a single Bf 109 that made one diving pass on the bomber formation, then streaked for the deck.

The routine of uneventful escorts was broken on August 8 during a mission that saw 53 Mustangs "ride herd" on the 5th BW as it bombed the Geyer aircraft and car works in Hungary. When in the vicinity of Banja Luka, in Yugoslavia, Lt Alfonso Simmons was last seen heading away from the rest of the group into clouds. After he bailed out of his flak-damaged P-51C, Simmons joined up with a band of partisans and eventually returned to the group. Two days later, 62 Mustangs escorted the 304th BW's B-24s to Ploesti to attack the Campina Stevea Romana oil refinery. No enemy aircraft were spotted during the mission. After almost ten days without directly confronting the Germans, the group was itching for more contact with the enemy. It would soon get more than its share.

ON THE DECK AND ABOVE THE CLOUDS

In support of the coming Allied invasion of southern France, codenamed Operation *Dragoon*, the 332nd FG was ordered to conduct a series of ground attack sorties in addition to its seemingly endless schedule of bomber escort missions. And the first such operation it carried out, on August 12, would prove costly.

The group was tasked with knocking out radar stations surrounding the harbor at Marseilles in advance of the invasion, and all four squadrons were assigned specific targets. These turned out to be well defended. The 99th FS attacked targets in Montpellier and Sète, destroying both stations, but during his strafing run, recent arrival 2Lt Dick Macon had his fighter shot out from beneath him and he was forced to bail out at low altitude just before his Mustang crashed into a house. With a compound fracture of his shoulder and four broken vertebrae in his neck, Macon was quickly captured.

The 302nd FS strafed radar installations at Narbonne and Leucate, scoring hits on the primary targets and on nearby installations. As they bore in on the stations, the four-ship flight of Alton Ballard, Virgil Richardson, John Daniels and Alexander Jefferson encountered heavy flak at 15,000ft. "I looked back to find Jefferson and noticed that Daniels, who was flying in front of me, was going up in smoke," said Richardson. Daniels' Mustang pancaked into the harbor. Richardson pulled up and had just started following Ballard when Jefferson was also hit. Forced to bail out of his flaming Mustang, the latter pilot was quickly captured by the Germans and ended up in captivity with Macon and Daniels.

The 100th FS went after three targets around Marseilles and Cape Couronne, and all were believed to have been destroyed. The 301st FS, meanwhile, attacked four targets in the Toulon area, including a radar station. The antenna installations were seen to topple over under the weight of the squadron's fire, but flak claimed Lt Joseph Gordon and Langdon Johnson, both of whom were killed.

The following day, after first completing a 61-airplane escort for the 304th BW attack on the railroad bridges at Avignon, the group was assigned yet another strafing mission. The 301st and 302nd FSs attacked the radar facilities around Cap Blanc, Camerat Capet and La Ciotat, while the 99th and 100th flew fighter sweeps of the Toulon area. Lt Luke Weathers and two of his fellow pilots from the 301st hit one radar installation and were rewarded by the sight of the antenna crumbling. The second flight overshot the target, so they strafed six small buildings nearby instead.

Meanwhile, the 302nd's first flight attacked a 6cm wavelength-type antenna from deck level and observed hits and sparks from the target, then continued to fire on a nearby heavy machine gun position. Two aircraft were lost in the strafing mission, Lt Clarence Allen bailing out of his damaged machine over Elba. He was soon rescued, as was Robert O'Neil, who crash-landed on the beach near Toulon and was rescued by the Free French.

The nearby fighter sweep, meanwhile, became a strung-out affair, with one of the 100th's flights becoming lost. While they were trying to regain their bearings, two Bf 109s and two Fw 190s bounced them from "five o'clock high." The Mustangs turned into their attackers, and in the process of extricating themselves from the ambush, Lt George Rhodes found himself in position to fire several short 15- to 20-degree deflection shots at an Fw 190. The Focke-Wulf's left wing disintegrated and the airplane cartwheeled into the ground.

On August 15 the group was back at high altitude with the heavy bombers, 64 Mustangs escorting the 55th BW to Point St Esprit, Douzare, Le Teil, Bourg and St Andeal, in southern France. Two enemy fighters were observed, but they were too far away to be intercepted. Lt Wilson Eagleson's fighter was hit in the engine by flak and started losing coolant, but he stayed with the Mustang until the Merlin froze up and then he bailed out. By then he was over Allied territory, and a squad of American troops saw him jump. By the time Eagleson had walked the half-mile to a nearby road, the soldiers were waiting for him in a jeep to provide him with a lift back to Ramitelli!

The next day, during a bomber escort mission for the 55th BW to the Ober Raderach chemical works in Germany, another pilot was forced to jump. 1Lt Herbert V. Clark of the 99th FS, who was one of the unit's flight leaders, was shot down by flak. He evaded capture and ended up commanding a band of partisans conducting raids against the Germans in northern Italy. Clark was reunited with the group eight months later on May 7, 1945, just as the war ended.

On August 17, 55 Mustangs escorted the 304th BW on a mission to Ploesti. Two aircraft, including the Mustang of Louis Purnell, were damaged by flak and landed on the island of Vis, off the coast of Yugoslavia, where an emergency strip had been established. Two days later, 50 P-51s escorted the 47th BW on yet another Ploesti mission. One Mustang was lost when Lt William Thomas crash-landed on Pianosa Island 20 minutes after taking off. Thomas was returned to the group by the air-sea rescue boat.

August 20 provided evidence of both the 332nd's growing reputation and of the declining aggressiveness of the enemy. A fleet of 59 Mustangs escorted the 5th BW on a raid on the oil refineries at Oswiecim, in Poland. The group was menaced by 18 Bf 109s and Fw 190s that lined up to attack the last P-51 flight, but when the four Mustangs turned into them the German fighters scattered and ran.

Following a day off, Capt Erwin Lawrence led 52 Mustangs aloft to shepherd the 55th BW to the Korneuburg oil refinery in Vienna on the 21st. The bombers were 18 minutes late to the rendezvous point, so Lawrence ordered the group to orbit until they arrived. During the escort, 20 Bf 109s were spotted near Lake Balaton, and three more at a higher altitude made a move toward the bomber formations, but they were chased off by a flight of Mustangs.

The closest the group came to actual combat was when a solitary Spitfire stumbled across the combined formation in the target area and made the mistake of pointing its nose at the bombers. A flight of Mustangs made one firing pass before the unharmed Spitfire waggled its wings and sped away. That same day, 18 Mustangs escorted six C-47s to Yugoslavia on an afternoon mission to drop supplies to the local Partisans. The mission was uneventful and all the aircraft returned safely.

On August 22, a 60-Mustang formation guarded the 55th BW during an attack on Markersdorf airfield, in Germany. Over the target, the bombers were set upon by 14 Bf 109s. Seven were seen to enter a Lufbery Circle, then dive through the bomber formation with no apparent success. Lts William Hill and Luke Weathers tagged onto the tail of one of the Bf 109s and, from 250 yards, fired from 24,000ft all the way down to the deck. Whether or not their claim would be verified had to wait, but after their gun camera film was developed, each was credited with half of a confirmed kill on August 28.

SCREENING AIRFIELD ATTACKS

Screening heavy bomber attacks on Axis airfields seemed to be the best way to scare up fighter opposition in August. On the 24th, 52 P-51s escorted the 5th BW to Pardubice airfield, in Czechoslovakia, and although the escort to the target proved uneventful, on the way home a Bf 109 attacked Lt John Briggs' flight from "six o'clock." The Mustangs turned sharply into their attacker, and Briggs positioned himself behind and below the now-fleeing and climbing fighter, firing bursts from 250 yards at a height of 24,000ft. Seeing no results, he pressed as close as 25 yards and opened fire again at 35,000ft. Pieces of the Bf 109 flew back toward Briggs, followed shortly by the pilot, who bailed out.

Meanwhile, Lt Charles McGee had spotted an Fw 190 flying 180 degrees to his course, so he peeled off to attack. The German pilot saw the red-tailed Mustang and abruptly headed for the deck, using a series of evasive maneuvers to try to shake off McGee before finally resorting to a steep dive toward the airfield at Pardubice. "I recall as we flashed over the field proper in a right turn, there was a hangar and several aircraft fires brightly blazing," McGee said. He maneuvered in behind the Fw 190 and fired a burst that he suspected hit the aircraft's control cables, because the German fighter made two erratic turns and slammed into the ground. McGee's wingman, Roger Romine, saw the airplane crash and confirmed the victory.

Although he had got his kill, McGee was now in trouble, as the airfield's antiaircraft guns were all trained on him. "I made a low-altitude dash out of the area to avoid ground fire," he recalled, and for good measure he "got a good burst off on a locomotive at a railroad stop," before climbing to rejoin the group.

About five minutes later, at 1235hrs, Lt William Thomas spied another Fw 190 at 24,000ft at about the same time that the German pilot spotted him. Instead of turning into Thomas, he tried to dive to safety, but the Mustang pilot caught up to him at an altitude of about 800ft and fired six times at him from 75–100 yards. Thomas' final burst was a 30-degree deflection shot, which caused the Fw 190 to hit the ground and crumple up into a tangle of smoking wreckage.

On August 25, 60 Mustangs returned to Czechoslovakian skies when they escorted the B-17s of the 5th BW sent to attack Brno airfield. The mission went exactly as briefed, but this time no enemy aircraft rose to challenge the bombers, and all the 332nd's P-51s were back at Ramitelli by 1315hrs. The next day, 56 P-51s accompanied the 304th BW to attack barracks near the Bulgarian airfield at Banasea. The bombers were ten minutes late arriving at the rendezvous point, and when they did eventually attempt to hit their target, the Mustang pilots saw that their ordnance had fallen harmlessly in some nearby woods. Worse still, 2Lt Henry Wise of the 99th FS was forced to bail out when his oil pressure dropped and his Merlin started to smoke heavily.

Taken prisoner in Bulgaria, Wise's fortunes changed dramatically when his captors severed their ties with Germany. While the latter marched a number of PoWs out of Bulgaria, Wise and hundreds of others were left behind. They were eventually evacuated through Turkey and Egypt, before finally making it back to Italy, where Wise returned to the group in September. He was immediately promoted to first lieutenant and issued with orders sending him home.

On August 27, the 57 Mustangs sent to escort the 55th and 304th BWs to Blechammer, in Germany, had completed their rendezvous and escort when Melvin Jackson spotted a single German aircraft taking off from an airfield near Prostejou, in Czechoslovakia. The group dropped down and attacked this site, along with an airfield at nearby Kostoleo. A lack of flak allowed the 332nd to strafe a large number of aircraft, and by the time the pilots had exhausted their ammunition, 13 Ju 52/3ms, four Ju 87s and three He 111s had been destroyed and four Ju 87s, four He 111s, nine Ju 52/3ms and an Me 323 Gigant had been damaged.

The chief contributors to German misery this day were Wendell Pruitt, who destroyed three Stukas and two He 111s, Spann Watson, who accounted for four Ju 52/3ms and an He 111, and Luther Smith, who destroyed three Ju 52/3ms and an He 111. For good measure, the group also strafed the airfield's barracks and an unlucky locomotive that happened to be near the airfield. The 332nd suffered no casualties.

Four dozen P-51s covered the 47th BW's raid on the Miskolc main railroad marshaling yard, in Yugoslavia, on August 28. All returned safely to base. The following day, 55 Mustangs escorted the 5th BW's attack on the Bohumin and Privoser oil refineries and the Moravska main railroad marshaling yard. Lt Emile Clifton developed engine trouble during the mission and bailed out of his Mustang over Yugoslavia, although he returned to the group a month later.

CARNAGE AT GROSSWARDEIN

If the Luftwaffe refused to come up, the 332nd was happy to come down, and on August 30 the group found about 150 aircraft at Grosswardein airfield, in Rumania, camouflaged rather poorly under stacks of hay. Despite moderate flak, the 302nd FS made seven passes, the 100th five passes and the 99th three passes. After several attack runs, the biggest hazard facing the Mustang pilots was the rising smoke from burning aircraft – the entire field was blanketed with an oily haze caused by flaming hay and gasoline. The kills were distributed among 46 different pilots, with Roger Romine of the 302nd destroying seven aircraft and Alfonso Davis and Freddie Hutchins four apiece.

The collection of destroyed aircraft reads like an inventory of German wartime aviation – 30 Ju 88s, 12 He 111s, seven Fw 189s, six Ju 87s, six Do 217s, five Ju 52/3ms, four Fw 190s, three Bf 109s, three Go 242 gliders, two Me 323s, two Me 210s, two Bf 110s and a single Ar 96. In all, the group destroyed 83 aircraft and damaged 31 more, making this the most destructive day in the 332nd's history. Adding to the carnage, a single Mustang destroyed four tank cars on a nearby siding. The only casualty was Lt Charles Williams, who was shot down in the target area and taken prisoner.

Escort missions resumed on August 31, when the 100th and 301st sent 32 Mustangs to shepherd second-wave B-17s in an attack on Popesti airfield. A similar mission was given to the 99th and 302nd FSs, which sent 31 fighters to cover the third wave of bombers. No enemy air activity was observed. The following day, the group again provided escort for B-17s attacking this airfield, but weather and poor navigation prevented the 301st and 302nd from completing the mission.

On September 2, 61 Mustangs conducted an armed reconnaissance of the road between Stalac, Cuprija and Osipaonica, in Serbia. During the mission, the group strafed goods wagons at the rail station at Krusevac and damaged a nearby truck – two aircraft attacked five wagons on a siding and scored hits on all of them. Later, a single unnamed pilot, who had taken off late and was hurrying to join the group, spotted a 30-truck convoy and raked it from end to end, setting three vehicles on fire and damaging ten more.

In an effort to prevent the Germans from shifting troops into northern Europe to repel the Allied advance, the Fifteenth Air Force turned its attention to the destruction of railroad bridges in northern Italy and Hungary. Some 59 P-51s were tasked with covering the 304th BW's attack on the Hungarian bridges at Szolnok and Szeged on September 3, while Capt Erwin Lawrence led an escort of 45 P-51s for the 304th BW's bridge-busting mission to Tagliamento Casarsa and Latisana, in Italy, the following day. A similar mission on September 5 was flown by the 5th BW, with Andrew "Jug"Turner leading the 54 Mustangs sent aloft. All three missions saw no German air opposition.

For a change of pace, the 5th BW attacked the main railroad marshaling yard at Oradea, in Rumania, on September 6. The 332nd sent 63 Mustangs as escort, and again there was no opposition. Two days later, Capt William Mattison led 42 aircraft to the Luftwaffe airfield at Ilandza, in Yugoslavia. About 20 airplanes were spotted, and 23 Mustangs dropped down to the deck to strafe them, covered by 14 others. The attack destroyed 18 aircraft, including five Ju 52/3ms, four Ju 88s, three Do 217s, three Fw 200s and a single Fw 190, Bf 109 and He 111. The Mustang flown by Lt James A. Calhoun was hit by flak, and while his fellow pilots thought that he had deliberately crash-landed his fighter in the target area, Calhoun was killed. The group then continued on to the airfield at Alibunar, where 15 P-51s attacked parked aircraft while 26 fighters flew top cover in expectation that the now-alerted Luftwaffe would respond. Instead, the group eliminated 15 Fw 190s, two Bf 109s and an SM.84 transport in the face of moderate flak. For good measure, the 332nd also destroyed a locomotive on its way home.

On September 10, the 332nd assembled at Ramitelli for a particularly meaningful ceremony. Gen Benjamin O. Davis Snr was on hand to award the DFC to his son, Col Benjamin O. Davis Jr, as well as Capt Joseph Elsberry and 1Lts Jack Holsclaw and Clarence "Lucky" Lester. After 48 hours off, the group sent 71 Mustangs out at 1039hrs as escorts for the 5th BW – four spares turned for home at 1220hrs.

On their way back to Ramitelli, two of the latter pilots sighted a twin-engined aircraft in the landing pattern at Udine South airfield and they dropped down to check it out. After the tower fired two red flares, the airplane disappeared into the haze. The two red-tailed Mustangs were already at low altitude, and they spotted ten aircraft hiding in sandbag revetments under camouflage netting near the base perimeter. The Mustangs circled to the right and made a solitary pass, damaging one single-engined and three twin-engined airplanes, before a small-caliber antiaircraft shell hit one of the fighters in the rudder, forcing them to abandon the attack.

On September 13, 57 P-51s escorted the 304th BW to the Blechammer North oil refinery. Although three German fighters were spotted in the distance, they did not attack the bombers. During the mission, 2Lt Wilbur F. Long went missing, his fellow pilots assuming that he had crash-landed his P-51C. Long was quickly captured by the Germans and spent the rest of the war in Stalag Luft VIIA.

Budapest was the target on September 17 and 18, 63 Mustangs escorting the 5th BW strike on the Rakos railroad marshaling yards during the first raid. While the bombers were on their run, a single twin-engined aircraft was spotted speeding over the city. The bogie was identified as an RAF Mosquito, which flew through the target area unmolested. The next day, the 304th BW attacked Budapest's Shell oil refinery and railroad bridges whilst under the protection of 51 332nd Mustangs. Once again a single Mosquito was observed flying over the target area during the B-17s' bomb run.

On September 20, 65 Mustangs escorted B-24s from the 304th BW sent to pound Malacky airfield, in Czechoslovakia. There was no aerial opposition. The next day, 62 Mustangs were sent out as an escort for the 5th BW's attack on the Debreczen railroad marshaling yards in Hungary, but weather delayed the fighters by 18 minutes and the bombers were ahead of schedule by ten minutes, ruining any chance of a rendezvous. The last two bomb groups were dropping their bombs just as the 332nd arrived over the target area. However, the Luftwaffe was unable to take advantage of the situation – again, no German aircraft were seen anywhere near the "heavies."

Two days later, another mission was completed in which the USAAF went unmolested by enemy aircraft, although while escorting B-17s away from a target in the Munich area, Chris Newman's Mustang *Goodwiggle* was hit by flak. He had nursed the crippled fighter as far as the Adriatic when his engine burst into flames and he was forced to bail out. Newman was quickly rescued by the efficient air-sea rescue service and returned to the group. 2Lt Leonard Willette was not so lucky, for about ten miles north of Lake Chiem, in Germany, he radioed that he was losing oil pressure and would be forced to bail out. Willette was declared killed in action in January 1945.

On September 23, 50 Mustangs accompanied the 5th BW's mission to destroy a synthetic oil plant in Germany. There was no air opposition. The following day saw another "milk run," with 37 P-51s accompanying the 304th BW to Athens airfield. Although the local flak batteries were assisted by four warships offshore, all aircraft returned to base. The missions were now becoming almost routine, with no enemy aircraft sighted for almost two weeks, and the intensity of combat having steadily slackened. This situation would be swiftly reversed in the coming month.

THE TOUGHEST MONTH

On the morning of October 4, 1944, a flight of four Mustangs escorted three C-47s to Sofia, orbited while they landed and shepherded them back to safety. It was an uneventful start to what would duly become a bloody day, and the start of the 332nd FG's bloodiest month in combat.

At 1058hrs, 37 Mustangs took off under the command of Erwin Lawrence, CO of the 99th FS, to strafe the Greek airfields at Tatoi, Kalamaki and Eleusis. At the assigned point, the 99th, 100th and 301st split off to attack the three target airfields. The pilots of the 99th strafed Tatoi from deck level, spotting 25 to 30 well-dispersed enemy airplanes as they ran in. Closing on the target, Lawrence, who was leading his final mission before rotating home, suddenly rolled over at low altitude in his fighter and crashed in flames.

Squadronmates believed that he had struck a cable strung across the airfield as a crude form of air defense. 2Lt Kenneth I. Williams also crashed in the target area, but he survived and was taken prisoner. "Four fires were seen on the airfield during the initial pass, but two of the fires are believed to have been from our own airplanes lost in the target area," Ray Ware wrote in his mission report. Almost all the German aircraft on the airfield were damaged, with Herman Lawson claiming a Ju 52/3m destroyed – small reward for the loss of a popular commander.

The 100th FS attacked Kalamaki airfield at much the same time, destroying three airplanes and damaging eight more. Meanwhile, the 301st strafed the base at Eleusis, destroying four Ju 52/3ms and an SM.79. While the other three squadrons were strafing in Greece, the 302nd FS was assigned the job of escorting 12 C-47s to Bucharest – 14 Mustangs completed this uneventful mission. The Greek airfields at Tatoi, Kalamaki and Eleusis, plus the strip at Megara, were once again the target on October 6, and this time the group was led by Col Davis. Soon after departing Ramitelli, Lt Elbert Hudson's sputtering Mustang belly-landed on the forward airfield at Biferno. It was a bad omen.

The 99th struck Tatoi, destroying two Ju 52/3ms, an Fw 200 and an He 111. The 100th again attacked Kalamaki, where George Rhodes destroyed an He 111. Two other German aircraft were damaged on the airfield, but during the attack 1Lt Carroll S. Woods' P-51 was hit by flak and, with its tail on fire, crashed on the air base. The pilot would spend the rest of the war in Stalag Luft VIIA.

At Eleusis, the 301st arrived to find that the Germans had evacuated all their aircraft except for one derelict Ju 52/3m. Even so, the squadron shot up the base and set a fuel dump on fire. In the process, however, 2Lt Andrew D. Marshall's fighter was hit by flak and he was eventually forced to bail out – Marshall would return to the group with slight injuries on October 18. 2Lt Joe A. Lewis, a veteran of 51 missions, was not so lucky. His aircraft was last seen trailing smoke on its way out of the target area, and after his Mustang went down, he joined Carroll Woods in captivity.

The 302nd found Megara similarly empty, but worked it over just the same. 1Lt Freddie Hutchins opened fire on what turned out to be an ammunition dump, and as the target exploded violently, his Mustang, *Little Freddie*, was raked with flak that blew off its right wingtip and shredded its tail. Hutchins could hear small-arms fire rattling against the airplane and he pressed himself down against the armor plate, only to have a burst come through the bottom of the cockpit and pepper his legs with fragments.

Now in agony, Hutchins nursed the Mustang to a spot three miles west of Megara and crash-landed whilst still traveling at 250mph. Knocked unconscious, he eventually awoke to find that he was still strapped into the cockpit of his fighter, but that its engine was now several hundred feet away and the wings and tail had been ripped off. His goggles were smashed against his forehead and his legs hurt terribly. Greek civilians rushed to the site and lifted Hutchins out of the cockpit, placing him on the back of a donkey and leading it to the home of a doctor. The doctor rubbed him with olive oil and bandaged his wounds, before putting him to bed. Hutchins awoke after being bitten by dozens of fleas, and the itchy pilot decided to make it back to friendly forces under his own steam. Managing to avoid capture, he returned to the group on October 23.

Despite losing five Mustangs the day before, 53 P-51s under the command of "Spanky" Roberts escorted the 5th BW to the Lobau oil refinery in Vienna on October 7. During the outbound leg, 1Lt Robert Wiggins survived the crash-landing of his Mustang at Vis, but Flt Off Carl J. Woods and 2Lt Roosevelt Stiger went missing and were never heard from again. Fuel became a major issue during this mission, with the 23 pilots that were forced to land at forward fields having to be collected by a fleet of trucks.

After a three-day break to rest and reequip, the group was sent out on an interdiction mission from Budapest to Bratislava, in Czechoslovakia, in an effort to cut off German troops retreating from the Eastern Front. Weather prevented all but 20 of the 72 Mustangs that set out from finding targets, but those who managed to penetrate holes in the cloud at Esztergom, on the Danube River in Hungary, were rewarded with the destruction of 17 enemy aircraft at three airfields. The Mustang pilots also wrecked two locomotives, an oil wagon and a fuel dump, whilst six barges, a locomotive and a goods wagon were damaged. Lt George Gray of the 99th destroyed two Me 210s, an He 111 and a biplane trainer on the ground during this mission, while Lt Richard S. Harder also claimed a pair of Me 210s and an He 111. The only thing that marred the day was George Rhodes' forced landing at Ramitelli, which wrote off the Mustang but left the pilot safe.

On October 11, 63 Mustangs set out again for the area between Budapest and Bratislava. While on patrol over enemy territory, the 99th FS sent 14 aircraft down to investigate a report of a biplane overhead Kaposvar airfield. Although 35 to 40 aircraft were seen parked in or near revetments, no biplane could be found. Nevertheless, the 99th attacked the airfield just the same. The first pass was made from east to west, with each of the nine subsequent passes being flown in a counterclockwise manner. The attack left 18 airplanes burning, including four Bf 109s, five He 111s, five Ju 88s, an Fw 200, an Fw 190, an unidentified trainer and an unidentified twin-engined aircraft. Five other airplanes were damaged. Lt George Gray bagged five on the ground, while Lt Hannibal Cox ignited three others.

The 302nd also received a radio report that an enemy aircraft – this time an He 111 – had been spotted near another landing field. As Capt Wendell Pruitt's flight was looking for the Heinkel, Lee Archer spotted a group of enemy aircraft climbing at "two o'clock low." Pruitt gave the order to attack, but before his flight could peel off, it was jumped by nine Bf 109s that were covering two He 111s.

"Two Messerschmitts were flying abreast," Archer reported. "I tore the wing off one with a long burst. The other one slid in behind Pruitt. I pulled up, zeroed in, hit the gun button and watched him explode." Pruitt, who had already bagged an He 111 and a Bf 109 by this point, was giving chase to another Messerschmitt fighter when his guns jammed. Archer took up the chase, following the fleeing fighter to the deck. "He appeared to be trying to land," the Mustang pilot recalled. "I opened up at ground level, hit him with a long volley and he crashed." Flak and small-arms fire in turn drove Archer back to higher altitude. He would conclude his three-kill day with a landing on the island of Vis, during which his aircraft ran off the perforated steel planking runway and damaged the propeller.

In just 15 minutes, all three He 111s and six of the nine Bf 109s had been destroyed, with Milton Brooks, William Green, Roger Romine and Luther Smith downing the four enemy aircraft not accounted for by "the Gruesome Twosome." The fight had raged from 7,000ft all the way down to the deck, and pilots reported that the Germans used very poor and, in some instances, no evasive tactics. After countering the enemy fighters, the 302nd turned its attention to the nearby airfield, destroying three He 111s, two Bf 109s, a Ju 88, a Bf 110 and an unidentified biplane trainer. Four more aircraft were damaged.

The 100th and 301st FSs continued on toward their assigned targets, only to be disrupted by several yellow-tailed Mustangs (probably from the 52nd FG), which turned into them as if to attack. The 100th was sent to counter the P-51s, and fortunately the two sides avoided any acts of fratricide. Once the "threat" from their fellow Mustangs had gone, the 100th strafed a railroad siding and a factory, damaging three locomotives, three passenger cars, 30 goods wagons, 25 trucks on the nearby highway and the factory itself, which was surrounded by three parking lots filled with an additional 45 trucks.

While the 100th strafed the factory and railroad line, the 301st set its sights on 50 oil barges in the Danube. Three were sent to the bottom and a further 11 were shot up during the attack by 18 Mustangs. 1Lt Walter L. McCreary was hit by flak whilst making his strafing run, and he was forced to bail out of his stricken P-51 over Kaspovar, in Hungary. McCreary would spend the remainder of the war at Stalags Luft III and IVA.

On October 13, after the primary task of escorting the 304th BW to the Blechammer oil refineries had been completed, the group's 60 Mustangs dropped down to replicate the previous day's strafing successes. A four-ship flight from the 99th attacked a train headed east from Bratislava, damaging two locomotives and a flat car loaded with trucks. Three of the 100th's Mustangs also shot up six previously damaged goods wagons, while four other P-51s from the 302nd strafed a train, destroying a locomotive and damaging goods wagons and coal cars. They also strafed a small house alongside the track, and this exploded so violently that it was undoubtedly being used to store ammunition.

Two flights from the 302nd swooped in on Tapolcza airfield, destroying seven airplanes, including three He 111s and two Ju 52/3ms – six more aircraft were damaged. The mission proved costly, however, as two Mustangs were shot down by intense flak. 1Lt Walter Westmoreland was killed and 1Lt William Green parachuted into a field near Sisak, and returned to the group after spending a week with Tito's Partisans in Yugoslavia.

A short while later 1Lt Luther Smith's P-51B caught fire over Hungary after suffering damage from an exploding ammunition dump. He rolled the fighter over in order to bail out, but the airplane snapped into an inverted flat spin, snagging Smith half-in and half-out of the cockpit. He tried to clamber back in to free himself, but jammed his right foot between the rudder pedals and the floor. At that point, the slipstream tore off Smith's oxygen mask and he passed out, but somehow he was thrown free of the Mustang and his parachute deployed. When he came to, he was suspended in a tree, his right foot and hip badly broken. Smith spent time in a series of German hospitals, suffering from bone infections and dysentery, before being sent to Stalag Luft VIIA. When he was finally liberated, he weighed just 70lbs.

On the morning of October 14, 52 aircraft left Ramitelli to escort the 49th BW's B-24s to the Odertal oil refineries in Germany. The Luftwaffe offered no opposition, but losses continued just the same, as Lt Rual Bell of the 100th FS suffered mechanical problems an hour from the target and bailed out of his P-51C. He returned to the squadron in December.

After Bell's bail-out, the group received a much-needed respite from the losses. On October 16, Col Davis led an escort for 5th BW bombers sent to attack the Brux oil refineries, and although no aerial opposition was met, one Mustang was holed by flak.

The next day, three P-51s accompanied a single B-17 to Bucharest at 0720hrs, followed by a 51-airplane mission escorting the 5th BW to the Blechammer South oil refinery. The only other aircraft spotted during the mission was a lone Mosquito south of Brno.

On the 20th, a second 51-airplane mission to escort the 5th BW to the Brux oil refineries again met with no resistance. The only aircraft spotted this time were B-26s near Venice. Later in the day, two Mustangs escorted an OA-10 Catalina to rescue seven survivors from a ditched B-17, shepherding the amphibian as it flew back to Rimini. The 304th BW was treated to a 55-airplane escort to Gyor in Hungary on October 21, while Capt Vernon Haywood led four P-51s to search for downed fliers in the Gulf of Venezia that afternoon. They spotted two men in Mae Wests, and their report brought an RAF Walrus to the scene 75 minutes later, and the downed aviators were soon rescued.

MORE LOSSES

Losses resumed on October 23 during an escort mission for the Regensburg-bound 304th BW. A total of 64 Mustangs rendezvoused with the bombers despite bad weather, but during the run in to the target 2Lt Fred Brewer of the 100th FS was seen spinning into the clouds, having possibly fallen victim to flak. Brewer was killed in the subsequent crash. In addition, Robert C. Chandler and Shelby Westbrook's P-51Cs were lost when the former suffered engine trouble and his escort, Westbrook, had his instruments malfunction. At low altitude and with a descending ceiling, the pair crash-landed in Yugoslavia, but evaded capture and returned to the group after 31 days on the ground.

On the 29th, Capt Alfonso Davis, who had assumed command of the 99th FS upon Lawrence's death, was himself killed during a three-ship mission escorting an F-5 Lightning in the Munich area. He had possibly fallen victim to oxygen deprivation. William Campbell, who at 25 was the oldest member of the squadron, became the new CO.

The 332nd had lost 15 pilots in October, which was a rate of attrition that Col Davis admitted was "hard to take." Additionally, "the Army Air Force screwed up the pilot training production so very much that by the winter of 1944-45, there weren't any replacements, and our pilots were doing 70 missions while other fighter groups' pilots were going home after 50 missions. You can imagine the effect this had on morale." Thanks to the still-segregated nature of training, these manpower shortages would continue until war's end.

TIGHTENING THE NOOSE

After a trio of missions on November 1, escorting the 304th BW to Vienna and covering two supply drops to partisans in Yugoslavia, the group prepared for a change of command. On November 3, Col Davis returned to the USA and Maj "Spanky" Roberts once again assumed command. Weather slowed the pace of operations slightly, but on November 4, 61 Mustangs, led by Capt Andrew Turner, covered the 5th BW's attack on the Regensburg/Winterhafen oil storage facility.

Mysteriously, 20 minutes after taking off from Ramitelli, a Mustang with the same group markings as the 332nd FG, but without side numbers, joined the formation for 45 minutes before turning northeast at Trieste and disappearing. Elsewhere, Louis Purnell and Milton Brooks each led fighter escorts for lone reconnaissance F-5 Lightnings during the afternoon. The next day, 48 Mustangs again "rode herd" on the 5th BW, this time to the Floridsdorf oil refinery in Austria. Lee Rayford led the uneventful mission, which was followed in the afternoon by two more F-5 escorts.

Missions in support of the 5th BW's B-17s continued on November 6, when 63 P-51s escorted them to the Moosbierbaum oil refinery in Vienna. During the mission, the P-51C flown by Capt William J. Faulkner of the 301st was seen falling in a tight spin near Reichenfels, in Austria. He was classified as killed in action.

Capt William Campbell commanded the 63 Mustangs that escorted the 55th BW to Trento and Bolzano, in Italy, on November 7, and four of the P-51s suffered slight flak damage during the course of the mission. The group was then grounded by weather for 72 hours, but on the 11th, 52 Mustangs escorted 5th BW "heavies" that struck the Brux oil refineries. Flak over Salzburg was heavy, and although 2Lt Elton H. Nightengale's P-51B was last seen over friendly territory in no apparent trouble, he never returned from the mission. Turner W. Payne's airplane also ran into trouble, and he was forced to crash-land at Lesina, destroying the Mustang but emerging from the incident unhurt.

Weather prevented any further missions being flown until November 16, when the group escorted the 304th BW to the Munich West railroad marshaling yard. During take-off, a farmer absentmindedly drove a herd of sheep across the end of the runway at Ramitelli, and the animals were hit by Roger Romine's P-51D. The machine (one of the first D-models to be issued to the group) was in turn rammed by William Hill's P-51C, causing an immense explosion. Hill, although badly burned, was rescued by Woody Crockett, who was not scheduled to fly but was watching the take-off. Sadly, Romine died in the tangled wreckage of his flaming aircraft.

The mission pressed on, meeting up with the B-24s at Masseria. South of Latisano, a pair of Bf 109Gs (almost certainly ANR aircraft flown by Capitano Ugo Drago and Tenente Renato Mingozi) positioned themselves up-sun and at "six o'clock" to a formation of six Mustangs and made a diving attack. They succeeded in damaging George Haley's airplane before P-51s from the 52nd FG chased them off. This was not the only enemy activity the group would see on the 16th, for after the bombers had hit the target, Melvin Jackson, Louis Purnell and Luke Weathers spotted a crippled B-24 in the Udine area. Whilst attempting to protect the bomber, the three pilots were jumped by eight Bf 109s, which attacked in a string but then broke into a Lufbery for mutual defense.

Weathers charged into the formation and closed to within 100 yards of the last two, firing short bursts with zero to 20 degrees of deflection. One of the Bf 109s began smoking and Weathers followed it from 24,000ft down to 1,000ft, where he saw it hit the ground. As tracers suddenly arced past his canopy, he realized that another Bf 109 had followed him down. "It looked like they had me, so I decided to follow the falling airplane," Weathers said. "I made a dive, came out of it and looked back. One airplane was still on my tail. I was headed back toward Germany, but I didn't want to go that way. I chopped my throttle and dropped my flaps to cut my speed quickly. The fellow overshot me, and this left me on his tail. He was in range, so I opened fire." Several bursts resulted in the Bf 109 slamming into the side of a mountain.

The next day, Ed Gleed led 44 P-51s as escorts for the 5th BW on an attack on the Brux refineries, and while the 332nd FG reached the escort area 40 minutes late, the bombers were themselves a further ten minutes behind them because they too had been delayed by the same headwind that had slowed down the fighters.

On November 18, Maj Roberts headed 44 Mustangs escorting a bombing strike on airfields near Verona and Vicenza. Francis Peoples launched late and he was last seen hurrying to catch the group. He never rendezvoused with the 332nd and never returned to base. Lt Alva Temple's landing gear malfunctioned and he had to belly his Mustang in at Ramitelli after the mission.

STRAFERS

The next day, the group was ordered to strafe railroad, road and river traffic around Gyor, in Hungary, and Vienna and Esztergom, in Austria. While the 302nd provided top cover, the 99th worked over a stretch between Gyor and Veszprem, destroying 15 horse-drawn vehicles and 20 goods wagons, and damaging a further 100 horse-drawn vehicles, two locomotives, 40 goods wagons and ten trucks.

The 100th also strafed rail and road traffic, destroying one tank wagon and damaging 30 goods wagons. It then turned its attention to river traffic between Esztergom and Gyor, damaging six barges and a tugboat. During one pass, Lt Roger B. Gaither's Mustang was hit by flak, and he spent the rest of the war as a PoW.

The 301st had been providing top cover for the 100th throughout their strafing attacks, and when the latter squadron had used up its ammunition, the former dropped down and resumed wreaking havoc on the river traffic. Its pilots shot up two 88mm guns on a German lighter and damaged an additional six barges. On the way home, a burst of flak disrupted Quitman C. Walker's flight from the 100th FS, damaging his aircraft enough to force him to bail out near Lake Balaton. He was never seen again.

On November 20, Capt Rayford led 50 Mustangs covering the 5th and 55th BWs' attack on the Blechammer South oil refinery. At about the time of the rendezvous with the bombers, 1Lt Maceo Harris went missing in his P-51C and was never seen again. Weather limited the group's activities for the rest of the month to an escort of two B-25s to Yugoslavia on November 22 and a photo-reconnaissance escort to Grodenwoh and Nürnberg four days later.

December 2 saw 51 aircraft under "Red" Jackson's control escort B-24s of the 49th and 55th BWs to Blechammer's oil refineries. Just before leaving the bombers, Lt Cornelius P. Gould's coolant system gave out, belching white glycol vapor. Gould parachuted into the hands of the Germans and spent the remainder of the war in Stalag Luft I. The next day, 64 Mustangs shepherded the 49th BW through the Udine area. On this day, the only German aircraft spotted were six aircraft on the bombed field at Maniago. There were losses, nevertheless. During a routine transition flight onto the Mustang, 302nd FS newcomers 2Lt Earl B. Highbaugh and Flt Off James C. Ramsey were killed in a mid-air collision near Ramitelli.

Weather prevented operations until December 9, when the group mounted a 57-airplane escort of the 5th BW on a raid on Brux. As the B-17s and Mustangs approached the target, a single aircraft made a fast pass at the fighters, then split-essed into a cloudbank, before climbing steeply back through the formation. The group had just seen its first Me 262 jet fighter. Minutes later, over Mühldorf, a second Me 262 made a head-on pass at a flight of Mustangs, and two groups of Me 262s were then spotted east of the formation. On the way home, Lt Robert Martin's Mustang suffered engine trouble, which forced him to make a wheels-down landing at the gunnery range at Cutelo, north of Termoli. The P-51 nosed over on the rough ground and damaged the propeller.

The mission to Moosbierbaum on December 11 saw 51 Mustangs under the command of Capt Walter Downs covering the 47th BW. The rendezvous was made cleanly, and the mission's only notable incident was the sight of a B-24 exploding suddenly near Vienna. That same day Capt Claude Govan led a five-ship escort for an F-5 mission to Prague, which went without a hitch. This run of uneventful missions continued four days later when the 47th BW's strike on Innsbruck was covered by 48 Mustangs.

On December 16, 49 Mustangs led by Maj Roberts shepherded the 5th BW's B-17s on a mission to Brux. Two of the group's aircraft were despatched to escort a crippled B-24 that stumbled along the mission's path. Other than having to divert to a secondary target at Karlovac, the mission was a "milk run." That afternoon, Capt Mattison led a five-ship escort for a B-25 headed for Mrkopij, in Yugoslavia. The following day, 40 P-51s escorted the 304th BW to Olomouc, where the group spotted about 40 airplanes on an airfield that had been immobilized due to a lack of fuel – caused by the Fifteenth Air Force's continual punishment of the German oil and lubricants infrastructure.

Another mission to Blechammer on December 18 saw 45 Mustangs arrive at the rendezvous point, which was bereft of B-24s from the 49th BW. After orbiting for 15 minutes, Capt Lee Rayford sent 32 P-51s to the target area, while the remaining 13 circled in the rendezvous area. Five minutes later, one bomb group of B-24s arrived, and they were escorted to the target. That same day, Capt William Campbell led six Mustangs on an F-5 escort to Innsbruck, where they found no flak and were not enticed lower by the sight of three locomotives running in broad daylight.

Blechammer South oil refinery was targeted 24 hours later by B-24s from the 55th BW, the bombers arriving 17 minutes late. This in turn forced the group's 57 Mustangs to give up the escort just after the wing reached the target area. Elsewhere, 1Lt Alva Temple led five Mustangs that morning to cover an F-5 mission to Dresden which proved uneventful. The next day, another mission had to be cut short when the 5th BW was 15 minutes late arriving at the rendezvous. The briefed target was Brux, but one group broke north for the secondary target of Salzburg, while the rest of the "heavies" headed for Regensburg. Two Mustangs were forced down at forward airfields through a shortage of fuel.

The group's reconnaissance escort missions were by now becoming commonplace, and on December 20 Lt Charles Dunne's flight covered an F-5 sent to overfly Prague. Two days later Lt George Gray and his five Mustangs protected another F-5 photographing Ingolstadt. On the 23rd it was Capt Andrew Turner's turn to lead a five-ship mission escorting yet another Prague-bound F-5. On the latter flight, Capt Lawrence Dickson's P-51D developed engine trouble near the target area and he bailed out over the Alps. Although Dickson's parachute was seen to open, he was later found frozen to death.

On Christmas Eve, the group received a present when Col Benjamin Davis returned from the USA and resumed command of the 332nd. The next morning, 42 Mustangs, again led by Turner, covered the "heavies" visiting Brux. On the way home, the group spotted four Bf 109s below them chasing seven B-26s, and a section of fighters peeled off to intercept. As the Mustangs dived on them, the Messerschmitts broke off their attack and fled the area.

December 26 saw the group provide a two-pronged escort for the 5th and 55th BWs, sent to attack targets in Odertal and Blechammer. The 100th and 301st sent 23 Mustangs in one group and the 99th and 302nd provided 21 Mustangs for withdrawal cover. Both groups found the bombers' formations to be good and tight, making them easy to cover. This contrasted markedly with the 5th BW's B-17s the next day, which the escorting force of 52 P-51s, led by Capt Ed Gleed, found strung out over several miles on the way to their targets in Vienna. Luckily, no enemy aircraft rose to take advantage of the situation.

On the 28th, the 304th BW hit the oil refineries at Kolin and Pardubice, in Czechoslovakia. Fifty 332nd FG Mustangs covered the mission, and when the bombers split into two groups, they split with them – another example of their excellent escort tactics. A replay of that mission was scheduled for December 29, with the targets this time being Mühldorf and Landshut, in Germany. The 304th BW rendezvoused with the 332nd, and almost immediately 11 Mustangs were detached to escort a single 49th BW B-24 in an attack on Passau. Over the target, Lts Frederick D. Funderberg and Andrew Marshall of the 301st were last seen at around 1155hrs. Minutes later they fell victim to either flak or a mid-air collision, and both were killed. On the return flight to Ramitelli, Lt Robert Friend's aircraft entered a spin and he bailed out over Larino, and Lt Lewis Craig bailed out over Termoli. Both men duly returned to their squadron.

The weather moved in on December 30, giving the pilots of the 332nd FG a brief respite from this grueling series of four-hour bomber escort missions. In his year-end message to the group, Col Davis stressed that the 332nd's record for escort was not going unnoticed. "Unofficially, you are known by an untold number of bomber crews as those who can be depended on, and whose appearance means certain protection from enemy fighters," Davis wrote. "The bomber crews have told others of your accomplishments, and your good reputation has preceded you in many parts where you may think you are unknown."

GRINDING DOWN THE REICH

Weather limited the group to just 11 missions in January 1945, but it brought no respite to the comings and goings of personnel at Ramitelli. The first to go was Maj Lee Rayford, CO of the 301st, who returned home and was replaced by Capt Armour McDaniel. Just days later, Capt Melvin Jackson turned command of the 302nd over to Capt Vernon Haywood. The group also managed to temporarily ease its pilot shortage when 34 new aviators arrived from the USA.

The 332nd remained grounded until January 3, when Lt Alfred Gorham led a three-Mustang flight that accompanied an F-5 to Munich and Linz. However, cloud cover over Austria and southern Germany forced the mission to be abandoned. A second attempt to make the same run, this time with a photo-reconnaissance Mosquito, also ran into bad weather and yielded no results.

Weather continued to foil the group's efforts on January 8, when the 47th BW attempted to strike the Linz railroad marshaling yard. The 51 Mustangs that reached the rendezvous point found no bombers, for the B-24s had made a 360-degree turn when they encountered solid overcast upon making landfall. The bombers and fighters never spotted each other, and the Mustangs were all back on the ground by 1450hrs. One week later, the group tried again. Col Davis led 52 Mustangs to the rendezvous point, only to find no trace of the 304th BW's B-24s. The colonel had the group orbit once, before rendezvousing with a wing of B-24s – oddly enough, from the 47th BW! The Liberators were escorted as far as the Mustangs' fuel would allow, before being turned free.

Freddie Hutchins led the photo-reconnaissance escort mission on January 18, and once again the F-5 and its escorts reached the target – Stuttgart – only to find it completely covered in cloud. At about the same time, six more Mustangs commanded by Capt William Campbell chaperoned an F-5 to Munich, where the weather allowed the Lightning to make its photo run. Elsewhere that same day, Lt Howard Gamble and his wingman escorted an F-5 to Prague. Cloud cover up to 34,000ft forced the reconnaissance pilot to give up the mission, and ten minutes later the F-5's right engine started to splutter. The escorts could only watch helplessly as the Lightning descended inexorably toward the undercast. At 29,000ft the pilot radioed, "This is it – I'm going to bail out. Tell them back at the field that I will be alright."

On January 20 the 99th FS came close to suffering its own non-combat losses during a reconnaissance mission. Capt George Gray had led four P-51s and an F-5 Lightning to Prague, but during the withdrawal from the target area, the five aircraft ran into a snowstorm while flying at just 300ft above the ground. The pilots became separated, and somehow they all managed to navigate their way home in terrible weather – the last airplane landed after seven and a half hours in the air.

Twenty minutes after Gray's photo-reconnaissance flight took off, Capt Gleed led 46 Mustangs on an escort mission for the 5th BW, which was attacking oil storage facilities near Regensburg. Although no enemy aircraft rose to challenge the group, flak was heavy, damaging a P-51 and perhaps also accounting for Flt Off Samuel J. Foreman and 2Lt Albert L. Young. Both were recorded as missing, and were later confirmed as having been killed.

On January 21, 44 Mustangs provided high cover for the 5th BW's attack on refineries in Austria. When the bombers radioed ahead that they were 30 minutes late, the group proceeded to the target area and the "heavies" caught up with them there. On the way to the target two Me 262s were spotted, but they remained out of range.

Following this mission, the weather closed in. Ten days would pass before the Fifteenth Air Force could again mount a major attack on Axis targets. Finally, on the 31st, the 47th and 55th BWs struck the Moosbierbaum oil refinery, in Austria. The wings arrived 15 and 30 minutes late to the rendezvous point, but Capt Vernon Haywood and his 42 Mustangs reacted flexibly, splitting into two groups to cover both formations' approaches to the target.

On February 1, the Fifteenth Air Force launched a "one-two" punch on Moosbierbaum. Col Davis led an escort of 100th and 301st fighters for the 49th BW, whose bomber crews seemed confused when it came to determining their target. With the minutes ticking by as the "heavies" circled over Austria looking for their initial point, Davis had to pass responsibility for withdrawal escort cover over to another Mustang group. An hour after this first mission started, the 99th and 302nd FSs launched their fighters from Ramitelli under the command of Capt Gwynne Peirson. Their job would be to escort the 47th BW, which had to switch targets from Moosbierbaum to Graz because of worsening weather.

Four Mustangs, led by Lt Harold Morris, flew an uneventful F-5 escort to Salzburg two days later, and on the 5th, the group escorted the 47th BW as its bombers attacked the Salzburg main railroad station using reconnaissance photographs from this mission. Terrible weather en route to the target area scattered the fighters and prevented an effective escort from being flown. Luckily, no enemy fighters challenged the unprotected bomber formations.

Three days later, weather again disrupted a planned fighter sweep to clear opposition for a supply drop to partisans in Yugoslavia, the 12 Mustangs sortied finding clouds that stretched from the mountain tops up to 30,000ft. Communication problems also meant that the pilots could not contact the transport aircraft by radio.

On February 7, the Fifteenth Air Force again tried a two-pronged attack on Moosbierbaum. The early flight, under Capt George Gray, saw 33 99th and 302nd FS Mustangs escorting the 304th BW, and an hour later Capt Andrew "Jug" Turner led 29 fighters from the 100th and 301st FSs accompanying the 47th BW's B-24s. The latter formation came under antiaircraft fire around Vienna, and two Mustangs shepherded a flak-damaged bomber to the safety of the forward field at Ancona.

BETTER WEATHER, MORE MISSIONS

As the weather cleared, the pace of operations quickened. Following another F-5 escort on February 8, Lt Spurgeon Ellington led a replay of the weather-plagued supply drop mission to Yugoslavia. This time, the 12 fighters found the weather favorable, and after the Mustangs had verified the absence of German forces, they watched as an RAF Lysander came into the area and landed in a field. That same day, 41 Mustangs under Maj Roberts' control escorted the 55th BW's attack on the Vienna South goods and ordnance depots.

Although combat fatalities were now in decline, the 99th lost a new pilot on February 11 when 2Lt Thomas C. Street was killed when his Mustang crashed during a transitional flight. The next day, Capt Alva Temple led a six-aircraft escort of an F-5, which made three runs over Linz – the final one coming after it was discovered that its primary target, Prague, was socked in. Capt Freddie Hutchins led the next day's reconnaissance escort, shepherding an F-5 to Munich. That same morning, 45 Mustangs accompanied the 49th BW to the Vienna central railroad repair works, followed two hours later by a separate 12-ship escort for bombers attacking targets in Zagreb, Maribor and Graz.

February 14 saw plenty of activity for the wing once again, with Col Davis leading 30 Mustangs as escorts for the 5th BW raid on the Vienna Lobau and Schwechat oil refineries. During the course of the mission, two Mustangs were detached to cover a group of B-17s that had become separated from the main force while dodging flak, and the rest of the 100th and 301st FS fighters became separated from the bombers in the target area by cloud cover. Fortunately, they were able to rejoin after the bomb run. A B-17 and a B-24 that were straggling behind the main formation were also chaperoned to safety.

Once the bombers were safely out of Austria, three other Mustangs dropped down and strafed five small craft on the Drava River, although no damage appeared to have been inflicted on the vessels. "Spanky" Roberts led the uneventful second half of the mission, with 36 Mustangs from the 99th and 302nd escorting the 55th BW to the same targets.

Another staggered mission was flown on February 15, this time to the Penzinger railroad marshaling yard in Vienna. Capt Vernon Haywood led 32 Mustangs of the 99th and 302nd aloft at 1030hrs to escort the 49th BW's Red Force, and a hour later Andrew Turner's formation of 100th and 301st P-51s lifted off to accompany the 49th BW's Blue

Force. Turner's formation saw the only "hostile" aircraft to present themselves – a pair of confused P-38s which made two ineffective passes at the Mustangs. Again, the 332nd provided cover to cripples from the 451st and 461st BGs.

Spann Watson led the escorts for a photo-escort mission on February 16, during which a Mosquito made several passes over Memmingen airfield, and Lt Alfonso Simmons led the second six-airplane escort which took an F-5 to the Munich area. Just after Watson's formation departed, the group launched 49 Mustangs for a 5th BW escort mission to Lechfeld airfield, but weather scattered the 332nd so badly that only nine P-51s, led by Lt Emile Clifton, rendezvoused with the bombers. 2Lt John H Chavis of the 99th FS went missing in his P-51C shortly after the group departed from Ramitelli, and he was never seen again.

Two reconnaissance escort missions were performed on the morning of the 17th – a six-airplane escort of an F-5 to Nürnberg and a four-fighter escort of a Mosquito to Munich. An hour after these missions were launched, 44 P-51s took off from Ramitelli and headed for the Linz–Vienna railroad line, looking for targets to strafe. Once in the area, the squadron formations took turns in strafing and providing top cover for each other as they attacked four trains. The 99th and 302nd made three passes on targets while the 100th and 301st each made two. The group claimed two locomotives, two trucks on flat cars, three tank wagons and a power transformer destroyed, plus three locomotives, seven tanks on flat cars, 15 trucks on flat cars, five tank wagons, 15 goods wagons, five armored cars on flat cars, a railroad control tower and a small factory damaged. No Mustangs were lost during the mission.

The next day, Lt Elwood Driver led the by now routine reconnaissance mission, his three Mustangs taking an F-5 to Linz. Col Davis, meanwhile, led 53 P-51s later that day on an escort mission for the 47th BW as it attacked the Wels railroad marshaling yard. However, after a hazardous climb out through thick overcast, the pilots heard the weather aircraft transmit the recall signal to the bombers, scrubbing the mission.

On February 19, the group sent 48 Mustangs aloft, and this time weather permitted a rendezvous, although it was a sloppy one thanks to headwinds that delayed both the fighters and bombers. At one point, a single Spitfire started to make a pass on the formation, but when three Mustangs dropped tanks and broke into him, the British fighter split-essed away.

Driver again commanded the photo-reconnaissance escort on the 20th, which saw five Mustangs shepherding an F-5 to Nürnberg, One of the F-5's engines began running rough before reaching the target, however, and the formation turned back – the Lightning landed safely at San Severo. That afternoon, Capt Turner commanded 43 Mustangs escorting the 47th BW to Vipitento and Brenner railroad marshaling yards. The 332nd was on time for the rendezvous, but no bombers could be found. Turner ordered one-third of his fighters onto the target area, while the rest orbited over the rendezvous point – they were joined by the Liberators six minutes later. The weather again proved difficult, and the bombers finally headed for their number five target (Fiume), at which point the escorts had to leave for home. The first group of 11 fighters provided penetration escort to a group from the 49th BW, which was attacking the original target.

Armour McDaniel led the February 21 mission, which sent 39 Mustangs north with the 304th BW to the Vienna central railroad marshaling yard. One of the B-24s had mechanical difficulties and left the formation just as the fighters rendezvoused with the bombers – two Mustangs were despatched to see the Liberator safely to Trieste. The rest of the mission progressed without incident.

On the 22nd, the group was tasked with escorting the 5th BW's attack on railroad marshaling yards in southwest Germany, followed by a strafing mission against rail targets. The 44 Mustangs shepherded the bombers to the target, but the strafing mission was called off when the target area was found to be completely socked in. Reconnaissance escorts later in the day targeted Prague and Stuttgart, with 1Lt Clifton and Capt Driver leading the Mustangs. The next day's mission to cover the 304th BW's attack on the Gmünd West railroad marshaling yard was again hampered by weather – the B-24s were forced to split up and hit two alternate targets, but Col Davis kept the escorts in place for both groups of B-24s.

1Lt Spurgeon Ellington commanded a five-airplane escort for a Mosquito reconnaissance mission to Munich on February 24, and a six-airplane escort for an F-5 visit to the city the next afternoon. Some of the information gathered on these flights may have led to the mission of February 25, when 45 P-51s were despatched to strafe traffic in the Munich–Linz–Ingolstadt–Salzburg area. The 99th, 100th and 301st FSs assumed their usual strafing tactics, with squadrons alternating between strafing and providing top cover. The 100th started the destruction, dropping down to strike the line running between Rosenheim, Mühldorf and Landshut. The attack destroyed four locomotives and damaged three others, and five passenger carriages, six oil wagons, four goods wagons and a pair of ore wagons were also damaged. Unit records also note that three soldiers were hit. In the midst of the attack, an airfield was spotted with 15 aircraft scattered about – in short order, two He 111s were in flames and a third He 111 and a Bf 109 were damaged.

As the 100th rose to assume top cover duties, the 99th descended on the railroad line, destroying six locomotives and shooting up 40 goods wagons, five passenger cars, four trucks and an additional locomotive. In the process, however, 2Lt George Iles' P-51 was hit in the coolant system by flak and he bailed out. Although the pilot attempted to escape to Switzerland, he was captured in southern Germany. 2Lt Wendell Hockaday was so intent on hitting a locomotive that he actually flew into it, ripping off part of his wing. He nursed the Mustang as far as the Alps before bailing out near Vitendorf, but he was never seen alive again. Flak also damaged 2Lt Daniel L. Rich's P-51 – he crash-landed in a valley north of Campomarino, in Italy, and escaped with second-degree burns to his face.

The 301st came down next, but fuel limited them to five minutes of strafing. An electrical power station was damaged, another destroyed and an electric locomotive was peppered with .50cal machine gun rounds. While the 99th was making its passes, 1Lt Alfred Gorham's P-51 suffered an engine failure and he was forced to bail out just east of Munich. He was soon captured and spent the rest of the war as a PoW.

In the wake of this costly mission, the group was thankful to return to a round of photo-reconnaissance escort flights and bomber escort duties. 1Lt Richard Harder led the three-airplane escort for a photo-reconnaissance Mosquito to Munich on February 26, whilst the following day, 32 Mustangs under Maj Roberts' command accompanied the 49th BW to Augsburg railroad marshaling yard. The last day of February featured an F-5 escort to Prague, led by 1Lt Chris Newman, a second reconnaissance escort to Prague later that same day, led by 1Lt Albert Manning, and a 34-airplane escort of the 5th BW to Verona, led by Col Davis.

The personnel problems that continued to plague the group had led to a virtual deactivation of the 302nd in February, and on March 6 the unit was officially taken off the mission roster and its pilots assigned to the three remaining squadrons. In the final weeks of the war, as German forces were squeezed into an ever-shrinking area, the group would see increasing opposition.

JETS AND JUBILATION

Although it was becoming clear that conflict in Europe was nearing its end, German resolve showed no sign of cracking. Similarly, the pressures on the group from operational accidents continued unabated. During March, Flt Off Thomas L. Hawkins was killed when his Mustang crashed on take-off and, even more disheartening, 1Lt Roland W. Moody died of burns that he received when a drop tank fell off an aircraft as it taxied by and burst when it struck the pilot's tent.

The month started with the now-routine reconnaissance escorts to Prague and Stuttgart, complementing a 39-airplane escort to Moosbierbaum for the 55th BW. When the Vienna area was found to be completely socked in, the wing bombed the alternate target at Amstetten. The situation facing the Germans was highlighted by the sight of a dozen Il-2 Sturmoviks spotted in the air just prior to the P-51s rendezvousing with the bombers.

On March 2 the group sent out Mustangs to protect an F-5 mission to Prague, followed by an uneventful 34-airplane escort for the 304th BW to the Linz railroad marshaling yard, led by Capt Jack Holsclaw. The next morning, the 100th and 301st sent 23 airplanes to scour the area between Bruck and Wiener Neustadt, in Austria, for trains to strafe. Flying along the Maribor–Graz line, the 100th sent four airplanes down to shoot up parked rolling stock, and seven goods wagons and a passenger car were damaged.

Seven more Mustangs overflew the area between Gliesdorf and Radkersburg but found nothing. A second section continued north past Bruek, then turned south and finally found parked goods wagons on a siding near Langenwang, damaging two of them. Eight more of the 100th's Mustangs remained in the Graz area, and two of them, flown by Lts Robert Martin and Alphonso Simmons, dropped down to attack an airfield south of Graz. Both men, who were last seen starting their strafing runs, quickly fell to flak. Simmons was killed, but Martin, who radioed, "I will walk in from here" just after his airplane was hit, made good on that statement, returning to the group in April.

Col Davis led the mission of March 4 which saw 42 Mustangs escort the 49th BW to the Graz railroad marshaling yards yet again. The next day, five P-51s escorted a Mosquito to photograph the area around Munich – a mission duplicated on March 7, but this time with an F-5. Forty-eight hours later, the photographic subjects were Linz and Munich – all these missions passed without incident.

The third mission on March 9 took 39 Mustangs to the Bruck marshaling yards with the 5th BW, the escorts splitting into two forces to give the bombers coverage over the target for the full duration of their attack.

On March 12, another pair of F-5 escorts was carried out, again to Linz and Munich, followed by a 48-airplane mission led by Capt William Campbell to the Floridsdorf oil refinery, near Vienna. While escorting the 47th BW on the latter operation, two bogies were spotted on the deck. A pair of Mustangs were sent down to investigate, but they lost the aircraft in ground haze. Later, the group heard over the radio that a B-24 was being attacked by enemy fighters, but it was unable to ascertain where the bomber was located.

From March 13, the routine F-5 escorts started to become more interesting. The early flight to Stuttgart that day went as planned, but one member of a six-airplane escort for the photo-reconnaissance mission to Nürnberg found more action than he expected. The unnamed Mustang pilot took off late and was hurrying to catch up with the rest of his formation when a single Fw 190 dived on him. When the pilot dropped his tanks and turned into the enemy, he spotted a second Focke-Wulf diving out of the sun from about his "four o'clock." The pilot split-essed for the deck, with the Fw 190s in pursuit, but upon reaching the coast the German pilots abandoned the chase. Ed Gleed led the day's escort mission, taking three groups of bombers from the 5th BW to the Regensburg railroad marshaling yard. The formation spotted two Fw 190s, but they were too distant to be engaged by the fighters.

March 14 proved to be an exceptionally busy day for the group, with four missions scheduled. Two were photo-reconnaissance escorts for Mosquitoes heading to Munich about one hour apart. The day's major assignment tasked the 100th and 301st with shepherding the 47th BW to the Varazdin railroad bridge and marshaling yard. That mission went without incident, but the 21 aircraft of the 99th assigned to strafe targets on the Bruck–Leoben–Steyr railroad line that morning saw enough action for the entire group.

Despite moderate, accurate, light flak at Hieflau, the squadron destroyed nine locomotives and nine goods wagons, and damaged a further nine locomotives, 127 goods wagons, 37 flat cars, eight oil wagons, seven trucks on flat cars, three railroad stations, two railroad buildings, a power station and a warehouse, which was left burning.

During one pass, P-51D 44-25070, flown by 99th FS pilot Harold Brown, was hit and the latter was forced to bail out. Pilots saw him running for cover in the snow halfway up the side of a mountain, but only 30 minutes after he had landed, two constables apprehended him and marched him back to Hieflau, where an angry mob awaited. The mob had a rope, and they dragged Brown to a small tree and prepared to hang him. Luckily, a third constable arrived with a rifle and forced the mob to back down. The constable delivered Brown to the military police in a nearby town, who interned him in Stalag Luft I for the remaining weeks of the war in Europe.

The next day, Capt Downs led eight Mustangs on a "special mission" to Yugoslavia. While on station, Downs spotted eight B-24s and five Halifaxes, plus another escorting group of four Spitfires, all of which were participating in yet more resupply sorties for partisans. Just before this mission was launched, 49 additional Mustangs under Capt Woodrow Crockett had set out to rendezvous with the 5th BW, which was attacking Zittau, in Germany.

On March 16, 31 aircraft were sent to strafe rail targets in Austria and Germany. Eight airplanes from the 99th attacked a stretch of track between Ebersberg and Neumarkt for more than an hour, while three others provided top cover. The fighters destroyed two locomotives, four trucks on flat cars and five goods wagons, and damaged a further 45 goods wagons, five locomotives and four trucks on flat cars, as well as eight buildings.

The 100th attacked a stretch of railroad line to the west, sending three airplanes down to strafe while six others kept a lookout for the Luftwaffe. The three Mustangs destroyed two locomotives and damaged two more, as well as five goods wagons and a baggage car. The 301st strafed Plattling, with 11 Mustangs destroying three locomotives and a flak car and damaging 15 goods wagons, nine locomotives, six coal wagons, three passenger carriages, an oil wagon and the railroad station.

The 301st found more targets when it reached Mettenheim airfield, where five Mustangs strafed the assembled aircraft. One fighter lined up a Bf 109 that was trying to take off, sprayed it with machine-gun fire and saw it collapse back onto the airfield. The official score was three Fw 190s and a Ju 52/3m destroyed, and nine Fw 190s, two Bf 109s, one Fw 200, an unidentified biplane trainer, two barracks buildings and an operations building damaged.

The group also repeatedly strafed a large reinforced concrete structure, which the Germans called Project *Weingut I* (Wine Estate I) – a massive building planned as a plant for the manufacture of Me 262 engines and parts. The facility was being built by concentration camp inmates and Russian PoWs from Dachau. Only half-finished, the site was overrun by the Allies on May 2. The attack was not without losses, however, for 2Lt Robert C. Robinson of the 100th FS was lost when, during a low strafing pass north of Muhldorf, his Mustang struck its left wing on a tree and exploded.

The next day, after more Mosquito escort missions to Munich and Prague, Lt Manning led a six-ship mission to cover the withdrawal of 70 B-24s attacking Monfalcone Harbor, in northern Italy. F-5s received escorts on March 17 too, with Prague and Linz being documented, and Mosquitoes were taken to the same targets 48 hours later.

That same day, Col Davis led a 44-airplane escort of the 55th BW to the Mühldorf railroad marshaling yard – the only enemy aircraft sighted was a single Me 262 fighter heading away from the formation over the Brenner Pass.

A photo-escort mission to Linz and Munich in the early afternoon of March 20 and covering a supply run by a C-47 to Sanski Most, in Yugoslavia, were overshadowed by a two-part escort launched that morning. The first wave, under Capt Bill Campbell, was broken up by rough weather, but ten Mustangs rendezvoused with the 304th BW on its way to the Kralupy oil refinery – six of the fighters were subsequently forced home because of a lack of fuel. When the bombers ran into even worse weather and turned south, the four remaining Mustangs stayed with them as long as they could before turning for home and dropping to deck level. They found a seven-wagon train at Buchkirchen and destroyed the locomotive, before shooting up a pair of goods wagons.

A dozen other Mustangs missed the rendezvous entirely, and as they searched for the bombers, the engine of Lt Newman Golden's P-51B seized, forcing him to bail out. He floated down into German captivity. As fuel ran low, this group of Mustangs began to lose sections and flights as they broke for home, but four fighters stumbled across a 34-airplane formation of 49th BW B-24s and provided an opportunistic escort for them.

The second wave, led by Capt Ed Gleed, saw none of the problems of the first wave. The group joined up with the 304th over Lambach as assigned, and they provided an escort all the way to the alternate target – the Wels railroad marshaling yard.

The seven-and-a-half-hour missions of the previous day did not keep the group down on March 21, when 38 P-51s, commanded by Col Davis, escorted the 47th BW to another airfield in southern Germany. On the way home, two Mustangs found a lone B-24 of the 376th BG struggling along with its number two engine feathered, so they nursed it back to the airfield at Zara. Group pilots also flew three photo-escort missions that day, and another on March 22 to Ruhland, in Germany.

Twenty minutes after this mission had departed Ramitelli, 50 Mustangs launched in two forces to cover another attack by the 304th BW on the Kralupy oil refinery. The only action seen came when a trio of 52nd FG Mustangs turned into an element of the 332nd, causing a brief moment of anxiety.

The photographs taken on March 22 helped prompt the 5th BW's attack on the Ruhland oil refinery the following day, which was accompanied by 43 P-51s from the 332nd. Although no enemy aircraft were spotted, one P-51 suffered mechanical problems and its pilot, 2Lt Lincoln Hudson, turned east toward Russian lines because he lacked the altitude to cross the Alps. Eventually, Hudson bailed out of his P-51C in the vicinity of Tropau, in Czechoslovakia, and was beaten badly by civilians before German soldiers could take him into custody. He was imprisoned in Stalag Luft III and later Stalag Luft VIIA.

LONGEST MISSION

On March 24, the Fifteenth Air Force launched its longest mission – a 1,600-mile round trip to the Daimler-Benz tank assembly plant in Berlin – which was being flown in an effort to help draw pressure off Operation *Varsity*. The latter was the codename for the Allied airborne assault on the eastern side of the Rhine. Supporting this mission were 59 Mustangs from the 332nd FG, which were tasked with escorting B-17s from the 5th BW. The group departed Ramitelli at 1145hrs, and five aircraft aborted soon after take-off. The remaining 54 continued north, and 38 of them rendezvoused with the bombers over Kaaden, in southern Germany. Here, they relieved the P-38s of the 1st FG. A short while later Col Davis' Mustang developed a vibration at high manifold pressure, and he relinquished the lead of the mission to Capt Armour McDaniel, CO of the 301st.

The group was scheduled to turn its escort duties over to the 31st FG on the outskirts of Berlin, but the latter group was late and the 332nd continued toward the German capital. As the combined formation neared the target area at 1208hrs, some 25 enemy fighters (mostly Me 262s from JG 7) engaged the American bombers. The 332nd immediately came to the aid of the "heavies," intercepting the first pass made by a string of four Me 262s on the lower right echelon of the lead group of bombers from "five o'clock high." The leader of the four-ship formation continued down, while the next two rolled to the right and dived away from the bomber stream. The fourth Me 262 broke high and to the left.

1Lt Richard Harder tried to follow the second two jets, firing several bursts from 1,000 yards down to 300 yards – he claimed to have damaged one of the aircraft. Meanwhile, Capt Edwin M. Thomas had spotted the same attack. "My entire section of eight aircraft broke after the jets," he said. He and 2Lt Vincent I. Mitchell pursued the two Me 262s trying to dive away, and they also believed that they had managed to hit one of the German fighters as it fled, although there is no mention of any damage being inflicted on JG 7's Me 262s on this date in the unit's official wartime records.

Two minutes later, 1Lt Reid E. Thompson of the 100th FS spotted another jet making a pass at the bombers from "two o'clock high," so he peeled away to attack it. Another flight cut between him and his original target, so he broke off his pursuit. Thompson then saw another aircraft which he almost certainly misidentified as an Me 163 (the only Komet launch sites within range of this combat had been overrun by this time). After Thompson fired a short burst from long range, the enemy airplane went into a steep dive in an effort to escape his pursuer. "He was almost vertical in his dive," Thompson reported, and "no smoke appeared from his jets." The Mustang pilot pulled out of his pursuit at 6,000ft, and although he said he did not see the jet crash, he claimed that he saw smoke on the ground, "where I estimated he had hit."

At the same time, an Me 262 made another pass at the bombers in a 30-degree dive, after which he flew right across the nose of 1Lt Earl R. "Squirrel" Lane. "He appeared as if he was peeling off from an attack on the bombers," the pilot recalled. "I came in for a 30-degree deflection shot from 2,000ft away. He didn't quite fill my sight. I fired three short bursts and saw the airplane emitting smoke. A piece of it, either the canopy or one of the jet orifices, then flew off."

Lane achieved complete surprise over his foe, seven-kill ace Oberleutnant Alfred Ambs in Me 262A-1/R1 Wk-Nr. 110999, who had already completed two successful passes against the B-17s. "As I flew away from the bomber stream, phosphorus shells suddenly struck my cockpit," Ambs later wrote. "My oxygen mask was riddled and splinters struck my face. I quickly jettisoned the canopy and pulled up the nose of my Me 262 to lose speed. I bailed out at approximately 350kph at an altitude of about 6,000m."

Lane broke off his attack at 17,000ft, then pulled up and circled over the spot where Ambs' Me 262 had begun its final dive. He was rewarded with the sight of "a crash and a puff of black smoke," followed by a second smaller impact two seconds later. Ambs came down in a tree near Wittenburg, tearing ligaments and breaking his kneecap. It would be his last flight of the war.

Meanwhile, two more Me 262s zoomed through the formation, only to find 1Lt Robert Williams and wingman Samuel Watts Jnr waiting for them. As they turned into the Me 262s, the two jets fired on Watts, whose maneuverability was hampered by a hung-up drop tank. When the Me 262s passed below the Mustangs, Williams split-essed after them and got on their tails at a range of about 1,500ft. As the Me 262s opened the distance, he fired at the trailing jet and claimed damage to its tail.

1Lt Richard Harder, climbing back up to 26,000ft after his earlier fruitless chase, spotted three more Me 262s attacking the bombers from "five o'clock high." The jets "did not reach the bombers, as I turned my flight into them," he later explained. The jets made a quick right turn as Harder's "Blue Flight" turned inside of them. They then split up, with one diving away and a second entering a steep climb. The third continued its turn, and Harder fired at him from 2,000ft down to 900ft, observing hits on the fuselage for a second damaged claim.

Flt Off Joseph Chineworth claimed a probable at about the same time after three Me 262s turned into his flight. "We broke right and down on them, pursuing them through a series of turns while descending," Chineworth explained. "When I got to within 1,500ft, I started firing on the rearmost enemy aircraft. I fired three bursts and my guns stopped." Chineworth saw pieces come off the jet and it started trailing smoke, before entering a dive at 15,000ft.

A few minutes later, Me 262A-1a/R1 Wk-Nr. 111676 "Yellow 6," with Oberleutnant Ernst Worner at the controls, lined up for another pass on the bombers. He cut in front of Flt Off Charles Brantley's Mustang, and the young pilot firewalled his Merlin engine to close the distance. "He was well within range when I fired four bursts," Brantley said.

He then broke off his attack, but another 100th FS pilot saw Worner's jet erupt in flames and lurch out of control. The wounded German pilot was able to bail out, but his injuries prevented him from flying again.

1Lt Roscoe Brown spotted four jets heading north below the bombers and he peeled off to attack them, but "almost immediately I saw a lone Me 262 at 24,000ft climbing 90 degrees to me some distance from me," Brown said. "I pulled up at him in a 15-degree climb and fired three long bursts from 2,000ft at 'eight o'clock' to him." Almost immediately, the jet's pilot, Oberleutnant Franz Kulp, bailed out of "Yellow 5" as flames burst from the engines of the stricken jet. The wounded Kulp floated down to safety, but like his fellow pilots, the severity of his injuries meant his war had come to an end.

Despite these successes, the group did not escape unscathed from the battle, however. At 1215hrs, flak blew off the outer right wing of Leon "Woodie" Spears' P-51 *KITTEN*. "Looking at that wing and hearing how the engine was running, I knew there was no way I could get over the Alps to Italy," Spears recalled. Instead, he turned east and headed for the Soviet lines in Poland. Losing altitude, he selected a field near a river for a landing, only to discover that he was flying directly into a skirmish between Soviet and German troops, who held opposite banks of a nearby river. "Between the two of them, they shot my airplane to pieces," Spears said. "While I was flying down this river, I could feel shells hitting my fighter."

Spears dropped the landing gear, then hurriedly decided to raise it again to prevent the Mustang from falling undamaged into enemy hands. After the badly damaged P-51 had finally slid to a halt, German troops drove up to the fighter and duly captured Spears, but "they seemed to be trying to be as nice as they could," he said. "If they had a name badge, they'd shove it right under my nose so I wouldn't miss it. They knew that the war was coming to an end, so they did not want to be involved in any war crimes or any cruelty."

The Germans gave Spears a half-hearted interrogation. "They knew full well that any information they got would be useless to them," he said. After just three days in captivity, Spears heard a commotion outside. "I pulled a board off a window and the first thing I saw was this huge Russian tank." Soviet troops were firing into buildings at random, so Spears began shouting and waving at them to avoid being hit. One Soviet soldier heard him above the din of battle. "I had an A-2 flying jacket on with a large American flag on the back. I put my back to the window so he could see it. I heard him yell, 'American! American!' He rushed up and gave me a big bear hug!" Spears subsequently returned to the group on May 10.

James T. Mitchell, who had stayed with Spears as he headed for Polish territory, had landed on the Soviet side of the frontline, while Arnett Starks had been killed in action near Berlin. Armour McDaniel, who had assumed command when Col Davis' P-51 acted up, was forced to bail out when his own Mustang suffered engine trouble, and he ended the war as a PoW. Capt Walter M. Downs was appointed to lead the 301st in his absence.

On their way home from the German capital, the group strafed rail traffic, claiming two locomotives and three goods wagons damaged. Gen Lawrence of the 5th BW sent a telegram thanking the group for its extraordinary efforts on the Berlin mission, which resulted in the 332nd being awarded a Distinguished Unit Citation. The latter was awarded to units of the armed forces of the United States and its allies for extraordinary heroism in action against an armed enemy.

March 25 saw the group conduct a photo-escort for an F-5 overflying Linz, and this was followed up by a 39-airplane escort of the 49th BW to Prague/Kbely airfield under the leadership of Capt Jack Holsclaw. Whilst in the target area, the group spotted a Soviet Pe-2 bomber, which rocked its wings as it flew below the American formation. The group maneuvered to avoid the Russian aircraft, but then watched in horror as two P-51Ds from another unit swooped in and opened fire. The Pe-2 caught fire and dived into the ground.

Hannibal Cox led the next day's F-5 escort to Munich, which was followed by an escort of the 5th BW to the Wiener Neustadt railroad marshaling yards. The bombers were forced off course by weather, but they rendezvoused with the 332nd over the target area and were safely shepherded home.

Weather kept the group grounded until March 30, when Holsclaw led the morning's photo run to Munich. Cloud prevented the F-5 from getting any good photographs, however.

MORE AERIAL VICTORIES

The last day of March 1945 would bring the 332nd its biggest haul of aerial kills in World War II. With Col Davis in the lead aircraft, 47 Mustangs conducted a fighter sweep of the Munich area, followed by a strafing mission against rail targets. Four aborts brought the number of P-51s to enter German airspace down to 43, and Davis ordered the squadron formations to cover equal thirds of the target area.

Just after the three squadrons split up to look for things to strafe, five Bf 109s and a single Fw 190 suddenly broke out of a cloudbank above a flight of seven Mustangs from the 99th. The pilots, who were in the process of lining up strafing targets, broke off their attack and engaged the fighters instead. The Fw 190 fell to the guns of 2Lt Thomas Braswell, while the Bf 109s were downed by Maj William Campbell, 1Lt Daniel Rich and 2Lts John Davis, James Hall and Hugh White. Five minutes later, pilots from the 100th spotted eight Fw 190s and three Bf 109s at 3,000ft. Although these fighters engaged the Mustangs with some aggression, their tactics were haphazard and they failed to allow the German pilots to work as a team. The 100th took full advantage of this.

"I dived into a group of enemy aircraft," reported Robert Williams, who turned onto the tail of one of the Fw 190s. "I shot off a few short bursts. My fire hit the mark and the enemy airplane fell off and tumbled to the ground. On pulling away from my victim, I found another enemy airplane on my tail. To evade his guns, I made a steep turn. Just as I had turned, another enemy fighter shot across the nose of my airplane. Immediately, I began firing at him." Williams' aim was true, for the Focke-Wulf went into a steep dive and crashed. While Williams was engaged, 1Lt Roscoe Brown and 2Lts Bertram Wilson and Rual Bell each despatched a Bf 109, while 1Lt Earl Lane and Flt Off John Lyle downed an Fw 190 apiece.

After dealing with the German fighters, the group resumed its strafing mission. The 99th FS destroyed two locomotives and damaged a third, whilst 15 passenger cars were also shot up. In the process, however, Clarence Driver was brought down – he bailed out within view of several of his fellow Tuskegee airmen in Stalag Luft VIIA, located in nearby Moosburg. The burned "Red" Driver soon joined his friends in the PoW camp.

On its strafing runs, the 301st destroyed three locomotives, two goods wagons and a house, and damaged nine locomotives, 14 goods wagons, six passenger cars, five oil wagons, five hopper cars, a factory, a roundhouse, a railroad station and a truck. Meanwhile, the 100th destroyed two locomotives, eight oil wagons, three passenger cars and a warehouse, while damaging a locomotive, two tank cars, a truck and ten goods wagons. The squadron lost 2Lt Ronald Reeves over the target area when his fighter went into a spin while making a tight turn – he was too low to recover and died in the crash. A second Mustang ran low on gas and went missing during the return flight.

April Fools' Day 1945 saw 45 Mustangs rendezvous with the 47th BW's B-24s for a mission to the marshaling yards at St Pölten, in Austria. Eight fighters from the 301st, led by Lt Harder, preceded the bombers through the target area before turning west and conducting a fighter sweep around Wels and Linz. This flight spotted four Fw 190s below them in the neighborhood of Wels airfield and dived to the attack. The four low aircraft were bait, as there were two other Fw 190s trailing the first four, with an additional ten Fw 190s and Bf 109s positioned above the six low aircraft to spring the trap. A series of swirling dogfights ensued, with the Germans trying virtually everything to beat the Mustang pilots – head-on passes, Lufberys, turning attacks, deflection shots.

Despite the German aggressiveness, the 301st came out on top in most engagements, with Harry Stewart bagging three Fw 190s and Charles White a pair of Bf 109s. Single kills went to Carl Carey, John Edwards, Walter Manning, Harold Morris and James Fischer. The latter pilot's airplane was shot up when he chased his victim across an airfield, and while struggling to bring the Mustang home, he took another shell through the wing over a small town in Yugoslavia which forced him to bail out, although he landed among friendly partisans. Manning was shot down after he scored his kill, as was Flt Off William Armstrong. Both pilots were killed.

The April 1 photo-escort to Prague was uneventful, but the next day's trip to Munich, featuring an F-5 and four 99th P-51s led by Lt Hannibal Cox, had just arrived in the target when the formation was jumped by a lone Me 262, which made a single pass from "seven o'clock high." The Mustangs turned into the Me 262, but the F-5 failed to drop into the No 3 position in the formation as briefed and continued toward Regensburg. While on the way home, two Mustangs gave chase to an Fw 190, but they failed to catch the German airplane. Without a Lightning to escort, Cox led the P-51s down to the deck and strafed six river barges during the trip back to Ramitelli.

The mission for April 2 called for an escort of the 304th BW to the marshaling yard at Krems, followed by a fighter sweep by the 99th of the area west of Vienna. All 47 Mustangs returned safely. After a short break, the group was up again on April 5, taking an F-5 to Linz in the morning and shepherding the 5th BW to Udine airfield in the afternoon. The anticipated Luftwaffe response from the latter base never materialized.

On April 6, the 304th BW attacked the marshaling yards at Verona and Porta Nuova, and 39 of the 332nd's Mustangs went with them, led by now-Maj Andrew Turner. No enemy aircraft were spotted, nor were they during the afternoon's photo-reconnaissance escort to Prague. The next day, six groups from the 5th BW attacked bridges in northern Italy, and the 332nd provided cover. One aircraft, flown by 2Lt William Walker of the 100th, landed at Zara, in Yugoslavia, and the pilot and P-51 returned to Ramitelli two days later.

The escorting of photo-reconnaissance missions continued to occupy pilots who were not assigned to protect bomber formations. On April 7, Lt Gentry Barnes led the escort of an F-5 to Munich, and the next day's missions took six-airplane escorts to Linz and Munich with a Mosquito and to Prague with a Lightning. Hannibal Cox led the 34-airplane bomber escort mission flown on April 8, as three groups of the 5th BW flattened the railroad bridge at Campodazzo. No flak or fighters were seen, although one B-17 was spotted ditching in the Adriatic Sea.

On April 9, a six-airplane escort for an F-5 to Prague, led by Lt Carl Ellis, saw evidence of the Luftwaffe's presence, but never had a chance to engage. During the approach to Prague, 16 twin-engined aircraft were seen on the deck, along with a half-dozen single-engined fighters at about the same time, and 45 minutes later a single Me 262 flew past the formation on a parallel course. A second photo-escort to Prague that afternoon found no sign of these enemy aircraft. Col Davis led the day's big mission – a 39-airplane escort of groups from the 5th and 304th BWs to Bologna. The mission was notable in that there were no aborts, which was a tribute to the groundcrews who had worked hard to master the Mustang.

Bologna was the next day's target as well, with Lt Chris Newman commanding the 34-airplane escort. April 10 also saw yet another uneventful photo-reconnaissance escort to Munich. The next day, 35 Mustangs covered the 304th BW's attack on the railroad bridge at Ponte Gardena – a mission that required the detachment of four P-51s to chaperone a pair of crippled B-24s to safety.

Jack Holsclaw led the escort of an F-5 to Munich on April 11, seeing no sign of enemy aerial resistance. Two uneventful escorts the next day, to Linz and Munich, were followed by a mission for the 100th and elements of the 301st to escort the 47th BW to the Casara railroad bridge, and the 99th and the rest of the 301st to take the 49th BW to St Veith, in Germany. During the latter mission, tragedy struck when 2Lts Samuel Leftenant and James L. Hall Jnr collided. Leftenant was killed, although his airplane was seen to continue flying south, seemingly under control. Hall bailed out of his damaged P-51 and was captured by the Germans in Rumania. He would rejoin the group after war's end.

On April 14, Lt Robert Williams led the F-5 escort to Munich and Lake Chiem, and a second six-airplane escort provided cover to supply-dropping Halifaxes later that morning. April 15 was a busy day, beginning with F-5 escorts to Bolzano, Prague and Munich. Next came a 29-airplane escort of the 304th BW to the Ghedi ammunition factory and storage area. Other than the repeated hostile response of some P-38s to a lone Mustang's efforts to join up with them, the mission was wholly unremarkable.

That same day, Col Davis led 37 P-51Ds on a strafing mission against rail targets in the Munich, Salzburg, Linz, Prague and Regensburg areas – the three squadrons split up and attacked targets in pre-assigned locations. Despite flak from two trains that they harassed, the Mustangs strafed the railroad unmolested for over an hour. A dozen Mustangs from the 99th destroyed four locomotives and damaged four more. Fourteen goods wagons, four motor transports on flat cars and two railroad buildings were also damaged. Flak guns mounted on flat cars peppered Flt Off Thurston Gaines's P-51, forcing him to bail out near Munich – he quickly became a PoW. A dozen P-51s from the 100th strafed the railroad line from Plattling to Passan to Klatovy, destroying five locomotives and damaging four more, as well as five goods wagons cars, a passenger car and a house near the tracks.

The 301st had the most interesting time of it. First, their Mustangs strafed river traffic, damaging two barges, a steam crane and a house near the river, then they attacked a railroad line, destroying an oil wagon and damaging six others. Four 301st P-51s dropped down from flying top cover and attacked a second railroad line, destroying three locomotives and eight oil wagons and damaging a flat car and a goods wagon. The four Mustangs made another pass and claimed four locomotives destroyed and 15 goods wagons, nine locomotives and a passenger car damaged, and they also shot up a gun emplacement.

As they pulled off this run, Jimmy Lanham and his wingman spotted a Bf 109 painted dark blue, and lacking German markings – a possible Italian ANR holdout. The Bf 109 tried to turn inside the speeding Mustangs, but Lanham fired a series of deflection shots and saw hits around the cowling. The fighter burst into flames and hit the ground – inexplicably, Lanham was subsequently credited with only a probable victory. On the way home, Flt Off Morris Gant radioed that he was low on fuel, and he was ordered to land at the nearest airfield as the group passed Ortona, in Italy. Gant was never seen again.

April 16 continued the hectic pace. Lt Henry Peoples led a four-ship escort of three C-47s to Yugoslavia, and small groups of Mustangs flew three photo-reconnaissance escort missions to the Munich area. A 37-aircraft escort of the 49th and 55th BWs to Bologna took place in the early afternoon. The next day's F-5 escort to Linz and Munich was followed by a 49-airplane effort escorting the 5th and 304th BWs to Bologna. This mission was repeated the next day by 38 Mustangs under Maj Gleed, which took the 304th back to its Italian target. The fighters were supposed to cover the 5th BW, but confusion surrounding the rendezvous time left the 332nd with no one to escort, so Gleed led them to the assistance of the 304th's B-24s.

Col Davis led the mission of April 19, when 47 P-51s "rode herd" on the 304th BW, which split into two groups and attacked railroad marshaling yards at Wels and Puchheim. Davis put 19 airplanes over Wels and 16 over Pucheim, with the last seven set free to conduct a fighter sweep. Unfortunately, no fighters could be seen in the air, but as the pilots were preparing to climb back to altitude, they encountered the astounding sight of 35 to 40 Me 163 rocket aircraft piled together in a large pasture – mute evidence of the effects of the Allies' bombing campaign on German industry. Six Mustangs also accompanied an F-5 Lightning to Munich that morning.

On April 20, two groups of 25 aircraft left Ramitelli 49 minutes apart to cover penetration, target cover and withdrawal of 49th BW "heavies" attacking the Lusia railroad bridge and the 55th BW's attacks on the Boara and Gazare railroad bridges in northern Italy. Despite delays on the part of the bombers, the mission went without a hitch. Jimmy Lanham led the similarly smooth F-5 escort to Prague.

That afternoon, Col Davis received a letter from Wendell Pruitt in which he pleaded with him to allow him come back to combat. Pruitt was now at Tuskegee as an instructor, a job that he had little patience for. Ironically, the very day his request arrived at Ramitelli, Pruitt and a student were performing a low-altitude roll when the airplane fell out of the sky and smashed into a field. Pruitt, the survivor of 70 combat missions, and his student were both killed.

The following morning, 23 aircraft from the 99th and 301st were assigned to escort the 49th BW to the Attang/Puchheim railroad marshaling yards. Because of poor weather, the group never rendezvoused with the bombers during their approach to the target, but it was able to pick them up coming off the bomb run on the second alternate target. 2Lt Leland Pennington's P-51 left the formation en route to the rendezvous near Zara and, foregoing an escort, proceeded home alone. Pennington never made it, and he was later classified as killed in action.

Capt Emile Clifton led a second mission that day – a 25-airplane fighter sweep of the Udine area. Initially, the Mustangs were tasked with attacking an area around Augsburg and Munich, but a wall of cloud prevented them from getting too far north. The group also squeezed in another escort of a Lancaster and a Halifax as they dropped supplies to partisans in Yugoslavia.

After an aborted photo-reconnaissance mission on the morning of April 22, 32 Mustangs of the 99th and 100th FSs carried out an armed reconnaissance between Stanghella, Monselice, Padova, Nogara, Verona and Nantova, in northern Italy. The 100th encountered weather that prohibited it from hunting for targets, but ten P-51s from the 99th completed their mission. The unit claimed a passenger car destroyed and eight others damaged. Capt Chaskin, A-3 of XV Fighter Command, flew the mission in the ironically coded position of "White Leader."

April 23 brought more escort work. Two forces from the 332nd accompanied the 55th and 304th BWs on missions to Padua and Cavarzere, in northern Italy. After completing their escort, 16 airplanes of the first force conducted an armed reconnaissance of the areas around Verona, Morostica, Padua, Cavarzare, Stanghella and Legnana. Three aircraft strafed a railroad line, damaging one car and a small factory. Hugh White was hit by flak at about 1,000ft, but he had enough speed to climb to 4,500ft before bailing out, coming down near Padua, where he was captured. Eventually, with the war's end clearly in sight, his captors surrendered to him! White returned to the group on May 6, 1945. The 332nd also flew two photo-escort missions to Prague and Brno.

Ed Gleed led the first part of the April 24 mission to northern Italy, escorting the 47th and 49th BWs to the Rovereto and San Ambrogio railroad bridges. The second element was commanded by 1Lt Gordon Rapier. The German forces failed to so much as fire a single round of flak at either group of attacking airplanes.

The next day, the 332nd sent up four eight-airplane forces on an armed reconnaissance mission in the Verona area. One flight, led by Gentry Barnes, spotted a convoy and made a firing pass, damaging a truck before red crosses were spotted on three or four of the 50 vehicles in the convoy. April 25 also saw three more photo-reconnaissance escort missions flown, including one led by Lt Rapier to Munich. The six Mustangs and one Mosquito stumbled across a single Fw 190 14,000ft below them, which immediately split-essed away and dived for the deck.

The third mission of the day – an F-5 escort to the Pilsen area led by Lt Leon Turner – was interrupted by the arrival of a lone Me 262, which closed on the F-5 from "six o'clock." Three of the Mustangs turned to intercept the jet, and they were joined in their pursuit by three P-38s. With the odds against him, the Me 262 broke for home.

LAST AERIAL VICTORIES

With the war winding down, it was apparent that few enemy airmen relished the idea of becoming the last pilot killed in the service of the Reich. Just the same, the F-5 escort of April 26 resulted in the 332nd's final scores, and the final aerial victories for the Fifteenth Air Force.

Six Mustangs, led by Lt Charles Wilson, escorted an F-5 Lightning to the vicinity of Linz, Prague and Amstetten. At 1205hrs, 15 miles east of Prague, three of the Mustangs spotted an aircraft and dropped down to investigate. The airplane turned out to be a lone Mosquito.

As the Mustangs climbed to rejoin the formation, they stumbled across five Bf 109s, which initially rocked their wings to appear friendly. When the Mustangs broke into them, two Bf 109s pulled up as if to dive. A P-51 pilot fired two bursts at one of the fighters and it spiraled into the ground and exploded. The three other Messerschmitts split-essed for the perceived safety of the ground, but two other Mustangs, with their advantage in the dive, despatched two of these Bf 109s, one of whose pilots bailed out. The remaining fighters were caught after a short chase, and one was promptly destroyed while the other was claimed as a probable. Thomas Jefferson scored one kill and the probable and Jimmy Lanham, William Price and Richard Simmons each bagged a fighter apiece. That same day, Col Davis led a complicated five-part escort for the 47th and 55th BWs to the Casarsa and Malcontenta ammunition dumps. The 332nd had fighters over the bombers for two and a half hours, having staggered take-off times to ensure coverage of the bomber stream.

April 30 saw a fitting end to the 332nd's war. Lt Herbert Barland led a four-airplane escort of an F-5 to Balzano, in Italy, which went entirely without incident. With the war's end a few days later, the group moved to a much more comfortable field at Cattolica, and participated in the Fifteenth Air Force Review over Caserta and Bari on May 6. While preparing for a return to the US and a possible redeployment to the Pacific, there was a simmering pride in the men at their achievements. The 99th FS and the 332nd FG had destroyed 111 aircraft in the air and 150 on the ground, wrecked 57 locomotives, damaged or destroyed more than 600 goods wagons and flown 15,533 sorties. Moreover, as far as anyone could determine, they had never lost a bomber under escort to enemy aircraft.

The latter claim is hard to verify, for although mission reports do not mention the loss of any aircraft under escort, it is all but impossible to determine which groups the 332nd was covering at specific times. Even Col Davis expressed uncertainty about this now-famous claim. "I don't say that, or if I do say it, it's not an overenthusiastic statement. I question that privately," he told USAF historian Alan Gropman in 1990. "But so many people have said it that a lot of people have come to believe it."

The most important believers in the 332nd's claim were the bomber crews of the Fifteenth Air Force, many of whose veterans to this day proclaim that the most beautiful things they ever saw in the skies of southern Europe were the red-tailed Mustangs of the 332nd FG.

LOCKBOURNE AND THE END

On June 8, 1945, the group held a ceremony at Cattolica during which Col Davis was awarded the Silver Star for his leadership during the April 15 mission. Within hours of the ceremony, Davis and a cadre of 40 officers and airmen were on B-17s on the first leg of their return trip to the USA. Their task was to rebuild the 477th Medium Bombardment Group, which would be merged with the 332nd FG to become the 477th Composite Group (Colored).

The 477th was subsequently bounced from base to base – far worse, it was the victim of overt racism that kept it from becoming a deployable unit. The slights ranged from substandard facilities to exclusion from the PX and officers' clubs to the outright hostility of Gen Frank O. D. Hunter, commander of the First Air Force. "As long as I am commander of the First Air Force, there will be no racial mixing at any post under my command," Hunter proclaimed in 1944.

Col Robert Selway, who was the white CO of the 477th, helped enforce Hunter's prejudicial policies. Upon arrival at Freeman Field, in Indiana, Selway divided the officers' clubs along racial lines. In an effort to disguise this, he said Club No 1 was open to "trainees," which was how all black officers were classified at Freeman Field, and Club No 2 was open to instructors and supervisors. The men of the 477th made plans to "integrate" Club No 2, and on April 5, 1945, Lts Marsden Thompson and Shirley Clinton entered the club and were arrested. Next came Roger Terry. Throughout the next day, 58 more black airmen tried to exercise their rights as officers, only to be taken into custody by white MPs. On April 9, Selway ordered the black officers to sign a statement that they understood his orders regulating segregation of the officers' clubs. A total of 101 officers refused to sign, and they were bundled off to Godman Field on April 13.

Selway's belief that he had quelled the rebellion was toppled the next day when he learned that every black officer left at Freeman Field planned to enter the club that night. Selway closed the club, the 101 non-signers were released, and only the original three entrants to the club were held in custody. They were submitted to a court martial, which concluded by fining Terry $150 for forcing his way past an MP at the club door. In the 1990s, an official order dismissed charges against all the participants in what became known as "the Freeman Field Mutiny."

Following the court martial, Selway was relieved and Davis took over the group on June 24. For the first time, the group had black officers in responsible positions, namely Ed Gleed as group operations officer, Andrew Turner as deputy group commander and former 332nd flight surgeon Vance Marchbanks as base surgeon, among others. William Campbell assumed command of the newly attached 99th FS. On July 1, Davis took charge of Godman Field itself and appointed Lee Rayford as base operations officer.

The group trained for deployment to the Pacific, with the Mustangs being replaced by P-47N Thunderbolts, but the war's end saw the wholesale departure of pilots back to the civilian world and the group shrank accordingly, leaving just 16 B-25H/Js and 12 P-47Ns on strength by February 1946. In March, the group was transferred to Lockbourne Field, near Columbus, Ohio, which became the only all-black base in the Army Air Force.

Their welcome at the airfield underscored how pervasive racism was, even in Ohio. The editor of the *Columbus Citizen* objected to the arrival of the black airmen, insisting that "this is still a white man's country," and that it was totally unacceptable for America's wars to be fought by "servants."

Caught between the hostile members of the community and the 332nd were a group of white civilian employees who feared that they would lose their jobs as a result of the arrival of the black airmen. Col Davis held a meeting for these employees and assured them that as long as they did their jobs they would remain in their roles at the base. "They became our very great allies and public relations-types with the local people," Davis later said.

Davis also spelled out his expectations of his men. "I made the statement early on that we were going to make Lockbourne the best base in the Air Force," Davis said. "And, by 1948, in an inspection report, there is a statement that said it could well serve as a model for bases in the Air Force."

In May 1947, the 477th reverted to being the 332nd FG after disposing of its B-25s. Three months later, the group became the 332nd Fighter Wing, and shrank even further in size. The segregated nature of the USAAF meant that there was little room for advancement for black officers and enlisted men. Instead of competing for promotions against all others in their specialities, the men competed against all black men in their area – in other words, the men they worked with at Lockbourne.

After two years of this, there was a light at the end of the tunnel – President Harry S. Truman, engaged in the difficult 1948 election campaign, decreed that the armed services of the USA would provide, "equality and opportunity for all persons without regard to race, color, religion or national origin." It would take a while, but segregation in the US military would become a thing of the past – due in large part to the outstanding wartime exploits of the 332nd FG.

In the meantime, the unit continued to fly training missions. On March 28, 1948, a five-ship formation took off from Shaw Air Force Base in Greenville, South Carolina, on a simulated armed reconnaissance. The final destination of this flight would be Lockbourne for four of the pilots, but Harry Stewart would not be among them.

"We were flying in formation over Eastern Kentucky, passing through a thunderstorm, when I had engine failure at 20,000ft," he said. "I rode the airplane down to 10,000ft, but I was still in the clouds, and I knew there were mountains in the area."

Rather than risking an unexpected rendezvous with a mountaintop, Stewart, a veteran of 43 wartime missions, elected to bail out. He opened the canopy, unbuckled his seat belt, and, "trimmed the nose forward so that when I let go of the stick, the nose would dip and eject me forward," he explained. "Unfortunately, the slipstream hit me and I flew back, hitting my left leg on the tail of the airplane, breaking it in two places between the calf and ankle."

While the injured Stewart floated down over the Kentucky coal mining town of Van Lear, his P-47N hurtled over the Webb family cemetery and crashed into a hilltop overlooking the home of the soon-to-be-famous country singer Loretta Lynn, exploding and leaving a crater 10ft to 15ft deep.

"I'd lost my shoe on the leg I broke, which was bleeding profusely," Stewart said. "I must have been in shock, because I remember wondering why I had got up that morning and put on one red sock and one brown one." He used his white silk flying scarf to improvise a tourniquet for his bleeding leg. Then he began to wonder how he was going to save himself. "Just then, I heard a voice from afar, yelling out, 'Hello, hello!'" Stewart said. "Of course, I replied with a frantic 'Hello!' of my own. I didn't want to take a chance on them not hearing me."

A man named Lafe Daniels found Stewart beneath a rock cliff and loaded him onto his horse. Daniels took the aviator home to his wife, Mary, who cleaned and bandaged his wounds. To treat Stewart's pain, the Daniels employed a clear, all-purpose mountain remedy that Stewart mistook for water. Daniels then took the pilot to a clinic in nearby Paintsville. The doctors gave him morphine for his pain and, Stewart said, "the combination of moonshine and morphine put me in another world."

"I remember people lined up outside the door to see this apparition," Stewart said. "The mayor came in and introduced himself," he said, "followed by the police chief, county sheriff and a reporter from the *Paintsville Herald*." Tellingly, the story in the local paper about the crash did not mention that the pilot was black.

Stewart's Thunderbolt became an item of interest for the community as well. By the time Air Force officials showed up to investigate the crash site, nearly every scrap of the wreckage was gone. The locals picked up what they could find – Stewart's cap, machine gun rounds, even the propeller, which one witness said was last seen lashed to the side of a jeep owned by Loretta Lynn's husband. Eventually, residents hitched three mules to the wreckage and hauled the entire airplane off the hill and onto a cattle truck. The P-47's carcass was taken to Ashland, where it was sold as scrap for $70. Once his broken leg had healed, Stewart returned to active duty.

In May 1949, the newly established US Air Force held its first continental gunnery meet, with teams from every fighter group in the country congregating at Las Vegas Air Force Base. The 332nd team was made up of Stewart, Alva Temple and James Harvey. These veterans competed against other pilots in six categories — air-to-air gunnery at 10,000ft and 20,000ft, rocket-firing, skip-bombing, dive-bombing and strafing. Each team's scores in these events would be averaged out to determine a winner.

In the skip-bombing phase, each man scored a hit in all six passes for a perfect score. In the rocket-firing competition, Temple scored hits with eight of eight, while Stewart and Harvey scored seven of eight. The competition continued in this vein until the trio compiled the best score as a team for "conventionally-powered" aircraft, with Temple finishing second in individual scores. About a month later, perhaps not coincidentally, the 332nd FG was disbanded and its personnel transferred to various commands within the Air Force.

For many, the idea of leaving an all-black unit was daunting, but Col Davis was convinced that desegregation was the only way to cement the progress his units had made. "I told them that when you join those units, you're going to outshine them," he said. "That's exactly the way it turned out. They were far in advance of their contemporaries in the white units. They had the combat experience, they had the flying background and they had the knowledge. What more is there?"

Part Three
475TH **FIGHTER GROUP**

The Pacific Elite

INTRODUCTION

There were two clearly crack P-38 Lightning fighter groups in World War II, namely the 82nd FG in the Mediterranean and the 475th FG in the Southwest Pacific. Both were credited with more than 500 confirmed aerial victories apiece in a remarkably short period of time, and both were staffed with an impressive cadre of highly trained and motivated pilots who transcended the difficulties inherent in their particular operational conditions to create outstanding combat records by war's end.

In the case of the 475th FG, the key to making it an elite combat unit was the personality of Maj Gen George Churchill Kenney, commander-in-chief of the USAAF's Fifth Air Force. His dynamic personality and vision for conducting the air war in the Southwest Pacific were responsible for creating a unit that was despised and feared by the Japanese, and despised and envied by other USAAF units within V Fighter Command.

The list of distinguished accomplishments garnered by the 475th FG is impressive, with perhaps the speed at which its pilots scored aerial victories being the most notable of them all. Averaging about 20 victories a month during the 23 months that it was on operations, the 475th was the fastest-scoring fighter group in the Pacific, and among the top ten in the USAAF by war's end. Both of America's leading aces scored at least some of their victories with the group, and, indeed, the two most successful pilots in the Southwest Pacific claimed all of their kills with the 475th.

The hatred toward the group in Allied ranks came about because Maj Gen Kenney insisted on taking the best personnel from other units, which were in the throes of austere staffing themselves, and creating an instant cadre of elite fighting aviators and groundcrews. Just as Maj Gen Claire Chennault had hastily gathered a group of professional and experienced pilots to become the famed "Flying Tigers" of the American Volunteer Group in China, Kenney brought together a tough body of men who guaranteed that a whirlwind would be hurled against the enemy once they entered combat.

Many of the best fighter leaders were transferred in to the group from hard-pressed squadrons elsewhere in the Fifth Air Force. These units also had to be satisfied with combat-weary Lightnings, or other fighter types that were thoroughly obsolescent by 1944, whereas the 475th was equipped with factory-fresh Lockheed fighters. Rivalries with other P-38 groups ensued, but in the end the record of the 475th justified every sacrifice made on its behalf by V Fighter Command.

"BE JOYFUL IN BATTLE"

If circumstances had taken their normal course, the 475th FG would have been activated in the middle of 1943, equipped with the P-40N Warhawk and left to become an ordinary line unit without being given the chance to write the distinguished military history that it eventually did. As it happened, the combination of a firebrand commanding general (Maj Gen George C. Kenney) conferring with an equally resourceful US Army Head-of-General Staff (Gen George C. Marshall), along with an unusually talented group of combat pilots and crews, would severely challenge the enemy and write a remarkable page of history in the Southwest Pacific air war.

The 475th was activated by special authority granted to the Fifth Air Force on May 14, 1943, one day before the group was constituted within the auspices of the USAAF. Maj Gen Kenney had his work cut out when it came to staffing his new fighter unit, since he had to find the pilots and groundcrews from within V Fighter Command. In addition to seeking out good people for the unit, he had to locate pilots who could fly ultra-long-range escort missions, which would be the norm from then on in the Southwest Pacific. Few aviators had the training or experience to conduct such 300-plus mile flights, whilst still defending the bombers against very potent Japanese defenses.

There were three essential sources for the first cadre of 475th aircrew. The core of the new unit would come from the already painfully understaffed groups of V Fighter Command. Five or six pilots would have to be sliced from the lean flesh of each of the nine hard-pressed operational squadrons within the command at the time, and Kenney had specified that none of the choices could be sub-par material. The first groans of displeasure were soon heard from harried squadron commanders who were required to part with men that they felt were the lifeblood of their units.

Another avenue explored by Kenney was the relatively dormant Seventh Air Force based in Hawaii. Following its action during the Pearl Harbor attack on December 7, 1941, the 15th FG had been less than fully utilized from an operational standpoint. Kenney had already benefited from the Seventh Air Force in the late summer of 1942, when he brought in future aces 1Lt Harry Brown, who had claimed a "Val" dive-bomber during the Pearl Harbor attack and scored further kills with the 49th and 475th FGs, and 1Lt Verl Jett, who initially joined the 8th FG and would eventually command the 475th FG's 431st FS.

A number of pilots transferred directly from the 15th FG to the 475th in July 1943, including 1Lts John Cohn, John Knox and Paul Morriss, who went into the 431st, 1Lts Billy Gresham and Howard Hedrick, who joined the 432nd, and 1Lts Ralph Cleague and Robert Tomberg, who were assigned to the 433rd. These pilots were not given any details about their new assignment, but the tacit promise of action appealed to them more than the scant opportunities to fight the enemy in the quiet sector of the Central Pacific. Others transferring into the Fifth Air Force were 1Lt Martin Low, who would briefly serve with the 40th FS/35th FG before taking command of the 433rd FS/475th FG, and 1Lt Joe McKeon, who scored a victory in the P-39-equipped 35th FS/8th FG, before becoming an ace with the 433rd.

Despite bringing in these pilots from the combat backwaters, V Fighter Command primarily relied on the sacrifices made by existing squadrons in-theater when it came to staffing the 475th FG. The 8th FG's 39th FS contributed six pilots, in addition to veteran groundcrews and its own commander, Lt Col George Prentice, who was made CO of the 475th on May 21, 1943. The 431st FS was a direct beneficiary of this infusion of talent from the 49th FG, with its first commanding officer being Maj Franklin A. Nichols, late of the 7th FS. 1Lts David Allen, Harry Brown, Jack Mankin and Arthur Wenige, who all joined from the 49th at this time, duly made their mark by achieving ace status with the 475th.

Frank Nichols already had four aerial victories to his name following his service with the 7th FS's piquantly named flight, "Nick Nichols' Nip Nippers." Nichols was perfectly suited to the spirit of the new 475th FG, and his exuberance and tenacity eventually saw him become a full general in the postwar USAF. His dynamic personality and whirlwind nature served the 431st FS well during its first days in action, and many of the remarkable records set by the 475th in its first actions were largely made possible because of Nichols' energy at the head of his squadron. Indeed, he was only slightly fatigued when he handed the reins of the unit over to Maj Verl Jett in November 1943.

Equally talented personnel came to the 432nd FS between May and July 1943, with Maj Frank Tompkins, Capt James Ince and 1Lt Noel Lundy being transferred in from the 80th FS/8th FG. Tompkins was the 432nd's first CO, and Ince served as interim commander for a time too. Future 432nd FS CO 1Lt John Loisel joined from the 36th FS/8th FG at this time too, and he would subsequently rise through the ranks to become the 475th FG's final wartime commander.

Loisel was a tall and lean officer with a taciturn but genial manner. He was, in fact, a signal leader in the orientation and training of pilots into service with the P-38. With brisk aplomb, Loisel was largely responsible for assuring that pilots assigned to the new group were indoctrinated in the efficient operation of the Lockheed fighter, as well as the unusual air discipline needed for aerial combat tactics. His stewardship ensured, for example, that pilots knew how to use the emergency features of the P-38, like single-engine operation and the manual employment of hydraulically operated functions, as well as the importance of maintaining flight integrity and radio discipline in the combat area.

Naturally, the formation of a new offensive fighter force was heavily wrapped in secrecy, so those selected for the unit were unaware of the specific reason for their transfer. It was theater policy to weed out pilots who had been involved in more than one aircraft crash, or who had shown undisciplined behavior in operational conditions. Some of the men selected for the 475th were therefore convinced that they had made some indiscretion which marked them for banishment. Only when large groups of highly qualified pilots and other personnel were gathered at air depots for transportation to Australia did the exciting rumor spread that exceptional crews were being assembled for a special assignment. One of the mechanics involved was Sgt Carl A. King, formerly of the 9th FS, where he had worked on both P-38 and P-40 engines, before he and the others selected from his unit were packed off to Australia on June 29, 1943;

> We took off from Port Moresby and landed at Seven-Mile airfield at about 0815hrs, and then went to Ward's airfield to get an airplane to Townsville, in Queensland. By 1128hrs we were in the air once again in a C-47 headed out to sea – at Ward's, we saw four of the new four-engined Douglas C-54 transports. We landed at Garbutt Field, in Townsville, at 1600hrs, ate and then got a train south at 2200hrs that same night. We stayed on the train for two days and two nights, and at 0630hrs on Thursday, July 1, 1943, we pulled into Brisbane. There were trucks there to take us to Amberly Field, and by 0730hrs we were at our new home, which was cold as hell.

Sgt King would soon find himself working on one of the 75 brand-new P-38Hs assigned to the 475th, which would arrive at Amberly Field in gradual increments over coming weeks.

If the remaining squadrons of the Fifth Air Force had reason to resent the preferential treatment given to the new group, then there would have been justification for open revolt from other USAAF commands had they got wind of the deployment of scarce P-38s to the Pacific. Three groups in the Mediterranean, with two more scheduled to relieve the long-range bomber escort shortage in England, had to be content with what they could scrounge from the meager stocks of available P-38s. The formation and equipping of the 475th had to be kept secret from the USAAF's overseas commands, as well as the enemy!

At unit level, Sgt King was assigned to "B Flight" in the 431st FS, and he saw his charge for the first time on July 8, 1943. He and his fellow groundcrew immediately began working on the P-38, which gave them "holy trouble" until the 432nd FS borrowed it and reported no trouble. The latter squadron received its first Lightning – a combat-weary P-38G-5 presumably from a service unit that repaired worn and damaged aircraft and assigned them to different units – which was charged to the care of the squadron's engineering section on June 23. By the end of that month the 432nd had taken delivery of an additional six P-38Hs.

The squadron's personnel strength was also increased with the addition of Capt Danny Roberts as operations officer, Capt Arsenio Fernandez as adjutant and Capt Ronald Malloch as intelligence officer. Roberts had already enjoyed success with the 80th FS, scoring two kills with the P-39 and two with the P-38 before his old unit reluctantly gave him up to the 475th FG. Roberts would go on to attain legendary status with the 432nd FS, claiming three more victories before joining the 433rd FS as its CO in October 1943. He downed a further seven Japanese fighters with his new unit prior to being killed in a mid-air collision with another P-38H shortly after securing his 14th victory on November 9, 1943.

Things were not quite as felicitous in the formation of the 433rd, however. A perfectly sound line pilot who had little in the way of administrative experience was selected to command the new squadron, newly promoted Capt Martin Low, formerly of the 40th FS/35th FG, making some immediately unpopular decisions, not the least of which was an unfortunate choice for first sergeant. The new top enlisted man in the squadron showed an immediate disdain for subordinates, and his treatment of the enlisted grades made him greatly disliked, subsequently causing morale on the line to drop precipitously.

The disfavor extended, justly or unjustly, to the squadron commander himself, who had a reputation as a fairly good combat formation leader, but was forced to take increasingly tough measures on the ground in order to retain some semblance of control of his unit. One of Low's most hated orders was the removal of names from the promotion lists unless the individual concerned was shown to be well-deserving.

Veteran pilots from the 433rd generally saw Capt Low in a more kindly light, and he eventually went home on rotation in early October 1943 and subsequently saw further combat as CO of the Eighth Air Force's P-38-equipped 55th FS/20th FG in 1944, during which time he won a Silver Star. The first sergeant has remained nameless over the decades, enlisted 433rd veterans being reluctant to mention him. The squadron's early combat results suffered because of the generally low spirit of the 433rd, but things would dramatically improve once Capt Danny Roberts took charge on October 3, 1943.

TRAINING AND FIRST COMBAT

Although events at Amberly slowly began to evolve into some sort of military order as July 1943 progressed, Col Prentice drew concern from his veteran pilots for his apparently clueless approach to aerial combat. He was reputed to be a fearless fighter pilot, but some of his wingmen claim that they were often left to frantically deal with enemy aircraft that he had allowed to get onto his tail.

Fortunately, Prentice apparently saw the light (or was shown it!) and left leadership of group combat formations to more capable pilots, instead preferring to focus his attention on his penchant for ground organization. One of the important points that Prentice tried to emphasize early on was group coherence and integrity of formations in the air. However, when the author mentioned this focus on group integrity to random veterans from the 475th, he was greeted with baffled shrugs. There was fierce loyalty within the squadrons, but apparently no desire to identify closely with the other units.

Having said that, the matter of formation discipline was stressed to the point of reflex action from the minute the group was established. There were a few mavericks who ventured off on their own at times, but in general the 475th was distinctive in its adherence to maintaining at least flights of four. As a result, the Japanese came to recognize the red, yellow or blue spinners of large flights of P-38s diving down on their formations, and referred to this dangerous enemy in unkind terms – even before they had an inkling of the 475th's real identity.

Training began as soon as P-38s were available for service. Sgt King mentioned in his journal that he had many difficulties with the first Lightnings given over to his charge. Frequently, he would work throughout the night to bring his aircraft to flying status, only to have supply shortages force him into inactivity for days when he could not get the right parts to fix his fighter. Sgt King's experience was common for the servicing crews of the neophyte group, but the intervals of inactivity were not periods of great suffering since the pleasures of Brisbane were easily available, and popular with crews used to the privations of jungle camps.

Of course there were unfortunate results to the initial disorder of the organization. One of the first caused the death of 431st FS pilot 1Lt Richard Dotson, whose P-38 crashed and burned during an attempted landing on July 5, 1943. Records indicate that four days later fellow squadron pilot 1Lt Andrew K. Duke was killed when he crashed flying 431st FS P-38 "136" at Mareeba, in northern Australia. Capt Harry Brown damaged "118" by running into a tree, and "122" had a taxiing accident at around the same time.

One positive feature of the organization of the group in Australia was the presence of resourceful requisitions people. The first 475th camp was established at Amberly in June 1943, with the appearance of neat rows of tents and several buildings of wood, canvas, concrete and screening to fend off the various insects that dominated the area. Talented supply officer Capt Claude Stubbs, aided by 1Lt Davis and Sgts Bryant and Joseph, developed reputations for gathering materials necessary for the group to attain operational status. By the end of July the 475th was beginning to look like a frontline organization on the ground, although its formations in the air still left a lot to be desired.

Technical inspection of group engineering was initially entrusted to World War I veteran Capt Albert Dossett. He had served in the Army for 26 years by the time he finally rotated home, and was reputed to have taken no leave while assigned to the 475th. His place was taken by Capt Bill Pruss, who had been doing the job for the 432nd FS. Pruss, in turn, was replaced by CWO Greg Kowalski in the 432nd FS, and the latter was eventually succeeded by redoubtable nine-kill ace 1Lt Joe Forster when Kowalski also returned home on rotation.

Training of pilots and groundcrews progressed in Queensland until late July 1943, when the pressing state of the Pacific War dictated that the group be thrown into action now that they had achieved an acceptable standard of operational proficiency. By the end of the month the 475th had begun its ponderous movement northward, sending air and ground echelons to Port Moresby, on the southern coast of New Guinea. Sgt King watched his P-38 leave Amberly on July 29, and he was now anxious to get back into action following his brief time in Queensland. In the interim, King received another brand-new Lightning:

> I got a new ship today and she is a "beaut" – P-38H-5-LO 42-66742, complete with a new paint job. I also loaded ten 2½-ton trucks today with equipment to be sent by boat on our trip north.

King's new Lightning would see action in the very first engagement fought by the group, the aircraft clashing with Japanese fighters on the afternoon of August 16, 1943 when future five-kill ace and ex-9th FS/49th FG pilot, 1Lt Jack Mankin, was credited with the destruction of a "Zeke" and a Ki-43 "Oscar" over Marilinan. Two days later Capt Verl Jett used King's 42-66742 to destroy a pair of "Zekes" over Wewak.

Perhaps because the personnel involved with the group were a cut above the ordinary combat crews in-theater due to their previous frontline experience, the final stages of the 475th's training and organization rapidly took shape once it reached New Guinea in early August. Tension built in anticipation of the first operational mission, and 431st FS records suggest that the unit's provision of escorts for transports heading to Tsili Tsili on 12 August marked the group's combat debut. However, the lack of any documentation surrounding this operation suggests that it was either canceled or assigned to another group.

The 432nd FS had followed the 431st FS to Port Moresby by the 12th, and the unit flew its first mission the very next day when Capt Danny Roberts led 15 P-38s on a three-hour escort of transports again bound for Tsili Tsili. Although this proved to be little more than a routine flight, seven future aces (Roberts, James "Impossible" Ince, Fred "Squareloop" Harris, John Loisel, Paul Lucas, Billy Gresham and Grover Gholson) got some valuable operational flight time in the P-38 under their belts.

Theater-wide, aerial opposition was certainly heating up as aggressive American combat formations sought to engage Japanese fighters and bombers over their home bases. For example, just 24 hours after the 432nd FS had completed its escort mission to Tsili Tsili, P-39s from the 35th FG downed more than ten Japanese aircraft in exactly the same area. On the 16th it would be the 431st FS's turn to take on the enemy – and thus provide the 475th FG with its first victories – during yet another transport escort mission, this time to Marilinan.

Squadron Mission No 5 began at 1225hrs when 15 P-38s took off to rendezvous with their charges. The first sight of the enemy came at about 1520hrs over Marilinan, when the 431st's pilots, who were cruising at 21,000ft, looked up just in time to spot 15-plus Japanese fighters diving down on them from the northeast. The P-38 pilots immediately dived away and took violent evasive action in an effort to avoid a disaster at the hands of the enemy in their very first encounter.

Capt Harry Brown was listening to warnings from his fighter controller when he heard 1Lt David Allen shout over the radio that he was being attacked from the rear. Brown then saw eight enemy fighters descending towards him too, so he pushed the nose of his P-38 down and led his flight out of harm's way. Once he thought that it was safe to turn into the sun so as to regain the initiative, he wheeled the Lightnings back in the direction of Marilinan.

Brown was able to see 1Lt Allen shoot the wing off an "Oscar" and send another aircraft, tentatively identified as a B5N "Kate" torpedo-bomber, down in flames. When other Japanese fighters began closing in on the remaining flights, Brown led his own P-38s down into the fight and chased away at least one enemy aircraft with an inconclusive burst of fire.

Climbing once again to regain the advantage of altitude, Brown sighted another "Oscar" (he identified it as a "Zeke") above him and carefully aimed from dead astern until his fire caused an explosion in the fighter's cockpit. He then lined up a second Ki-43 in his gunsight and shared in its destruction with another P-38. Finally, a third "Oscar" pulled up into a hammerhead stall directly in front of Brown's fighter, which hit the Japanese fighter so hard with cannon shells and machine-gun fire that the Ki-43 exploded while it was almost motionless at the top of the stall.

1Lt Lowell Lutton was leading the last Lightning flight into the heart of the fight when he and his wingman, 2Lt Orville Blythe, were separated from the second element. They charged head-on at two "Oscars," and the first Japanese fighter turned away while Lutton shot off part of the engine and canopy of the second – Blythe saw the Ki-43 spin away into the jungle below. The latter's P-38 had been so badly damaged in the head-on pass that he had to make a forced landing at Marilinan's airstrip. Prior to setting his fighter down, Blythe had also witnessed the crash of the second "Oscar" credited to 1Lt Art Wenige during the course of the mission.

As previously mentioned, 1Lt Jack Mankin had taken Sgt King's P-38 into the fray and shot down an "Oscar" that burst into flames after the Lightning pilot had opened fire from close range. Then Mankin and his wingman, 2Lt Paul Smith, attacked another Ki-43 and an aircraft that looked like a "Kate" dive-bomber. Mankin destroyed the "Oscar" and Smith set the B5N alight. Mankin was impressed with Smith, who had managed to stay with him throughout the entire engagement.

Good fortune allowed the 431st FS to claim 12 victories following this clash, with only 1Lt Blythe's P-38 being damaged in return. It had been a morale-building engagement which had reinforced the training and tactics drummed into the 475th's pilots by the group's senior officers. Among the future aces claiming their first kills on this day was 1Lt Warren Lewis, who would subsequently destroy a further six aircraft and lead the 433rd FS from November 1943 through to August 1944. His combat report for August 16, 1943 detailed the action as follows:

At 1525hrs I saw two flights of Zeros attack "Red Flight" over the strip, so I dropped tanks and led "White Flight" on a rear quarter pass. Zeros broke off climbing. I then turned to the north and saw a flight of Zeros attacking a P-47 flight. I made a 60-degree deflection pass on a Zero chasing a P-47, firing from 150 to 350 yards. The Zero, which was of the "Oscar" type, went into a roll as if hit. I passed over him, and after turning, I could not find him. I do not make any claim for the destruction of enemy aircraft.

Nonetheless, Lewis was given credit for a kill as Allied personnel at Tsili Tsili had seen the Ki-43 crash following his attack. Confirmation reached the group through eyewitness testimony that was transmitted via the 40th FS/35th FG. This victory only added to the 475th's jubilation, and the group went on to claim even greater successes in coming days.

WEWAK CAMPAIGN

475th FG formations mounted the group's first bomber escort to the Japanese fortress at Wewak on August 17, although they took the enemy by such surprise that very few enemy fighters managed to get into the air to oppose the strike. The P-38s covered B-25s that were sent in at low level to drop parachute bombs on the parked enemy aircraft at the main airfield in the area. Some 50 Japanese fighters and bombers were destroyed, although only a handful of these were actually shot down.

The Wewak mission took five hours to complete, draining the fuel tanks of the escorting fighters – five 432nd P-38s had to land at Marilinan to refuel prior to heading back home. Although the 475th FG still had much to learn about conserving gasoline for future long-range escort missions, the group nevertheless sent more fighters to Wewak just 24 hours later. Some 48 P-38s started taking off from Port Moresby at 0700hrs on August 18, these aircraft providing low cover for more B-25s attacking Dagua airfield. Fifteen P-38s of the 431st were the first USAAF aircraft over the target, overflying the mission objective a few minutes before 1000hrs at an altitude of just 4,000ft.

Once again, the Japanese seemed to have been caught flat-footed, as only a handful of "Oscars" from the 24th Sentai were encountered on patrol. These aircraft reported spotting a force of 40 American aircraft heading north over Hansa Bay, which in turn resulted in the immediate scrambling of seven more "Oscars" from the 24th Sentai, five Ki-61 "Tony" fighters from the 68th Sentai and two twin-engined Ki-45 "Nicks" from the 13th Sentai – all these aircraft were based at Borum. Nine Ki-43s from the 59th Sentai at But airfield also intercepted the raid.

The 431st FS pilots soon sighted enemy fighters above them as they raced over Dagua airfield in an effort to sweep it clean of any aerial opposition for the approaching B-25s. They all switched to internal fuel before dropping their external tanks in preparation for the impending fight. The weather had been reasonably clear en route to Wewak, but now it was clouding over. Sporadic showers were encountered as the P-38 pilots watched the Japanese fighters dive down on them.

1Lt Lowell Lutton was an old hand from the 8th FS/49th FG, and he was leading "Blue Flight" when he followed "Red" and "White" flights up into the enemy attack. The B-25s had just hit their target, and the 431st was inland of the Japanese airstrip, so Lutton felt confident that he could concentrate on the enemy fighters while the bombers retreated over the sea. An "Oscar" pulled up in front of Lutton's P-38, allowing him to fire inconclusively before having to break off his attack. He then saw another Ki-43 falling in flames, and Lutton later learned that flightmate 1Lt Don Bellows had shot it down.

Lutton had lost his flight in the subsequent wild maneuvering over Wewak, so he quickly found two other P-38s that were soon the focus of attention for a determined "Oscar" pilot who made a head-on attack. When the two Lightnings broke after passing the enemy fighter, Lutton succeeded in getting in a good shot at the Ki-43, which burst into flames and fell away into the jungle below.

Now alone once again, Lutton quickly joined up with two more P-38s which, coincidentally, endured yet another head-on pass from a solitary "Oscar." This time, however, all three Lightning pilots got on the tail of the wildly gyrating enemy fighter, but only Lutton managed to follow him long enough to get in some good shots when the Ki-43 turned away from Dagua airstrip and headed out to sea. The P-38 pilot overshot the "Oscar," and when Lutton looked back he could not find his foe. He did, however, see flames on the surface of the water from what must have been a crashed enemy aircraft. Lutton then joined up with other P-38s to cover the retreating B-25s.

The first two Lightnings that Lutton had tried to formate with early on in the engagement had been flown by 1Lts Tom McGuire and 2Lt "Fran" Lent. Lutton had seen at least one "Oscar" shot down by the pair, and it is a matter of record that McGuire was credited with the destruction of two Ki-43s and a Ki-61 and Lent a "Hamp" for their first victories.

One indication of the confusion inherent in aerial combat comes from the combat reports lodged by Japanese fighter pilots that survived the August 18 action. 475th records indicate that enemy pilots were skilled and aggressive in this engagement, and Chutai (flight) leader Nanba Shigeki of the 59th Sentai was certainly that. He was leading six "Oscars" into the battle when he was cut off from his charges by a large number of P-38s. This was his first real encounter with the Lockheed fighter, and he wrote in his report that he was dismayed to find that he could not outrun or outclimb it.

Although Shigeki's Ki-43 was hit several times, he was skilled enough to evade destruction by using the breathtaking maneuverability of his fighter. When his attackers turned away, apparently satisfied that he was shot down, Shigeki chose to engage his pursuers rather than escape. It can be assumed from some of the 431st after-action reports, therefore, that the P-38 pilots were convinced that they were being bounced by an entirely different fighter, rather than the one they had just shot up. Shigeki was finally able to crash-land his "Oscar" on But West airfield after the raid subsided. Again, following a careful study of 475th FG after-action reports, it is possible that as many as four pilots claimed to have shot the resourceful Shigeki down!

The 432nd FS was also heavily engaged over Wewak on the 18th, and the unit scored its first victory when Capt William Waldman claimed an "Oscar." 2Lt Paul Lucas did not manage a kill on this mission, although he filed an after-action report that reflected the fury of the clash:

I was flying the wing of 1Lt Grover Gholson and had just come within sight of But airfield when I heard someone report "Zeros at 'ten o'clock'" and everybody began dropping belly tanks. I dropped mine and made a wide half-circle to the left and came back over But on the land side. A Zero was diving away from another P-38, and 1Lt Gholson made a high, tight turn and came in on the Zero's tail. I cut inside and down and got a short full-deflection shot at the Zero. I don't think he was hit. The Zero was a bright natural aluminum color, and had evenly rounded wingtips and a radial engine.

In pulling out of my dive, I lost 1Lt Gholson and had lost too much altitude, so I went wide and started to climb back up. While climbing, I saw a P-38 chase a Zero in a vertical climb up into a cloud – the Zero did a tight Immelman turn and nosed down into a head-on attack on the P-38. The P-38 broke off and dove away. There didn't seem to be any Zeros left, so I joined seven P-38s headed for Marilinan. I landed there.

With the destruction of an additional 15 Japanese aircraft by its pilots following this mission, the 475th had achieved an impressive 27 kills in its first two encounters with the enemy. The effort expended by Maj Gen Kenney in creating an elite offensive unit was paying immediate dividends. The group had suffered its first loss on August 18, however, when 2Lt Ralph Schmidt of the 431st FS failed to return to Port Moresby – he was last seen flying alone after becoming separated from his flight.

Yet another sparkling performance was put in by V Fighter Command's P-38 force during the third strike on Wewak, flown on August 21. The 475th sortied 33 P-38s for a high cover mission over a force of B-25 Mitchells that left their base at 0730hrs and arrived overhead the target at 1000hrs.

1Lt Tom McGuire was leading "Blue Flight," with 2Lt "Fran" Lent once again flying as his wingman, when calls came in from the low cover fighters requesting help in fending off Japanese interceptors at 3,000ft. McGuire finally sighted the milling dogfight below, and he took his flight down to attack. One "Oscar" (claimed as a "Zeke") fell to a 45-degree blast from McGuire's guns, and Lent watched the fighter crash in flames into the jungle below.

Although the second element of McGuire's flight had become separated during this initial contact with the enemy, 1Lt David Allen made short work of another "Oscar" that appeared ahead of him. Both this aircraft and a second Ki-43 that fell to McGuire's fire – giving him ace status – were seen to crash by Allen (who also "made ace" later that day with three fighters destroyed to add to his previous four kills) and Lent.

McGuire then confirmed the destruction of a twin-engined fighter (possibly a Ki-45) for Lent, which he saw crash into the jungle below. McGuire also claimed to have damaged a twin-engined aircraft after he observed hits on its wing, engine and cockpit. There was in fact only one "Nick" of the 13th Sentai listed as lost in Japanese records, although no fewer than four American pilots claimed to have destroyed one apiece.

It seems from the language used in the after-action reports from the 21st that most of the attackers were firing at the same target, and simply claiming that their fire was doing the job of destruction! In spite of the subsequent controversy that surrounded the legendary Tom McGuire, it may at least be said of him that he was prudent in making his claims on this particular occasion.

Capt Danny Roberts also had a fruitful day whilst leading the 432nd FS's "Clover" (unit call-sign) flights. Ordering his 14 Lightnings down to protect the B-25s, which were under attack by "Oscars" and "Tonys," his flight became embroiled in a swirling dogfight when still more Japanese fighters bounced the P-38s. The 432nd FS pilots claimed 12 enemy aircraft shot down, two of them confirmed for Roberts (he stated that they were "Hamps" rather than Ki-43s), which gave him ace status – he already had four kills to his name from his P-400/P-38 days with the 80th FS/8th FG.

1Lts Fred "Squareloop" Harris and John Loisel each claimed two "Tonys," 1Lt Campbell Wilson downed two "Nicks," and 2Lt Billy Gresham and 1Lt Grover Gholson a "Nick" apiece. Finally, 2Lts Elliott Summer and Paul Lucas each destroyed single "Oscars," which they identified as "Zekes" at the time.

1Lt Loisel had been leading the second element of "White Flight" on the approach to Wewak when he heard Roberts give the order to drop tanks over the radio. He later reported:

I saw P-38s and enemy fighters at a distance straight ahead of me. We all dropped our tanks when our leader dropped his at 9,000ft. I made successive passes at an inline fighter (a "Tony"), two Zeros (probably Ki-43s) and a twin-engined fighter. Then I saw a yellow-nosed Zero, high at "seven o'clock," close and shooting. I dived with my wingman across in front of another element and lost him. I then made a head-on pass at a twin-engined fighter and fired at a Zero in a slight bank at "two o'clock." He passed close under my left wing. My wingman, 2Lt Lucas, also fired and hit him – he saw him burn.

I made my next pass at an inline fighter and followed up with a head-on pass at close quarters. I saw the wing of my foe peeling off in large pieces, and I believe that one of these pieces struck 2Lt Lucas' wing. I claim this aircraft destroyed.

A single P-38 was then spotted in the general vicinity of Borum, with five or six enemy aircraft dodging in and out of the clouds just over the hills behind it. I dived down on a "Tony" just as it began to roll out on the tip of an Immelman. I pressed home my attack to within 50 yards. The pilot never completed the full roll. Instead, he fell away trailing smoke and out of control. As he was at low altitude (1,500ft), I am sure that he could not have pulled out. The clouds were at my level, and as he fell one passed between us, so I did not see him crash. I claim this aircraft destroyed. Shortly thereafter, I ran out of ammunition and followed my leader away. Initially landing at Tsili Tsili, I returned to base after refueling.

Squadronmate 2Lt Elliot Summer recorded a spectacular victory about five minutes after he saw "Squareloop" Harris destroy his first "Tony" – aside from the two Ki-61s that he shot down, Harris also damaged four more "Tonys." Summer's victim smoked badly for several seconds before bursting into flames and exploding. He then witnessed Harris shoot another Ki-61 off the tail of 432nd FS pilot 2Lt Tom McGuire (not the 431st FS ace). The latter's P-38 was one of the few to suffer any kind of damage during this mission when one of its engines was shot out. Several others were also holed, but all 475th FG aircraft eventually made it home.

As 2Lt Summer left Wewak, he looked back to see at least five Japanese aircraft heading to their bases trailing smoke behind them. At that point he was too occupied with staying with the other P-38s and vacating the area to note if any of them subsequently crashed.

August 21 had seen the group fly yet another long mission that required a number of pilots to land at Marilinan short of fuel. To a man, they were glad to be down on solid ground after a hard fight.

Sgt King noted the mission, and its cost on his efforts to keep aircraft operational, in the following entry in his journal:

> Got my ship in commission and we pulled the ninth mission today to Wewak. Capt Nichols (in P-38H-1 42-66540) got one and then almost got killed – his ship is shot all to hell, but he is now an ace. 1Lt Allen got three, which made him an ace too. 1Lt McGuire claimed two to become an ace also. 2Lt Lent got two for his first kills, and the squadron now has a total of 35 aircraft shot down in just two weeks of combat time. We only have 19 P-38s left, however. So far we (431st FS) have lost "110," "111," "114," "117," "122" and "123."

The 431st FS's Capts Frank Nichols and Harry Brown and 1Lts David Allen and Tom McGuire were all now aces with at least five aerial victories to their credit, although only McGuire had claimed all of his kills with the 475th FG. Allen was the leading ace in the group with seven confirmed victories, five of them having been scored with the 431st, while Brown had become the group's first ace on August 16 when his three Ki-43s were combined with two victories he had scored in 1941–42. Nichols' solitary P-38 kill was added to four victories he had claimed while flying P-40Ks with the 7th FS/49th FG in 1942–43 to give him ace status. The 475th FG had paid a modest price for this success – two pilots killed in training, one lost in an operational accident and another posted missing in action.

The 14th and final mission flown to Wewak in August 1943 was mounted on the 29th, when 30 P-38s from the 475th FG helped escort B-24s on a high-altitude strike. Seven Japanese interceptors were claimed to have been destroyed by the group, three of which fell to the 431st FS. One "Oscar" was claimed by 1Lt Harold Holze and another Ki-43 and a Ki-61 were downed by 1Lt Tom McGuire (flying his favorite Lightning 42-66592) to give him seven confirmed aerial victories. He was now tied with 1Lt David Allen as the group's top scorer.

This mission showed a remarkable aspect of Tom McGuire's emerging nature as a pilot. A veteran of combat in the Aleutians and New Guinea with the 54th PG and 49th FG respectively, his numerous experiences in action seemed to have instilled in him an utter fearlessness when it came to engaging the enemy. Some of McGuire's squadronmates became convinced that he was almost eerily talented, while others believed that he was not much more than an ordinary pilot with an enormous amount of drive to become the leading American fighter ace of all time. McGuire's combat report for the August 29 mission gives some indication of the enigma that he would become:

I was leading "Blue Flight." We took off from Berry airfield [Port Moresby] at 0615hrs. My wingman "snafued" shortly after take-off so I led a three-ship flight over the target. I saw three medium-sized ships in or near Bogia Harbor.

At 1050hrs I saw two Zeros making a pass at the bombers at 17,000–18,000ft. We dropped belly tanks and I led my flight in – the Zeros ("Oscars") saw us and dived away to the left. I lost my flight at that point. The lead ship pulled up and I got several good bursts at him. The Zero started straight down smoking, then blossomed into flames. This Zero was silver-colored with a dull finish. I made a pass at another Zero but with no results observed.

At this time I saw a "Tony" start in at the bombers. I made a head-on pass and then, turning, got several shots in deflection, seeing him lose height whilst smoking and on fire. Being at 13,000ft, I started back for altitude when I noticed three Zeros and a "Tony" coming down on my tail. Tracers started going by as I stuck my nose down and gave it the throttle. The Zero farthest to the left shot out my left engine, setting it on fire. I shut the engine down and let the propeller windmill, slipping down to 9,000ft and thus putting the fire out – I also used this slipping as an evasive tactic. Two of the enemy fighters followed me down shooting, and I continued on in a 45-degree dive. They left me just before I entered clouds at 4,000ft.

I continued on toward the mountains under scattered clouds, then on to Marilinan, where I made a one-engine landing. I left my ship there and returned to base by transport the next day. Flak during this mission had been intense, and it appeared to be accurately aimed at the bombers flying between 16,000ft and 20,000ft. Enemy tactics were studied and effective. They sent some fighters down at the bombers, but kept others back which eventually dived on us when we attacked those aircraft trying to reach the B-24s. They also had some fighters positioned below the heavy bombers, attacking their vulnerable undersides. The Japanese fighter pilots appeared to be both experienced and eager.

Tom McGuire's first Lightning (P-38H-1 42-66592, which he nicknamed *PUDGY*) was written off charge at Marilinan following the August 29 mission. Stuck miles from home, McGuire hastily made his report to the 35th FG. 41st FS intelligence officer 1Lt Samuel Yorty made a final general remark to describe the cool nerve of the young 475th fighter ace after debriefing him:

This pilot remained calm in spite of the fire in his engine, and thereby successfully brought himself and his airplane safely to this base.

HUON GULF AND RABAUL

Both Japanese and Allied records agree that Wewak endured a series of hard blows that had left it reeling by September 1943. Maj Gen George Kenney was satisfied that his air forces could now take the war to the enemy, at least on a limited scale, and he reported this fact to Gen Douglas MacArthur, Supreme Commander of Allied Forces in the Southwest Pacific Area. MacArthur was ultimately determined to make a triumphant return to the Philippines, and the route to his objective had to be over the northern coast of New Guinea in order to both clear the enemy from his flanks and to be within bombing range of the myriad Philippine islands occupied by Japanese forces.

One immediate logistical problem that had plagued the 475th FG throughout the Wewak offensive was eased on the last day of August when the group began its relocation from its various Port Moresby airstrips to Dobodura, on the northern coast of New Guinea. This new base was at least 20 minutes flying time closer to Wewak, and was much more in the sphere of action for the vital areas of New Britain and the Bismarck Sea. The 432nd FS's Capt Danny Roberts led the first air contingent to Dobodura on August 31.

By September 1943 the Fifth Air Force was well poised to support an Allied offensive against Japanese bases in eastern New Guinea, as well as those further along the northern coast. Attacks against Wewak continued, nevertheless, and the 433rd FS at last achieved its first aerial kills during one such operation on September 2, when it was tasked with escorting B-25s sent to bomb the still-formidable stronghold. Elsewhere, formations of V Fighter Command P-38s covered B-17s and B-26s attacking Cape Gloucester, on the island of New Britain.

Amongst the pilots conducting the Wewak escort was 2Lt Calvin "Bud" Wire, who was wingman to Capt Herbert Jordan in the last "Possum" (the 433rd's call-sign) flight. Known as a "little scrapper," Wire had commenced his military flying career with the Royal Canadian Air Force in 1941, prior to transferring to the USAAF in the wake of the Pearl Harbor attack. Whilst performing his duty protecting his leader, Wire would shoot down an "Oscar" (misidentified as a "Zeke") for the squadron's first confirmed claim.

As "Possum" flight neared Wewak, Wire was distressed to find that he had fallen several hundred yards behind his leader. It was then that he spotted Japanese fighters closing in from astern and on both sides of the lead P-38, and Jordan seemed oblivious to Wire's cries over the radio for the two of them to rejoin their formation.

When two "Oscars" rolled into a split-ess in an effort to trap Wire while he was separated from his leader, he decided on turning into the enemy fighters. The drill of never maneuvering with Japanese fighters – especially when separated from other Americans – raced through Wire's mind as he pulled hard into the Ki-43s, but he felt that the situation demanded unconventional tactics. And this time it worked, as one of the "Oscars" began to fall apart when accurate fire from the P-38's concentrated nose guns hit it. The other Japanese pilot was apparently unnerved and flew away.

Jordan, meanwhile, had at last spotted Wire's predicament, and he joined up in time to discourage additional enemy fighters from closing on his tail. Wire took up his position on Jordan's wing, shooting at another "Oscar" when the two Lightning pilots flew over the target area at just 4,000ft – he subsequently told the debriefing officer that he saw the Japanese fighter flying away trailing smoke. Minutes later, Wire heard over the radio that the bombers had dropped their loads on the target and were heading home, so both P-38 pilots decided to follow them back to base, with low fuel and ammunition as an added inducement to retreat.

2Lt John Smith was the only other 433rd FS pilot to score a kill during this particular mission when he claimed a "Hamp" (actually a Ki-43) shot down and a twin-engined Ki-46 "Dinah" reconnaissance aircraft badly damaged. Although he had previous combat experience flying reconnaissance missions in New Guinea, Smith was nominated by his squadronmates as being most likely to become a casualty because of his reckless attitude towards combat, and on this mission he almost fulfilled the prophecy.

Becoming separated after tangling with the Ki-43 and Ki-46, Smith soon lost his way whilst trying to get back to Dobodura. His compass was out, and the fix given to him by the Bena Bena radar station was not much help either. Afraid that he was flying into enemy territory, he made a 90-degree turn to the right and continued on until he was almost out of fuel. Smith crash-landed in a field just by the coast, being knocked senseless and suffering some cuts and bruises as the fighter ground to a halt.

Later, he hiked to an Australian radio station at Siabai, which was not on the northern New Guinea coast, but across the bay from Port Moresby! He made it back to his base a few weeks later. Incidentally, Smith's P-38 was recovered in 2005 from its final resting place and is now a possible candidate for restoration.

INTRUSION NORTHWARD

Allied pressure was now building against Japanese positions defending Lae and Salamaua, with Australian ground forces and American paratroopers threatening from the east and north. As part of the military build-up in-theater, radar stations had also been installed in places like Tsili Tsili and Bena Bena to give effective direction to the Allied air forces that would cover the invading convoys approaching from the sea off Lae in early September.

Maj Gen Kenney was confident that his forces could protect the vulnerable troop convoys, in spite of the fact that few replacement pilots or aircraft were available to make good any losses suffered in the immediate future. He also felt that the gamble he had taken in setting up the 475th FG as an elite unit had already paid off, and he stated that the standards set by the group in combat during its August engagements over Wewak were unmatched.

September 4 saw heavy fighting over the invasion beaches in the Huon Gulf, on New Guinea's northern coast, and Maj Gen Kenney's impression of the quality apparent in his aircrews was reinforced during the day in spite of the successes achieved by determined Japanese air attacks.

The 475th FG experienced its first action at 1315hrs, when P-38s of the 433rd FS were scrambled to join Lightnings from the 80th FS/8th FG and P-47s from the 39th FS/35th FG and the newly arrived 348th FG in response to a heavy Japanese bombing attack on the invasion convoy. By the end of the engagement several barges and beachheads had been hit, but the American fighters had accounted for 20 fighters and bombers shot down. Five of these victories were credited to the 475th, with two bombers and two fighters falling to pilots from the 433rd FS, and a Zero, according to official lists, being claimed by Col Prentice himself.

Capt Joe McKeon was an old hand in-theater by the time he waded into the Japanese formations near Lae on September 4. Indeed, he had been one of the pilots transferred from the 15th FG to the 8th FG in August 1942 following Maj Gen Kenney's call for additional pilots for V Fighter Command. Assigned to the 35th FS, McKeon had downed a Zero whilst flying a P-39D over Buna on December 7, 1942 – a fitting way to mark the first anniversary of the Pearl Harbor attack. Transferred to the 475th FG in June 1943, and promoted to captain shortly afterwards, McKeon's after-action report for September 4 read as follows:

Three flights were scrambled on an alert at 1315hrs. I was leading "Blue Flight" in trail of "Red" and "White," and once on course, we headed in a fast climb in the direction of Hopoi. We cut straight across the sea, and at an altitude of 15,000ft, immediately across from Natter Bay, contacted the enemy attacking our shipping. Before reaching the vicinity, "Red" and "White" flights initiated the attack, and from my position I couldn't distinguish the type and number of enemy airplanes. However, I saw two large puffs and trails of white smoke indicating destroyed airplanes, presumably enemy.

On reaching the area, I attacked a group of fighters milling in a circle toward us. Singling one out, I hunted him down for a closing deflection shot, approaching from nearly head-on. He was seen to leave a huge trail of smoke by my wingman. With the exception of a few P-38s, the area was occupied by 30 or more enemy fighters. I circled and climbed outside the area, and then made a head-on pass at several flying at the same level. One made a half-hearted pass at myself and my wingman, who had stayed with me throughout the fight. As we closed to about 150 yards, he half-rolled, straightened out and dove. I fired on him, pushing over at the same time to keep my sights on him – no results were observed.

The preceding action took about 15 to 20 minutes. The area then cleared of all action, and after cruising around for an additional 30 minutes, I headed for home.

2Lt Walter Reinhardt was flying on McKeon's wing, and he added some notes to the action from his perspective:

After Capt McKeon's burst, the "Oscar's" engine caught on fire and smoked heavily. The "Oscar" went into a very steep dive from 14,000ft. This "Oscar," in my estimation, was burning too much to ever reach its home base. He then made a pass on another "Oscar," firing from 100 yards down to 50 yards, without any results noticed. The enemy airplanes then left the area, and after circling we returned home. I got in two passes, but achieved no results. Both "Oscars" came at us head-on as we attacked, then peeled off. The "Oscars" did not seem to press home their attacks. After an attack, they peeled off and got out. I thought I saw one barge afire on the water below us.

Following this clash, a lull fell over the Huon Gulf area during the next few weeks. A few Japanese raiders were claimed by patrols over the landing grounds, but the effectiveness of the fighter control system must have discouraged enemy interference with the operations to secure Lae. V Fighter Command instead turned its attention once more to Wewak, scheduling a series of bomber missions during which P-38 escorts from the 475th FG downed a number of Japanese fighters.

Future aces were amongst the pilots who enjoyed success over Wewak during September, with Capt Verl Jett claiming a "Nick" and 2Lt Vincent Elliott an "Oscar" (again claimed as a "Zeke") on the 13th. The Ki-45 was Jett's fifth confirmed victory (his first had come in a P-39D on December 28, 1942 whilst serving with the 36th FS/8th FG), whilst the Ki-43 was the first of seven for Elliott. 1Lt Warren Lewis got his second (of seven) when he claimed an "Oscar" on September 28, and 1Lt Tom McGuire claimed two more Ki-43s on the same day to raise his total to nine destroyed – once again, both pilots had stated that these aircraft were "Zekes."

Over in the 432nd FS, 2Lt Billy Gresham got two Ki-61s over Marilinan on September 20 for his second and third of six victories. And it was the 432nd FS that set a new record for the 475th over the Lae–Finschhafen invasion area when it tallied 18 victories for the loss of a single pilot on September 22.

The Imperial Japanese Navy (IJN) had been largely ignoring New Guinea and focusing instead on what it considered to be the greater threat in the Solomons, but the loss of Lae–Salamaua and the imminent assault on Finschhafen demanded some sort of response. It duly came in the form of G4M "Betty" bombers from the 702nd and 751st Kokutais, covered by Zeros of the 201st, 204th and 253rd Kokutais, which were despatched on September 21/22 to find and attack the invasion convoys.

When the convoys were finally discovered on the morning of September 22, a force of eight torpedo-armed "Bettys" was sent off in three waves, covered by some 35 Zeros from the three fighter units. It was this force that was engaged by the 432nd, as well as other units, during the early afternoon of September 22 near the Finschhafen invasion area. The Allied fighter controller tracking the approaching Japanese formation gave the US pilots updated plots every five minutes until they finally spotted the enemy aircraft at about 6,000ft, their wings glistening through the broken clouds.

Capt Fred "Squareloop" Harris was the high-scoring P-38 pilot for the day, and his after-action report described his mission experiences on the 22nd:

I saw six "Betty" bombers, with ten Zeros as close cover, and above us were 20 to 30 more Zeros as high cover, doing aerobatics. I immediately told the squadron to drop belly tanks, and we started down on the bombers, trying to head them off before they reached their target. During our dive, we attained a speed of 500mph indicated. As we were approaching them they were also diving at a very high rate of speed, and they went under a thin layer of clouds, temporarily obliterating their whole flight. We went over the top of the thin layer of clouds and ended up right in the middle of their close cover, with their top cover hitting us from above. One of them got on my tail, pouring lead into me. My wingman, 2Lt Zach Dean (in P-38H-1 42-66504), shot the Zero off my tail – I saw it spin into the water.

This attack split up the Zeros completely, and they left their bombers. This left 1Lt Ince's and 1Lt Loisel's flights with a clear pass at the bombers. Our second pass was made at three bombers that were off by themselves. On that pass we got two bombers – I got one which caught fire amidship and went right into the ocean, and my wingman, 2Lt Dean, hit a "Betty" to our left which apparently had not dropped its torpedo because the bomber exploded in mid-air.

Following this attack, we gained a high rate of speed. As we could not see any more bombers, I peeled off after a Zero that was slightly lower and ahead of us. After I fired, he went straight into the ocean. We then climbed up for more altitude in search of more Zeros. We saw a few more Zeros floating around, but they were taken care of by P-38s and P-47s.

At the time that the P-38s and P-47s were mixing it up with the enemy fighters, I saw four Zeros go down. I believe three were hit by the 39th FS and one by the P-47s. At this time I saw a straggler, very low, trying to sneak home. I roared up on him and shot him down. 2Lt John Rundell, who was in my second element, saw him crash after 2Lt Dean and I had passed by.

We circled for about 15 minutes while "Duckbutt" (area fighter controller) searched for more Zeros. The controller then called us and said everything was okay. He next reported that pilots were down in rafts, so we went down to search the area. While we were searching, "Duckbutt" reported that 1Lt Vivian Cloud (in P-38H-1 42-66575) had been rescued and was okay. 2Lt Dean called me and said he was low on gas and out of ammunition, so we assembled our squadron and came home.

Many "Bettys" and Zeros were claimed, even though Japanese losses were limited to seven bombers shot down and an eighth that was forced to crash-land upon reaching its base, while at least eight fighters failed to return from the mission. American claims amounted to 40 Japanese aircraft shot down in total, giving some idea of the complexity and confusion surrounding this large engagement. Whatever the actual totals, the 432nd FS earned a record 18 confirmed claims for a single squadron in a single engagement, for the loss of two P-38s, with one of the pilots being recovered safely.

RABAUL

One of the key Japanese positions that threatened all Allied forces in the South and Southwest Pacific was the fortress of Rabaul, on the Gazelle Peninsula of New Britain. Aircraft operating from airfields surrounding Rabaul could strike at Allied targets either in New Guinea or the Solomons, in addition to maintaining a position of key strategic defense for much of the Pacific theater. The Japanese had put considerable effort into fortifying Rabaul, and the Allies knew full well that it would be a difficult nut to crack.

Gen Douglas MacArthur argued for the invasion of Rabaul, but most other Pacific strategists explained that sanity dictated such a formidable objective be isolated and bypassed. Privately, MacArthur was not keen on invading this Japanese fortress either, but publicly he felt he had to push for such an attack in order to build up his own case for the invasion of the Philippines, which was his primary strategic goal for the theater.

Allied plans were to take enough territory such as the Admiralty Islands, in the nearby Bismarck Archipelago, in order to isolate Rabaul, and then bomb the existing forces on the airfields in the area and in Rabaul's Simpson Harbor to ineffectiveness. Every air commander wanted a crack at the place, so all units assigned to the Fifth and Thirteenth Air Forces, as well as Navy land- and carrier-based aircraft, were poised to attack.

Maj Gen Kenney again led the way by scheduling a bombing raid on October 12, 1943. Upwards of 200 B-24s and B-25s, joined by 16 Australian Beaufighters and an escort of more than 100 P-38s (including a provisional squadron), flew the 300-plus miles to the airfields at Vunakanau and Kokopo (the latter called Rapopo in Allied contemporary reports for some unknown reason) and apparently caught the enemy completely by surprise.

The only fighter claim on the day was made by 1Lt John Fogarty of the 432nd FS, who was flying with the provisional squadron. The 432nd's war diary described the mission as follows:

Today was the day that our pilots have been waiting many months for. The day when they would at last fly over the Japanese stronghold of Rabaul – 100 B-24s, 115 B-25s, 120 P-38s and 16 Beaufighters were to participate in the largest strike ever made against this Japanese base. Twenty of our airplanes took off at 0730hrs to escort the fast-flying, strafing B-25s that were to sweep over Vunakanau and Rapopo airfields. Maj Tompkins, 1Lts Hedrick and Wilson and Flt Off Ratajski were in "Red Flight," Capt Byers and 1Lts Hanson, Summer and Ritter flew in "Blue Flight," Capt Waldman and 1Lts Fostakowski, Gholson and Gresham made up "Green Flight" and 2Lts Farris and Lawhead made up the spares, with 1Lts McGuire and Fogarty flying in the provisional squadron.

The strips at Vunakanau and Rapopo were strafed by the B-25s, and our fliers noticed several fires which might have been burning aircraft. The B-25s also strafed a "Sugar Charlie" and two barges. No interception of any kind was met. 1Lt Fogarty, flying in the provisional squadron, destroyed a stray "Betty" bomber after his flight leader, Maj Smith of Group Headquarters, made the initial pass. All airplanes stopped at Kiriwina for refueling. All bar three returned to base at 1445hrs. The three that remained did so because of small mechanical problems.

Not a round of ammunition was expended, except by 1Lt Fogarty, but 36 belly tanks were dropped. Naturally, all of our pilots were disappointed because they didn't see combat, but they were well satisfied with the results of the mission. Maj Tompkins and Capt Harris were perturbed considerably because the Aussies broke radio silence en route to the target and the crews of the B-25s were guilty of the same act. Shortly after the mission had been completed, Capt Byers was hospitalized with possible malaria.

Two small airstrips on the island of Kiriwina had been prepared as emergency refueling depots for the P-38 escorts, and many aircrew owed their survival to these bare bases created at the north and south ends of the island to receive combat aircraft in need of fuel or repair.

1Lt Ferdinand Hanson was on hand in the 432nd FS at the time of the Rabaul raids, and he made some interesting notes in his diary about the value of Kiriwina, as well as the state of mind of some of the great American aces in-theater:

I remember that we are going to Rabaul in the morning. We have overnighted at Kiriwina so as to be closer to the target. We are standing around waiting at the ready shack for the signal to scramble. The 475th and other fighter groups are involved.

Capt Bong is in full flight gear, sitting on a stump or rock digging into the ground with his survival knife. He is "Mr Cool." Capt MacGuire is just the opposite. Man, he is nervous and jumpy. We all are. He is saying – "Let's get this show on the road – Now!" Dick Bong just looks up, grins a little and then continues digging into the ground. We later get the signal and we take off.

JAPANESE RESPONSE

This first heavy raid on Rabaul demanded some sort of counter-blow from the Japanese, which was delivered quickly but without sufficiently heavy force on October 15 and 17. The target hit was the critically important harbor facility at Oro Bay. This was used as a key staging point for Allied troops and equipment waging the offensive in New Guinea, and a concentrated blow here could have stalled the campaign in the Southwest Pacific for some considerable time.

Fifteen "Val" dive-bombers of the 582nd Kokutai, escorted by 39 Zeros of the 204th Kokutai, took off from Rabaul in the early morning hours of October 15 to attack shipping in Oro Bay. Even with the improved warning network of radar stations and coast watchers, the force was able to penetrate deeply into Allied airspace, partly because they flew some of the way at lower altitude to avoid radar detection.

Amongst the men to enjoy success on this day was prewar fighter pilot Maj Charles MacDonald, who had only joined the 475th FG two weeks earlier after completing a stint as CO of the P-47-equipped 340th FS/348th FG. Posted to the group's headquarters unit, he was just leaving the 475th's HQ building shortly before 0800hrs on October 15 when Capt Jesse Ivey drove up in a jeep and excitedly told MacDonald that a Japanese bombing force was on its way in. The two officers tore off in the jeep and were disappointed at first when they could find no P-38s in the 432nd's dispersal area. However, they soon came across two Lightnings that belonged to the 433rd FS, and MacDonald ordered Bud Wire's crew chief to get his P-38 (aircraft "193") ready for flight.

Wire himself got to the alert tarmac just as MacDonald and Ivey were taxiing across the airfield for the fastest possible take-off. The crew chief, who received some unremitting wrath from his pilot, told Wire that he was not going to argue with a headquarters major, leaving the future ace to watch in frustration as his P-38 took off to meet the enemy without him at the controls.

MacDonald did not even have time to raise his landing gear before he saw that he was going to cross flightpaths with the Japanese dive-bombers. Quickly shooting one down, he then lost Ivey when the latter went after several other "Vals." Another dive-bomber was destroyed by MacDonald, and two others were hit by his fire, before the Zero escort badly damaged his P-38. Although MacDonald was now far out to sea, and unable to spot any other friendly aircraft, he somehow managed to coax the damaged Lightning back to Dobodura, where he made a textbook wheels-up crash-landing.

The mechanics who raced up to the battered P-38 as it steamed on the runway wondered at the major's sanity as he emerged from the shattered cockpit laughing maniacally at the thought of his narrow escape, as well as his first claims as a fighter pilot in combat after four long years in the frontline.

The most successful pilot to emerge from this action was 2Lt "Fran" Lent, who took off in the second element of the first 431st FS formation to depart Dobodura:

We were scrambled from No 12 strip at 0810hrs. I was leading the element in the first flight. We climbed to about 18,500ft over Oro Bay, sighted the enemy and dropped our belly tanks. 1Lt Kirby (in P-38H-1 42-66593) dived down on a "Val" and I saw it burst into flames and fall into the water. I broke away and followed a second "Val" which was heading out to sea. I fired five bursts from approximately 500ft, directly from the rear, and my fire was returned by the rear gunner. Then the "Val" burst into flames and crashed into the sea. This "Val" is confirmed by 2Lt Hedrick.

At this time I saw two Zeros being followed by three P-38s, and I headed out to sea after them. Before I could catch up, both "Zekes" had burned and crashed. I then saw another "Val" about 1,000ft above the water, and as I attacked I was joined by a flight of three more P-38s. I fired a 90-degree deflection shot at this "Val" and missed. The other P-38s got him. I flew on out to sea looking for enemy aircraft, and spotted a "Zeke" heading for home, right down on the deck. Evidently, he didn't see me, because I got right on his tail and fired and he burst into flames and dropped into the water.

After this I saw about three P-38s chasing two "Zekes" and I joined in this fight. One of the "Zekes" did a loop and a half-roll and I got a good deflection shot at him until I got on his tail and kept firing until he burst into flames. After this I was out of ammunition, so I headed home.

By then the 432nd FS had also managed to break into the confused battle, and in just a matter of minutes its pilots accounted for six "Vals," four Zeros and an "Oscar" that had possibly blundered into the engagement. Capt John Loisel got two Zeros to give him five confirmed victories overall, Capt Fred Harris also got two "Vals" to take his tally to seven victories and 1Lt Frank Tompkins destroyed a Zero and a "Val."

Frustratingly for Bud Wire, he had missed the 433rd's best day so far, as his squadron claimed 15 fighters and dive-bombers, including the four racked up by MacDonald and Ivey. One of those to score a kill was Capt Joe McKeon, who got a "Val" to give him ace status.

Two days later, the Japanese again attempted to hit Oro Bay in much the same way that they had done on the 15th. A force of Zeros ranged out over the water toward the base from Rabaul, perhaps with nothing more in mind than to pick a fight with Allied aircraft. There is some evidence to suggest that seasoned pilots from the crack 253rd Kokutai were among the Zeros' pilots in action on this day. There is a chance that one of them might have been CPO Hiroyoshi Nishizawa, Japan's third-ranking ace of World War II, who was flying with the 253rd Kokutai at the time this engagement took place.

At about 0930hrs the alarm was sounded at Dobodura, and P-38s from the 431st and 433rd FSs were scrambled off airstrip No 12 to intercept the force that was reported to be approaching from the direction of Rabaul. Coincidentally, the 432nd FS was just returning from a mission to Lae at the time, and its pilots sighted the enemy formation off in the distance. However, a shortage of fuel demanded that they skirt around the Japanese fighters and land first in order to replenish their tanks.

For the 433rd FS, this would be the unit's first encounter with the enemy under the leadership of Capt Danny Roberts, who had replaced Maj Low as CO on October 3. Capt Marion Kirby was leading the 431st at the head of "Hades Red Flight," with 1Lt Kenneth Richardson as his wingman, and 1Lt Edward Czarnecki, with 2Lt Vincent Elliott as his wingman, in the second element. "Red Flight" was patrolling between Tufi Point and Buna Point when the squadron ran head-on into the Japanese formation. Kirby's after-action report detailed his flight's engagement:

We were at 22,500ft when we saw about 20 "Zekes" at 20,000ft, heading south-southwest. We circled and attacked from the rear. The flight I was leading attacked the foremost "Zekes." I fired at one on this pass but missed, or perhaps damaged it slightly. I then turned to my right (heading towards shore) and made a pass at a "Zeke" which three other P-38s were engaging. I made one pass and then turned to see 1Lt Czarnecki shoot the "Zeke" down. I then headed out to sea again and ran into a number of "Zekes" in a Lufbery circle. I made a pass on three of them, hitting one. 2Lt Elliott saw him go down. I then banked my airplane around and saw 2Lt Elliott hit one, which burst into flames almost immediately.

I was looking for more airplanes when I saw a "Zeke" being chased by a number of P-38s. They all made a pass at it and the last one either got the "Zeke" or it fell to a lone P-40 that was sitting directly overhead the fighter as it came out of a split-ess maneuver – I could not tell from my position. As the "Zeke" was going down, a parachute fell away from it, and as the parachute neared the water I noticed an airplane circling it. I thought it was yet another enemy aircraft, and I went to investigate it, but as I neared the 'chute I identified the circling fighter as friendly.

By now I had gotten a long way away from the fight, and with my motors detonating at high manifold pressure, I decided not to rejoin the engagement. I duly returned to base.

Czarnecki was credited with two Zeros destroyed following the fight, taking his tally to six kills overall. He was forced to bail out of his P-38H over enemy territory six days later and spent three months evading capture until meeting up with other aircrew evaders and being rescued by a US submarine in February 1944.

The successes of October 17 meant that "Red Flight" had accounted for four of the nine Zeros tallied by the 431st on this day. Three of the remaining five claims were submitted by 1Lt Tom McGuire, but he nearly paid with his life for his daring attacks.

Among the positive things to be said about McGuire amid claims that he was reckless and overbearing is the fact that he was a consistent team player who scrupulously followed the policies of his unit, and service in general. In this fight, he was responsible for saving the life of a fellow pilot with such utter disregard to his own safety that he was himself shot down into the sea.

The first of his three victories for the day was observed by Navy Corpsman Arthur Kemp and Marine Corps TSgt J. B. Pruett. McGuire had scrambled at the head of "White Flight," with 2Lt Hunt again on his wing, when the P-38 pilots ran straight into the enemy formation. Kemp and Pruett were watching the progress of the battle through field glasses, and later jointly signed the following statement:

On October 17, 1943, I was watching the aerial combat which took place over Buna Bay. I was standing on the beach looking through field glasses, and had a clear view of the combat. At the beginning of the combat I saw two P-38s attack a "Zeke." One of the P-38s pulled away, but the other one followed the "Zeke" down, firing several bursts, until he too broke away. This second P-38 was the one piloted by 1st Lt Thomas B. McGuire, Jnr, and I saw the "Zeke" on which 1Lt McGuire fired go down smoking and explode just before it hit the water.

McGuire kept diving in and out of the fight, shooting or dodging the fire from the Zeros behind him. He observed one P-38 in apparent mortal danger with two Zeros behind him. Despite McGuire being the target of seven more enemy fighters, he took a 90-degree deflection shot at one of the Zeros menacing his squadronmate and it burst into flames. The ace then closed in on the tail of the second enemy fighter and set this aircraft alight too after opening fire from close range.

By now the seven Zeros immediately behind McGuire were in a perfect position to inflict telling damage on the latter's Lightning – this aircraft was actually assigned to Maj Frank Nichols, since McGuire had yet to receive a replacement for 42-66592, which had been written off in combat on August 29. The Japanese fighters wrecked the P-38's left engine and damaged the right one, as well as shooting out the radio immediately behind the pilot. Shrapnel from the latter hits wrecked the cockpit and wounded McGuire in the arm, wrist and backside.

Desperately fighting for his life, McGuire dived away, knowing full well that he would have to abandon the airplane. He ripped himself free of the jagged cockpit and managed to open his parachute, despite its D-ring handle having been shot away. Now free of his stricken fighter, McGuire floated the short distance down into the water.

Despite being wounded, and bobbing around in a partly inflated, bullet-damaged raft in shark-infested waters, McGuire was more concerned about what his commander was going to say to him in respect to the loss of his airplane than about his imminent rescue. That rescue did come about 45 minutes later when PT boat No 152 plucked the ace from the water. McGuire's luck even extended to the fact that his rescuers had watched the last part of the fight, and Lt George Westfeldt signed another statement verifying that the second pair of Zeros engaged by McGuire had indeed crashed into the sea.

Despite the successes of the 431st FS on October 17, for once the unit's exploits were overshadowed by the 433rd FS thanks primarily to the efforts of new CO, Capt Danny Roberts (who claimed two "Zekes"). Since transferring in from the 432nd FS, he had been instilling the concept of teamwork into his charges, telling his pilots to "hunt like a pack of wolves." This idea so inspired the unit that it claimed ten Zeros for the loss of just one P-38 and its pilot. The 431st had also suffered a single fatality, but had been fortunate in having Tom McGuire returned so expeditiously to the fold. Thus, for the net loss of two pilots and three Lightnings, the 475th FG had added an impressive 19 victories to its tally.

As for Maj Frank Nichols, he took the loss of his P-38 with equanimity since his squadron had now claimed more than 65 victories in just two months of operations, and Tom McGuire had become the leading ace in-theater with 13 kills. Also, Nichols was virtually tour-expired, expecting to turn his squadron over to Operations Officer Verl Jett by the end of the next month.

Despite these attacks on Oro Bay, the Allied offensive against Rabaul went on, and weather conditions permitted a high-level bombing mission by B-24s on October 23. Ten of the approximately 13 claims submitted in the wake of this mission were made by the 475th FG, with the 433rd FS being credited with four of them. Capt Roberts once again led the way with two "Zekes," to boost his tally to 11 kills.

It was the duty of the 433rd FS on this mission to sweep ahead of the bombers and clear away any enemy fighters that were attempting to hinder the B-24s' progress to the target. Roberts related the details of his engagements with the Zeros in his after-action report:

We reached the target area a little early, so we made several circuits outside before entering the target area, at 1215hrs. Several Zeros were observed at 15,000ft in the center of the harbor, and approximately ten single-engined airplanes were between Rapopo and Vunakanau. Twelve Zeros headed out over the water toward Kavieng, but they then turned back and climbed up into our area.

For several minutes, the two squadrons charged with providing the B-24s with low cover were sufficient in number to adequately take care of the Zeros. However, about 15 enemy fighters then appeared, so our squadron dropped its belly tanks and dived down from 25,000ft to 20,000ft. My radio messages were not received by the balance of my squadron, however, and as a result, two of the flights stayed too high, with only "Red" and "White" flights going down.

One flight from the 431st FS delivered an attack on approximately eight Zeros, and when several of the enemy pursued them, I flew directly behind a "Zeke," giving him three short bursts. As the "Zeke" turned right, I fired another burst, which left his left wing very ragged and the airplane burning furiously. I then executed an attack on another "Zeke" from a quarter head-on, firing a long burst. The "Zeke" immediately burned, rolled over and some large object appeared to drop from the cockpit. However, I saw no parachute open. This action took place at 19,000ft. The Nips half-rolled when being attacked. We were too high to do effective work.

This was the most intensive phase of the escorted bombing campaign against Rabaul, with another low-altitude mission being flown the very next day. The low-level raids flown by B-25s and covered by P-38s were usually the most effective, as they elicited the greatest response from the Japanese. October 24, 1943 proved to be yet another fruitful day for the Lightning escorts, who claimed 40 Japanese aircraft shot down, including 12 for the 80th FS/8th FG and 18 for the 475th FG.

On 25 October the B-24s were again unleashed on Rabaul in a high-altitude mission, but on this occasion the often-treacherous weather in the area served the target well, as it forced most of the P-38 escorts to turn back before reaching the objective. In point of fact, only seven Lightnings from the 432nd FS, led by Maj Charles MacDonald, managed to stay with bombers from the 43rd and 90th BGs long enough to protect them from interception.

It was a peculiarity of this mission that Japanese records supported the single fighter claim made by Maj MacDonald (his fourth kill) and credited to the P-38 escort on this date. Those records admit to the loss of two "Zeke" fighters, one of which fell to bomber gunners and the other to the escort, during an interception that was not pressed home with determination.

2Lt Zach Dean (who had claimed two kills the previous day to "make ace") was flying on MacDonald's wing, and he reported witnessing his leader's victory:

The ack-ack was surprisingly accurate, bursting right at our level, which at this time was 28,000ft. It is my belief that they had Zeros calling in our altitude. I saw about eight or ten enemy aircraft at our altitude, or slightly above. One of these foolishly tried to make a pass on seven of us unaided. Maj MacDonald made a beautiful deflection shot and the Nip exploded in mid-air. His complete tail assembly flew to pieces and burned furiously.

Despite poor weather closing down operations against Rabaul for the next few days, Maj Gen Kenney was ecstatic over what he perceived to be the trouncing that his air forces were giving the enemy fortress. In point of fact, only modest damage had been inflicted on the area, and the Japanese quickly repaired their facilities. Indeed, Rabaul would continue to be an effective roadblock to Allied advances in the region for the rest of the year.

Maj Gen Kenney's view that the defenders of Rabaul were now a spent force was challenged on October 29, 1943, when a high-altitude raid by B-24s against Vunakanau provoked a fierce response from Japanese fighters. The 431st and 432nd FSs escorted the "heavies," losing 2Lt Christopher Bartlett from the latter unit to either flak or enemy aircraft. The latter also forced 2Lt Robert "Pappy" Cline to land at Kiriwina with approximately 30 bullet holes in his P-38.

The star performers once again were the pilots of the 433rd FS, ten of whom dived down from 28,000ft over the target to engage an estimated 35 to 40 enemy interceptors harassing the bombers from below. With such numerical inferiority, it was necessary for the Lightning pilots to use conservative tactics, being content to simply divide the attention of the attacking enemy fighters rather than seeking out individual kills.

Nevertheless, six Japanese interceptors were claimed destroyed, including a "Zeke" credited to Capt Danny Roberts for his 13th victory. 2Lt John Smith also downed a "Zeke" for his sixth and final kill – he would perish in action over Alexishafen 11 days later.

1Lt John Babel was at the head of his flight as they dived into the massed ranks of Zeros, and his element leader, 1Lt Donald King, recorded their successes in his after-action report:

As the bombers were withdrawing after finishing their run, we peeled off in pairs and engaged the 35–40 "Zekes," "Oscars" and "Tonys" that were circling loosely through the area at about 18,000ft, attempting to intercept bombers from below. I followed my flight leader, 1Lt Babel, on one deflection pass at a "Zeke," and was about to follow him on another pass when a "Zeke" came down upon us from above and to the left at "eight o'clock high". I wheeled up into him and fired from 200 yards, head-on. We closed very fast, and the "Zeke" clipped my wingtip as he passed by. The "Zeke" was smoking very heavily and went down, followed by 1Lt Babel. The "Zeke" crashed into the ground smoking without having burst into flames. I received no injuries, but the wingtip of my airplane was damaged and must be replaced.

The enemy pilots were better than usual today. They were wary, but fearless once they began a pass on a P-38.

Other Lightning squadrons from V Fighter Command were credited with a dozen more claims, and Maj Gen Kenney was satisfied that the Japanese air forces in the Rabaul area must have been badly crippled following this engagement. He would get the shock of his life four days later.

On November 2 weather conditions finally allowed another massive escorted raid to be undertaken, and Maj Gen Kenney hoped that this would knock out any remaining air power defending Rabaul. The mission called for 75 P-38s to escort B-25s to Simpson Harbor, where the latter would bomb and strafe whatever shipping was present. What the escorting P-38 pilots did not know was that the fighter units in the immediate area had not only made good their losses, but they had been bolstered by reinforcements flown in from aircraft carriers or on temporary deployment from Japanese Army Air Force (JAAF) units in the surrounding areas.

The 431st FS bore the brunt of the action when its Lightnings entered the harbor area at 1340hrs on November 2. As the unit's nine P-38s headed up the Warangoi River toward the harbor itself, they were fired on by destroyers anchored in its mouth. Having been bracketed by heavy flak, the 431st's flights had been forced to loosen their formations, thus making them vulnerable to attack by Japanese fighters. Sure enough, as they raced over the harbor at 2,000ft, the P-38 pilots spotted enemy interceptors diving down on them from 6,000ft. A wild fight ensued, with the Lightning pilots striving to defend themselves and the bombers.

1Lt Art Wenige was leading "White Flight," and he claimed two "Zekes" destroyed to take his overall tally to five kills. His wingman, 2Lt Frank Monk, who also claimed a "Zeke" for his second confirmed victory, described the encounter in the following after-action report:

We followed the bombers as they went across the beach at Cape Gazelle, at which point we were attacked by approximately 60 to 70 enemy aircraft. Moments later I saw 2Lt Lent shoot down a "Zeke," which burned and then crashed. The enemy aircraft dived down to attack both us and the bombers, and we engaged the enemy to divert their attention away from the B-25s.

While 1Lt Lutton was engaged in destroying a "Zeke," which I saw crash in flames, he was attacked from behind by two more "Zekes." 1Lt Wenige attacked one of the enemy aircraft and I attacked the other "Zeke." I saw the "Zeke" that 1Lt Wenige was shooting at spin down out of control and crash into the sea. I fired a long burst at the other "Zeke," but it broke away and I did not see the results of my fire. We made many passes on enemy aircraft that were diving on 1Lt Lutton, 1Lt Wenige and myself. 1Lt Wenige fired at one of them which I saw burst into flames and explode. I fired a short burst at the other "Zeke," but did not see any damage.

Another "Zeke" attacked us from above at approximately "one o'clock." 1Lt Wenige ducked under him and turned left, and I fired a burst into the "Zeke" and saw it start to burn. 1Lt Wenige saw this "Zeke" go down in flames and crash. Again seeing two "Zekes" diving on 1Lt Lutton, 1Lt Wenige and I dived on them. The two "Zekes" broke away and I got in a short burst, but saw no results.

At this time there were approximately five or six enemy aircraft above and on both sides of us. One of those on the right made a diving attack and passed within 50ft of us. This was the last pass made at us by enemy aircraft. We were over the mouth of Wide Bay by this time, and continued on our way to Kiriwina.

1Lt Marion Kirby was leading the 431st FS's "Red Flight" on November 2, and he shot down two "Zekes" to take his finally tally to five kills. One of these aircraft was almost certainly being flown by 11-kill Zero ace Lt Yoshio Fukui. Several P-38 pilots reported seeing a Zero move in to finish off a B-25 and then be shot down by Kirby. Although suffering from burns, Fukui survived the encounter by parachuting from his blazing fighter at low altitude.

Thirteen 432nd FS P-38 pilots split up into three "Clover" flights followed the 431st FS into the dogfight over Rabaul, and they too were forced to scrap for their lives just as the "Hades" flights had done minutes earlier. 1Lt Grover Gholson had led the unit into battle, and he soon succeeded in latching onto the tail of an "Oscar" long enough to send it down in flames. Minutes later he destroyed a Zero for his fifth, and final, victory since arriving in New Guinea in May 1942 – he had claimed his first kill (also a Zero) on May 14, 1942 whilst flying P-39Fs with the 36th FS/8th FG.

Six Japanese interceptors were claimed in total by the 432nd, including a "Tony" for 2Lt Leo Mayo. Unfortunately, Mayo pressed home his attack to such an extent that a large chunk of the Ki-61's wing broke off and mortally damaged his P-38. Seen to bail out just offshore and last observed walking into the jungle, Mayo was never seen again.

The 433rd FS also got into an inconclusive scrap on the 2nd, with probable victories being awarded to Capt Danny Roberts and 1Lt Donald Revenaugh. 2Lt Donald King, who had claimed his fourth aerial victory on October 29, was posted missing in the wake of this mission.

Although the 431st FS had made the most claims with nine confirmed kills, it had also suffered the most casualties with two pilots missing. 1Lt Kenneth Richardson went down near Rabaul, while 1Lt Lowell Lutton, who had just claimed his fifth victory, was spotted joining up at the tail end of 1Lt Wenige's "White Flight" as it left the target area, but he then disappeared sometime after clearing Simpson Harbor. Postwar, in November 1948, Art Wenige made this statement about Lutton's loss:

Again and again on the November 2 mission 1Lt Lutton was singled out for attack by two or three enemy fighters at a time, and he was saved from destruction only by the valiant efforts of other members of the squadron. Despite this, 1Lt Lutton continued to lead his men in passes at the enemy aircraft attacking the bombers, thus showing that he had his squadron's focus and cohesion uppermost in his mind throughout the action.

On the return flight to base, 1Lt Lutton lost his squadron in the overcast and a storm which barred the way back to Kiriwina from Rabaul. Unable to reach Kiriwina, 1Lt Lutton crashed into the ocean, and although a search was made, no trace of him was ever found.

To the best of my knowledge, 1Lt Lutton's P-38, having been hit repeatedly by enemy fire over Wide Bay, went into an extremely shallow dive, struck the surface of the water and sank about 50 to 100 miles southwest of Rabaul.

Fellow 431st pilot 2Lt Owen Giertson enjoyed better luck, however, for after he was shot down during the engagement, he managed to meet up with squadronmate 1Lt Ed Czarnecki. As previously mentioned, the latter pilot had survived a dunking in the same area on October 23, and both men evaded capture until collected by the Allies and transported to Open Bay, on the northwest side of the Gazelle Peninsula. From here, they were eventually picked up by submarine in February 1944. Although both men survived their ordeals and were sent home, Czarnecki was subsequently plagued by ill health after he contracted a tropical disease whilst evading in New Britain. He eventually succumbed to tuberculosis in 1976 following three decades of deteriorating health.

Sgt Carl A. King of the 431st FS made the following entry in his journal after the November 2 mission:

> 1Lt Morriss "Snafu" in "120" (the P-38 serviced by King for Capt Verl Jett) from a Rabaul mission. We got into them and got nine, lost three including 1Lts Richardson and Lutton. That makes 74 Nips shot down.

CHANGES

Two new squadron commanders and a new group CO changed the face, but not the spirit, of the 475th FG in the weeks following the November 2 mission. Sgt King again recorded events in his journal when Maj Frank Nichols left the 431st FS on November 19, 1943:

> We had got the troublesome right engine in "120" all ready to come out when up walked the group CO, who told us not to pull it. I wish they would make up their minds! Maj Nichols then told us that he was going home, and that Capt Jett – my pilot – would be our

next CO. Later that day we all went over to the visiting USO show and saw Gary Cooper, Una Merkel and Phyllis Brooks in person.

Change of command for the 433rd FS was a more somber affair. Capt Danny Roberts had been in charge of the unit for a mere 37 days when he led the November 9, 1943 mission to Alexishafen, situated on the north New Guinea coast. He had just claimed an "Oscar" at low altitude (originally listed as a "Hamp") for his 14th victory, and was chasing another when he made a sudden turn that caused him to collide with his wingman, 2Lt Dale Meyer. Both men perished in the subsequent crash, and as previously mentioned, six-kill ace 2Lt John Smith was also shot down in the same area on the same mission to give the squadron one of its grimmest days in World War II. Mild-mannered future ace Capt Warren Lewis took over command of the 433rd, and he led it until he was declared tour-expired in August 1944.

Maj Charles MacDonald, who claimed two "Zekes" in the same engagement to take his overall tally to five kills, witnessed the aftermath of the collision between Roberts and Meyer. Within three weeks MacDonald would replace Prentice as CO of the 475th FG, thus changing the group's style of leadership – MacDonald was a truly great fighter leader in the air – but not its primary focus of protecting Allied bombers or hunting down enemy aircraft. MacDonald would lead from the front and eventually become the only other pilot besides Tom McGuire and Dick Bong in the Southwest Pacific to surpass the mythical 26-victory mark of World War I ace Eddie Rickenbacker. Men like Lewis and MacDonald would ensure that the 475th FG's valiant legacy would go on despite the terrible losses inflicted on the group in the final months of 1943.

That unlikely legacy went a long way to convincing Maj Gen Kenney that he was right to remain on the offensive, even though his pugnacious spirit had been shaken by recent events in-theater. He was now ready to implement the Allied grand plan for the Southwest Pacific theater by attacking strategic points along New Britain's southern coast, as well as outlying positions in the Rabaul salient. Kenney's ideas on strategy had not fulfilled his most sanguine hopes to date, but even doubters in other commands had to be impressed with the adverse effect the campaign in the New Britain and New Ireland areas was having on Japanese forces in the Solomons and Central Pacific.

For the rest of November, the 475th FG continued to fly bomber escort missions, covering "heavies" sent to attack Rabaul on the 11th and Wewak five days later. Maj Meryl Smith from group HQ claimed two "Zekes" (actually Ki-43s) during the latter operation for his first of nine victories, although three 431st P-38s failed to return from the mission after the squadron was jumped by an estimated 30 Japanese fighters. Two of the pilots were eventually recovered, but 1Lt Robert Smith was apparently killed in action. The group's two other squadrons claimed a pair of enemy fighters in return.

By the time the Fifth Air Force assault on Rabaul had ended, the Marine Corps had landed on Bougainville in the Solomon Islands and seized Cape Torokina after bitter fighting. Thanks to these successes, the Thirteenth Air Force now had airstrips within 250 miles of Rabaul, allowing it to take the fight directly to the Japanese fortress.

In December the Allies made a direct land assault on New Britain when 3,000 troops of the 112th Cavalry Regiment landed on the Arawe Peninsula during the morning of the 15th. Numerous diversionary and support attacks were carried out by both American and Australian aircraft over the next few days, and the 475th enjoyed its most successful period in combat since the Rabaul raids when it patrolled over Arawe on December 16. Poor weather initially delayed the 432nd from taking off on a B-24 escort to Cape Gloucester until 1230hrs. About 90 minutes later, however, one flight was sent up to 24,000ft to investigate unidentified aircraft, whereupon its pilots found 30 to 40 "Oscars" and "Tonys" covering seven Ki-49 "Helen" heavy bombers. Continuing their climb in order to have the advantage of height, the "Clover" squadron P-38s eventually fell on the Japanese escorts and drove them down to the same altitude as the bombers, claiming one of the "Oscars" as damaged in the process.

At about this time the 431st showed up and attacked the bombers before they could escape into cloud. 1Lt David Allen led the squadron into the action, and as he pulled up after making his first pass, he noticed that there were still five Japanese bombers in formation trying to reach cloud. He fired at one on the outside right, and saw pieces fly off before he had to break away beneath his target to avoid colliding with it. 2Lt Bill O'Brien was flying behind Allen, and he saw the "Helen" (misidentified as a "Betty") burst into flames, fall away and crash.

1Lt "Fran" Lent attacked another bomber head-on and watched as pieces flew off from the canopy area. Squadronmate 1Lt Carl Houseworth, who had led the flight down in the attack, was able to see the aircraft drop away trailing smoke. Lent erroneously claimed a "Betty" destroyed, and was awarded a kill to take his tally to ten victories. Future five-victory ace 2Lt John Tilley, who had only joined the unit a matter of days earlier, also attacked the bombers and watched one go down in flames after he broke off his pass.

Now fully recovered from his wounds of October 17, newly promoted Capt Tom McGuire was back in action during this engagement, although he suffered from his usual problem of sighting the enemy in time to allow him to effect an attack. A number of his compatriots in V Fighter Command had been relieved when McGuire was confined to a hospital bed, for it meant that the airwaves had been free of his incessant chattering as he called for the location of enemy aircraft. The ace was obsessed with locating Japanese aircraft once contact had been made by Allied units so that he could participate in the fighting.

On December 16, McGuire arrived too late to attack the bombers before they had reached the cloud cover, but he did manage to hit one of the "Oscars" (he reported it as a

"Zeke") with a few bullets before it, too, escaped – he was credited with having damaged the aircraft. The 433rd FS also tangled with the enemy on the 16th, Capt Warren Lewis leading from the front by claiming two "Bettys" (actually Ki-49s) before they could reach cloud cover. Two more Ki-49s and a pair of Ki-43s were also claimed by the "Possum" squadron to give the 475th credit for all seven bombers and at least two of the fighters downed during the engagement.

1943 ended spectacularly for the entire Fifth Air Force when the 1st and 5th Marine Divisions invaded the Cape Gloucester area of northwest New Britain on December 26, 1943. Fighting over the southeastern corner of the island had also been heavy in the wake of the Arawe landings on December 15, with all Lightning and Thunderbolt pilots involved finding opportunity to increase their scores.

The Marine Corps had seized control of several airstrips in the Cape Gloucester area by the afternoon of December 29, these having been targeted by Japanese forces desperate to repel the invaders during the previous 72 hours – both the JAAF and IJN sortied aircraft against the invasion beaches and shipping offshore. Three squadrons of P-47s, two of P-38s and another of P-40s countered enemy attacks during the afternoon of the 26th, claiming more than 60 aircraft – mostly Zeros and "Vals" – shot down. Japanese records are obscure for the day, but they do reflect the loss of a number of "Helen" and "Val" aircraft, as well as fighters.

Capt Tom McGuire led the 431st FS into the fight, with the redoubtable 1Lt Frank Monk on his wing. The fighter controller handling the interception ordered the P-38s of the 80th PS/8th FG and 431st FS to attack a formation of enemy aircraft detected coming in from the northeast. The Lightning pilots were instructed to ignore the bombers and go after their fighter cover at 22,000ft, so McGuire took his squadron up to 23,000ft before engaging them head-on.

For some reason the unit tasked with intercepting the "Vals" below the Zeros was late in arriving, leaving the dive-bombers in a perfect position to attack the shipping off the coast just as McGuire dived down on their fighter escorts. The latter could clearly see the Aichi aircraft through the formation of Zeros, so he ordered his squadron to ignore the fighters and to intercept the "Vals" instead.

In the wild maneuvering which ensued, Monk lost his flight leader, but tacked onto the wing of an 80th FS P-38 engaging the Zeros. One fighter went down in smoke and flame after Monk's pass, and McGuire looked back to see the Japanese fighter crash into the sea.

"Hades White Flight" ran into "Oscars" below the Zero cover and 1Lt Vince Elliott shot one of them down, as well as a Navy fighter, for his final confirmed victories (his tally now stood at seven kills). Capt Verl Jett, who was leading "White Flight," also managed to damage a solitary "Val."

2Lt Herman Zehring, who was also a part of "White Flight," experienced a great deal of difficulty in releasing one of his drop tanks, but he nevertheless managed to engage the "Vals" and score his first two (of four) victories:

I heard Capt McGuire say, "Let's get the dive-bombers!" I then peeled off and followed my leader down. As I lost altitude, I saw the "Zeke" that 1Lt Monk had hit burst into flames and crash into the sea off Gloucester strip. When I was about 1,000ft above the water I came upon a "Val"-type aircraft and fired a short burst which caused it to burst into flames and explode. 2Lt Powell saw it, too. After this, I caught a "Val" heading out, down near the water. I gave it a burst and the dive-bomber crashed into the water. 1Lt Elliott saw this airplane crash. After this, I couldn't find any more enemy airplanes, so I returned to base, where I landed at 1630hrs.

McGuire became wild in the midst of the "Vals," which were disrupted by the American attacks to the point that only one hit was scored on a US Navy destroyer, which sank a few minutes later. At least seven "Vals" were claimed by the 431st and two by P-47s of the 36th FS/8th FG, plus several others were listed as probably destroyed or damaged.

McGuire himself caused one to explode in mid-air, and watched three others hit the water following his attacks – one of these kills was eventually credited to a P-47 pilot from the 36th FS. It would be months before McGuire would erase the Japanese victory flag denoting this "Val" kill from the side of his fighter, in spite of the victory having been officially awarded to the pilot of the Thunderbolt.

That mission on December 26 signaled the end of the 475th FG's scoring run during the first five months of its operational service. More than 275 Japanese aircraft had been claimed destroyed in air-to-air combat, with 25 pilots having lost their lives in return to all causes. Thus, the group had established an eleven-to-one victories-to-losses ratio, and achieved an outstanding average of 55 victories per month. Although this record would certainly not hold throughout the war, the group had already exceeded the expectations of its "creator," Maj Gen Kenney.

LONG RANGE OVER WATER

January through March 1944 saw the complete strangulation of Rabaul as an offensive base. Manus Island, in the Admiralty Islands northwest of New Britain, was taken at the end of February to seal a ring around the Japanese base. Elsewhere, areas taken in the Solomon Islands were also consolidated at much the same time, and early the previous month the Saidor region just north of the Huon Peninsula had fallen as Allied forces seized their first territory north of the Huon Gulf.

The 475th FG was heavily involved in the fighting during this period, with six pilots being killed in action. One of those lost was 1Lt William Ritter during a fighter sweep to Wewak on January 18. Lt Col MacDonald led four squadrons of P-38s that day, which claimed 13 "Oscars" and "Tonys" (including an "Oscar" each to aces MacDonald, Jett and Gresham). Ritter, of the 432nd FS flew too close to the "Tony" that he was shooting down and a piece of the disintegrating fighter flew back and tore off one of the P-38's wings. 2Lt John Michener, who was Ritter's wingman, saw the Lightning fall in flames without any sign of a parachute. Ritter, who was an amiable and well-liked pilot, apparently managed to escape from his flaming aircraft, only to fall into the hands of a pitiless enemy. Word eventually reached the Allies that he had been summarily beheaded by his captors.

Attacks on Wewak continued throughout February and March in an effort to further reduce the base's potential to hinder Allied advances along the northern coast of New Guinea. The Wewak area would finally be invaded by Australian forces in May 1945, by which point the base was barely functioning. With Wewak effectively sidelined, the Fifth Air Force began supporting a new offensive against the former Dutch colonial capital of Hollandia, which represented the enemy's last viable defensive point south of the Vogelkop Peninsula.

Allied aerial claims were admittedly exaggerated following the battles which took place over the town, with American pilots perhaps being the worst culprits. As claims were made in the heat of large-scale combat, it is easy to see how honest mistakes were made. A decidedly unscientific survey estimates that as much as 40 percent of all American claims could be discounted. Be that as it may, the JAAF had certainly been weakened by the time it was forced to consolidate its units around Hollandia.

On January 16, for example, the newly deployed "Oscars" and "Tonys" of an inexperienced *sentai* reported losing ten fighters over the Saidor area to the P-40s of the highly regarded 35th FS/8th FG. The Warhawk pilots in turn claimed 19 victories to set the high-scoring record for a single V Fighter Command squadron in an engagement in World War II.

By the time of the assault on Hollandia there were fewer experienced Japanese pilots available to oppose Allied aircraft, and even those who were veterans now showed signs of trying to survive in combat, rather than taking on an ever more formidable enemy. Therefore, when American bombers finally appeared over the Hollandia area at the end of March, Japanese forces were already primed for defeat.

Only four squadrons of P-38s remained in V Fighter Command following the grueling battles fought out over Rabaul and Wewak that finally ended in November 1943. In the weeks that followed, the 475th again incurred hostility from other fighter units in the Southwest Pacific when replacement P-38s newly arrived in-theater were concentrated in the 80th FS/8th FG and the three squadrons of the 475th FG. Pilots assigned to the 49th FG's 9th FS were especially unhappy about giving up their Lightnings for the generally despised P-47, which the unit was forced to keep well into 1944.

As a point of fact, the 49th considered itself the seminal fighter group of the Southwest Pacific, and its crews resented the fact that the 475th had taken its "lifeblood" in terms of skilled pilots, maintainers and replacement P-38s. Ex-49th FG CO Brig Gen Paul "Squeeze" Wurtsmith, who was rapidly becoming a decisive force in Fifth Air Force operations in his capacity as commander-in-chief of V Fighter Command, and who considered his old unit with more than just a modicum of affection, stated publicly that he intended to give the 49th its head in P-38s and pilots when allocations were eventually increased.

Thus, leadership of future operations would probably go to the 49th FG, with lesser opportunities going to other groups such as the 475th. And this was indeed what transpired during the Philippines offensive, as the 49th was given territory to patrol in the promising Luzon area, while the 475th had to be content with leaner pickings in the Mindoro–Leyte–Negros triangle.

But all this lay in the future. The Hollandia threat had to first be neutralized, and the offensive began with four squadrons of P-38s available to the Fifth Air Force for bomber escort. The one Lightning squadron – the 80th – not controlled by the 475th in the campaign commenced escort operations when it took B-24s to their target as part of the initial attack mounted on Hollandia on March 30, 1944. All US aircraft returned from the successful raid, and 80th FS "Headhunters" pilots claimed seven Japanese interceptors destroyed.

The following day it was the 431st FS that was given the job of escorting the "heavies," 21 "Hades" squadron aircraft departing Nadzab airstrip No 3 at 0755hrs and rendezvousing with B-24s 20 minutes later. Once all the Lightnings were correctly positioned above the bombers, the force headed for the target.

About 15 minutes before the formation reached Hollandia, the Lightnings were jumped by 15 Japanese fighters. "Yellow Flight" was the last formation in the escort, and 1Lt Frank Monk ordered his pilots to drop their tanks when he saw enemy aircraft some 1,000ft above them, diving from the right towards the Lightnings in front of him. The "Oscars" were heading for the tails of "Green Flight," which was immediately in front of him, so Monk forced the Japanese pilots to turn away from their intended targets by breaking into them head-on. One Ki-43 broke to the right, presenting Monk with the chance to rip away pieces of its canopy, engine and wing with a well-aimed burst of fire.

2Lt Horace "Bo" Reeves was a new pilot in the squadron flying on Monk's wing throughout the mission, and he saw the Ki-43 burst into flames and disintegrate moments after it was hit. 2Lt Herman Zehring was leading "Yellow Flight's" second element when he followed his leader into the fight. Looking around to clear his tail, Zehring saw his wingman, 2Lt Robert Donald, leaving the formation to chase after another "Oscar." He was later seen to join up with other P-38s in the area, and Zehring mentally promised him a tongue-lashing for leaving him in the middle of a dogfight when they got back to base. However, Donald ultimately paid a much higher price for breaking up section integrity, as he was subsequently listed as the only American loss for the day.

Later in the fight, 2Lt Zehring sighted 15 more enemy fighters attempting to attack the B-24s, and 1Lt Monk turned leadership of the flight over to him when he could not locate the "Oscars" over Humboldt Bay. Zehring made the most of the opportunity and shot down two Ki-43s, one of which crashed on the shore of Humboldt Bay – these victories took his final tally to four kills.

1Lt "Fran" Lent downed a pair of "Oscars" (claimed as "Zekes") to tally the last of his 11 victories, and other squadron pilots were credited with two more. One unconsummated attack was attributed to Capt Tom McGuire, who was beginning to feel the frustration of striving to become the leading US ace – he had not claimed a kill since December 26, 1943:

I was leading "Green Flight." We made contact with the enemy 25 miles southeast of Hollandia at 1015hrs. There were ten to 15 "Oscars," "Zekes" and one "Tony." My flight was jumped from behind and above. "Yellow Flight" drove them off as I turned underneath and to the right to drive enemy aircraft off 1Lt Monk's flight ("Yellow Flight"). I got a short burst in, but the "Tony" half-rolled before I could do any damage. My second element snafued at that time.

We stayed over the bombers and target area until 1110hrs. The enemy pilots seemed non-aggressive, and appeared to be trying to escape after their first pass. A/A was very light. We covered the bombers back to 50 miles from Tadji, where we left them and proceeded home, landing at 1335hrs.

It was the 432nd FS's turn to shine when the weather improved enough for another strike to be made on Hollandia on April 3. Some 17 P-38s (with the addition of Capt Richard I. Bong, who tacked on to the unit on its approach to Hollandia in his V Fighter Command Lightning and went on to score his 25th victory in the ensuing engagement) guarded a mixed force of A-20s and B-25s that struck the target from 1135hrs onwards.

Two pairs of "Tony" fighters slipped behind the rear elements of "Green Flight" and made separate attacks, 1Lt Clifford Mann, who had just gone into battle formation with Flt Off Joe Barton, spotting them at the very last minute. Mann ordered the flight to drop their external tanks, and watched in horror as two enemy fighters closed quickly on the inexperienced Barton. A violent roll and dive to the right lost the first two Ki-61s at 4,000ft, but the second pair of fighters then latched onto Barton's tail. Mann evaded again by diving steeply to the left, and he glanced back to see Barton rolling away in the same direction into a nearby bank of cloud. Subsequent visual sweeps and radio calls failed to find any trace of him, however, and Mann eventually had to head home when his fuel level became critical. Barton was the mission's only casualty.

Elsewhere, other flights were enjoying much better fortune. Capt John Loisel was leading "Blue Flight" over the target when he heard calls from the A-20s that they were being attacked. He led his flight down to intercept a formation of eight "Oscars," one of which fell to Loisel's guns. Future five-kill ace 1Lt Henry Condon, who was leading "Green Flight," witnessed the first of Loisel's two victims crash into Sentani Lake just before he shot down his own Ki-43 on the south side of the lake.

The rest of "Blue Flight" was also making its mark, with 1Lt Perry Dahl accounting for two more "Oscars" (one claimed as a "Zeke") to give him ace status. His wingman, 1Lt Joe Forster, gave the most impressive performance of the day, however, claiming two "Tonys" and an "Oscar" for his first confirmed victories. His after-action report stated:

The flight leader (Loisel) made an attack on the lead enemy fighter while I attacked the two-ship flight. My pass was to the front of the aircraft from the port side. The first enemy airplane – a "Tony" – was carrying aerial bombs. An explosion flashed immediately behind the engine, but I observed no further results. I continued my fire through the second "Tony," which was also carrying aerial bombs. It immediately burst into flames and crashed on a hillside. 1Lt Dahl observed this action. Pulling back into string with my flight, I made several passes without effect. Following through, I made a head-on attack on an "Oscar." As it passed over, I saw smoke streaming from the engine. Banking into a turn, I saw another P-38 finish it off.

After pulling back into string, I saw an "Oscar." I made several frontal and stern attacks and saw cannon flashes on his fuselage. I trailed him across Hollandia airfield and cornered him against a mountain. After a head-on pass, he began trailing smoke. Turning back,

I closed in as the airplane began diving out of control. As the pilot got out on the wing I gave him a short burst. Both the pilot and his airplane continued in the dive and crashed. 2Lt Temple observed this airplane crashing into the mountain.

Elsewhere on April 3, 475th FG CO Lt Col MacDonald was leading the escort at the head of "Clover Red Flight" with his usual 432nd FS wingman, 1Lt John Hannan. Although MacDonald scored no kills on this mission, he did file an illuminating after-action report:

Approaching the southeast side of Sentani Lake, I observed six "Oscars" on the deck making for the A-20s. They were in loose string formation. We attacked and split them up. One "Oscar" got down over a swamp and kept turning and twisting as everyone made passes. 1Lt Summer ("White Flight" leader) shot him down. We attacked another "Oscar" who worked his way over Hollandia airfield before he was shot down by 1Lt Hannan. He crashed in the revetment area. I saw three crashed airplanes on the south side of the lake.

Numerous small fires and dense smoke covered Hollandia airstrip. Light caliber A/A was intense. I observed a large ship in the harbor and numerous barges and luggers. The airstrips looked like junk yards.

The "Possum" flights of the 433rd FS duly added two more "Oscars" to the 12 claimed by the "Clover" flights. An additional ten claims were made by the "Headhunters" of the 80th FS, and these victories combined virtually eradicated Hollandia's air defenses. Granted, the actual losses suffered by the Japanese were certainly lower than those claimed by the P-38 pilots, but the decline in the enemy's aerial strength following this mission was marked nevertheless.

BLACK SUNDAY

Although April 3 saw the 475th FG claim its last victories over the Hollandia area, sadly the group would lose more pilots in the region in the coming days. And these losses would be inflicted by the turbulent New Guinea weather rather than by the enemy, for the latter was now all but beaten. Proof of this came in intercepted messages sent by the Japanese garrison in Hollandia that urgently complained of dwindling supplies and an inability to counter Allied attacks.

Despite this intelligence, the Fifth Air Force was instructed to conduct one final airstrike on Hollandia prior to the Allies launching an invasion on April 22. A relatively large force of B-24s, B-25s and A-20s from seven bomb groups would be sent against targets in and around the town, with the bombers being protected by 70-plus P-38s from the 475th and the 8th FGs – all three squadrons in the latter group having recently converted to the Lightning. These aircraft could have delivered a mighty blow had the weather cooperated.

The morning of April 16 dawned with gloomy and overcast skies that promised to have the mission scrubbed. The P-38 pilots were already planning to spend the day on the ground when sunshine eventually appeared to herald fine conditions to launch the mission. Just before noon, the Lightnings were sent aloft and rendezvoused with the bombers with little difficulty. For the previous two days Allied weather services had been recommending that the mission be canceled, but clear blue skies all the way to the target area seemed to prove the "met men" wrong.

No interceptors were encountered over Hollandia, and the few antiaircraft bursts that appeared soon after the bombers had made their devastating run on the target emphasized the poor condition of the Japanese defenses below. It was an encouraging sign for the aircrews now returning home, and the P-38 pilots were especially ebullient thanks to the extra fuel they had in their tanks due to the absence of Japanese aerial opposition.

Rat-racing and dodging in and around the "heavies," the fighter pilots frolicked to the delight of the bomber crews, who enjoyed the impromptu aerobatics show. Some distance away, however, ominous black clouds topping out above 30,000ft were rapidly building up, and before long, the playful P-38 pilots would be sweating in terror as they desperately tried to find airstrips where they could land safely in an effort to escape the worst of the New Guinea weather.

Then the full scope of the deadly storm front was revealed to the American force when dark storm clouds descended from the north to trap them in a disappearing pocket of clear weather. When the horrifying truth dawned on them, the Lightning pilots tried to get radio fixes from nearby ground stations, while desperately attempting to follow the bombers which were already breaking up into individual flights so as to better rely on their own navigation equipment.

432nd FS pilot 2Lt Robert Hubner was heard by Capt Loisel making frantic calls for help, and although the veteran ace tried his best to calm his excited squadronmate down, the desperate radio calls eventually faded out and Hubner, and his element leader, 1Lt Jack Luddington, were never seen again. They were not the only Lightning pilots to be lost during this ill-fated mission.

The 433rd FS suffered the most grievously when five of its P-38s failed to return. 2Lts Louis Longman, Austin Neely and Lewis Yarbrough were simply lost somewhere in the murk, while 1Lts Bob Tomberg and Bud Wire had harrowing escapes. The latter pilot was flying in company with new 433rd FS pilot 2Lt Mort Ryerson when they unsuccessfully attempted to join several bomber formations in the hope that they would guide them home. Having lost one group of B-25s when they broke up to make it through the weather individually, Wire then failed in his attempt to lead Ryerson above the storm. He then tried to find a clear path along the shore, following the coastline until he reached the Saidor area, where he tried to land at the tiny Piper L-4 Cub airstrip at Yamai.

Whilst maneuvering his big fighter in high winds for an approach over the sea, Wire mushed his Lightning into a wave and was lucky to emerge from his sinking P-38 without serious injury. He bobbed about in his flotation gear until a small boat picked him up. Ryerson was fortunate enough to make it all the way back home.

Having been in-theater since 1942, 1Lt Robert Tomberg of the 433rd FS knew just how treacherous New Guinea weather could be, so he took to his parachute and was lucky enough to land in a clearing near thick forest. Although suffering minor injuries on landing, he was able to walk to an airfield in the Saidor area, where he hitched a ride back to Finschhafen in the gunner's position of an A-20.

Tomberg's squadronmates 2Lts Joe Price and Stanley Northrup managed to crash-land at Saidor, where their P-38s were handed over to service squadrons for repairs while they returned to duty with minor injuries. 2Lt Milton MacDonald of the 431st FS was less fortunate, however, and the wreckage of his Lightning was eventually discovered near Efu village. The young pilot's remains were not reclaimed until after the war. Ten P-38s from the 475th FG crashed, killing six pilots, during the most devastating day the Fifth Air Force would ever endure. Overall, 54 aircrew and 46 aircraft were lost.

SECURING NEW GUINEA

Between April 22 and the beginning of June, enemy forces along the previously impregnable northern coast of New Guinea were swept aside by the Allies. The 4th Japanese Air Army was all but wiped out during this period, with its bases being seized and surviving aircraft shot down as they attempted to escape to the northwest Vogelkop Peninsula.

The Fifth Air Force was combined with the Thirteenth Air Force during this campaign to form the Far East Air Forces (FEAF), which would in turn be responsible for supporting campaigns in the Philippines, Central Pacific, Borneo and the former Dutch East Indies.

Despite these significant organizational changes, within V Fighter Command the great "ace race" continued unabated. Indeed, on April 12, Maj Dick Bong had broken the long-standing World War I record of Capt Eddie Rickenbacker when he took his tally to 28 kills following the destruction of three Ki-43s over Hollandia.

Capt Tom McGuire was Bong's closest living rival (22-victory ace Col Neel Kearby having been killed in action on March 5, 1944), but as mentioned earlier, he was enduring a barren run that had started, following his 16 kills, on December 26, 1943. He had still not added to his tally by the time Bong was sent home on leave in mid-April. However, in May and June McGuire claimed four victories to take his tally to 20 kills.

McGuire and his fellow pilots in the 475th FG would get more opportunities to add to their scores in June, when reports from Allied reconnaissance aircraft and submarines suggested that a strong Japanese naval force was lurking off the coast of Biak Island, northwest of New Guinea. The enemy were resisting Allied invasion attempts with remarkable vehemence, fighting hard to retain control of its strategically important airfields. Several sweeps were made by the 475th FG of the waters north of the island but no Japanese vessels were located.

An enemy troop convoy did indeed exist, however – naval vessels carrying 2,500 troops from the Philippines to reinforce Biak. Ducking in and out of weather fronts, the reinforcement force dodged back and forth with little hope of breaking through the waves of Allied aircraft searching for it.

On June 7, Col MacDonald led an escort force of 432nd FS P-38s that were covering B-25s sent to find and attack the Japanese convoy. However, the mission fell foul of poor weather and the Lightnings landed on Wakde Island instead. The next day the enemy vessels made a determined bid to reach Biak in better weather across open seas, and this allowed ten B-25s, covered by 17 P-38s from the 432nd and 433rd FSs (again led by MacDonald), to intercept the ships near Manokwari Island.

Col MacDonald claimed his 11th kill during the engagement which ensued, and details of this victory were outlined in his after-action report:

We approached at the same level as the B-25s and then climbed to the right in order to divert antiaircraft fire away from them as they turned to the left to begin their bombing runs. At the same time we sighted enemy aircraft about 3,000ft above us, so we started climbing towards them. Three more enemy aircraft then came from behind the clouds and passed about 1,000ft above us. We waited for them to make a move, but they did not seem anxious to engage us. Then we sighted four "Zekes" and started after them from "nine o'clock."

The leader turned into me as though to make a head-on pass, but he seemed afraid to try it. I got a 30-degree head-on shot, led him two radii, and then fired a two-second burst. As I looked back I saw that he had burst into flame around the engine. Capt Zach Dean saw him crash into the water. This action took place at 5,000ft directly over the destroyers, where the "Zekes" apparently thought we wouldn't follow them.

When we entered that area the enemy formation broke up and ran. I followed what I think was an "Oscar." As I was overtaking him, he dived through an overcast at 3,000ft. I followed, fired a short burst and saw him start smoking. I could also see where part of his wing peeled back from a cannon shot. He pulled back into the overcast and I followed him in, but losing sight of him in the soup, I dived out. Then I saw him again, and as I closed in, he flew into a large cumulus cloud. I went right in behind him, and as we came out the other side, I got another burst at him. He did a quick 180-degree turn and again headed back into the cloud. I fired another shot at that time, and as the enemy aircraft entered the cloud I followed him, still shooting. I then saw a bright orange flash in the mist, and when I came out the other side of the cloud I could no longer see the Nip aircraft.

A steady build-up of cloud cover over the convoy made the confirmation of several certain victories impossible to achieve, although 1Lt Perry Dahl managed to confirm one "Oscar" destroyed and another probably destroyed, while 1Lt Clifford Mann also destroyed a Ki-43. Dahl subsequently lived up to his nickname "Lucky" when his landing gear failed and he simply walked away from what should have been a serious crash when his fighter speared into trees and was totally destroyed.

Luck was not entirely with the bombers, however, for three of their number were shot down over the target ships and the remaining seven were all badly shot up. One vessel was sunk and three others badly damaged, and this was enough to discourage the Japanese convoy from trying to reach Biak. Eight days later, on June 16, recently promoted Maj Tom McGuire claimed two victories when he led the 431st FS on a B-25 escort to Jefman Island. The squadron initially flew from Hollandia to Wakde Island to refuel, where Col MacDonald experienced electrical problems in his P-38 that forced him to relinquish the role of mission leader to a delighted McGuire. Having refueled, the P-38s took off again at 0930hrs and rendezvoused with the bombers over Roon Island at 1140hrs. Within 90 minutes they had intercepted Ki-43s and a solitary Ki-51 "Sonia" tactical reconnaissance aircraft.

To the astonishment of his squadronmates, McGuire actually maneuvered with the "Oscars," following one of the agile Japanese fighters into a reverse turn and claiming it destroyed after it blew up under the weight of his fire. With a "Sonia" also shot down during this engagement, McGuire's score now stood at 22.

Other "Hades" pilots added an additional six "Oscars" to the mission tally, including two for Capt Paul Morriss to take his final tally to five kills. 1Lt Frank Monk also scored his fifth, and final, kill, while 2Lt "Bo" Reeves claimed the first of his eventual six victories. Capt Bill Gronemeyer downed the third of his four victories, and McGuire's wingman, 2Lt Enrique Provencio, claimed his first of two kills.

LINDBERGH VISIT

Col MacDonald had just finished a refreshing dip in the cold stream behind his quarters on Hollandia and was settling down for a game of checkers with his executive officer, newly promoted Lt Col Meryl Smith, when a tall civilian came up to introduce himself. MacDonald was so involved with his game that he initially paid little attention to the presence of this mildly irritating stranger. When the man began asking them intelligent and very technical questions, both MacDonald and Smith looked up and recognized the eminent aviator Charles Augustus Lindbergh.

During his time in the Pacific, Lindbergh put his infamous antiwar sentiments behind him by offering technical advice that extracted amazing performance from US combat aircraft in-theater. V Fighter Command benefited greatly from his expertise in long distance flying, Lindbergh's suggestions allowing its pilots to extend the range of their existing P-38 and P-47 fighters to such a degree that they could confidently operate over the unbelievable distances that their command now had to contend with.

Lindbergh spent time with virtually every P-38 and P-47 squadron in-theater between May and late August 1944, passing on some extremely useful tips and techniques that increased their fighters' endurance. He explained how it was possible for Lightnings, for example, to fly mission distances in excess of 800 miles, which tested the limits of the pilot more than the machine itself. Lindbergh quickly became a legend once again to men who had been little more than idolizing boys when he flew the Atlantic in May 1927.

Although revered in the front line, it must be said that Lindbergh was less than completely taken with the 475th FG during his stay with the group. He certainly came to admire the skill and bravery of individual pilots and commanders, but his sensibilities were offended by some of the group's practices. One of the things that caused him the most concern was the 475th's general attitude towards the enemy. Lindbergh felt that most of the personnel in the group acted like pirates rather than professional soldiers when dealing with the enemy. Indeed, even the Japanese at Rabaul became aware of the "Satan's Angels," as the aviators in the 475th were called, and "Radio Tokyo" nicknamed the group the "Bloody Butchers."

Many pilots thought it part of the rules of the game to gang up on damaged Japanese aircraft as they tried to reach the safety of home. Lightning pilots also routinely strafed their enemy counterparts as they dangled helplessly in their parachutes. Several downed Japanese pilots bobbing in Rabaul's Simpson Harbor also had to dive for safety when marauding P-38s sporting distinctive red, yellow or blue tails threatened to strafe them. Considering the generally pitiless regard that the Japanese had for their prisoners of war in the Pacific, Lindbergh's criticism seems unusually harsh.

Lindbergh also objected to the unusually graphic artwork that adorned many of the group's P-38s. Drawings of unclad women and barbarous maledictions against their opponents were the usual subjects of this artwork, which was carried on both sides of the aircraft's nose. In general, the 475th crews shrugged when they were made aware of Lindbergh's complaints, and took it as something of a compliment that they were rough on the enemy.

Lindbergh's first flight with the 475th came on June 27, 1944, just 24 hours after meeting Col MacDonald and Lt Col Smith. The latter pilots accompanied Maj

McGuire and Lindbergh on a reconnaissance mission to Jefman and Samate islands, where they managed to inflict some damage on a pair of Japanese barges during a series of strafing passes.

The second mission that Lindbergh flew with the 475th was another reconnaissance to Nabire and Sagan, situated along the coastline of Geelvink Bay, in northwestern New Guinea. When Lindbergh landed and his P-38 was checked out, the groundcrew was amazed to find that he had considerably more fuel left in the tanks of his fighter than the other members of his flight. Lindbergh noted the reason for the low fuel consumption in his postwar book, *Wartime Journals of Charles Lindbergh*:

> I landed on the Hollandia strip at 1708hrs after a six-hour-and-fifty-minute flight. All during the day I had been holding my engine down to get a check on minimum fuel consumption. Landed with 210 gallons in my tanks.

Any reservations held by group pilots about how the ideas of this aviation pioneer could benefit a modern combat organization disappeared in the face of actual practice over coming days. It soon became common for pilots to get pointers from Lindbergh on the art of reducing manifold pressure during combat flights in order to reduce fuel consumption by almost half. The 475th FG's already hard-worked groundcrews were less than enthusiastic, however, when they realized that the methods suggested by Lindbergh would inevitably foul their fighters' Allison V1710 engines, thus both hastening and complicating servicing.

Some pilots who flew long missions with Lindbergh became excited when the usual halfway point was reached for a P-38 mission and he would calmly order engine settings for an extended flight. Inexperienced Lightning pilots would then sit in cold dread of an engine sputtering into lifelessness until the flight would land as much as eight hours after take-off. A grinning Lindbergh would jump up on the wing of the newly initiated pilot to declare, "See, didn't I tell you we could do it?"

For most of his time with the 475th, Lindbergh was under the care of Maj Tom McGuire, much to the consternation of some of the pilots in the 431st FS. McGuire would routinely treat Lindbergh with apparent disdain, ordering him to do menial tasks or speaking to him as an underling. Lindbergh, knowing that he was a guest under already trying conditions in a combat zone, had little recourse for any slight that he received.

However, other veterans remember that the interplay between McGuire and Lindbergh was on the light side, with the venerable practical joker Lindbergh giving as good as he got. One pilot recalled McGuire ordering Lindbergh to fetch his beloved battered service hat, and Lindbergh returning with a flight cap that was far too big for him, and which was adorned with the single gold bar of a second lieutenant!

Lindbergh was right in being discreet about the fact that he flew combat missions. He even furtively claimed to have destroyed a Ki-51 "Sonia" of the 73rd Independent Chutai over the island of Ceram, off the west coast of the Vogelkop Peninsula, on July 28. MacDonald was leading the 433rd FS formation which included the aircraft flown by Lindbergh, so the eventual fallout when the incident was revealed to Fifth Air Force HQ came down heavily on him. Being a civilian, Lindbergh was forbidden from partaking in combat missions, even though tacit approval for the flight had been tendered. MacDonald was duly sent home on leave as punishment.

Aside from the embarrassment caused to V Fighter Command by this incident, Lindbergh's range development work with the 475th FG had also raised further problems for the command when it was publicly revealed that it had been telling V Bomber Command for weeks that it could not facilitate their requests for long-range fighter escorts! In reality, the Lightning groups had been flying freelance sweeps in search of enemy aircraft, as Lindbergh's kill had shown.

Col MacDonald shrugged off being made the scapegoat for the failings of senior officers in V Fighter Command, instead making the most of his enforced leave by seeing his newborn son. He would return to the group in October, but just prior to his departure for the USA, he managed to fly one more long-distance mission to Palau Island on August 1 and claim an A6M2N "Rufe" floatplane fighter and a "Val" dive-bomber to take his tally to 13 kills.

Lindbergh left the 475th FG in mid-August and continued to offer advice to several other units prior to being taken out of theater later in the month. He had done yeoman service for the Allied cause in the Pacific, even though he stated that he would not accept a commission whilst President Franklin D. Roosevelt was in the White House. Roosevelt, in turn, is quoted as saying that he would never offer one to Lindbergh in any case! The great aviation pioneer had done as much as anyone could as a civilian to aid the Allied cause in the Pacific, and the results were immediately obvious in the ever-widening scope of 475th FG operations.

BALIKPAPAN

In mid-June 1944, the group moved to Biak Island, near Geelvink Bay, in the Vogelkop Peninsula. Although battles were still raging nearby to ensure the security of this strategically positioned island, V Fighter Command felt that it was worth the risk basing one of its most prized units close to the enemy. Thanks to its location so far west, and with Lindbergh's advice on fuel monitoring being rigorously adhered to, the 475th, with careful staging through other "bare base" airstrips in the region, could now escort heavy bombers sent to strike targets as far away as Mindanao or Borneo. These missions would allow the Allies to knock out the all-important oil production facilities at Balikpapan, in the former Dutch East

Indies, which the Japanese had been so anxious to seize in 1941. Oil was the lifeblood of the enemy's war effort, and virtually all of Japan's supplies came from refineries in this area.

The first escorted mission to Balikpapan was mounted on October 10, 1944, and the Lightnings involved staged through recently captured bases on Morotai Island. It was a generally successful operation, with P-47 pilots claiming 12 Japanese fighters destroyed and their P-38 counterparts six. Envious pilots from other groups, including the 475th, would get their chance to tangle with enemy fighters over Balikpapan just four days later.

On October 14, Lightnings from the 9th FS/49th FG would cover Fifth Air Force B-24s, as would 13 P-38s from the 432nd FS, led by deputy group CO, Lt Col Meryl Smith. Flying a P-38L-1, he took off from Biak with "Clover Red Flight" at 0645hrs and flew through clear weather until the Lightning pilots reached the target area four hours later. As Smith neared Balikpapan, he could hear that the P-38s of the 9th FS were busy tangling with a large force of enemy fighters through the pilots' excited radio chatter.

Six A6M3 "Hamps" were soon spotted above the milky white clouds, and Smith interposed his fighters between them and the bombers so as to prevent the latter from being attacked. The enemy pilots were skilled enough to dodge in and out of the clouds, thus stopping the "Clover" pilots from successfully engaging them, but also ruining any chance they had of repelling the bombers.

Smith made several passes at individual interceptors before he at last got a good burst in at one of the "Hamps." His flight leaders were behind him, and they saw the enemy fighter burst into flames and fall away for Smith's seventh kill. 1Lt Joe Forster also successfully engaged a "Zeke," thus bringing up his fourth victory. The kills claimed by the 475th FG's leading scorer on this mission were not added to the group's overall total, however. When Maj Tom McGuire discovered that the 431st FS were not involved in this operation, he had somehow managed to get himself onto the mission roster of his former unit, the 9th FS/29th FG, as wingman for 11-kill ace Maj Jerry Johnson!

Johnson and McGuire had duly led their force of 17 P-38s into a group of about 25 Japanese interceptors that were trying to reach the B-24s. Both men sparred with the enemy fighters until McGuire got in behind an "Oscar" that had been damaged by Johnson before excess speed had made the latter overshoot the target. Anxious not to make the same mistake, McGuire throttled back and set the Ki-43 ablaze, convincing the Japanese pilot to bail out. In turn, Johnson shot down a second "Oscar" and a Ki-44 "Tojo," and McGuire also claimed a "Tojo" after chasing the fighter in a dive through cloud down to about 1,500ft above the water, where the Japanese aircraft burst into flames and crashed. Minutes later he destroyed a third fighter that he identified as a "Hamp," the A6M3 bursting into flames and going down, as witnessed by Johnson.

Unknown to McGuire, his fruitful but furtive mission with the rival 49th FG was being monitored by Col MacDonald, who had arrived back in-theater that very day and resumed command of the group from Lt Col Smith. McGuire had left for the 9th FS camp elsewhere on Biak on the evening of October 13, so he was unaware of MacDonald's return until he himself came back to the 475th on the 15th. Veterans swear that McGuire virtually rolled out of MacDonald's office after the wrathful commander had finished admonishing him, but MacDonald himself always gallantly denied any memory of dealing with his squadron commander (McGuire had become CO of the 431st FS on May 2, 1944), who had added three kills to the scoreboard of an arch-rival fighter group.

McGuire's problems were minor in comparison to those of Capt Joe Forster, who had an engine shot out in his successful bid for a fourth aerial victory. The future ace subsequently set a record for single-engined flight in a P-38 when he covered the 850 miles back to the nearest friendly landing strip. 1Lt Ferdinand Hanson remembered the mission some 50 years later with an understandably hazy command of details, but an interesting and lighthearted view of the dangers involved:

We landed at Halmahera fighter strip on our way back and started to count noses. "Where is Joe Forster – he's late?" Word was out that he was on a single engine, having been shot up and leaking coolant. As I recall, most of us quickly fueled up and flew back to Biak. Joe was a good pilot, and we knew he'd make it. There was no use in missing our whiskey ration just for him, and the sack would feel good after such a long flight.

Well, Joe made it back and landed in the evening twilight at Biak. He later asked "Why didn't you guys wait for me? I could have been shot down, my only engine was overheating, I could have crashed at sea, I might have run out of gas – Jeez – it was getting dark!" We simply shrugged our shoulders, went and got some G.I. soap and headed for the beach, intent on discovering how good the fishing was!

THE PHILIPPINES

Following the long-range strike on Balikpapan on October 14, 1944, and the successful commencement of the campaign to retake the Philippines six days later, the 475th FG began moving from Biak to Dulag, on the island of Leyte, on the 28th of the month. The initial invasion of Leyte had taken the Japanese completely by surprise, and the naval battle of Leyte Gulf which raged from October 23 to 26 virtually eliminated the IJN threat, after four fleet carriers and most other major warships of the Japanese fleet were sunk. Fully aware of how quickly the campaign was progressing, and anxious to see action, the 475th FG had to wait until November 1 to take on the enemy over the Philippines.

In the vanguard of the action was Maj Tom McGuire, who, earlier that same day, had led 17 "Hades" pilots in a ferry flight with elements of the 49th FG to the newly won Tacloban airstrip. His unit had departed Morotai Island, in the Dutch East Indies, at 0730hrs and arrived overhead Tacloban three hours later.

Upon making radio contact with a fighter controller at the base, McGuire was asked if he and his squadronmates had sufficient fuel remaining to patrol over the airfield, as Leyte was on red alert at the time. He readily agreed to help out, and his after-action report reveals details of the first of 14 kills that the 475th FG's ranking ace would claim over the Philippines in two months of near-constant action:

I took up patrol ten miles southwest of Tacloban at 10,000ft with two flights, sending "Blue" and "Green Flights" up to 15,000ft. At 1115hrs we sighted one probable "Tojo" about 1,000ft above us. The enemy aircraft turned south and started a shallow dive for cloud cover. I gave chase, catching him just south of San Pablo. I fired one burst at 45 degrees deflection from 300 yards, getting hits and observing an explosion around the cockpit. I closed up to 50ft, firing another two bursts. The "Tojo's" tail came apart and he started straight down, spinning and crashing into the hills. Flt Off Edward J. O'Neil witnessed this action. We resumed patrol for a short while, after which we landed at Tacloban at 1200hrs.

This action signaled the beginning of a momentous two months of combat for the pilots of the 475th FG. When the JAAF and IJN recovered sufficiently from the shock of invasion and the decisive defeat of the Imperial Fleet, they responded by attacking Allied forces in the Philippines with every airworthy aircraft that they possessed, hoping to check the invasion.

From the end of October 1944 until early January 1945, many aerial victories were scored, especially by the pilots of the 49th and 475th FGs. However, these engagments would be the last great air battles fought in the Southwest Pacific, and they would ultimately cost the 475th the life of its foremost fighter ace.

The group first's large-scale clash with the JAAF over the Philippines occurred during the morning of November 10, and the clash almost saw the 432nd FS's 1Lt Perry Dahl lose his life. Dahl was the pride of his hometown on Mercer Island, Washington State, having claimed six Japanese aircraft shot down in seven months of combat. Nicknamed "Lucky," he had negotiated every hazard of aerial combat with a buoyant spirit, which he would need in abundance on this particular operation, which almost proved to be his last.

Col MacDonald was once again leading the 432nd FS on this date, the unit having been scrambled to attack aircraft detected approaching Ormoc Bay. Twelve P-38s encountered a flight of four Japanese fighters, and MacDonald chased an "Oscar" in and out of the clouds until he caught the Ki-43 with a concentrated burst of fire that set the airplane burning. MacDonald's wingman, 2Lt Calvin Anderson, subsequently reported witnessing the enemy pilot bail out.

MacDonald then noticed that his Lightning was inexplicably running low on fuel, so he turned the leadership of the squadron over to Dahl and hastily returned to Tacloban with Anderson. Dahl continued patrolling the area with his nine charges, and eventually he chased a lone Zero into a nearby bank of cloud. His initial frustration at having lost a certain kill gave way to elation when 16 enemy fighters were sighted flying serenely through the broken, dark undercast. Dahl had his P-38s stalk the enemy aircraft until they broke out of the cloud cover into clear air, whereupon they were quickly identified as "Tony" fighters.

Making sure that his squadronmates carried plenty of airspeed into the engagement, Dahl dived on the Ki-61s from some 500ft above the hapless JAAF fighters. He singled out the leading "Tony" and fired a burst at it with about 45 degrees of deflection. Dahl watched the bullets hit the engine cowling and cockpit, then saw the Ki-61 fall away out of control, trailing smoke all the way down until it hit the water northwest of Ponson Island. No fewer than ten other "Tonys" followed this aircraft down, with 2Lts Henry Toll and Richard Kiick both claiming two Ki-61s apiece.

Dahl's after-action report describes with laconic detail the harrowing events he then had to endure after claiming his seventh kill:

I then broke left and looked over my squadron. I was then hit by another airplane from below, and I supposed it was an enemy "self-blaster." I learned later, however, that it was 2Lt Grady Laseter. He was evidently hit, or in some kind of trouble, for he was out of formation, flying in the opposite direction to the rest of the squadron. My airplane was on fire and I was forced to bail out. My left wing and both tail booms had been severed from the rest of the aircraft.

I landed in the water near some Japanese shipping, and after nine hours in the water, I reached the west coast of Leyte Island. I was strafed twice while in the water – once by a destroyer and once by a lone "Tony." I suffered a hit in the hand by the destroyer's fire, and first, second and third degree burns on the face, neck and right arm due to the crash. It took me until December 10 to get back to my outfit (via the Filipino guerrilla network).

Small actions continued to be fought throughout November, sending V Fighter Command victory scores up in fits and starts. Two days after Perry Dahl had claimed his seventh victory and then been obliged to run for his life through the Leyte jungle, the 431st FS fought a small but significant action while patrolling over Allied naval vessels operating in Leyte Gulf.

Capt Fred Champlin, who was leading "Hades Red Flight" on this mission, was an old hand in the squadron, having scored four confirmed victories between September and December 1943. Holding a similar position to the 432nd's Perry Dahl in the central core of pilots in the 431st FS, he had been waiting almost 11 months to "make ace." Champlin's chance would come on November 12, 1944, when he would find that his duty included protecting US Navy vessels, as well as destroying his fifth and sixth Japanese aircraft:

We took off from Buri Strip at 0630hrs. Our mission was to protect a naval force in Leyte Gulf from aerial attack. During the two hours of patrolling, we were given continual plots to the south and east. After the last plot, we returned to the convoy at a height of 9,000ft. When we were almost on top of the convoy, I spotted three enemy aircraft approaching the ships from the northeast at our altitude. I immediately turned into them and recognized them as a [Ki-48] "Lily" twin-engined bomber, escorted by two "Oscars." I made a head-on pass at the "Oscars," which pulled up and around to the rear of my flight. This maneuver left the "Lily" alone. I turned to the left and closed on the "Lily" from 45 degrees astern. When well within range I fired a short burst, and the "Lily" immediately burst into flames and crashed in the ocean.

I then noticed that the "Oscars" were closing on my last man. I made a sharp 180-degree turn and came at them head-on. When almost in range, they both split-essed. I nosed straight over after the first. My second short burst hit him in the belly and he burst into flames, crashing into the sea. The pilot bailed out but his parachute did not fill with air. My last man followed the second "Oscar" through his split-ess and scored a hit. This last enemy airplane started burning and crashed in the ocean. 2Lt James A. Moreing accomplished this victory. I circled the area for several more minutes, but no more enemy aircraft were in sight. I then returned to base and landed at Buri Strip at 0915hrs.

Another local patrol in the afternoon netted four J2M "Jack" fighters for the 431st FS, including two that fell to McGuire, one for Capt Robert "Pappy" Cline and the fourth for Col W. T. Hudnell, who was flying as a guest pilot with the unit. These kills took McGuire's tally up to 28 confirmed victories. He was beginning to feel the frustration of competing with Maj Richard Bong, who had taken his score to 36 confirmed kills when he had destroyed two "Zekes" 24 hours earlier.

It was at this point that somebody high up in the FEAF had the bright idea that public relations would benefit from Bong and McGuire flying together on operations. Thus, the two great rivals would often fly together, and even bunk together, for the rest of Bong's time in combat, which lasted until the third week of December. This PR "dream team" turned out to be a disaster for the 475th FG, as the pressure of striving to be the top-scoring American ace of all time rasped the nerves of all who came into contact with either Bong or McGuire, and in turn soured the already strained relationship that existed between the two pilots.

CLIMAX IN THE PHILIPPINES

The 433rd FS arrived at Tacloban a few days after the 431st and 432nd FSs, by which point the latter two units had already commenced operations in earnest. Capt Campbell Wilson had taken command of the 433rd from Capt Warren Lewis in August, and he led the unit on its first patrol over Leyte on November 14. Five days would pass before the 433rd FS managed to claim its first kill. This honour fell to 1Lt Pierre Schoener on the afternoon of the 19th, when he shot down a dive-bomber that he identified as a "Val" south of Dulag.

Five-kill ace 1Lt Calvin Wire led the squadron's last mission of the day when he took four P-38s out on a patrol of the local area around Dulag. The formation's fighter controller directed Wire's flight toward another group of friendly fighters that were already embroiled in a dogfight with Japanese aircraft. The ace described his claims for two "Oscars" destroyed (the final kills of his combat tour) in his after-action report:

Unable to find this action, we patrolled the west coast of Leyte Island, and at 1615hrs, while heading southeast, sighted eight single-engined Japanese fighters heading due south. There were six above and in no particular formation, merely bunched. About 1,000ft below them, and to the rear, were two others. Both ourselves and the six Japanese fighters above were at 14,000ft, and we were approaching this formation from about "five o'clock." When we were nearly within range, the two airplanes below the main group apparently saw us and went into 45-degree dives straight ahead.

About 15 seconds later one of the six spotted us and signaled to the others by rocking his wings. At this signal, four of the "Oscars" climbed steeply, whilst the one on the extreme left went into a gradual level turn and the one on the far right executed a slight turn to the right. I went after the latter aircraft, opening fire at about 200 yards. The Nip then rolled over into a split-ess, but I was able to follow him using my diving flaps (fitted to all P-38Ls). Closing to about 100 yards, I fired a long burst of about two seconds. He went straight down and crashed into the water at full speed. This action ended between the Camotes Islands and Bulacan (on Leyte Island).

We continued our patrol, going south along Leyte's west coast. At about 1625hrs we observed a single bogey headed north and flying at approximately our level. I turned immediately, got on his tail and approached to within 200 yards before he saw us. In an effort to flee into the overcast, he turned straight up, but I followed him, closing to within 50 yards during this maneuver. My 20mm fire smashed into his engine and cockpit, whereupon he burst into flame, spun on into the ground and exploded south of Baybay.

The 433rd FS also ran into several wild fights on November 24, emerging with one Zero and four other single-engined fighters identified as "Tonys" or "Jacks" claimed destroyed. The latter fighters could have been the first examples of the new N1K-J "George" naval fighter encountered by the 475th FG, as this aircraft was in the throes of being introduced into IJN service on the Philippine front. The 433rd FS's afternoon patrol of four P-38s had run into "Georges" of the 701st Hikotai, and two Lightnings had soon been forced down by the agile Japanese interceptor – both pilots were eventually recovered, however. In return, the 701st Hikotai lost its veteran CO, and nine-kill ace, Cdr Aya-o Shirane. His demise has been studied by Japanese historians postwar, and they are convinced that his N1K Shiden fell victim to an attack by a 433rd FS P-38.

The bitter fighting over the Philippines continued into December 1944, with the 433rd FS scoring a further 25 kills. 1Lt John "Jack" Purdy was one of those pilots to enjoy success during this period, claiming no fewer than six victories in three clashes with Japanese aircraft. Having downed an "Oscar" for his first victory in May, he destroyed two "Vals" for his second and third kills on December 5 whilst leading a patrol of four P-38s between Albuera and Baybay, on Leyte.

Six days later, Purdy "made ace" with two "Oscars" shot down and another damaged, before he in turn was forced to bail out of his P-38L when he ran out of fuel over Cabugan Grande Island. He managed to make it back to base that same day after hitching lifts aboard a Catalina flying-boat and an L-3 Grasshopper.

Four days prior to Purdy achieving acedom, the FEAF's fighter force was tasked with protecting new Allied landings in Leyte's Ormoc Bay. In the fierce fighting which ensued, V Fighter Command pilots claimed more than 50 Japanese aircraft shot down in a day-long series of engagements. Almost every American fighter ace in-theater added to his score, and the 475th FG had one of its greatest days when it was credited with the destruction of 26 enemy aircraft.

In various clashes which took place from early morning to late afternoon, the fighters of the FEAF parried every thrust and inflicted frustrating losses on JAAF and IJN formations attempting to disrupt the invasion. The 49th FG's Maj Jerry Johnson claimed four victories during a morning patrol when he shot down three "Oscars," which crashed almost simultaneously into Ormoc Bay, and a "Helen" bomber in the space of just five minutes.

Col MacDonald was the 475th FG's top scorer on December 7, claiming three "Jack" fighters between 1125hrs and 1430hrs during the course of two flights. Lt Col Meryl Smith also enjoyed success against the J2M fighter, claiming a pair (to take his tally to nine kills) on the same morning mission that MacDonald had been credited with one destroyed. These would be his last victories, however, for Smith was posted missing following another clash with "Jacks" over Ponson Island at 1430hrs that same day.

1Lt Joe Forster of the 432nd FS had been the first 475th FG pilot to see action on the 7th when, at 0750hrs, his flight had run into a Ki-46 "Dinah" reconnaissance aircraft snooping around west of Dulag. His fire caused one of the aircraft's engines to smoke badly, although the "Dinah" escaped when it flew into heavy ground fog at low altitude – the veteran ace knew that it would have been suicidal to have continued the pursuit. Although certain that the Ki-46 was doomed, Forster had to be content with only a probable victory.

Three hours later, on his second patrol of the morning (the same one that McDonald and Smith participated in), Forster was more certain about the end result of his attacks. Leading the second flight of four 432nd FS aircraft, he managed to get in behind a Zero that was subsequently observed to fall burning into the sea between Ponson and Poro Islands. Forster then hunted down yet another Ki-46 after a squadronmate had burned out his guns trying to bring it down. Slipping in behind the fleeing reconnaissance aircraft, he opened fire from very close range and knocked out one of its engines. Clearly unable to escape, the Japanese pilot crash-landed on Ponson Island. These victories boosted Forster's tally to eight kills.

Dick Bong and Tom McGuire flew together several times during the day, and each pilot scored two victories. Bong claimed a Ki-21 "Sally" bomber and a "Tojo" fighter during an afternoon patrol, while McGuire got an "Oscar" in the morning and a "Tojo" in the afternoon. Both pilots witnessed and confirmed at least one victory for the other, and 1Lt Floyd Fulkerson witnessed one victory for each pilot, as well as confirming a "Tojo" for himself.

As an incidental point, Fulkerson emphatically believed that McGuire was a superior pilot to Bong. This may very well have been the case, but it was quite the rage at the time to compare Bong favorably or unfavorably to various other leading pilots in-theater – yet another factor that perhaps contributed to friction between Bong and McGuire. Indeed, soon after December 7 Bong packed up his kit and moved out of the tent that he had briefly shared with McGuire.

The 431st FS's 1Lt Ken Hart claimed two "Oscars" during a late afternoon patrol on the 7th, thus making him the 475th FG's newest ace. Although his after-action report was very brief, it accurately revealed the sort of fighting the group's pilots had participated in during this day of heavy action:

Capt Champlin, with 2Lt Martin on his wing, 1Lt Provencio as element leader and myself as the No 4 man took off from Dulag at 1600hrs. While flying south near Leyte, we spotted a "Zeke" to the west of us, heading north at about 8,000ft. We gave chase, and Capt Champlin shot him down in flames from dead astern off the north tip of Cebu. Flying north at 4,000ft near the Camotes Islands, we sighted and gave chase to an "Oscar" at 6,000ft, heading southwest. At a height of about 3,000ft, I fired from 0 to 30 degrees deflection from astern, observing a flash of flame on the right side of the engine and the Nip rolled over and went in just east of Olango Island.

At approximately 1800hrs we tagged an "Oscar" at 6,000ft, headed northwest, and chased him to the deck. He broke to the right and I fired from 30 to 60 degrees deflection, scoring hits on his engine and cockpit, setting him afire. He crashed in flames into the Camotes Sea at about 1810hrs. We then proceeded to home, landing at 1830hrs.

2Lt Chase Brenizer of the 433rd FS registered the 475th FG's final victory of December 7 when he claimed a "Helen" bomber shot down over the sea off Leyte at 1750hrs. The day ended on a poignant note for Col MacDonald when he and another pilot sortied just before dusk, after most of the missions had been completed for the day, to look for any sign of Lt Col Meryl Smith. They searched the Camotes Sea for an hour at altitudes from 1,000ft down to wavetop height without success, before landing back at base at 1810hrs. Smith was never found.

GROUP RIVALRY

The rivalry between the 49th and 475th FGs, which were co-located on Leyte in November–December 1944, was at its height during the Philippines campaign. Both groups scored heavily during the invasion, and by war's end the 49th FG came out on top with 664 victories thanks to its early war service. The 475th totalled 552 kills, its pilots having set some impressive records during its brief 24 months in the front line.

Dick Bong, who flew with both groups (although he was officially attached to V Fighter Command during his time with the 475th FG) scored his 40th, and last, victory (a Ki-43) on the afternoon of December 17 when he and 2Lt Fulkerson were patrolling over the new Allied beachhead on Mindoro Island. He had been presented with the Medal of Honor by Gen MacArthur five days earlier, and he would be sent home for good as America's premier ace just prior to Christmas. Driven on by the attention lavished on his great rival, Tom McGuire was straining at the bit to surpass Bong, and his exploits over Clark Field almost saw him snatch top spot.

The 475th FG played a key role in the first attacks on the airfield complex at Clark Field, which had been in Japanese hands since Luzon had fallen in early 1942. The 72 hours of fierce fighting that took place in this area between December 24 and 26, 1944, effectively broke the back of JAAF and IJN air power in the Southwest Pacific.

Air battles on Christmas Eve saw 33 Japanese fighters attempting to defend Clark Field fall to P-47 pilots from the 348th FG, whilst on December 25 the P-38s of the 49th and 475th FGs accounted for 40 more enemy aircraft. For the latter group, the 431st once again scored the lion's share of the kills, with 18 aircraft being claimed for the loss of three P-38s and two pilots. Both 2Lt Robert Koeck and 1Lt Enrique Provencio were killed over Clark Field, but squadronmate 1Lt Floyd Fulkerson, who claimed two "Jack" fighters before he was downed, successfully evaded capture.

1Lt John "Rabbit" Pietz also shot down two J2M fighters on Christmas Day to take his tally to five victories, while 1Lt John Tilley downed yet another "Jack" to leave him just one short of acedom. Unlike Fulkerson, who would end the war with four kills, Tilley would get his crucial fifth kill just 24 hours later.

Maj Tom McGuire, to adopt the vernacular of the time, "went wild" and successfully attacked three Zeros in the space of just 15 minutes before his guns were literally burned out by the long bursts that he had used in his zeal to down as many Japanese aircraft as possible. He was in the process of attacking a fourth enemy fighter down near the ground when all of his guns ceased to function. Out of options, McGuire ordered his wingman, 1Lt Alvin Neal, to shoot down the frustratingly vulnerable target.

The 432nd FS added six kills to the total, one of which provided 1Lt Joe Forster with his ninth – and last – victory. The 433rd claimed just one "Zeke" destroyed and Col MacDonald got two "Jacks" and a Zero to increase his tally to 24. A repeat operation over the same area the following morning saw McGuire fly his most successful mission in terms of aerial victories, the group's leading ace knocking down four "Zekes" in just ten minutes near Clark Field. His score now stood at 38, and he was seemingly within touching distance of Bong's 40 kills. Current or future aces Capt Fred Champlin and 1Lts "Bo" Reeves and John Tilley also claimed a "Zeke" apiece, with Tilley's kill making him the group's newest ace.

The Clark Field clash of December 26 proved to be the last great aerial battle of the Philippines campaign, and although other victories would be claimed by the 475th FG into 1945, the group's pilots would never again encounter massed ranks of Japanese aircraft as they had done in 1943–44.

SOUTHEAST ASIA AND BEYOND

January 1945 started off on a brisk note for the 475th FG when its last attack on the Clark Field complex in strength on New Year's Day netted the group three victories, as well as six more for the 49th FG. This proved to be the last sizable action to be seen by V Fighter Command in the Philippines, aside from the astonishing Medal of Honor mission in which Capt William Shomo of the 82nd TRS/71st PRG claimed seven victories in a single action in his F-6D Mustang over northern Luzon on January 11.

The fighter groups in the Philippines were still blissfully unaware that Japanese aerial resistance in the region had collapsed, leaving the 49th FG, in particular, unable to cash in on its exclusive assignment of the previously lucrative hunting ground over Luzon by V Fighter Command chief Brig Gen Paul "Squeeze" Wurtsmith.

One of the 475th pilots who did well on January 1 over Clark was Col Charles MacDonald, who shot down a "Dinah" and a "Tojo" to boost his tally to 26 aerial victories. The group CO had taken command of a five-airplane flight from the 432nd FS, MacDonald relishing this position at the head of a formation of P-38s on a fighter sweep. His after-action report contains some interesting details about the mission:

We approached the target at 18,000ft, but let down to 14,000ft because of the overcast. I sighted a lone "Dinah" coming in from the northwest at 12,000ft. I tried for a head-on attack but he was in a slight dive, and turning. I could only get a 40-degree angle-off shot in. I fired an extremely short burst with two radii lead, then turned to get a stern shot, but discovered that he was already on fire. He rolled over and went into a vertical dive. As his speed and the fire increased, he disintegrated, shedding large pieces before he crashed.

The next enemy airplane to go down was a fighter, which was destroyed by the element leader (Capt Paul Lucas) of a flight of four P-38s over Clark Field. I then observed two P-38s (from the 49th FG) destroy another fighter ten miles west of Clark Field.

I sighted a single enemy fighter at 4,000ft, heading west, and dived down on him from the stern. A series of short bursts set him flaming. This enemy airplane, which was a "Tojo," crashed eight to ten miles west of Clark Field. Immediately after this I saw a parachute descending, and thinking it might be one of ours, I investigated. It turned out to be an extremely nonchalant Nip in a dark green flying suit, floating down with his legs crossed and his elbow propped up on the shrouds. I returned to home base via Mindoro, where two airplanes from my formation landed for gas.

As mentioned in this report, the other pilot from the 432nd FS to claim a kill on January 1 was Capt Paul Lucas, who shot down a Zero for his sixth, and final, victory – he would be killed in action exactly two weeks later.

Tragedy struck the 432nd FS during the early morning sweep sent out on January 2, when squadron CO and five-kill ace Capt Henry Condon was shot down and killed whilst at the controls of Col MacDonald's P-38L-1 44-24843. The unit had originally been tasked with escorting B-25s that had been sent to bomb Porac and Floridablanca Airfield, but when the P-38 pilots lost contact with the bombers in the heavy overcast, Condon took his 11 Lightnings to the target area independently of the Mitchells.

A few miles north of Manila, Condon led two flights down to strafe a train, which exploded after he passed over it. Moments after Condon attempted to turn to make another pass on the target, his fighter began to trail smoke. Other pilots from the 432nd FS then saw Condon open the canopy, probably in preparation for bailing out, but the Lightning crashed into a field some ten miles north of Manila before the ace had a chance to take to his parachute.

Sadly, Henry Condon, who had served with the 475th since June 1943, would not be the group's only ace to be killed in action in January 1945.

DEATH OF TOM MCGUIRE

As January progressed, V Fighter Command pilots began to grow frustrated at the lack of action in the skies over the Philippines. Perhaps the most frustrated of them all was Maj Thomas B. McGuire, who since December 26, 1944 had been only three kills short of becoming the all-time American "ace of aces." To make matters worse for the 475th FG, the new division of territory between it and the 49th FG saw the latter group better positioned to oppose any Japanese aggression thanks to it being given responsibility for the northern part of Luzon, where JAAF units were still active. The triangle reserved for the 475th between Mindanao and Mindoro was now something of a backwater for the Japanese.

As if this was not bad enough for McGuire, his anxiety was further fueled by the knowledge that he would be rotated home in the very near future. The ace had already been on operations for almost two years, and he had suffered wounds in combat as well as tropical illnesses such as malaria. The only way McGuire could possibly stay in-theater was to accept a more senior position within the 475th, and it was unlikely that he could go any higher than the job he now held, which was group operations officer.

These matters weighed heavily on his mind when he organized "Daddy Special" flight, consisting of four 431st FS P-38Ls, for a sweep of Fabrica airfield on Negros Island on the morning of January 7, 1945. Officially, squadron mission number 1-668 took off at 0620hrs, with McGuire in the lead position in P-38L "112," which was usually flown by either Capt Fred Champlin or 1Lt Hal Gray – he had all but worn *PUDGY (V)* out, having flown it very hard during the previous weeks of combat. Capt Ed Weaver was assigned 1Lt Tom Oxford's P-38L "122," and was flying on McGuire's wing, while Thirteenth Air Force veteran Maj Jack Rittmayer (who had four kills to his name) led the second element in 1Lt Rohrer's P-38J "128," and 2Lt Doug Thropp was "tail-end Charlie" in P-38J "130."

An undercast prevented the pilots from observing any activity on Negros, so McGuire led his formation down to 1,700ft. The flight then circled boldly over Fabrica in an attitude of belligerence, hoping to provoke a spirited response from Japanese aircraft on the airfield. However, nothing seemed to be happening at Fabrica, so McGuire set course for airstrips in the western part of the island. Shortly after leaving Fabrica, Weaver called out what he thought was a "Zeke 52" about 1,000 yards ahead of them at an altitude of 500ft. McGuire immediately started a diving turn to the left to trap the enemy fighter.

Unbeknown to the Americans at the time, the "Zeke 52" was actually an "Oscar" of the 54th Sentai, piloted by combat veteran Wt Off Akira Sugimoto. He had been flying a frustrating mission over weather-obscured seas in search of an American supply convoy. When he spotted the P-38s trying to encircle him, he began to turn tightly to the left so as to get onto the tail of 2Lt Thropp's P-38.

In his eagerness to score a kill, McGuire had failed to order his formation to jettison the still partly filled external tanks hung beneath the wings of their Lightnings prior to attacking the lone enemy fighter. Thus, Sugimoto in his nimble Ki-43 was able to easily turn inside the P-38s and begin a firing pass on Thropp. Yet despite his clear advantage over his foes, the Japanese pilot inexplicably missed with every shot he fired!

Shaken by the threat posed to his wingman, Maj Rittmayer tried to turn his overloaded Lightning in behind the pugnacious "Oscar." Sugimoto responded by simply tightening his turn to get in behind Rittmayer's heavily laden P-38, which was flying low and slow over the lush Negros landscape. Capt Weaver survived the mission, and later wrote a report that outlined what happened next:

> I radioed that the "Zeke" was directly behind us, and Maj Rittmayer, in the No 4 position, fired a burst sufficient to make the enemy turn even more tightly and lose 2Lt Thropp. That put the "Zeke" in range and inside of me, in the No 2 position. I radioed Maj McGuire that I was being attacked, and increased my turn, diving slightly. The enemy stayed with me, but I was now inside and a little below my leader.

At this time Maj McGuire, attempting to get a shot at my attacker, increased his turn tremendously. His airplane snap-rolled to the left and stopped in an inverted position, with the nose down about 30 degrees. Because of the attitude of my airplane, I then lost sight of him momentarily. A second later I saw the explosion and fire of his crash. The "Zeke" broke off his attack just before Maj McGuire's crash, and climbed to the north. It is my opinion that the enemy did not at any time change his attack from me to my leader. I believe that Maj McGuire's crash was caused by his violent attempt to thwart my attacker, although it is possible that the major was hit by ground fire, which had now begun.

Whilst Sugimoto concentrated on Rittmayer and Weaver, Thropp had somehow managed to come around enough in the ever-tightening circle to get in behind the "Oscar" and fire a three-second burst. McGuire crashed moments later, and the plucky Japanese pilot took this opportunity to make good his escape to the north. However, his aircraft had perhaps already been damaged by fire from one of the American fighters because he duly made a crash-landing and was immediately shot dead by Filipino partisans.

A few minutes after Sugimoto fled north, the surviving American pilots believed that the fighter they had originally engaged had impudently returned to attack them again when a Ki-84 "Frank" of the 71st Sentai, flown by Sgt Mizonori Fukuda, appeared on the scene. It had intercepted the Lightnings from the opposite direction in which Sugimoto had fled, and Fukuda had used the element of surprise to get onto the tails of the three P-38s that were now at last rid of their drop tanks.

With the latter encumbrance gone, the 431st FS pilots responded more effectively to the attack, but not effectively enough to stop Fukuda from firing an accurate 90-degree shot that brought down Maj Rittmayer's P-38 (killing the pilot) and damaged 2Lt Thropp's fighter. In return, Weaver and Thropp damaged the "Frank" sufficiently enough to write it off when Fukuda crash-landed at Manalpa airfield.

The death of Tom McGuire struck a heavy blow to American morale in the Philippines when news of his death was announced, especially with the rotation of Dick Bong back home less than three weeks earlier. He had been the symbol of invulnerability, and in spite of his controversial nature, McGuire was universally regarded as the spirit of valor in the skies in the Pacific. His fearlessness was inspiring, but in the end he was vulnerable to the law of averages which plagued all fighter pilots on operations.

THE END IN THE PHILIPPINES

It was a remarkable repeat of history when American forces landed in Lingayen Gulf on January 9, 1945, for the Japanese had used much the same route to conquer Luzon in the opening stages of the Pacific War some three years earlier. Now the enemy they had vanquished was following in their footsteps as the Allies completely reversed the situation in the Philippines. And just as Japanese forces had swept into Manila in early 1942, the Americans were now threatening to take back the capital in 1945. Although Manila fell soon after the invasion, Luzon itself was not declared secure until June 1945. By then, of course, the Philippines had long stopped supporting the purposes of the Japanese Empire.

Coincidentally, two days after the loss of Maj Thomas McGuire, the entire FEAF was committed to the invasion of Luzon, including the fighter groups assigned to other areas of the Philippines. On the day that US troops stepped ashore at Lingayen Gulf, four P-38s of the 432nd FS flew a disappointing dive-bombing mission against a bridge north of Manila, as was recorded in the squadron's operational diary:

> Our first bombing mission of the month was flown today, and it was a dismal failure. Our task was to skip-bomb a bridge at Calumpit, on Luzon. Four airplanes took off from Dulag at 0615hrs, carrying one 2,000lb bomb each. When our P-38s reached the target area, the skies above the bridge were already overcrowded with friendly aircraft. B-25s were strafing the railroad from an altitude of 25ft, before heading off the target directly toward our Lightnings. Elsewhere, the roads were being strafed in both directions by A-20s. Anxious to avoid us being hit by a medium bomber, our flight leader continued on past our original target and led us in to bomb a bridge approximately one mile above Melolos.
>
> It was quite evident from the results of the bombing that our pilots needed a little more practice, as two bombs fell short, one overshot and one was jettisoned by accident. All airplanes landed back at Dulag at 1245hrs.
>
> All the aerial activity up in Luzon today was due to the fact that our troops were making a landing at Lingayen. At last we have a foothold on Luzon, the enemy's principal base in the Philippines.

With little aerial opposition now to speak of, the 475th FG began loading up its P-38s with bombs – on the mission just detailed, each of the four P-38s carried a single one-ton weapon. Lt Gen Ennis Whitehead had recently become head of the Fifth Air Force, and one of his new innovations was the fitment of heavier bomb loads to P-38s in order for them to be more effective in the ground-attack mission. Col MacDonald lauded this decision, stating after the war that it was one of the most effective and original orders issued by a commander during the Pacific campaign.

But just as the P-38 was set to embrace a new mission in the Pacific, units operating the Lockheed fighter began to feel the effects of a shortage of airframes in-theater. This problem was nothing new to the Fifth Air Force, as throughout 1943 and well into 1944, the Lightning had been the fighter of choice for USAAF commanders worldwide, yet it had been produced in far fewer numbers than any other American single-seat fighter type. When an overall reduction in demand for P-38s in Europe lessened the strain on the Pacific units, the relatively modest demands in the Southwest Pacific were at last satisfied in the summer of 1944. However, for some inexplicable reason the shortage occurred once again, and this time worse than ever, in early 1945.

Fortunately, with the virtual defeat of Japanese air power in the region, the FEAF did not suffer too badly due to the reduced number of P-38s in-theater. Nevertheless, the shortage affected the 475th FG to the degree that its squadrons had to put up mixed flights of, say, two "Hades" and two "Clover" P-38s in order to fulfil convoy cover duty during this period, simply because no single unit in the group could consistently muster four serviceable Lightnings at any one time.

Although the FEAF was suffering its own problems at this time, these were nothing compared to those besetting the enemy. Surviving Japanese forces in the Philippines were both fragmented and undersupplied because of the Allied air and naval dominance in-theater. Slowly, enemy troops were forced south into isolated pockets of resistance and to the north through the Balete Pass, where they could only hope to repeat the previous American delaying tactics of battles fought in 1942.

One objective of special interest to US forces was the resort town of Baguio, situated midway up the western coast of Luzon. Aircrew flying over Baguio spotted golf courses, swimming pools and other recreational facilities which ensured that they did not inflict serious damage to the town, lest they destroy a prime rest and leave spot for future use!

The 432nd FS was spared the possibility of inadvertently causing damage to Baguio on January 17 when four of its P-38s were each scheduled to drop a 2,000lb bomb on a road south of the town, only to have the mission scrubbed by weather. The Lightning pilots went after the alternate target of Silay airstrip on Negros Island instead, only to find that none of the bombs exploded when they were dropped. In frustration, they then strafed the strip, with unobserved results. Flak over this target had claimed the unit's Capt Paul Lucas two days earlier, and although the six-kill ace had managed to crash-land his damaged fighter, he was found dead in the cockpit of his machine by friendly Filipino partisans when they ran to help the downed American pilot.

The squadron again had no luck when sent to bomb Baguio on January 21, poor weather over the target area obliging seven "Clover" P-38 pilots to take their 14 1,000lb bombs to an alternate target on Negros Island. A pier was completely destroyed at Bacolod, and the P-38s strafed buildings and other structures in the area. Baguio was finally bombed with more success the following day when flights from both "Hades" and "Clover" squadrons attacked the nearby airstrip. After-mission assessment judged that the airfield and its runways were now inoperable for Japanese aircraft, which could have used the base to oppose the impending US invasion of the region.

Poor weather further impeded operations to some extent over the next few days, limiting flights to local convoy patrol or short-range armed reconnaissance missions. Maj John Loisel had inherited the job of group operations officer following McGuire's death, and he led the 432nd FS, which he had previously commanded, on a convoy patrol south of Leyte on January 27. He took off at 0715hrs in typically rainy weather with three other "Clover" squadron P-38s for a three-hour flight, and was back at the sodden airfield at Dulag by 1045hrs.

The mission would have been entirely routine except that Loisel parked at the end of the slippery runway to observe the landings of his relatively inexperienced flight members. Sure enough, 2Lt Arnold W. Larsen skidded badly on his landing run and struck a helpless Loisel, sat in Col MacDonald's fourth *PUTT PUTT MARU*, as the skidding Lightning ran head on into the commander's aircraft. Neither man was hurt, but both P-38s were written off and sent over to the 10th Service Squadron for disposal.

This particular *PUTT PUTT MARU* had only been in service for about three weeks, thus having what must have been the shortest service life of any P-38 flown by Col MacDonald. His reaction was very mild, considering the loss of one of his precious P-38s – after some understandably negative comment by the CO when he was first told about the accident, he simply commented, "Johnny should have been more careful, and not have sat so close to that crowded and slippery runway." MacDonald was known for being a tough commander, but he was also ultimately fair.

The 121st and last aerial victory scored by the 433rd FS during the Pacific War had come a few days before the accident, on January 24, when 1Lt LeRoy Ross confirmed a Japanese fighter shot down over a convoy just east of Negros Island. The unit report of the action is typically understated, but nevertheless informative:

Patrol convoy south of Sequijor Island, completed. One "Zeke 52" definitely destroyed, our losses nil. Two "Zeke 52s" sighted, headed southeast at 9,000ft about 40 miles south of Sequijor Island. P-38s headed 90 degrees at 9,000ft. Remaining three "Zeke 52s" escaped to the southeast during combat. "Zekes" were carrying belly tanks and did not appear to be attempting to attack convoy.

Flight leader and wingman handling high cover approached from "six o'clock" at 9,000ft, flight leader closed to 120 yards and fired short burst, causing right wing and right belly tank of enemy aircraft to explode. Enemy pilot bailed out and airplane crashed into water 18 miles northeast of Plaridel, Mindanao.

En route, four-tenths scattered cumulus 4,000–10,000ft. Eight belly tanks dropped. "Zeke 52s" were painted a dark green and had large red roundels. One "Zeke" had a wide orange band running around fuselage just to rear of cockpit.

The identification of the enemy types encountered as A6M5 Zeros was probably in error, for these fighters were more likely to have been Ki-84 Hayates, known as "Frank" to the Allies. This victory would have been even more gratifying to Ross if he had realized at the time that he would be the last 433rd pilot to claim an enemy fighter – and one of the best Japanese types to boot.

In February the 475th FG continued with its near-daily routine of flying patrol and ground attack missions throughout the region. The operational diary of the 432nd FS for February 2, 1945, which noted the tedium of operations at this time, also lamented the sorry state of the unit's operational strength:

> Today's flight was a good indication of the type of missions being meted out to our squadron due to our shortage of airplanes. Four airplanes escorted C-47s to Mindoro and back. Take-off was at 0900hrs and landing time 1530hrs. There were nil sightings during the mission.

On February 4 the squadron was reinforced with new personnel and a handful of replacement aircraft, which allowed it to fly nine P-38s to its new base on Mindoro over the next few days. Although routine missions continued during this period, the unit's pilots hoped for more action in the immediate future. And they were not disappointed when Col MacDonald visited the 432nd to fly with the squadron on February 13.

The CO led a flight of five P-38s on a bomber escort mission that began at 0730hrs, the P-38s departing from Elmore Field, on Mindoro, to cover the "heavies" as they went after Japanese shipping off the coast of China. Although a number of vessels were discovered in the target area, heavy cloud saved them from being attacked, and forced the bombers to jettison their loads harmlessly into the water. MacDonald, however, made the most of the situation when he sighted a Ki-57 "Topsy" transport aircraft and shot it down in flames. One horrific detail from the engagement recounted by the pilots involved upon their return to base was the sight of passengers jumping without parachutes to escape the flames and imminent crash. The destruction of this machine gave MacDonald his 27th and final victory.

The 431st FS found good hunting during a Navy PB4Y escort on February 25 when, just off the coast of Indochina near Cam Ranh Bay, a number of A6M2-N "Rufe" floatplane fighters were caught in the process of taking off. Two of the Japanese aircraft boldly attacked the 12 P-38s from different directions and altitudes and were promptly shot down, whilst two others were destroyed in strafing runs on their ramps. Having destroyed all of the "Rufes," as well as their base, the Lightning pilots then set about strafing any ship or installation along the nearby coastline.

The group also commenced napalm firebombing missions at the end of February, with the 432nd FS flying its first such operation on the 26th when 12 of its P-38s attacked

Puerta Princessa, on Palawan Island, in preparation for a forthcoming invasion. Several hours later, four 432nd FS fighters were sent to Busuaga Island to strafe and bomb a crashed B-25 that had force-landed in a fairly intact condition. This proved to be one of the more unusual operations flown by the unit, and flight commander Capt Joe Forster subsequently reported "a souvenir hunter couldn't have salvaged enough aluminum to make a decent set of earrings for his lady fair" after the four P-38s had worked over the hapless bomber.

March started much to the liking of seven-kill ace Capt Perry Dahl when he led the 432nd FS on a seven-airplane fighter sweep of Formosa on the 5th. This mission was the first squadron operation flown by the unit from its new base at the Clark Field complex, the group having occupied the site on February 28. The 432nd found itself camped between airstrip No 4 and Fort Stotsenberg, and declared itself operational in just a matter of days so as to be available to fly this potentially lucrative sweep.

Dahl made the most of the opportunity when he led his P-38s down in an abortive run on what turned out to be a civilian fishing fleet. However, soon after leveling off at just 1,500ft, Dahl spotted a Ki-21 "Sally" bomber flying in the opposite direction to him at his altitude just inland from his present position. The ace quickly reversed his course and came up directly behind the enemy aircraft, whose pilot was diving frantically in a futile effort to escape the P-38. Dahl fired a few bursts that set an engine on fire and caused large pieces of the Ki-21's fuselage to fly off. The "Sally" exploded upon hitting the ground, but to the utter amazement of the circling P-38s above it, five surviving crew members were seen to escape from the wreckage and run for cover.

The next day the Japanese welcomed the 475th FG to Clark Field by staging a rare air raid on the base. For 90 minutes in the early hours of March 6, enemy aircraft roared back and forth over the area totally unopposed since antiaircraft defenses had not yet been put in place. From 0300hrs until 0430hrs, the raiders sought out targets and dropped at least two sticks of bombs. However, they inflicted little physical damage of note, although they certainly frayed the nerves of the group personnel who huddled in whatever shelter they could find.

Missions continued unabated throughout March, with bomber escorts to the Southeast Asian coastline punctuating patrols and ground support operations. All the while, US troops were advancing along the western Luzon coast and east into the Cagayan valley, and on March 15 the 475th flew its first missions in support of ground forces advancing northward toward Baguio. By the end of the month, targets around Manila were also being hit as the Allies attempted to drive a wedge between the Japanese Army's northern Kembu group and the southern Shimbu group. By April, Japanese forces had become heavily fragmented, just as the US resistance in the Philippines had been three years earlier, with no hope of reinforcement or resupply.

The 433rd FS's two ground attack missions on March 28 illustrate how the 475th FG was implementing its role as the harasser of retreating Japanese forces in the Manila area. The first mission saw P-38s attack a motor pool south of Santa Fe just after 0900hrs, 12 1,000lb bombs hitting the target and two others damaging a building 600 yards away. Two more bombs were jettisoned in Pampanga Bay when no more suitable targets could be found. All eight P-38s involved in the operation also made two strafing runs to complete a successful mission. Later that same afternoon, eight Lightnings from the 433rd FS dropped a further 16 1,000lb bombs to knock out a field artillery position northeast of Santa Fe.

LAST AERIAL VICTORIES

As previously mentioned, the glory days of aerial combat in the Southwest Pacific had ended with the campaign against Clark Field in late December 1944. The Fifth and Thirteenth Air Forces had claimed more than 100 Japanese aircraft shot down during December alone, and almost as many again would be claimed by the entire FEAF during the remaining eight months of the war.

For the 475th FG the final 16 victories claimed by the group came during two long-range B-25 escort missions flown on March 28 and 29, 1945. These engagements provided a fitting end to a remarkable run of success for the group, which had seen it claim 552 aircraft shot down, 61 probably destroyed and 36 damaged in just 19 months of aerial combat. The 49th FG had secured top-scoring honors in the Pacific with 664 kills, but the 475th had achieved its kills at a faster rate than any other unit in-theater, and had one of the highest average rates of claims for any fighter group in the entire USAAF.

The swansong for the 475th as a fighter group began on March 28, when 24 of its P-38s rendezvoused with B-25s over Capotes Island at 0725hrs, before proceeding to what was then the Indochina coastline in search of Japanese shipping; landfall was reached at 1045hrs. The aircraft approached the mainland at low altitude (between wave-top height and 2,000ft), although the P-38s had reportedly climbed to 10,000ft by the time numerous enemy fighters were spotted stacked up in loose formations from 18,000ft down to the water at about 1130hrs. The latter were circling overhead a Japanese convoy that was sailing just off the Indochina coast.

By the time the engagement ended, nine more enemy fighters had been added to the 475th's tally, including the last victories for Maj John Loisel and Capt Perry Dahl. Loisel was leading the entire 475th FG formation at the head of the 433rd FS, and his after-action report details how the dogfight started:

On March 28, 1945 I was flying in the No 1 position in "Red Flight" in a formation of 20 P-38s. At 1150hrs, we sighted 12 (unidentified) enemy aircraft milling around between

18,000ft and the deck. The enemy aircraft were circling over a convoy of vessels just north of Tre Island. I started into a climbing turn, dropped tanks at 7,500ft, began a diving turn and approached two probable "Franks" from astern. The first "Frank" did a sharp left turn as I fired a sighting burst. The second "Frank" continued straight ahead in a slight climb. I gave him a good burst, getting hits immediately on his fuselage and right wing. He burst into flames from the wing-root, did a left turn and headed down steeply, flaming badly. This "Frank" crashed just off the enemy convoy.

A few minutes later I saw my number four airplane attacked by an unidentified enemy aircraft. One airplane from another flight drove the enemy aircraft off. 2Lt Wesley Hulett called me and said that his engine was out. I then turned eastward, only to see him diving with another enemy airplane on his tail. I scared this one off with a short burst and lost sight of the P-38. I looked around for him after he said both engines were shot out – I couldn't locate him, but told him to head due east and that I would call the Catalina. I then returned to the fight, which had drifted eastward from Tre Island.

I got in several desultory passes with no observed results. Saw 1Lt C. Wacker of the 432nd FS shoot down an enemy aircraft. I left the target area at 1210hrs, and on my way home I searched the area where 2Lt Hulett had gone down. I also contacted "Cat" and all other aircraft in area, giving them the location of the downed airplane. I landed at San Marcelino at 1540hrs.

As Maj Loisel noted in his after-action report, he had encountered the Ki-84 for the first time, and he gave the fighter high marks. The 11-kill ace recalled his "desultory" passes long after the war, further commenting that he had a few tricks up his sleeve that did no good against the swift and sleek JAAF fighter that had appeared in the frontline late in the war.

Ace 1Lt Kenneth Hart of the 431st FS emerged from the March 28 encounter as one of the group's high scorers, as his after-action report explained:

I was leading a seven-aircraft flight, with 2Lt T. Martin flying in the No 2 position and 1Lt "Bo" Reeves at No 3. At 1155hrs we reached the target area at 11,000ft. About ten minutes later we made our first pass on two enemy aircraft, with no results. Shortly after, we were jumped from "seven o'clock," and after a short engagement, I shot one down. I fired a long burst from 30 degrees to 0 degrees as I was pulling up on him from below and he burst into flames. The pilot bailed out northwest of Ninh Hoa at about 1213hrs.

A few minutes later we were jumped by four more "Hamps." 1Lt Reeves split-essed and I broke sharply to the left, coming out on a "Hamp's" tail. He skidded and was doing rolls as I fired short bursts at him, knocking large pieces from his tail and hitting his fuselage. There was a flash of flame in the cockpit and the pilot bailed out, the ship crashing at 1217hrs just south of the first Nip I shot down. I looked over to my right and saw a Nip spinning straight in, which crashed just after, and to the north of where my second Nip had just crashed.

Upon calling on the radio, I found that the P-38 above it, who had just shot down the Nip, was being flown by 1Lt Reeves. We joined up and gave chase to another Nip to the west. I fired at him out of range, endeavoring to make him turn before he reached cloud cover, but had no success. 1Lt Reeves dove under the cloud as I pulled up above and latched onto the Nip as he came out below. I circled above and watched him shoot it down, the Nip crashing and burning a short distance west of Ben Coi Bay at 1220hrs. We left the target area shortly afterward and landed back at home base at 1605hrs.

It had been a most satisfying operation for the 475th, except for the loss of 2Lt Wesley Hulett, who was never found – the 433rd FS's Flt Off Charles DeWeese was also lost in a separate incident that same day.

The next day, the 475th FG again escorted B-25s to the Indochina coast as the long-range anti-shipping offensive continued. Unbeknown to the P-38 pilots involved, their mission on March 29, 1945 would be the last time that the group would encounter Japanese aircraft on the wing. Six 431st FS and four 432nd FS Lightnings arrived in the target area at around 1130hrs, and moments later 1Lt Laurence LeBaron called out 11 bandits approaching them from the same altitude – 4,000ft – slightly off to their right:

Our flight made a shallow climbing turn to the right and attacked from "six o'clock." In the initial pass, I fired on a straggler from 200 yards at 30 degrees deflection. However, he saw me at the instant I fired and started a fast turn to the left. I observed several cannon bursts along the right side of the fuselage and on the right wing root. The airplane began smoking slightly and slipping down toward the water. My wingman fired several bursts, getting several hits on the wingtip. The airplane was seen to hit the water just off shore by 2Lt L. Dowler.

I reversed my turn and swung in behind the main formation in time to see 1Lt Harold Owen hit the other straggler and follow him in a diving turn to the right. As yet, the main enemy force gave no indication of having seen us. I closed rapidly on another wingman from the stern and fired a burst from 150 yards, getting numerous hits on the wings, tail and fuselage, knocking pieces off the wing and tail, and causing him to smoke moderately. Because I overran him, and my wingman, 2Lt John O'Rourke, was attacking another at the same time, the enemy pilot was not seen to crash or bail out. As I overran him, I pulled slightly to the left and gave his leader a burst from astern from about 100 yards. He began smoking violently, with pieces coming off the trailing edge of his wing. He immediately plunged into the water. I also saw another fighter crash in the water about 200 yards to the right at about the same time – the result of 2Lt O'Rourke's attack.

By this time the rest of the Nips had started to scatter, and as I brought my element around to join 1Lt Owens's element, the remaining Nips slipped in behind us. 1Lt Owen crossed over and broke them up with a head-on pass. In the ensuing dogfight, I saw a Nip make a head-on pass from above on 2Lt Dowler, who pulled up and fired at him from below. The Nip passed over him and crashed into the trees half a mile inland.

After making several more passes and getting in a few scattered hits, I saw one making for the clouds inland and gave chase. After reversing his turns in several cumulus clouds, he apparently thought he had lost us and straightened out, heading south. I came up from below and directly astern, firing a long burst at about 150 yards. He began coming apart and smoking violently. He crashed and burned at the edge of a small clearing. We circled the area two times, and being low on gas, we returned to base, leaving the target at 1255hrs and landing at home base at 1530hrs.

Although flying with the 431st FS on March 29, 1Lt John O'Rourke was actually a 432nd FS pilot who had readily offered to fill in for a "Hades" pilot who had aborted earlier in the mission. This in-flight swap had later proved to be the main topic of discussion back at Clark Field when the two units argued about whether O'Rourke's "Zeke 52" kill should have been added to the 431st or 432nd victory tally. It was finally decided to award the victory to the former, giving the 432nd six victories for the mission and a single kill to the 431st.

Victory lists disagree on the exact number, but the group accrued at least 552 verified kills by any tabulation, giving it an impressive average of roughly 22 kills per month from the time it first engaged the enemy in aerial combat.

SUPPORTING THE TROOPS

From early April through to the end of June 1945, the 475th FG had to satisfy itself with less glamorous "ground pounding" missions, rather than the high-profile fighter-versus-fighter engagements that had effectively been the group's reason for being activated in mid-1943. Japanese positions both in the northern Kembu and southern Shimbu areas were gradually worn down with methodical certainty by the FEAF, with small formations of bomb-toting P-38s being used to attack positions stubbornly manned by diehard fanatics rather than ranks of organized troops. Perhaps the most threatening Japanese positions of them all during this period were those defending the Ipo Dam area, as they posed a greater danger to the civilian population in the area than to advancing Allied troops.

April 1945 was one of the worst months for the Japanese war effort, for on the 1st, US forces invaded the island of Okinawa. The subsequent basing of USAAF B-29s here duly exposed the Home Islands of Kyushu and Honshu to a series of devastating attacks by the long-range heavy bombers. Six days later, the mighty battleship *Yamato* was lost in a futile operation against US naval vessels off Okinawa, and on the same day fighter-escorted B-29s began to attack the Home Islands.

Although heavily committed to the ground war in the Philippines, the 475th was able to alternate tactical strikes with bomber escort and long-range ground attack missions against targets along the Southeast Asian coast, as well as the island of Formosa. For example, on April 1 the 432nd FS escorted a PBM Mariner that had been sent to patrol the sea around Formosa, and 24 hours later the unit flew an impressive napalm attack mission on the Villa Verde trail, west of Santa Fe. For the latter operation, five P-38s were loaded with 1,000lb general-purpose bombs and four armed with napalm. Large fires were started in the target area which caused a US forward air controller to comment over the radio that the group's bombing was the best he had ever witnessed.

The 475th experienced the heaviest mission schedule of its brief operational life during this period, for the short nature of the tactical missions in support of troops on the ground allowed squadrons to fly at least two or three operations a day. And pilots who flew these missions commented that they took great pleasure in attacking railroad-related targets in particular. Locomotives were especially gratifying, for when bullets and cannon shells struck the boiler plate of the engine, a spectacular fountain of steam would often whoosh up for hundreds of feet just as the successful P-38 passed overhead.

The 433rd FS got an unexpected crack at railroad targets on April 8, when eight of its fighters escorted B-24s that had been sent to bomb an airfield on Formosa. The P-38 pilots had been circling the area for 15 minutes when a locomotive pulling five freight cars was spotted on the main north-to-south line near the city of Taichu. The train was thoroughly strafed, and by the time the fighters had withdrawn, the locomotive was hidden in a cloud of steam and its cars shot to pieces.

Later that same month the 475th gave up its comfortable Clark Field quarters for the dusty and austere conditions at Lingayen. The Mustangs of the 35th FG had been suffering high attrition because of the unrefined surface of the hurriedly built airstrips and runways in the area. Compared with the P-51, the P-38 had somewhat sturdier landing gear that was better suited to operations from rough surfaces and landing grounds such as those found at Lingayen.

By April 19 the 475th had essentially traded places with the 35th FG, and three days later, the grousing and complaining by the Lightning pilots about the interruption in combat operations ended when the group flew its first missions. For the next few days sorties were flown against ground targets around Baguio until that entire area fell to two American divisions on April 26. Elsewhere, Japanese forces were found to be entrenching themselves along transport routes into the Cagayan Valley, thus presenting the FEAF's fighter and dive-bomber units with plenty of fixed targets to attack. The move to Lingayen meant that the 475th was now in a better position from which to attack long-range targets on Formosa and mainland Southeast Asia. And even though ground support missions would continue, pilots soon came to appreciate the possibilities offered by this more strategic location.

On May 3, P-38s from the 433rd FS were on a dive-bombing mission to the Bontoc area of the Cordilera Central Mountains when the aircraft of formation leader 1Lt Jerome Hammond was hit by flak. Although one of his engines was ablaze, the pilot managed to force-land his P-38 and escape from the wrecked cockpit before it was engulfed by flames. Moments after he had scampered clear of the Lightning, it exploded into a fireball.

For three days Hammond successfully evaded Japanese patrols, and also his own comrades when P-38s dive-bombed a nearby target, until he was found by friendly Filipino partisans. He was then taken to an Allied camp, where he received food, clothes and treatment for the burns he had received during the crash. Eager to help him out, the Filipinos had guided Hammond back to Lingayen by May 19, where he rejoined his comrades. He left the Pacific for good in July when he was rotated back home to Wichita, Kansas.

While Jerome Hammond was making his way back through enemy lines, the drive toward the Ipo Dam was progressing at great speed. The 475th was heavily involved in this offensive, flying numerous missions against enemy positions in the immediate target area between May 17 and 26. By this time the dreaded napalm was really beginning to have an effect on the morale of Japanese troops, and the latter wilted in the face of continual attacks to the point where the commander of the US Army's 43rd Division sent the 475th a commendation for its part in making the sweep through the area so effortless.

June 1945 saw the end of all organized resistance by the Japanese in northern Luzon, and with enemy forces in the south having been all but defeated, there was little for the FEAF's tactical units to do except strike at occasional targets in the Aparri region of northern Luzon. By month-end the Philippines had been declared secure, and only occasional mopping-up missions were now being flown. On June 18 the 475th would commence long-range napalm missions with a strike on Kari, in southwestern Formosa.

TOUR ROTATION

Gen Douglas MacArthur had officially declared the Philippines secure on June 26, 1945, thus tacitly approving a general rotation back home for all FEAF personnel. Although MacArthur never put much stock in pampering his troops, giving little thought to sparing soldiers from the demands of combat, his views were not shared by Lt Gen Kenney of the FEAF. Indeed, the latter had gone out of his way to protect his aircrew, believing that they could only be kept sharp in combat if tour limits were rigorously adhered to. In practice, this meant that a fighter pilot in the Fifth Air Force could typically expect to be eligible for rotation after about 300 hours in combat or about 15 months on tour, unless he accepted a position of advanced responsibility such as operations officer or squadron commander.

Aces Perry Dahl and Joe Forster had both joined the 475th FG's 432nd FS in late October 1943. Destined to be aces by the end of 1944, they had remained in-theater until mid-1945. The only break from frontline flying that Dahl had experienced during this period came in November–December 1944, when he evaded capture for a month in the Philippines after being forced down following a mid-air collision. Forster had spent several months in the US in early 1945 attending a gunnery class, but was back in the Philippines by July – just after Dahl had rotated home in late June. Both men had enjoyed great success with the 432nd FS, claiming nine confirmed kills apiece and surviving numerous combat missions.

Although Dahl had spent an impressive 21 months in-theater (he had agreed to accept the post of operations officer for the 432nd FS), this did not come close to the three years of service Lt Col John Loisel gave to the 475th FG. He had joined the group upon its formation in July 1943 after being given a six-month extension to his tour following nine months in combat with the 36th FS/8th FG. Loisel progressed through the ranks within the 475th, being operations officer and then CO of the 432nd FS in 1943–44, after which he became group operations officer when Maj McGuire was killed in January 1945. By then an 11-victory ace, he was finally made commander of the 475th FG when veteran CO Col MacDonald was sent home in July 1945.

Another pilot who completed an extended spell in the front line was five-kill ace 1Lt Marion Kirby, who agreed to extend for six months when he was assigned to the 431st FS in July 1943. He had already spent close to 12 months in New Guinea with the 80th FS/8th FG by the time he transferred to the 475th, and was glad to rotate home in December 1943 after completing some 126 combat missions. Although virtually all fighter pilots assigned to the 475th FG were keen to see action, Lt Col John Loisel told the author that nobody ever turned down a trip home when orders terminating a tour were received.

For enlisted groundcrew, tours tended to last a lot longer. One individual who took this to an extreme was MSgt Clay V. Cockerill, who had joined the 475th in Australia in July 1943 and remained with the group until he was rotated home exactly two years later. He had managed to successfully resist being sent home until he fell under the provisions of the "over 40 years of age" ruling.

Just prior to Cockerill being sent home, he participated in a group-wide gathering on June 20, 1945 at Lingayen, which saw the 475th finally receive its three Distinguished Unit Citations. The first of these had been awarded to the unit as long ago as August 1943 following its impressive introduction into battle over Wewak on the 18th and 21st of that month, when its pilots not only protected the bombers, but also claimed many Japanese aircraft shot down.

The second citation followed the group's gallant fight over Oro Bay on October 15 and 17, 1943, when ground personnel were able to witness for themselves the clashes in which the P-38s disrupted Japanese attacks and claimed many more enemy aircraft destroyed. The third award came in the wake of the whirlwind of action in which many more Japanese aircraft were shot down between October 25 and December 25, 1944, during the climactic air battles over the Philippines in the initial stages of the invasion.

In March 1946 the group received yet another honor when Maj Thomas Buchanan McGuire was posthumously awarded the Congressional Medal of Honor. Maj Richard Ira Bong's service with the 475th in December 1944 had also been mentioned in the citation which accompanied his Medal of Honor, presented to the American "ace of aces" that same month.

FINAL COMBAT

Following almost 24 months of near-constant action, July 1945 at last provided the 475th FG's hard-pressed groundcrews with a little respite from having to provide serviceable P-38s for the two to three missions that the group had typically been flying on a near-daily basis since mid-1943. With a lack of targets to be serviced, groundcrews now had seemingly unlimited time for maintenance and the replenishment of supplies. They were even able to take a break from the flightline and parade in front of Brig Gen Freddie Smith, who had traveled to Lingayen Gulf in order to present 151 decorations to the 75 pilots then serving with the group. This would be the last such presentation conducted by the 475th in wartime.

Combat operations had not entirely stopped, however, for the group was still occasionally attacking ragged pockets of resistance stubbornly and defiantly posed by exhausted Japanese forces, mainly in the extreme northern part of Luzon. By late July even these missions had tailed off, so the 49th and 475th FGs were relieved of combat duty on the 23rd of the month in preparation for their impending move to bases in the Japanese Home Islands area.

Forty-eight hours earlier, the latter group's three squadrons had flown what would prove to be their last combat missions of the war. The 431st undertook mission number 1-1008, the 432nd sent eight P-38s on a fire-bombing attack northwest of Kiangan for mission number 2-907 and the 433rd performed a convoy cover patrol for mission number 3-1047. All subsequent sorties from Lingayen over the next five days would be either training or operational administrative flights. Even these ceased on July 26, when the group commenced packing up in preparation for movement closer to Japan itself.

Personnel from the 431st FS were loaded aboard LST 793, the 432nd FS boarded LST 752 and the 433rd FS embarked in LST 1014. All three vessels left Lingayen Gulf on the morning of July 27, and they reached the naval base in Subic Bay, in the Philippines, the next day. By August 1, the group was sailing again, with the HQ aboard LST 752 and other elements of the 431st aboard cramped LSMs which accompanied the convoy.

On August 6 the group arrived in convoy off Okinawa, and the 432nd FS's operational diarist recorded this event, totally unaware of the significance of a bombing mission that had taken place that same morning – the atomic bomb "Little Boy" had been dropped on Hiroshima:

> Land was sighted this morning – Okinawa. Our LST dropped anchor in Yonobura Harbor at 1130hrs. Next to Naha, this is the second most important harbor on the island. The amount of shipping in Yonobura surpassed everything we had laid eyes on before. Almost every conceivable type of vessel and craft used by the Navy and Merchant Marine were either anchored or seen plying the waters between ship and shore. Our LST was anchored close enough off shore for us to be able to observe a few of the numerous strips reputed to be on Okinawa, and some of us had the opportunity of viewing for the first time the much-vaunted "battleship of the air" – the B-29.
>
> We remained in Yonobura Harbor, awaiting our turn to disgorge our load on the beach at Ie Shima, which is about a two-and-a-half-hour trip from here. Ie Shima has facilities for unloading only four or five LSTs at a time, and the arrival of our convoy is overtaxing those facilities. It will probably be four or five days before our turn to unload comes up.

The first air raid alert for the 475th since March 5 in the Philippines was heard in the early morning hours of August 7. Two more air raids later that day caused more anxiety, since news of the atomic bombing had drawn speculation that the war might be coming to a sudden end. A second atomic bomb dropped on Nagasaki, and the Soviet Union's declaration of war on Japan on the 9th, presaged the general collapse of Japanese will.

Ie Shima itself was described by a 475th officer as "a combination of Biak and Leyte. The roads, which were all constructed of coral, were marvels of engineering skill, but our camp area was a muddy morass that had to be covered with coral before it could become even halfway livable." When the group finally disembarked on August 12, everybody was immediately pressed into service to make the camp come to life in record time.

Capt Elliott Summer had been interim commander of the 432nd FS until July 28, 1945, when he was rotated home and Maj Dean Dutrack took over the unit just as it began its move to Ie Shima. Maj Ed Weaver, who had been part of the fateful "Daddy Special" flight on January 7, over Negros Island, was in command of the 431st FS at war's end, while 433rd FS records have the signature of veteran group pilot Capt William Haning as commander during the July–August 1945 period.

For the last few months of operations, the 475th dropped more than 1,400 tons of high explosives and 1,600 gallons of napalm at a time when few missions involved more than eight P-38s. As these figures show, the group had been highly active in its role supporting Allied ground forces. And whether the latter recognized the twin-boomed airplanes over their heads or not, the troops on Luzon and Leyte owed some gratitude to the persistent skill of the 475th pilots who bombed and strafed determined, if ragged, Japanese troops barring the way to clearing the islands.

Between August 1943 and the end of March 1945, the 475th's 552 aerial victories had cost it 80 P-38s lost in combat and 75 pilots killed in action. 1Lt William Hasty of the 433rd FS, who had been downed in June 1944 and captured on the Vogelkop Peninsula, became the only 475th prisoner of war to be repatriated after VJ-Day.

POSTWAR POSTSCRIPT

Members of the 475th FG were satisfied to see two white "Betty" bombers with their distinctive green crosses on their fuselage and wings land at Mocha strip on Ie Shima at around noon on August 19, 1945. Brig Gen Freddie Smith of V Fighter Command was on hand to greet the grim-faced Japanese delegation flown in aboard the aircraft, and he saw them off again aboard a C-54 some 90 minutes later. They would fly on to Manila, where the last details of the new peace were to be negotiated before the September 2, 1945 ceremony that was staged aboard the battleship USS *Missouri* officially brought World War II to an end.

Throughout the war in the Southwest Pacific, V Fighter Command had been a painful thorn in the side of the Japanese, and the 475th had been the barb end of that thorn for much of the time. As previously mentioned, final figures of enemy aircraft shot down grant the 49th FG top spot with 664 confirmed claims, followed by the 475th with 552, the 8th with 453, the 35th with 387 and the 348th with 349. The tactically assigned 58th FG managed 14 kills while flying under conditions that were not conducive to aerial combat.

The first postwar move for the 475th was to Kimpo, in South Korea, in September 1945. Those crews who had endured the last operations of the Pacific War now had to cope with the usual level of neglect associated with the reduction in the size of armed forces after any large-scale conflict. To make matters worse, the group was subjected to freezing winter weather in South Korea in 1945–46. Fortunately, the ravaged Japanese wartime economy came to the rescue when surplus fur-lined flying suits and barracks heaters were procured from the 475th's former adversaries.

In 1946 the group converted to the P-51 Mustang in an action that would have been anathema to the wartime veterans who had sworn by their P-38s. Finally, in 1948, the 475th moved to Itazuke and then Ashiya, both in Japan, before being deactivated in April 1949. The group remained dormant until mid-1953, when the 431st was activated within the 7272nd Flying Training Wing. Inadvertently, one of the first experiences the author had had with the 475th was when he observed the F-89s of the 432nd Fighter-Interceptor Squadron (FIS), based at Minneapolis/St Paul International Airport, flying over his teenaged head in the mid-1950s!

The 431st FIS converted to F-86D Sabres in the mid-1950s, after which it operated from Wheelus air base, in Libya, before the squadron moved to Zaragosa, in Spain, in 1958. There, it converted to the F-102 Delta Dart in 1960, and the squadron was still operating the type when it was transferred to Southeast Asia in the mid-1960s. At about the same time, the 433rd FS was reactivated and issued with F-4C Phantom IIs, prior to being assigned to the 9th Tactical Fighter Wing. During the Vietnam conflict, pilots assigned to the 433rd FIS scored a number of aerial victories, thus raising its historical tally to more than 130 enemy aircraft shot down.

As of late 2006, it is still possible to visit with some of the personalities who actually lived the colorful history of the "Satan's Angels," as the veterans of the group are pleased to call themselves. Col John Loisel still maintains a military bearing that constantly breaks down into cheery friendliness when he talks about those days. Perry Dahl is much the same, making me wonder who gave him the nickname "Pee Wee" whenever I shake his hand and feel the vicelike grip of his enduring arm muscle. Joe Forster is still a lean and efficient looking individual, and it is not hard to imagine the venerable fighter pilot guiding his battle-damaged P-38 the 800-plus miles from Borneo back to northern New Guinea.

Many of the others are gone, of course. Col MacDonald was the very spirit of the group, and it is hard to believe that his gently dominating presence is gone. Fred Champlin was a quiet chap who remained a standard of "Satan's Angels" valor and determination until he slowly succumbed some years ago. But we can imagine them all, from the charismatic Tom McGuire to the line mechanics glowing with fierce pride in their job of work that championed our cause in a terrible and unfortunate war.

Part Four

15TH, 21ST AND 506TH FIGHTER GROUPS

The Tokyo Club

INTRODUCTION

The pilots called themselves the "Tokyo Club." It was a simple task to become a member. All you had to do was strap yourself into a heavily loaded P-51 Mustang fighter; take off from Iwo Jima (a postage-stamp sized volcanic island in the middle of the Pacific Ocean); fly 650 miles north over the sea – sometimes through monsoon storms – in your single-engined aircraft to Japan; attack a heavily defended target in the vicinity of the enemy's capital city; then turn around and fly home, while fretting over your dwindling fuel supply and perhaps battle damage as well. If your fuel held out and you did not lose your way on the return trip, you landed back at Iwo after an eight-hour flight with your body so stiff and sore that you needed to be lifted out of the cockpit by your groundcrew.

Doing it once earned you membership to the club. But make one mistake, or have a touch of bad luck, and you had a very good chance of ending up dead.

The following pages tell the little-known story of these brave men and their efforts to defeat the forces defending Japan during the final five months of World War II. Used initially to provide fighter escort for B-29s bombing Tokyo and other cities on Japan's main island of Honshu, the Iwo Jima-based P-51 pilots enjoyed such success that they were soon called on to make low-level attacks against ground targets in preparation for the expected invasion of Japan. You will get to know the three Mustang-equipped Very Long Range (VLR) fighter groups of the USAAF's VII Fighter Command – the 15th, 21st and 506th FGs – and the men who made them so successful.

By any measure, the "Sun Setters," as VII Fighter Command called itself, did a tremendous job. Between April 7 and August 14, 1945, the Mustangs flew 51 Very Long Range missions targeting mainland Japan, of which nine were aborted due to weather. In addition, nearly 140 strikes were flown against targets in the Bonin Islands, principally on the island of Chichi Jima. In the course of those missions, Mustang pilots scored 234.5 confirmed aerial victories, plus another 219 Japanese aircraft destroyed on the ground. It would be impossible to produce an accurate tally of the ground targets damaged or destroyed by the marauding Mustang pilots, but suffice it to say they took a heavy toll on Japanese rail, road and water traffic, airfield facilities and ground emplacements. The cost was substantial, with 131 P-51s lost and 99 pilots killed, but it is worth noting that by far the majority of losses were attributable to ground fire and bad weather. Indeed, only a handful of VLR Mustangs was shot down in air-to-air combat.

Several factors contributed to the success of VII Fighter Command's operations. Good equipment was a crucial element, and here the "Sun Setters" shone. Their North American P-51D Mustangs were arguably the best propeller-driven fighters of World War II, combining speed, maneuverability, firepower and long range in an airplane that was usually ultra-reliable and relatively easy to fly even when fully loaded with fuel and ammunition.

VII Fighter Command was also a highly skilled unit. Many of the pilots in the 15th and 21st FGs came to Iwo Jima with prior combat experience, and most of the rest had spent long months in training while in Hawaii. The 506th FG had just a smattering of pilots with combat experience, but many others had spent several years as training command instructors and had hundreds of flight hours in their logbooks. On the ground, the technicians and support personnel who worked long hours keeping the airplanes flying were dedicated and highly competent as well.

Meanwhile, at the far end of the 650-mile trip to Tokyo, the defending Japanese Naval Air Force and Japanese Army Air Force air units were no match for VII Fighter Command. By 1945 few veteran Japanese pilots remained alive, and their replacements graduating from truncated flight school programs had barely enough experience to handle docile training airplanes, much less the high-performance fighters they were expected to fly in demanding high-altitude engagements with American fighters and heavy bombers. Lacking not only flying skills but also familiarity with combat tactics and techniques, these young pilots would be lucky to survive even a single encounter with VII Fighter Command Mustangs.

As a result of this volatile combination of factors, the "Sun Setters" were able to roam freely over central Honshu throughout the spring and summer of 1945, creating havoc wherever they went. Their contribution to the Allies' final victory in the Pacific War was a significant one. This is their story.

THE LONG ROAD TO TOKYO

Around midday on November 1, 1944, air raid sirens began to wail in Tokyo. The people who did not immediately take shelter would have strained their eyes to pick out a single silver airplane flying high over their city. Some six miles above them, Capt Ralph D. Steakley of the 3rd Photo Reconnaissance Squadron, USAAF, and his crew of the aptly named Boeing Superfortress *Tokyo Rose* flew on a steady course, unhindered by Japanese interceptors or antiaircraft fire. It was the first overflight of the Japanese capital by an American aircraft since Lt Col Jimmy Doolittle had led his daring B-25 raid against Tokyo in April 1942.

Fortunately for the citizens of Tokyo, no bombs fell from *Tokyo Rose* that day, for she was an F-13A camera ship, not a B-29 heavy bomber. But unfortunately for the people of Tokyo, the photographs taken by Capt Steakley's crew would provide valuable target intelligence for XXI Bomber Command mission planners in the recently captured Marianas Islands, some 1,300 miles south of Tokyo. More photo missions followed over the next few weeks, each one adding to the Americans' knowledge of potential targets in the Tokyo area. As future events would show, the Tokyo air raid alarm of November 1, 1944 signaled the beginning of the end of the Pacific War.

Through nearly eight years of war, dating back to the first clash with Chinese troops on the Marco Polo Bridge on the outskirts of Peking in 1937, Tokyo had been spared the horrors of the war that its leaders had instigated. While Japanese bombers had ravaged city after city in China and Southeast Asia, Tokyo remained virtually untouched.

Even the massive air attack against the great American naval base at Pearl Harbor on December 7, 1941, which drew the United States into the war, had only elicited in response the pinprick damage caused by Doolittle's raiders four months later. Indeed, the next raid by American bombers against Japan did not come until June 1944, when B-29s based in China attacked targets in northern Kyushu. But the logistics required to support the B-29s in China were horrific, and, in any case, the big Boeing bombers lacked the range to reach Tokyo and the other key industrial cities of central Honshu.

All that changed on November 24, 1944. After a typhoon had delayed them for a week, 111 B-29s of the 73rd BW, each laden down with two-and-a-half tons of incendiary and general-purpose bombs, began taking off from Saipan at 0615hrs for the six-hour flight to

Tokyo. By the time the formation reached landfall on the coast of Japan, 17 bombers had dropped out due to mechanical problems, but the rest bore in on the Nakajima aircraft engine plant at Musashino, in northwestern Tokyo – the bombers' primary target.

Fierce winds buffeted the big bombers over Tokyo as they strained to reach their assigned altitude of 35,000ft. As a result, only 24 airplanes were able to bomb the primary target, causing minimal damage to the Nakajima facilities. The rest dropped on the secondary target – dock and urban areas – with similar results. About 125 Japanese fighters intercepted the B-29s, which also encountered moderate flak, but only two of the bombers went down. Following a small night mission on the night of November 29/30, the 73rd BW sent another major force against the Musashino factory on December 3. Again, high winds hampered bombing accuracy, and the target suffered little damage.

A pattern was beginning to emerge. A year earlier the USAAF brass, dominated by bomber advocates, had figured correctly that the B-29s flying at high altitude over Japan would be able to defend themselves sufficiently to hold losses to an acceptable level. But the planners had not reckoned with the effect that the wind patterns over Japan would have on bombing accuracy. Sure, the B-29s could survive over Japan at 35,000ft, but could they bomb from up there and hit their targets? Increasingly, the answer appeared to be no.

By January 20, 1945, when Maj Gen Curtis E. LeMay arrived in the Marianas Islands to assume command of XXI Bomber Command, the B-29s had flown 13 missions against major targets in Japan, but had achieved successful results only three times. Something needed to change, and change it would. First, LeMay would try low-level night attacks; then, when fighter escort became available, he could get down to precision daylight raids that would finally lay waste to Japan's industrial capability.

"PINEAPPLES" AND "YARDBIRDS"

On the morning of March 6, 1945, a P-51D Mustang took off from Isely Field, on Saipan. The pilot of the sleek fighter, Brig Gen Ernest M. "Mickey" Moore, slowly circled the island as 24 Mustangs of the 47th FS took off in pairs and found their places in formation behind him. When Brig Gen Moore was satisfied that his Mustangs were formed up properly, he turned north and began climbing, all the while scanning the sky in front of him. Soon a black dot appeared. It quickly grew into the shape of a B-29 Superfortress, the mother hen that would lead Moore and his chicks to their destination – the embattled island of Iwo Jima, some 650 miles away.

If "Mickey" Moore was excited that morning, he had every reason to be. The 37-year-old West Pointer had been waiting more than three years to lead his pilots into combat against the Japanese, and now he was about to get the opportunity. As commanding officer of VII Fighter Command, Moore had been given the job of providing fighter escort for XXI Bomber

Command B-29s that had recently commenced an intensive bombing campaign against the Home Islands of Japan.

Moore was highly qualified for the job. A Midwesterner, he graduated from the US Military Academy in 1931 and earned his wings at Kelly Field, Texas, the following year. His early flying career included stints as a fighter pilot flying P-12s with the 77th Pursuit Squadron and a period on detached service as an airmail pilot in his home state of Illinois. In 1936–37 Moore attended a graduate course in meteorology at the Massachusetts Institute of Technology, followed by an assignment as base weather officer at Langley Field, Virginia. Then, in the summer of 1939, he was sent to Hawaii – an assignment that would set the course for his entire experience in World War II.

"Mickey" Moore was a major serving as assistant chief of staff for personnel in the Hawaiian Air Force (HAF) on December 7, 1941 when he watched helplessly as Japanese naval aircraft bombed and strafed American military installations in and around Pearl Harbor – the fateful attack that forced the United States into World War II. In short order, the HAF was redesignated the Seventh Air Force, and VII Fighter Command was formed under it, with Moore assigned to serve as its executive officer. Two years later, he was appointed commanding officer of VII Fighter Command – now nicknamed the "Sun Setters" for the effect its pilots expected to have on the Japanese – and was promoted to his current rank. Now, as the miles of empty ocean rolled by under the wings of his P-51, Moore had time to consider how far he and his command had come since the Pearl Harbor attack. His first two years with VII Fighter Command had involved a lot of hard work, and more than a few frustrations.

In the opening days of the war, the primary mission of the command was to provide air defense for the Hawaiian Islands in case the Japanese should attempt another air attack. With two fighter groups – the 15th and 18th – and a smattering of aircraft ranging from antiquated Boeing P-26 Peashooters to the latest model P-39Ds and P-40Es, VII Fighter Command deployed its squadrons to airfields throughout the islands and prepared for a repeat engagement with the Japanese. But the American victory at Midway in June 1942 changed the course of the war in the Pacific, and it became increasingly unlikely that the enemy would be able to strike at Hawaii again.

The focus of the Pacific War shifted south to New Guinea and then the Solomon Islands. With that, VII Fighter Command's focus shifted as well. The air defense mission remained in place, but now the main job was to put the final polish on the training of fighter pilots who were heading south to join the fighting with the Fifth and Thirteenth Air Forces. Hundreds of pilots rotated through the fighter squadrons in Hawaii, and eventually the entire 18th FG was transferred to the Thirteenth Air Force on Guadalcanal. The 318th FG arrived in-theater to fill the open slot left by the 18th FG's departure. Meanwhile, VII Fighter Command deployed squadrons to such remote spots in the Central Pacific as

Midway, Canton and Baker islands – all dead-end assignments where the chance of getting into action was absolutely nil.

Through it all, "Mickey" Moore and the other leaders of the "Sun Setters" stuck to their jobs, frustrating though it must have been to be cast in a supporting role for the main show down south. Finally, in the autumn of 1943, VII Fighter Command got its first major combat assignment – providing aerial support for the joint amphibious operation against the Gilbert Islands. Following the capture of Makin Atoll and Tarawa, the next campaign was Operation *Flintlock* – the taking of Kwajalein Atoll, in the Marshall Islands. Three VII Fighter Command squadrons (the 45th FS with P-40s, plus the 46th FS and 72nd FS with P-39s) took part in the campaigns.

Combined, the three squadrons flew more than 1,100 effective sorties, including bomber escort, strafing, dive-bombing, fighter sweeps and patrols. In one escort mission on January 26, 1944, the 45th FS encountered JNAF Zeros over Maloelop Atoll and scored ten confirmed victories and two probables for no losses. The P-39 pilots recorded several victories as well.

With the successful completion of Operation *Flintlock* in March 1944, the squadrons returned to Hawaii. Young fighter pilots who had left here six months earlier with more spirit than experience came back as blooded veterans. One such individual was Herb Henderson, whose experience was typical of the pilots who flew P-40Ns in the 45th FS in 1943–44:

I finished pilot training on March 15, 1943 and was commissioned a second lieutenant. I got ten hours of training in the P-40E before being sent to Hawaii, where I was assigned to the 15th FG, with subsequent assignment to the 47th FS (P-40s). I transferred to the 45th FS in August 1943 and remained with the 45th through the Baker Island, Marshall Islands and Iwo campaigns.

The Baker and Marshall islands campaigns were excellent training for the long over-water flights that were required at Iwo. They sure taught us to live "camping out." Since all of our flying was over water, we learned to trust our compass and other sparse navigation equipment. The Marshalls campaign provided the advanced training we needed to improve our skills in the dive-bombing and strafing of targets.

The experience of pilots such as Henderson would prove to be an important factor in the future success of VII Fighter Command, because many of these men would form the leadership core of their squadrons a year later when they commenced operations over Japan.

But in the spring of 1944, as these combat veterans got themselves resettled in Hawaii, there was no way of knowing this was in their future. Nor could they know that back in

Washington, DC, military planners were already looking ahead to the strategic bombing offensive against the Japanese Home Islands, and the role they had in mind for VII Fighter Command. And few, if any, of these young American pilots had ever heard of a remote island half an ocean away called Iwo Jima.

When "Mickey" Moore assumed command of VII Fighter Command in April 1944, he had two fighter groups – the 15th and 318th, with four squadrons apiece – under his wing. Almost immediately, each of these groups gave up one squadron to the newly forming 21st FG. In addition, VII Fighter Command was soon relieved of its responsibility to provide fighter pilots for the South Pacific. On top of that, new P-38 Lightning and P-47 Thunderbolts began arriving to replace VII Fighter Command's service-weary Airacobras and Warhawks. It seemed clear now that the"brass" in Washington, DC had plans for "Mickey" Moore's command, and proof was not long in coming. When American forces invaded the Marianas Islands in June 1944, the 318th FG was sent to Saipan to assist in the campaign.

This left the 15th FG (led by Col James O. Beckwith) and the 21st FG (under Lt Col Kenneth R. Powell) in Hawaii. Both men were veteran "Pineapples" – the term for men who had spent a long time serving in the Hawaiian Islands. To them would fall the responsibility of preparing their groups for the next assignment.

Beckwith, a Vermonter, was already an experienced pilot when he joined the USAAC in 1937. February 1941 found him offshore Hawaii aboard the aircraft carrier USS *Enterprise*, one of 31 Army pilots assigned to fly their P-36 Hawk fighters off the carrier deck for delivery to Wheeler Field, on Oahu. The pilots achieved this historic "first" for the Army on February 26, and stayed on to fill out the ranks of pilots in the Hawaii-based fighter squadrons. When the fighter force was expanded in October 1941, Beckwith was given command of the newly formed 72nd FS. Two months later he watched in horror as his squadron's new P-40s were wiped out on the ground by strafing Japanese fighters during the Pearl Harbor attack.

After spending the following year leading his squadron on various deployments around the Hawaiian Islands, Beckwith was sent to New Guinea in January 1943 to study the combat techniques that V Fighter Command was using successfully against the Japanese in the Southwest Pacific. He flew five combat missions during his stay and then returned to Hawaii. In September 1943 Beckwith was elevated to command of the 15th FG.

His three fighter squadrons – the 45th, 47th and 78th FSs – were equipped with P-47D Thunderbolts in 1944. As we have seen, the 45th had by far the most combat experience of the three. In fact, its commanding officer, Maj Gilmer L. "Buck" Snipes, had scored the unit's first aerial victory of the war in October 1943, and 14 other squadron pilots had flown with him during the Marshalls campaign. The 78th FS spent January through to

April 1943 on Midway Island, but saw no action there beyond friendly gunnery contests against the Marine Corps, which also had forces occupying the island. Among the 78th FS's four combat veterans were the CO, Maj James M. Vande Hey, who had scored two confirmed victories in the Marshalls, and Capt Robert W. "Todd" Moore, who had one victory to his credit.

The 47th FS, meanwhile, had been the top-scoring squadron on December 7, 1941 with seven confirmed victories, but had remained in the Hawaiian Islands throughout the war. The 47th had christened itself the "Dogpatch" squadron because the out-of-the-way airfields it had inhabited reminded the men of the home of comic strip character "Li'l Abner." As far as can be determined, its only combat veteran was 1Lt Dick Hintermeier.

Ken Powell assumed command of the 21st FG when the group was activated at Bellows Field on April 21, 1944, after serving under Beckwith in the 15th FG prior to that. A native of Oregon, he grew up in Tacoma, Washington, and got his first taste of military life in the Reserve Officer Training Corps while a student at Washington State College (now a university). On graduating from college in 1938, Powell joined the Army as an infantry officer and served in that capacity until the autumn of 1939, when he entered flight training. Powell graduated from Kelly Field in flying class 40D and was sent to Hawaii, where he joined the 78th FS in September 1940.

Like the other pilots in his squadron, Powell had no opportunity to get airborne during the Japanese attack on December 7, 1941. He transferred to the 46th FS as squadron commander in November 1942 and led the unit to remote Canton Island the following spring. Powell was appointed deputy CO of the 15th FG in April 1943, and held that post until he was assigned to organize the 21st FG a year later.

All three of Powell's squadrons in the 21st FG had seen combat in the Central Pacific during 1943 and early 1944, and all three contained combat veterans on their pilot rosters. The 46th and 72nd FSs had flown P-39s, but the 531st had been a fighter-bomber squadron, equipped with Douglas A-24 Banshees – the Army version of the Navy's famous SBD Dauntless dive-bomber. With its A-24 flight crews replaced by fighter pilots, the 531st FS flew P-39s with the 46th and 72nd FSs until midsummer 1944, when all three squadrons of the 21st FG received new P-38 Lightnings.

This was a period of transition for VII Fighter Command. Many of the old "Pineapple" pilots were sent back to the US for training, leave or reassignment, while replacement pilots – called "Yardbirds" by the old hands – arrived to fill the open slots. Combat veterans were transferred among the squadrons to try to create a balance of experience. As the year progressed, the training intensified.

Two of the many "Yardbirds" who joined the 15th FG from the USA during this period were Flt Off Bert Combs and 2Lt Bob Kriss. The former recalled:

My prior military experience consisted entirely of aviation cadet and post-cadet flight training in P-40s and P-47s. I joined the 15th FG in late October 1944 at Bellows Field, Hawaii. There were 12 of us fresh from the P-47 Replacement Training Unit at Abilene, Texas. We received a very "warm" welcome from the 15th FG CO, Col Jim Beckwith, who told us we were unwanted and unwelcome as we had no combat experience, but that they would make the most of it and do something with us. What a confidence-builder.

Kriss, who arrived in Hawaii with Combs and was assigned to the 47th FS, recalled:

Whatever we had learned about flying to this point was kindergarten. These people flew "balls-to-the-wall" all the time, and expected the same from us "Yardbirds." One day, Ed Markham, who was 47th ops officer at the time, had me flying his wing. I got as close as I felt was prudent and he kept motioning me closer. Just about the time I could read the second hand on his wristwatch, he turned into me! Lordy, the brakes didn't work and none of the controls were designed for the maneuver I had in mind. Eyes closed and bowels locked, I survived, and found myself in a fairly reasonable position on Ed's wing. I was learning how to take care of myself and how to make myself useful no matter what the situation called for.

After long months of training, the 15th FG was alerted for deployment to a combat area. Morale skyrocketed as the men packed in anticipation of joining the force being assembled for the impending invasion of the Caroline Islands. Col Beckwith departed with his staff for the Western Pacific, but two weeks later he returned with the bad news that the invasion had been canceled. The Allies would be taking the Philippines instead, and the Fifth and Thirteenth Air Forces had all the fighters they needed to do that job. Deeply disappointed, the men of the 15th FG went back to their mundane daily routines.

November 1944 brought more turmoil, when the 21st FG was given the unwelcome task of flying 36 of its Lightnings across the Pacific to Saipan. Here, the group would turn its near-new fighters over to the 318th FG for use on long-range escort missions against the bypassed Japanese stronghold at Truk. Twenty-four of the 21st FG pilots swapped into the 318th FG with their airplanes, but the rest returned to Oahu, and more dull duty.

On a brighter note, "Mickey" Moore returned from a trip to England, where he had gone in September to confer with Eighth Air Force commanders about long-range escort operations. In particular, Moore needed to learn all he could about the newest fighter in the USAAF arsenal, the North American P-51 Mustang, which the Eighth Air Force had been operating with great success over occupied Europe since December 1943.

The reason for Moore's trip to England became evident soon after his return to Hawaii, when the first shipment of brand-new North American P-51D-20 Mustangs was delivered to Hickam Air Depot on Oahu. At about the same time, VII Fighter Command advised its units to prepare to ship out for a combat zone. The pace of life picked up, for the introduction of a new aircraft into the squadrons meant nearly everyone – from the pilots and crew chiefs to the armorers, supply people and more – needed to familiarize themselves with the Mustang.

George Brown, assistant 21st FG operations officer, and a veteran of Makin operations with the 46th FS, recalled this period vividly:

We flew P-38s until December 1944, when we received our new P-51 Mustangs. We only had about six weeks to get to know the airplane. I did a lot of testing – fuel consumption, with five trips between Kauai and Hawaii nonstop, and testing the new homing radio. Our radios were four-channel transmitter-receivers, with an IFF [Identification, Friend or Foe] transmitter, plus a homing receiver to pick up the B-29 navigator airplanes that would lead us across the Pacific to our targets and then back home once again.

The P-51D had six .50cal Browning machine guns mounted in the wings. It had underwing racks to carry either bombs or extra drop tanks. It was a fantastic flying machine. It had a 1,695hp Packard-Merlin engine that only burned 40 gallons per hour on a long-range mission.

The experience of the 531st FS/21st FG during this period was typical of all the squadrons. Seven P-51Ds were delivered to the 531st in December 1944, and they were put to work immediately as the 40 pilots in the squadron checked out in them, logging from three to 13.5 hours apiece in the new airplanes. At the same time, the engineering department was hard at work installing IFF units in the fighters. To do this, they first moved the battery from its factory location under the canopy to a spot in the engine compartment, and then mounted the IFF under the canopy. Another key task was painting group and squadron markings on the airplanes.

More P-51Ds arrived in January, allowing the 531st to compile 1,121 hours of Mustang flight time during the month. Included in the flight schedule were four practice escort missions carried out with B-25 Mitchells of the 41st BG. Perhaps the most exciting event came on January 31, 1945, though few men of the squadron actually witnessed it. Maj Sam Hudson, 531st CO, and Maj DeWitt Spain from group headquarters embarked in an aircraft carrier, along with two P-51s, and were taken about five miles out to sea. From there, the two pilots made catapult take-offs from the carrier deck and flew back to their base at Bellows Field.

The 531st was now declared on mobile status, and the men began packing their gear and belongings. The squadron history observed, "Many of the ground personnel were with the 531st at Makin with the A-24s, which showed excellent results." Another indication that VII Fighter Command would be moving out soon was the change of address to APO 86, wherever that was!

The squadrons of the two groups reorganized themselves into air and ground echelons in preparation for the move. The 15th FG loaded its 82 P-51s aboard the escort carrier USS *Sitkoh Bay* at Ford Island, in Pearl Harbor, and cast off for the high seas on February 2, bound for Guam. The 21st FG did likewise with USS *Hollandia* a week later. At Guam, the P-51s were lifted off the carrier decks by cranes, relieving the pilots of the need to fly their airplanes off the ships. The 15th FG flew its fighters from Guam to Saipan on February 14, and the 21st headed to Tinian one week later.

Meanwhile, the ground echelons of both groups had boarded Liberty Ships for their treks west. The 15th FG ground echelon left Hawaii on January 27 and arrived offshore a small island in the Volcano group, about 650 miles south of Tokyo, about three weeks later. The island was called Iwo Jima.

ASSAULT ON IWO JIMA

One look at a map is all it takes to understand why a huge American invasion fleet carrying 30,000 battle-ready US Marines was standing off the coast of Iwo Jima on the morning of February 19, 1945. For nearly a year, military planners in Washington, DC had been focused on Iwo Jima as a key element in their strategy to take the air war in the Pacific directly to the Japanese Home Islands. In Allied hands, this pinprick of land in the vast ocean could prove invaluable during the upcoming strategic bombing campaign against Japan. It could provide not only a haven for damaged and fuel-starved B-29s returning to their bases farther south, but also a base for fighters that would provide protection for the big bombers over their target areas.

Conversely, Japanese strategists had recognized the value of the island as a bulwark in the defense of Japan. In mid-1944, Japanese bombers and fighters based on Iwo Jima had flown numerous missions opposing the Allies' invasion of the Marianas. At that time, the small island was little more than a stationary Japanese aircraft carrier, with two airfields defended by just a handful of troops.

Legendary JNAF fighter ace Saburo Sakai, arriving for duty on Iwo Jima in June 1944, was shocked to see the island's meager defenses, and was further surprised that the Americans did not invade it immediately after securing their positions in the Marianas. Instead, the Americans focused next on the invasion of the Philippines, giving the Japanese seven valuable months to build up their defenses on Iwo Jima.

And build up they did. By February 1945 there were approximately 23,000 Japanese troops dug in on the island. They had constructed a web of interlocking strongholds connected by caves from one end of the eight-square-mile island to the other, with

This photograph of 1Lt "Fran" Lent posing with his P-38H *T-RIGOR MORTIS* was taken in late October 1943. His score officially stood at seven at the time, but some enterprising soul scratched four more victory flags onto this print after Lent claimed his final kills in March 1944! (Michael Gregg)

Four 431st FS aircraft are seen on a patrol from Dulag in mid-January 1945. The pilot of P-38L "126" is six-kill ace 1Lt John Pietz, while P-38L "122" was normally flown by 1Lt Tom Oxford, although five-kill ace 1Lt John Tilley was at the controls when this photograph was taken. 1Lt Louis DuMontier is flying his P-38L *MADU V* and nine-kill ace Capt Fred Champlin is in his P-38L *EILEEN ANNE*. (John Stanaway)

This dramatic still taken from the gun camera cine film of a V Fighter Command P-38 reveals a familiar sight for 475th FG pilots in the final months of 1943 – a Zero in a head-on attack. (USAF)

Maj Tom McGuire's P-38L *PUDGY (V)*, photographed perfectly illuminated at Tacloban, immediately after its pilot had downed a "Tojo" to register his 25th confirmed kill on November 1, 1944. This aircraft proved to be McGuire's most successful fighter, with the ace claiming 14 victories in it between November 1 and December 26. (John Stanaway)

This overhead view of Amberly Field was taken in early July 1943, and shows the 475th FG's camp in the background and all six of the group's P-38Hs in the foreground. A further 69 Lightnings had arrived at the base by the month's end. (Glen Denis Cooper)

Personnel from the 432nd FS's Ordnance Department pose for a group photograph in early 1944. They are, from left to right in the front row, Sgt George L. Peters, unknown, Cpl K. C. Jones and Cpl Anthony L. Pometto Jnr. In the back row, again from left to right, are 1Lt Darrell W. Morgan, Sgt Louis Necke, unknown, unknown and TSgt Charles E. Bigelow (John Stanaway)

The Allies found various wrecked Japanese aircraft littering the Hollandia airstrips when they occupied them in mid-May 1944, including this Ki-43. Indeed, the invasion had progressed so swiftly that numerous crates full of aircraft parts were found still unpacked. Surviving Japanese personnel in the area were forced to evacuate towards the north, taking with them only what they could carry. (Norbert Krane)

Iwo Jima was not much to look at, even from the air. Mount Suribachi, in the foreground, with South Field just beyond, was an extinct volcano at the south end of the island, which measured about six miles long and two miles wide. (Ed Linfante)

Col James O. Beckwith, commanding officer of the 15th FG, leads the 45th and 78th FSs to Iwo Jima on March 10. Beckwith is flying the P-51D at upper left, *Squirt*, which boasted 47th FS markings. The fighter was subsequently destroyed on Iwo Jima in late April when a B-29 ran into it during a crash-landing. (Tom Ivie)

Conditions improved for VII Fighter Command personnel on Iwo Jima as the summer of 1945 wore on, but they could never be described as luxurious. Here, 45th FS officers (from left to right) Capts William J. Morrow and James W. Haglund, 1Lt William M. Parry, Maj David A. Kyzer, 1Lt Joseph A. Wanamaker and 2Lt Robert D. Wray relax in the tent area at South Field. (Jill Wanamaker)

Working on the line could be dangerous. A battle-damaged B-29 of the 504th BG crash-landed at South Field on April 24, 1945, wiping out four P-51s of the 15th FG, including Col Jim Beckwith's *Squirt*. A fire broke out following the accident, but all members of the B-29 crew got out safely and no groundcrewmen were hurt. Note how the men visible in this view are taking cover because ammunition in the burning B-29 has begun to cook off. (Leo Hines)

Sgt Chet Raun takes a break from his duties in the 457th FS photo section to pose next to the pin-up adorning his squadron's P-51D *Broadway Gal*. The pilots who shared this Mustang were 1Lts Ralph Gardner and Chet Jatczak (Chet Raun)

Maj Fred A. Shirley, CO of the 46th FS, had flown 16 missions in the Marshalls campaign without a victory, but made up for lost time when he got to Iwo Jima. On April 22, 1945, he shot down two J2M "Jacks" to bring his total to four victories. (Bob Louwers)

Twin-mounted 20mm antiaircraft guns are pointed skyward in this view of South Field, with Mount Suribachi in the background. On the field are P-51Ds of the 78th (closest) and 45th FSs, 73rd BW B-29s and P-61s of either the 548th or 549th NFSs. (Leo Hines)

The flying did not stop for the "Sun Setters" when peace came. Here, 1Lts William F. Killian and Joseph P. Gutierrez Jr take up 78th FS P-51s *JIMMY* and *Sweet Rosalie* for a postwar photoshoot over Mount Suribachi. Note that both Mustangs have been repainted in the all-yellow revised squadron markings adopted in midsummer 1945. (Bill Killion)

hundreds of steel-reinforced concrete blockhouses, pillboxes and communications centers. Camouflaged artillery positions and machine-gun nests covered every approach to the island, and the black sand beaches were sown with mines. Mount Suribachi, an extinct volcano at the southern end of the island, was honeycombed with caves connecting gun emplacements and observation posts.

American naval forces began pounding Iwo Jima with a steady barrage of bombs and heavy artillery in early December 1944. The island's airfields were quickly rendered useless, but the hardened positions suffered hardly a scratch in the 74-day assault. Thus, when the Marines went ashore on February 19, they were in for one of the bloodiest fights of the entire Pacific War.

Among those in the invasion fleet were the men in the ground echelon of the 15th FG embarked in the transport ships *Berrien* and *Lenawee*. Their job would be to go ashore as soon as practicable to prepare the airfield called Motoyama No 1 for the arrival of the group's P-51s. That was not possible until D-Day plus six. Two junior pilots of the 47th FS within the ground echelon were Bob Kriss and John Fitzgerald. The latter recalled:

We went ashore in two LCIs. The beach where we landed was a mess with destroyed LCIs and dead and wounded Marines. I believe we went in along with Marines of the 3rd Division, which was the back-up division behind the 4th and 5th. The 3rd was called on to go in early because of the heavy casualties suffered in the initial assault.

We went in at about noon as I recall, and immediately started digging two-man foxholes maybe 100ft up from the water's edge. Somehow or other we got some sand bags, because the black sand fell right back into the hole we were digging. Fellow pilot Merlin Kinsey and I dug a hole 3ft deep and covered it with two tent tarps. We crawled in there as it got dark and stayed put, even though the Navy threw up star shells all night, as the Japs would infiltrate our lines after dark. The Marines had .30cal machine guns set up around the area, and they fired at every sound and movement all night long.

Kriss had a similar experience:

The Marines hit the beach on February 19 while we cruised offshore, watching the bombardment. How anything or anybody could have survived it is beyond comprehension. Six days later the Navy kicked us off its boat. We landed on the northwest side of the bay as far away from Suribachi as possible, to protect the landing craft, I suppose. Then the powers that be marched us back into the shadow of Suribachi, pointed to the hillside and told us to dig in.

I was paired with John Scanlan (later killed in action). Each of us had a digging tool and one half of a pup tent. Digging in the black sand was not easy, however, for every shovelful you threw out of the hole, two more fell back in. By dark, John and I had a hole about 3ft deep and 20ft around. We pitched our pup tent in the middle of the excavation and went to sleep.

Some fool who couldn't stand the peace and quiet fired a round into Suribachi and the Japs got even. They dropped a few knee mortars and fired some light machine gun rounds into the area. John and I managed to dig our hole a little deeper!

After a week or so we left the beach and dug in at the northern end of Motoyama No 1 airfield. We spent most of our time setting up shop for maintenance, operations, parts etc., so as to be functional when the aircraft came in from Saipan.

Fellow "Yardbird" pilot Joe Wanamaker of the 45th FS gave this account:

We came ashore on the day the flag went up on Suribachi. Eyeball view, smell and sound of what war is like? No way I can describe it, but it does leave a lasting impression on you. Since the island was not yet secured, our assigned area near the airstrip was still under fire, so the Marines were kind enough to let us dig our foxholes in their artillery area. We were really prepared for the ground action – pistols and carbines with limited ammo, gas mask, tarp, blanket, canteen and two boxes of K-rations.

The overall master plan was slightly off schedule. The island was supposed to be secured before we went ashore, but it was about ten days before we moved to our assigned area on the airstrip. At this time we dug better foxholes and scrounged boxes and other materials to hold back the sand. Much later we were issued with floored tents and finally Quonset huts.

LEARNING THE ROPES

The Marine Corps' epic struggle to wrest control of Iwo Jima from its Japanese defenders is the stuff of legend. As the Marines came ashore on February 19 they found themselves bogged down in the island's loose volcanic ash and under fire from enemy positions they could not see. In the first few hours of the battle they were able to establish a beachhead on the southeast coast that was a mere 4,500 yards long and 500 yards deep. From there they began their bloody advance up the rocky hillsides of the plateau.

In the first 48 hours, fighting without sleep and often in pouring rain, the Marines suffered some 3,650 casualties. But they continued to push forward. By the end of the first week they had captured both airfields and were clearing out the Japanese defenders on 546ft-high Mount Suribachi cave by cave and pillbox by pillbox. With no hope of reinforcement or withdrawal, the Japanese fought back fiercely.

It was during this period that Associated Press photographer Joe Rosenthal snapped his famous picture of the American flag-raising atop Suribachi, but the fighting for the island continued for another three weeks before the island was declared secured. The cost in human lives was enormous. The Marines would suffer 20,196 casualties, including 4,189 men killed. Even that number paled when compared to the losses of the Japanese. Of nearly 23,000 defenders, only about 200 were taken prisoner. The rest perished.

Often working while under fire, the men of the 811th Aviation Engineer Battalion meanwhile had completed their work of clearing wreckage and patching the cratered runway at Airfield No 1, which was soon to be called South Field. Working alongside the engineers, the ground echelon of the 15th FG had set up a rudimentary air base, stocked with fuel, ammunition and bombs for the group's aircraft.

On March 6 the airfield was declared ready for operations, and Brig Gen "Mickey" Moore led his 25 Mustangs of the 47th FS to the embattled island that same day. Col Jim Beckwith followed from Saipan on March 7, with the 45th and 78th FSs in tow. Charles Butler was one of the 78th FS pilots who made the flight:

On arrival on Iwo, I was surprised by the lack of vegetation, which had been destroyed by air bombing, heavy offshore naval fire, ground fire and the creation of dugouts, built mostly by the Japs. Many dead Japs had been quickly buried and only partially covered, and some were still exposed.

Bob Scamara, a junior pilot in the 47th FS, was in the secondary group of pilots who flew from Saipan to Iwo Jima aboard a C-46 Commando transport. His first few days on Iwo left a lasting impression:

By then the Marines had taken about half of Iwo, with severe casualties, poor guys. We ended up in foxholes in our assigned area. We could watch the big guns lobbing shells over our heads into Jap lines. The guns were still at the southern end of the island. The front line was only a couple of miles away. We could see their shells in flight over our heads, they were going so slow. And at night they kept the island lit up with flares, just like daylight.

Action started almost immediately for the 15th FG Mustang pilots, when the Marines sent a message on March 8 requesting an airstrike against particularly stubborn enemy positions on the northern coast. Capt John Piper, the popular CO of the 47th FS, led two flights of P-51s aloft and made radio contact with a Marine ground coordinator, who directed him to the target using points on a grid map. The eight Mustangs duly strafed the area with .50cal machine gun fire.

After the first pass, the coordinator urged Piper to come closer to the Marine frontlines, which were marked with yellow panels. Piper could not spot the panels, but adjusted his next pass in their supposed direction. Again and again the coordinator requested him to move closer, and the leading Mustang pilot complied, each time fearing his airplanes would overshoot the line and hit the Marines. But by the time the Mustangs had expended all their ammunition, apparently they were right on the mark. The Marines later complimented Piper's flight, calling the mission the best job of close air support they had seen in two weeks.

That night, P-61 Black Widows of the 548th Night Fighter Squadron (NFS), also recently arrived on the airfield to defend Iwo Jima from nocturnal Japanese air attacks, flew their first two sorties. They made radar contact with two bogeys before losing them due to bad atmospheric conditions.

Col Beckwith got his first crack at the enemy on March 9, leading one of three 45th FS missions in support of the Marines on Iwo. The 45th FS also sent eight-airplane flights to attack Kangoku and Kama islands, which stood close off the west coast of Iwo, and may have been occupied. It was the turn of the 78th FS on March 10, and squadron CO Maj Jim Vande Hey made the most of it by flying three of the squadron's 45 sorties that day. The 10th also saw the 15th FG suffer its first battle damage, when 2Lt Gordon H. Scott's Mustang was hit in the tail section by ground fire. Scott managed to land his airplane safely, however. By this time the Marines had split the Japanese forces on the island, making the battle lines so close to one another that close air support missions were no longer feasible.

Now the Mustangs were ready to take the next step – an overwater flight to attack Japanese positions in the Bonin Islands. Located about 150 miles north of Iwo Jima, the Bonins had been a territory of Japan since the 1870s. One of the islands, Chichi Jima, featured an excellent harbor, and might have been considered for invasion instead of Iwo Jima except for the fact that its mountainous terrain allowed room for just one small airfield. Nevertheless, Chichi Jima served as an important watching and listening post, with its radio station providing early warning of B-29 raids proceeding north from the Marianas toward Japan. Its Susaki Airfield was also used on occasion as a staging point for Japanese night bombers on their way to attack Iwo Jima from Japan.

Raids by US Navy aircraft, beginning in June 1944, had eliminated Chichi's fighters, but the island was strongly defended by some 14,000 Japanese troops and fairly bristled with antiaircraft guns. In addition, Chichi had developed a nasty reputation among American fliers, who had heard rumors that downed flyers captured on the island were likely to be executed rather than held as prisoners of war. In fact, the word was that if you went down in Chichi you could expect to be clubbed, bayoneted and have your head chopped off by a samurai sword. Since rations were tight on the island, there was a good chance that your body would be cut up and tossed into the cook pot to flavour the evening's stew. Sadly, investigations after the war proved these rumors to be true.

So it was with high spirits, tempered by natural trepidation, that 17 Mustang pilots took off from Airfield No 1 on Iwo Jima just after 0900hrs on March 11, 1945 and headed north toward Chichi Jima. The pilots were all drawn from the 47th FS save two – Col Beckwith leading "Red Flight" and Brig Gen Moore, who tagged along to observe the attack while answering to the call sign "Chieftain One."

Flying in clear weather, the formation climbed to 10,000ft and throttled back to a cruising speed of 200mph. As would become common practice in the months to come, they passed a Navy PBY Catalina "dumbo" rescue airplane about halfway to the target. The dumbo's job was to come to the aid of any fighter pilot who might need to parachute into the sea due to battle damage or mechanical failure. Similarly, they passed a Navy destroyer that was positioned to pick up any downed fliers. Soon, Capt Ray L. Obenshain Jr, "Blue Flight" leader, spotted Chichi Jima off to his right and called it in. Brig Gen Moore stationed himself about a mile southwest of Susaki Airfield, where he would be in position to observe the attacks on the base, and the nearby harbor.

Col Beckwith, using call sign "Invader One," led the remaining 16 Mustangs, each carrying two 500lb bombs, across the island to a point southeast of the airfield, where they could attack it from out of the sun. Four parked airplanes, one lacking a tail, came into view after Beckwith pushed over in his dive from 10,000ft.

With 1Lts Fred T. Grover, Frank L. Ayres and Jules C. Mitchell Jr behind him, Beckwith led "Red Flight" down in elements toward two of the parked airplanes on the western side of the field and released bombs at 4,000ft. Six of the eight bombs hit in the target area as "Red Flight" continued its dive across the airfield and strafed the other two airplanes on the far side, before heading out to sea through the harbor entrance. Beckwith pulled up to 3,000ft about three miles offshore and circled while the other three flights made their attacks. He observed black puffs of flak at 2,000ft, but no one was hit.

By the time Capt Obenshain's "Blue Flight," including Capt Theon E. "Ed" Markham and 1Lts Charles J. Cameron and Joseph P. Brunette, made its attack, the flak defenses on Susaki Airfield had begun firing. After dropping their bombs at 2,500ft, Obenshain and Cameron flew out to join "Red Flight," while Markham and Brunette proceeded north across the harbor to take a look at Omura town, before also joining up with the rest of the formation.

Next came "Green Flight," led by Capt Lawrence T. Pepin. He and his pilots – Capt Walter H. "Sam" Powell and 1Lts Eurich L. Bright and Henry C. Ryniker – had a hard time picking up any specific target on the airfield because of the heavy smoke and dust kicked up by the previous attacks. They released their bombs at 5,000ft and then proceeded out to the join-up point.

"Yellow Flight," with Capt Piper leading, skipped the airfield in favor of attacking shipping in the harbor off Shiomi Point. Leading Capt Robert R. Down and 1Lts Oliver E. O'Mara Jr and Charles E. Jennings from northeast of the harbor, Capt Piper headed for a group of about 16 small vessels and let go of his bombs. The others followed, and the flight scored one direct hit, two probable hits and the rest near-misses. The Mustangs strafed the seaplane base, noting heavy flak, before also heading to the rendezvous point.

With his Mustangs reformed, Beckwith flew south toward the neighboring island of Haha Jima, which was also known to be defended. Arriving over the island at about 1030hrs, the formation dove down from 4,000ft in a series of strafing runs on the town of Kitmura. They then attacked the weather station and a warehouse at Okimura. Flak was heavy, particularly at Okimura, and the P-51s flown by Obenshain and Ayres both sustained damage. But the radio station was left smoking.

Continuing south after the pass over Haha, Beckwith picked up a homing vector from the rescue destroyer and headed toward it. Once overhead the vessel he was given a second vector back to Iwo Jima. "Mickey" Moore, meanwhile, had followed the formation to Haha Jima, but arrived there too late to observe the attacks and proceeded back to Iwo Jima on his own. All airplanes were back on the ground at Airfield No 1 by 1115hrs.

The remarks portion of the 47th FS mission report for March 11 was short and to the point:

Excellent mission. Towns in too good condition to satisfy "Invader One." Perfect performance of airplanes. Good weather and communications. Briefing good.

Col Beckwith went back to the Bonin Islands for more action on March 12, leading the 45th FS on a strike against Haha Jima. Then on March 13 he led the 78th FS on its first strike against Chichi. After this, operations were conducted almost daily over the Bonins, weather permitting.

Through the Iwo close air support missions and the first strikes against the Bonins, the 15th FG had yet to lose a pilot. Everyone knew this could not last, and indeed it did not. 1Lt Beaver A. Kinsel of the 45th FS, who was a combat veteran of nine missions during the Central Pacific campaign, went up for a combat air patrol on March 17 and vanished when the flight briefly entered some clouds. He has the sad distinction of being the first of 99 P-51 "Sun Setter" pilots who would lose their lives flying from Iwo during the course of the war.

The first loss to enemy action occurred nine days after Kinsel disappeared, when 2Lt John R. Shuler of the 47th FS was hit by ground fire while strafing the radar tower at Chichi Jima. He nursed his P-51 about ten miles out to sea, bailed out and was seen to land in the water. However, when the "dumbo" arrived on the scene about 15 minutes later, there was nothing to be found except Shuler's empty life vest floating in the dye-stained water.

NIGHT TERRORS

When the 15th FG arrived at Airfield No 1, the engineers turned their attention to Motoyama No 2, in the center of the island. For 16 days they worked to make the strip ready for operations, and then on March 22 the sky filled with the roar of 20 yellow-banded P-51s of the 72nd FS/21st FG as they circled to land after the long flight from Tinian. The 21st's remaining two squadrons followed two days later, landing at 1300hrs.

Now "Mickey" Moore had two complete P-51 fighter groups under his command – a big enough force to provide meaningful escort protection to the B-29 formations that were continuing to pound Tokyo and other targets in central Honshu. The newly arrived 21st FG was similar in make-up to the 15th, with a mixture of veteran pilots in the leadership roles and younger "Yardbirds" filling out the rosters. In particular, Col Powell had three strong "Pineapples" commanding his squadrons.

Maj Fred A. Shirley, CO of the 46th FS, had flown 16 missions and earned a Distinguished Flying Cross with the 45th FS in the Central Pacific. The 72nd FS CO, Maj Paul W. Imig, had flown P-39s in the squadron at Canton Island, and once offered to take a reduction in rank if he could get a combat assignment in V Fighter Command. When the offer was rejected, he agreed to stay on in the 72nd FS in the hope that he would eventually get to see the famous Mount Fuji, near Tokyo, from the cockpit of a fighter. Maj John S. "Sam" Hudson was the popular commander of the 531st FS, but was destined not to experience aerial combat over Japan.

George Brown, assistant group operations officer, was one of the first members of the 21st FG to arrive on Iwo Jima, and his initial impression of the place was anything but positive:

> I preceded the group and flew to Iwo in a C-46 to get things ready. There was only one way to describe Iwo Jima – it was the asshole of creation. It is a volcanic island that is still covered with volcanic ash. Well water comes out hot and has sulfur in it. It was difficult to keep a tent up in the wind because the stakes would pull out of the ash. Iwo was difficult! They were building the runway while we were operating. It was a clay surface with no asphalt.

The 21st FG's squadrons went right to work flying combat air patrols, even though the pilots had to service their own airplanes for the first few days before the groundcrews arrived from Tinian. In their off time, the pilots began exploring the island, despite the sporadic barks of gunfire in the distance that served as a reminder that Japanese troops were still holed up in caves and tunnels throughout the island. When Maj Imig learned that some of his 72nd FS pilots had been poking around up near the front lines, he ordered an end to their escapades. Shortly thereafter, his order would become unnecessary.

Maj Lloyd A. Whitley, operations officer of the 531st FS, woke up long before sunrise on March 26, 1945. He was scheduled to lead a flight in the squadron's first strike on Chichi Jima later that morning and wanted to be sure all was in readiness. Whitley was a popular figure in the squadron, and many pilots had been in attendance when he married Navy nurse Ens Dorothy L. Main in Hawaii on January 25. When Whitley finished his work in the operations tent at about 0515hrs, he began walking toward a truck about 30 yards distant, where his best man and buddy, fellow 531st pilot Capt William Benton, waited with the alert crew to drive them to the flightline. It was still quite dark, and the men could not help but notice the sporadic gunfire and explosions that had started at about 0400hrs.

What they did not know was that the Japanese had organized about 300 soldiers to stage a night raid against Airfield No 2. Sleeping in tents in a bivouac area on the north side of the field were the officers of the 21st FG and the just-arrived 549th NFS, plus an Army unit of African-American laborers who had just been posted to Iwo to take over clean-up efforts on the island.

As Maj Whitley climbed into Benton's truck, they noticed a sharp increase in the intensity of the gunfire and then saw a number of shadowy figures running through the area. Suddenly, a hail of gunfire slammed into the vehicle. The occupants of the truck quickly bailed out and took cover underneath it, as well as beneath several jeeps that happened to be parked nearby.

Only one of the alert crew was armed, but his gun quickly jammed, leaving the men defenseless until Whitley grabbed a carbine from a truck that pulled up next to them and returned fire. The Americans remained pinned down until relief arrived at about 0700hrs, but at some point in the fighting Whitley had been hit in the neck by a Japanese bullet and died instantly. Meanwhile, confusion reigned in the tent area, where most men had been sleeping when the attack began.

"We were caught barefoot and in our underwear," Jim Van Nada of the 72nd FS told the audience during a 2003 panel discussion at the Museum of Flight in Seattle. Van Nada, who was wounded by grenade fragments in the attack, was sent to Hawaii to recuperate and would return to Iwo in May to assume command of the squadron.

Fellow 72nd FS pilot 1Lt Horace Brandenberger recalled the morning this way:

We were awakened by gunfire, thinking the Marines were trying to make our stay appear more like combat. We quickly realized there were Japs all around. As we dug into the ashy ground in our tent with our helmets, a buddy crawled in shot up and bleeding. The Marines arrived and called out to evacuate the area. I lifted the center pole of our tent so we could get our wounded buddy out. After it was all over, I couldn't lift the pole!

1Lt James W. "Bill" Bradbury of the 72nd FS had just arrived on Iwo the previous day, and he was assigned to a tent whose other occupants included two ex-Royal Air Force pilots:

About 0500hrs I was awakened by explosions. The first RAF pilot was dressed and out into the darkness. I was almost into my flying suit and shoes and halfway toward the tent flap when the second RAF pilot (1Lt Burton Bourelle of the 531st FS) started out the door, but was blown back by a grenade. I changed my mind about going out. He was on his stomach in the entrance groaning, and I could see the wounds on his back and legs. I attempted to treat those superficial wounds, not knowing that he was badly wounded in the abdomen, and he died a few minutes later.

I was now alone in the tent, hunkered down in the lava ash with my Colt .45cal pointed at the door. I could hear the Japs running through the tent rows, talking and throwing grenades. Rifle rounds shredded the center post of the tent.

As daybreak approached, I could see light through dozens of small holes in the tent from grenade fragments. After it got good and light, I exited the tent and joined a young Marine a few yards away. He was throwing grenades over my tent, and Japanese grenades were coming back. We were hiding behind a stack of K-rations by the mess tent. There was a Japanese bicycle lying in the ash a few feet in front of us. This Marine threw a grenade over my tent, and after the explosion a Jap hand came flying back over the tent and landed in the spokes of the bicycle. This is a very vivid memory of mine.

Capt Felix Scott of the 46th FS was no stranger to sleeping in tents after having served with the squadron on Makin Island in 1943–44, but that did not prepare him for the events of March 26:

We were living in tents, four of us in each one. Explosions started going off all around. I thought we were being shelled from the sea. I figured they had their distance computed exactly on our tent, because explosives were hitting the tent, rolling off and exploding. There was a bomb crater about 4ft from our tent, so I yelled for everyone to leave the tent and get in the crater. I then realized what was happening – the Japs were in bomb craters all around the pilots and throwing grenades on our tents, not doing much damage. You could hear all the Japs chattering, then a "Banzai," and one of them would charge the tent and cut it with a sword so they could throw grenades through the hole. That's when we would shoot at them with our Colt .45cal pistols.

Our dawn patrol flight were on their way to get airborne when the Japs attacked. When they heard the explosions, they returned to see what was going on. The pilots saw that the officers' tents were under attack, but that the Japanese weren't bothering with the airmen's tents across the road. They told us to run for the airmen's tents at the count of three, and we did. I ended up in a bomb crater with the S-2 officer, Capt Snyder.

While we were waiting for the infantry to arrive, I heard a piece of shrapnel whistle through the air and hit Snyder on the leather jacket. He yelled, "They got me." I picked up the piece of hand grenade – about the size of a half dollar – and handed it to him. It hadn't penetrated his coat.

Then, a captain and sergeant came in a jeep with rifles and a flamethrower. They passed the rifles out and told us to follow them. The captain told the flamethrower to burn them out. They turned the flames on the bomb craters and burned all the tents that contained Japs. I think all the Japs were dead in an hour.

Another pilot in the 46th FS, 1Lt John F. Galbraith, received a citation for bravery exhibited on March 26. He wrote a detailed account of his actions in a letter to his brother just a few days after the action:

It was almost pitch dark outside when they charged into my tent, which was next to the road and near a Marine flamethrower dump. They ran down the rows of tents, pitching in hand grenades. I was in bed when the first one went off. Nearly a dozen exploded on and around our tent before I could get out of bed. Three of my buddies ran out into the area and jumped into foxholes – one came back about 0600hrs when it was getting light.

I took the responsibility of organizing a defense of our tent, putting one fellow at the northwest corner with an M1 rifle, another on the east side with a Colt .45cal pistol, and I took the south side and entrance myself – barricaded it with three sandbags, a B-4 bag, a five-gallon water can and a washstand for additional cover and concealment. I was armed with a .30cal carbine that I had only bought the night before from a Marine for one quart of whiskey!

At about this time a Jap officer stopped at the northwest corner, where we had left a cover open, and started to throw in a grenade. I fired three shots through the tent in machine-gun fashion, but Paul Schurr, a tent mate, dropped him with a .45cal "slug." The Jap was dressed in a US field jacket and carried a carbine.

Back to the front door, I laid down on the ground and rested my carbine on the sandbags. Soon the Japs started to cross the clearing between the tent rows. The range was roughly ten yards, and since I could hit a dime at that distance I opened up on them. Within five minutes I had killed four of them – simply waited until they got midway between the tents and shot them through the body about five inches below the heart. When they fell, I shot them once more to make sure.

Then I spotted two Jap officers running toward a tent two rows ahead of me. I motioned to the fellas in my tent, and we fired as they drew their swords. They wielded those swords with both hands and cut that tent like it was tissue paper. They never finished their job, though, for we opened fire with a hail of steel that would have killed a dozen of them. We then went back to our posts, and I killed four more that tried to cross the opening in the other direction.

At this point they got wary and only one more tried to creep by. I shot him once, probably injuring him. As he crawled back out of view I shot through the corner of the tent. I think I got him, but can't say definitely. Things quieted down for a while, except for a shower of hand grenades — they had only a few rifles, but bags of grenades.

Then I got a bit of a scare. A giant Jap — 6ft tall — walked around the tent directly next to me. He was looking around but failed to see me until it was too late. I shot him just as he turned to go into the tent, and he fell, but wasn't dead. He tried to get up on his elbows and I shot him twice more, the last time through his helmet just to make sure. About ten minutes later another walked up right behind his body and got the same dose. Maybe it sounds a bit gruesome, but it was easy to do. The screams of our guys that they hit alone was enough to give us the guts to do it, and besides, it was just what they were trying to do to me.

About 0710hrs, the Marines shouted to us left in the area to evacuate it and defend the enlisted men's area adjacent to ours. I told the fellas to follow me out at intervals, and I made a break for it, running at top speed, barefooted, with my carbine in my right hand and spare clips in my left.

Just as I neared a big foxhole they hit me. My steel helmet saved my life, as a hand grenade exploded on the front rim of it, bending it all out of shape, cutting the rim off and splintering the liner. The blast was terrible, but luckily the shrapnel took only the skin off the left side of my nose, plus a few nicks here and there. The blast hemorrhaged my left eye and hurt my ears, but they are okay, and I can fly tomorrow. I managed to see through the blood well enough to make it to our lines, where I was led to an aid station and taken to a hospital for two and a half days. The rest of my tent mates were okay, too, although two were hit with shrapnel while escaping the tent.

Others were not so lucky as Galbraith and his tent mates. By the time the Marines arrived to mop up the remaining Japanese attackers, the 21st FG had suffered 14 men killed and 50 wounded. Among the more seriously wounded were 21st FG CO Col Ken Powell, who like Van Nada was sent to Hawaii to recover, and would return to lead his group over Japan, and Maj Sam Hudson, CO of the 531st FS. Hudson's left hand was badly mangled by an exploding grenade early in the raid, and he was evacuated to the US for treatment.

In a letter to Galbraith shortly before his death in 1993, Hudson recounted how he spent a year in various hospitals receiving treatment, including tendon grafts, before returning to flight status in 1946. He subsequently served as a meteorologist in the Air

Weather Service before retiring from the military in 1961 and going on to a second career as a college professor.

The banzai raid of March 26 proved the closing action of the ground campaign to take Iwo Jima, although small pockets of enemy troops remained to be rooted out by the American infantry on the island. In the 21st FG bivouac area, the men hastily abandoned their tents to dig foxholes, and the ground echelon arrived later in the day. Meanwhile, a company of the 147th Infantry Regiment was assigned to the airfield to provide perimeter guards.

The 21st FG, with Maj Elmer Booth temporarily replacing Col Powell as CO, immediately began flying strikes against the Bonin Islands. On March 30 the group suffered its first aerial fatality when 2Lt Albert J. Tondora was killed in an airplane crash at Iwo.

But by this time all of "Mickey" Moore's pilots on Iwo Jima were asking themselves the same question – When are we going to Tokyo? The answer was not long in coming.

"LITTLE FRIENDS" OVER JAPAN

By late March 1945 XXI Bomber Command's B-29s had been firebombing Tokyo at night for several months, laying waste to vast sections of the city. But key industrial targets remained that could only be hit by precision daylight bombing. Experience had shown that bombing accuracy suffered on high-altitude raids, but if the B-29s came in at lower levels they became vulnerable to enemy flak and fighter interception. Gen LeMay needed "Mickey" Moore's Mustangs to provide escort for his Superfortresses, and the "Sun Setters" were eager to start providing it.

So as the last stench of battle from the Japanese banzai raid cleared from the air on Iwo Jima, on March 30 nearly 100 P-51s of the 15th and 21st FGs fired up at their airfields for their first long-range mission. However, the airplanes would not be flying north to Japan and possible air combat on this day. Instead, they would be heading south to Saipan and back on a final practice mission, before being turned loose against the enemy. The results of this flight might have given LeMay cause for concern, as less than half of the Mustangs completed it successfully. The rest fell victim to a variety of problems, some returning to Iwo early and others landing at Saipan for repairs.

At VII Fighter Command headquarters, the staff went to work studying the navigational problems, fuel consumption, weather, pilot fatigue, mechanical failures and other weaknesses revealed by the practice mission. Within a few days they had sorted out most of the issues, and were ready to commit the P-51s to battle.

Bad weather intruded during the first few days of April, but finally on the 6th everything was in readiness to send the Mustangs to Tokyo for the first time the following day. The mission given to VII Fighter Command tasked it with providing 108 P-51s from the 15th and 21st FG as escorts for 107 B-29s of the 73rd BW that were heading for Target 357 – the Nakajima aircraft engine factories on the west side of the city.

All six squadrons from the two Mustang groups were to take part, and it was a measure of the experience level in VII Fighter Command that only pilots with more than 600 hours in fighters were chosen to fly this important first mission. Mission leader Col Beckwith led four flights from the 47th FS aloft from South Field at 0655hrs on April 7, 1945, thus kicking off VII Fighter Command's historic first Empire mission. Maj DeWitt Spain, leading the 21st FG in place of the convalescing Col Ken Powell, took off from Central Field with his three squadrons at about the same time.

Following Beckwith as leader of the 47th's "Green Flight" was a familiar face – Brig Gen "Mickey" Moore. The groups formed up on Beckwith as he led them north to Kita Rock, where they would rendezvous with three navigating B-29s. Beckwith got no farther than that, as the oxygen system in his Mustang failed and he broke off to return to base. That left 47th FS CO Maj John Piper as mission leader. Soon, Brig Gen Moore discovered that the switch controlling the fuel tanks in his fighter was stuck, so he too was forced to head back to Iwo Jima. Two more disappointed senior officers would have been hard to find in the entire Pacific Theater that day.

In all, 17 Mustangs aborted the mission after take-off, and the rest settled down for the three-hour flight to Japan at 10,000ft. Fuel management was critical. The Mustang was equipped with internal fuel tanks in both wings, plus one behind the pilot's seat and a 110-gallon drop tank hung from each wing.

Normally possessed of good maneuverability, the P-51 became something of a tail-heavy slouch when the fuselage tank was full, so it was imperative to burn off most of its fuel before encountering enemy aircraft in the target area. Likewise, the drop tanks would be jettisoned prior to a combat engagement, so it was also prudent to burn off as much of the fuel in them as possible before that happened, leaving the internal fuel supply for combat and the return trip to Iwo Jima.

For maximum fuel economy, the engines were set to run lean at 1750–1900rpm, with manifold pressure of 34 to 35 inches. One pilot recalled that the propeller turned so slowly at this setting that he could almost see its four blades as they turned in front of him.

The Mustangs rendezvoused with the B-29s over Kozu Rock, just off the coast of Japan, at 1020hrs. The bombers were at 15,000ft, and the P-51s fanned out into combat formation several thousand feet above them, with the 21st FG on the left and the 15th FG on the right. The formation hit landfall within ten minutes, and soon enemy interceptors were spotted over Sagami Wan (Tokyo Bay) between Atami and Hiratsuka, 30 to 45 miles south of the target. The Mustang pilots quickly jettisoned their drop tanks and went to full power, gunsights switched on.

"Blue Flight" of the 46th FS/21st FG had the first crack at them when several pilots got hits on a Ki-44 "Tojo" in the vicinity of Yokohama. Before long, the Mustangs were scrapping with single- and twin-engined Japanese fighters all over the sky.

The 47th FS/15th FG made first contact at 1040hrs, when Maj Piper's "Red Flight" spotted a Ki-45 "Nick" about 900ft above them, flying a parallel course. The P-51 pilots gave chase until the twin-engined fighter did a split-ess and dove away, then they resumed their escort position.

Next, they spotted four dark green Ki-44 "Tojos" approaching head-on, but these fighters also broke away into a dive when the Mustangs approached. The flight was still over the bay, just off Tokyo, when the engine in Maj Piper's P-51 abruptly quit. He turned back out to sea with his wingman, 1Lt Joe Brunette, and by the time Piper's engine restarted the formation was long gone. The pair proceeded to the Rally Point, picked up a heading for Iwo Jima and settled down in their cockpits for the long flight home.

Capt Sam Powell and 1Lt Frank Ayres formed the second element of "Red Flight," and they also broke off early when the latter reported his fuel supply was running low. When 200 miles from Iwo Jima, Ayres was nearly out of fuel. Spotting the rescue destroyer USS *Cassin* at the "Warcloud" rendezvous point, he bailed out and was quickly picked up unharmed.

The 47th FS's "Yellow Flight," led by Capt Ray Obenshain, also had no opportunity to close with the enemy. The flight held its position as various enemy fighters made feints at the B-29s before breaking away. They noted heavy flak over the target and saw two B-29s blown out of the sky, with no parachutes spotted, before turning for home.

Capt Bob Down had assumed the lead of the 47th FS's "Green Flight" after Brig Gen Moore, followed by Maj Emmett Kearney, aborted the mission. While still over Sagami Bay at 18,000ft, Down and his element leader, 1Lt Dick Hintermeier, spotted a Ki-45 approaching from the northeast.

Hintermeier, a combat veteran who had scored a victory with the 45th FS during the Marshall Islands campaign, turned into the Ki-45 for a high frontal pass and put a burst into its right engine, which began to smoke. Then Down whipped in behind the smoking fighter and fired two bursts. The first hit the aircraft's canopy, and the second blasted the right engine again, causing the stricken fighter to fall away in flames. Down and Hintermeier were given shared credit for the Ki-45, which was deemed to be the first enemy aircraft shot down by USAAF fighters over Japan.

Capt Down shot down a Ki-44 a few moments later. Then his wingman, 1Lt Eurich Bright, got into the act by attacking a Ki-61 "Tony" from the rear and setting it on fire. Bright overran the inline-engine fighter, which was beginning to break apart, so he pulled up and saw it fall in flames. About then an A6M Zero made a pass at Bright, who maneuvered out of the line of fire and latched onto the Zero's tail as it dove away. With Capt Down keeping Bright's tail clear, the latter fired from dead astern. The Zero pulled up, burning, and then fell off in a final death dive.

Bright was not finished, however, as he then spotted a twin-engined aircraft and shot it down from behind for his third victory of the mission. Bright's last target was another Zero, but he lost it in a split-ess, so "Green Flight" turned south for an uneventful flight home.

Capt Ed Markham was leading "Blue Flight" of the 47th at 17,000ft out ahead of the B-29s, about 20 miles south of the target, when he encountered a single-engined two-seater that he identified as a Nakajima C6N "Myrt" JNAF reconnaissance aircraft.

"Blue Flight" approached it from behind, bracketing the airplane, which then turned into the second element, led by 1Lt Richard Condrick. He fired two bursts and hit the "Myrt" in the left wing root, setting it on fire. The C6N went down trailing smoke, and it was seen to crash into the ground. At this point, the two elements became separated.

As Markham approached Tokyo, he spotted two Ki-45s about 1,000ft below him, heading in the same direction. He closed in to about 250ft behind one of them and gave it a long burst. The airplane broke up in the air and fell away as Markham and his wingman watched. The "Blue Flight" elements made several more passes at enemy fighters but did not score again before turning south toward the Rally Point, where they joined up with B-29s for the three-hour flight back to Iwo Jima.

The 45th FS was led by its CO, Maj Buck Snipes. Like Maj Piper, he had trouble with his fuel tanks and lost power briefly just as the squadron began to encounter enemy aircraft. Snipes' P-51 lost several thousand feet before the pilot succeeded in restarting its engine, and he then climbed back up into position at the head of "Red Flight." Soon, he spotted a Ki-61 1,000ft above him, and so pulled his nose up for a shot. Snipes could not get proper deflection to hit the airplane, but his wingman, 1Lt Herb Henderson, put a few "slugs" into it before the Japanese pilot made his escape.

The Mustangs reformed, and soon Snipes put a burst from behind into a Ki-44, which began to smoke from the trailing edge of its wing before Snipes overran his target and lost it. Henderson, meanwhile, had attacked the Ki-44's wingman. The "Tojo" turned left, which put it right in front of Snipes, who promptly opened fire. The burst from the Mustang's six .50cal guns tore the Nakajima fighter apart, and the stricken machine dropped for several thousand feet before Snipes and Henderson saw the pilot bail out.

As this was going on, the second element of "Red Flight" attacked a Ki-61 that was attempting to make a pass at the B-29s. Capt Al Maltby, element leader, pulled straight up and put a good burst into the Ki-61 before stalling out. His wingman, 1Lt Wes Brown, followed the stricken enemy fighter long enough to observe it dropping out of control straight down, unlikely to recover.

The pair reformed and headed for Tokyo, where they saw a twin-engined Japanese airplane drop a phosphorus bomb on the B-29 formation. They latched onto the fighter, believed to be a Ki-45, and Brown sent it falling away in a tight spiral to its destruction.

Capt Art Bridge, leading "Blue Flight" of the 45th FS, lost contact with "Red Flight" after making landfall. All four members of this flight were highly experienced veterans of the Marshalls campaign, and it soon began to show. As the flight neared Tokyo, Capt George Hunter took a snap shot at a passing Ki-45 from his "Blue 4" position and was rewarded by seeing a sparkle of hits as the airplane passed from view.

Just west of Hiratsuka, a flight of four Ki-44s attacked "Blue Flight" at 18,000ft. "Blue 3," Capt Bruce Campbell, and Hunter turned into the attack and concentrated their fire on the same Ki-44, which went down in flames. Bridge and his wingman, 1Lt George Dunlap, also attacked, and the former saw his tracers rip into one of the Ki-44s at its wing root before the airplane made a split-ess and disappeared. Bridge became separated from the rest of "Blue Flight" during this encounter, but all four Mustangs returned home safely.

"Green Flight" of the 45th FS flew all the way to the target area without engaging enemy fighters. The flight was at 17,000ft when Capt Mort Knox, element leader, spotted a JNAF N1K "George" fighter flying parallel to the bombers down and to his right. He dove behind the naval fighter and gave it one good burst from dead astern, which tore up its tail and set the airplane on fire. The remaining three pilots in the flight also attacked the "George" as it began to fall out of control, but Knox was given credit for the victory. "Green 2," 1Lt Joe Walker, also got hits from 60 degrees deflection on a Ki-45 that was attacking the B-29s, but the airplane was able to complete its pass and dive away.

"Yellow Flight" leader Capt Walt Morey lost his wingman near the target when 1Lt Quentin McCorkle accidentally hit the mixture switch and killed his engine. McCorkle's airplane dropped 8,000ft before he managed to restart the engine. As he climbed back toward his flight, McCorkle crossed over the B-29s, and one of the American gunners opened fire on him. The P-51 took two hits but did not sustain serious damage. Otherwise, "Yellow Flight's" mission was uneventful. All airplanes from the 45th FS were back on the ground at Iwo Jima by 1745hrs.

The 78th FS, led by CO Maj Jim Vande Hey, was positioned at the right front quarter of the formation, and thus was able to claim the honor of being the first USAAF fighter squadron to fly over Tokyo. 1Lt Charles Heil claimed another distinction for the 78th by mistake. Losing contact with his flight at the outbound rendezvous, Heil latched onto the first formation of B-29s he saw and stayed with them all the way to their target and back. He did not find out until later that these B-29s were on a separate mission to bomb Nagoya without escort. By going with them, Heil became the first USAAF fighter pilot to fly over Nagoya, and the only pilot to escort an entire formation of B-29s by himself!

Maj Vande Hey, leading "Red Flight," was over Kiratsuka when he heard the bombers call in a bogey attacking from "12 o'clock high." With "Yellow Flight" providing top cover, he quickly spotted a Ki-45 making the pass, and damaged it with a deflection shot. The major described the twin-engined airplane as black, with orange zebra stripes on the wings and fuselage. He had better results a few moments later when he attacked a Ki-46 as it was making a shallow diving turn to the right.

"I closed rapidly, firing long bursts, and saw my hits strike the left engine and the wing root, causing debris to fly off the airplane," he reported. "The left engine then suddenly flamed and I had to break off." The "Yellow Flight" leader, Capt Vic Mollan, observed the Ki-46 falling in a steep spiral, trailing smoke, and Vande Hey was credited with a victory.

The leader of "Blue Flight" was Maj Jim Tapp, the 78th FS operations officer. Shortly after making landfall on the west side of Tokyo Bay, Tapp spotted a Ki-45 diving on the B-29s and gave chase. He closed in and opened fire at a range of 300 yards, putting a long burst into the fighter's right engine, and also getting incendiary strikes on the fuselage. Tapp's wingman, 1Lt Phil Maher, fired at the Ki-45 too, but the "Nick" did not catch fire or appear to go out of control as "Blue Flight" broke off contact and climbed back to position over the bombers at 20,000ft.

Tapp next spotted a Ki-61 "Tony" about three miles ahead and gave chase. He cut back the throttle as he approached from behind so as not to overrun and fired at the "Tony" from 800ft down to about 100ft. The fighter soon caught fire, and the pilot was seen to bail out for Tapp's first victory of the day.

He was far from finished, as the Mustang pilot next attacked a Ki-46 that was making a head-on pass against the bombers, but was unable to observe results. "Blue Flight" then dropped back to give support to a burning B-29 that was under attack from a silver two-seat enemy aircraft of unidentified type. Tapp began his pass at 90 degrees deflection, opened fire at 1,000ft and closed up right behind his target. He saw pieces of the aircraft breaking off and strikes all over the fuselage, before it flipped over into a spin. 1Lt Maher watched as the stricken airplane crashed into the ground.

"Blue Flight" moved back into its escort position, and then spotted six single-engined enemy fighters – four A6Ms and two Ki-44s – approaching at 18,000ft. Tapp made a head-on pass at one of the Ki-44s and saw his fire hitting the engine and cockpit. The airplane went into a violent spin as Tapp passed, and 1Lt Maher saw a 6ft section of wing break off as it fell from the sky, disintegrating as it went. When the mission reports were turned in, VII Fighter Command gave Tapp a victory credit for the first Ki-45 he attacked, plus the three single-engine victims, making him top scorer for the day with four confirmed victories.

"Green Flight" of the 78th FS was led by Capt R. H. "Todd" Moore, another veteran of the Marshall Islands campaign with one kill in P-40s to his credit. The flight didn't engage the enemy until reaching the Choshi area, where Moore spotted four A6M3 "Hamp" naval fighters doing "lazy eights" in string formation over the B-29s at 22,000ft.

Moore latched onto the end of the string and opened fire on the airplane in front of him from 20 degrees deflection, causing it to explode. At full throttle, he next closed in on the number three fighter in the string at the bottom of the "lazy eight" and hit it in the engine and cockpit with a short burst that set it on fire.

Capt Ernie Hostetler, "Blue Flight" element leader, then called Moore to warn him that the lead "Hamp" was about to attack, so Moore broke off into a dive. His wingman, 1Lt Robert Roseberry, noted that the entire bottom of the enemy airplane his leader had just attacked was blown out and burning as it fell from the sky for Moore's second victory of the day. All Mustangs of the 78th FS returned safely to Iwo Jima, the last landing at 1415hrs.

The 21st FG, in its position on the left side of the bomber formation, saw far less action than the 15th FG on April 7 because the Japanese interceptions came primarily from the east. Leading the 531st FS was its new CO, Capt Harry C. Crim Jr, the ex-72nd FS operations officer having assumed command of the 531st after Maj Hudson was wounded in the banzai raid. Crim had flown a combat tour on P-38 Lightnings with the 14th FG in the MTO during 1943 without scoring a victory and was eager to make his mark, as would soon become obvious.

Nine of the 20 P-51s in the 531st FS aborted the mission, leaving Crim with a short squadron to perform its share of the escort duties. His "Red Flight" was first into the target area, and soon spotted about 30 enemy fighters of various types, all apparently operating independently of each other. Crim made the following report of the ensuing action:

My flight was over a bomber box just south of Tokyo when a "Zeke" was reported at "six o'clock high." My flight turned 180 degrees and the "Zeke" passed overhead. At this time I saw a "Tony" going in the opposite direction about 1,000ft lower. I made an overhead attack on him but couldn't get the right amount of lead, so on the recovery from 500ft below I gave him a short burst from close range. Overshooting, I pulled up over him and rolled on my back. From this position, I could see the left side of his engine burning. He then started about a one-needle-width turn to the left, and I dropped back on his tail. From this position I fired a three- or four-second burst from about 300ft. His right wing came off at the middle panel.

I broke off to the right and saw a "Nick" at about two miles at "three o'clock" to me, same level, making a large circle to the left. I cut his circle and started firing at about 700ft at 30 degrees, and I fired until I overshot. I pulled up on the outside of his turn and then dropped back on his tail. His left engine nacelle and left wing were burning as I closed in on the second attack. I fired again until I overran, at which time his fuselage was starting to burn. I pulled up and circled once and headed for the Rally Point. I was looking back constantly, and saw him crash into the southeastern suburbs of Tokyo.

More than two years after flying his first combat mission, the aggressive pilot from Florida was finally on the scoreboard.

The element leader of "Red Flight," 1Lt Robert G. Anderson, was not so fortunate. Losing Capt Crim, Anderson led his wingman, 1Lt Lloyd Bosley, eastward across Tokyo Bay. Bosley reported:

I was flying with my element leader at 12,000ft when slightly to the right and below about 500ft I saw a silver airplane. It passed under us to the left and I recognised it as a "Tony." My element leader dived on him, and as he made a sharp turn to the right my element leader gave a short burst with no effects. I turned with the "Tony" and started firing with a two radii lead. Not seeing any hits I began increasing my lead. With about 2½ to 2¾ radii lead, I observed incendiaries bursting at and around his wing roots. Pieces of the airplane began pulling off. I kept firing for about 120 degrees turn, then the airplane turned over on its back and started spinning. I broke off and watched it spin down to about 5,000ft. Then I pulled up and rejoined my element leader.

Shortly after the engagement, Bosley observed 1Lt Anderson do a roll-and-a-half over onto his back as if entering a split-ess dive. But instead, Anderson's P-51 shed its wings and exploded for no apparent reason. The three remaining "Red Flight" Mustangs turned for home individually, but the other two 531st FS flights, which had not engaged the enemy, returned to Iwo intact. 1Lt Anderson was the only pilot of VII Fighter Command to be killed on the mission.

The 72nd FS, meanwhile, got four victories during the scrap. The squadron was the last to engage, with 1Lts Jacob W. Gotwals Jr and William E. Merritt each claiming a Ki-44 destroyed over Tokyo in engagements that began at 1055hrs. A few minutes later, Capt Adolph J. Bregar claimed a Ki-45 shot down, and Merritt scored again when he destroyed a Ki-61 while leaving the Tokyo area.

When the "Sun Setters" tallied the results of the mission, "Mickey" Moore had reason to be pleased, despite his personal disappointment at missing the action. The Mustang pilots were credited with 26 Japanese airplanes destroyed, one probably destroyed and five damaged, at a cost of two P-51s and one pilot. Only three Superfortresses went down during the mission – two hit by flak and one struck by an aerial bomb dropped on the formation.

If Gen LeMay had been concerned before the mission about the ability of Moore's P-51s to protect his B-29s, he could quit worrying now. The "Little Friends," as the B-29s crews called the escorts, could do the job.

LESSONS LEARNED

The men of VII Fighter Command had reason to feel proud, and maybe even a little cocky, after their success of April 7. But in war, a man's focus is on today and maybe tomorrow, not yesterday. In reality, April 7 was just the opening bell of Round One. There was a whole lot more fighting ahead in this bout.

The second VLR mission, on April 12, 1945, promised to be a near copy of the first, as the Mustangs again would escort B-29s of the 73rd BW attacking the Nakajima aircraft engine factories. The only difference in the plan was that the mission would kick off an hour later, with the Mustangs beginning their take-off rolls at 0800hrs. On this day, however, VII Fighter Command would learn that missions do not always go as planned.

Right off the bat there was trouble at Central Airfield, where the 21st FG Mustangs encountered windy conditions while taxiing out. Some had to switch runways before taking off, which cost them precious time and fuel. Maj Elmer E. Booth, deputy 21st FG commander and group leader, got off on time at 0755hrs with the 46th FS, but the last airplane of his third squadron (the 531st FS) did not bring up the rear until 0837hrs. By now, the 46th and 72nd FS were long gone, and eventually all three flights of the 531st returned to base without reaching Japan.

By the time the Mustangs reached Japan, various problems had reduced their number to just 82. They did their best to rendezvous with the B-29s, but the bomber formation was strung out and unwieldy. To add to that, the sky was hazy over Japan, with visibility down to four to eight miles. The two remaining squadrons of the 21st FG took the high lead position for this mission, and at 1130hrs the 46th FS began to encounter enemy interceptors.

46th FS commander Maj Fred Shirley made the initial contact. A combat veteran with 19 missions in the 45th FS during the Marshall Islands campaign, Shirley spotted a Ki-45 "Nick" below him attempting to attack the B-29s and shot it down in a diving pass. Reforming his flight, Shirley next spotted a V-formation of JNAF J2M "Jack" fighters and again swooped to attack. This time, kills went to Maj Shirley and 1Lts John W. Brock and Eugene V. Naber, with Capt Jack V. Garnett claiming a probable.

The 72nd FS, meanwhile, failed to close with the interceptors. But on the return flight to the Rally Point one flight was attacked by a particularly aggressive J2M pilot, and 1Lt James H. Beattie was shot down and killed. The 15th FG was led by Maj Emmett L. "Pilot Ben" Kearney Jr, deputy group commander, at the head of "Red Flight" in the 47th FS. One of the old "Pineapple" pilots of VII Fighter Command, Kearney was about to get his first and only crack at air-to-air combat.

"Red Flight" made landfall at 1150hrs and weaved over the bombers until just beyond the turning point, when the Mustang pilots spotted a lone Ki-45 passing below them, headed in the opposite direction. Maj Kearney and his wingman, 1Lt Harry M. Tyler, performed a split-ess onto the twin-engined fighter's tail and opened fire. The Ki-45 was hit, and they saw it fall off in a dive for 10,000ft trailing smoke. The Mustangs pulled back up and reformed with 1Lt Alex Trodahl, who had been flying solo as the second element since his leader aborted earlier in the mission.

At this point, they spotted two more Ki-45s behind and below them. Kearney led the Mustangs in a 180-degree turn that brought them out on the tail of the left Ki-45, which he and Tyler both shot up. The left engine caught on fire, and the stricken airplane went straight down trailing a plume of smoke. Trodahl was able to see it crash into the ground after he had fired at another Ki-45 on the right, which was out of range. "Red Flight" had one more encounter, when Kearney shot down an A6M Zero, before turning for home. In all, the 15th FG tallied 11 confirmed victories, five probables and two damaged for the mission. Of these, the 78th FS contributed just one victory and one probable, but the victory was historic.

Maj Jim Tapp, leading his flight at the extreme right flank of the formation, spotted a Ki-61 below him and shot it down in a diving pass. Unfortunately, Tapp's wingman, 1Lt Fred W. White, was following him so closely that the spent shells from Tapp's guns apparently got sucked into his Mustang's air scoop and damaged the radiator. White's engine failed on the flight home and he attempted to bail out, but his parachute did not open and he fell to his death. The 78th FS also lost 1Lt Gordon A. Christoe, who went down over Japan during the fight.

At the time, this was thought to be Tapp's fourth victory, because he had turned in one of the four claims on April 7 as a probable. Some weeks later, VII Fighter Command reviewed his claims and upgraded the probable to a confirmed victory, making Tapp's April 12 kill his fifth. This was a minor point, because Tapp would score again on April 19 to be recognized as the first ace on Iwo Jima anyway.

When he filed his report on the mission, Maj Kearney complimented 1Lt Trodahl for staying with him as a one-airplane second element, and maintaining a perfect supporting position throughout the mission. Sadly, Trodahl would be killed later in the month when his engine failed on take-off for a mission. Kearney also complained of continuing problems with gun stoppages on the P-51s in his report, stating that his own airplane was down to four functioning guns during the fight, and Trodahl had only two guns firing. This was perhaps attributable to the fine-grain volcanic dust on Iwo Jima, considering the P-51D had been operating in the ETO for nearly a year with minimal gun failures.

But the bigger problem was in the mission planning and execution. When the air fighting subsided, the Mustang pilots turned south for the long flight back to Iwo Jima. The problems at the start of the mission, and their "round-about" escort route now started to hound them, because many of the Mustangs had been operating on internal fuel at high throttle settings for nearly an hour during the combat engagement.

Desperate to get home, pilots began filling the radio channels with requests to the navigator B-29s for direct vectors to Iwo, or for directions to the nearest air-sea rescue units stationed along the route. In the event, only one more pilot went down on his way home – 1Lt Maurice F. Gourley of the 47th FS – but many others were flying on fumes when they landed at Iwo Jima that day. Maj Jim Vande Hey, 78th FS CO, felt his engine quit just as he touched down on the runway at Airfield No 1. He was out of gas, and had to be towed in to his parking place. Like many other pilots, he had been in the air for a little over eight hours.

The next Empire mission was scheduled for April 16, but the problems uncovered on the 12th were too complex to be sorted out in just four days. To make matters worse, the mission was changed at the last minute from another Tokyo escort to a sweep of enemy airfields in southern Kyushu, where kamikaze attacks were being launched against the

American invasion fleet off Okinawa. The 15th FG was assigned as the low-level assault unit, with the 21st FG providing top cover. The mission produced eight more hours of trauma for the Mustang pilots, and little else.

The 21st FG was late getting off, causing the rendezvous to be delayed, and then had no fewer than 17 aircraft abort the mission. Two 21st FG pilots experienced mechanical failures that forced them to bail out en route to Kyushu, and one of them, 1Lt Glenn Reagan of the 72nd FS, was killed. Reaching Japan, the formation encountered no enemy interceptors over the target area.

Only two of the 15th FG squadrons were able to find a target, Kanoya Airfield, and it was relatively bare of aircraft. The Mustang attack produced few results, but several P-51s were hit by ground fire and had to limp home. One more pilot, 1Lt James R. Wightman of the 78th FS, experienced engine failure on the return flight and bailed out, only to be killed when his parachute failed to open.

In mid-April, the USAAF's complex scheme for rotating pilots home based on points accrued during service in a combat zone began to take effect in VII Fighter Command, and it started near the top. Among the pilots to receive orders reassigning them to Stateside duty was Col Jim Beckwith, 15th FG CO. Despite commanding the group through its transition to the P-51, its training for the VLR role and its difficult first fortnight on Iwo Jima, Beckwith would return home without completing a single mission over Japan. The same was not true for the other reassigned 15th FG leaders – deputy group commander Emmett Kearney, 45th FS CO Buck Snipes and 78th FS CO Jim Vande Hey – all of whom had not only earned membership of the "Tokyo Club," but also had scored confirmed victories in the process.

Assigned as the new commanding officer of the 15th FG was Lt Col DeWitt Spain, who became available to move over from the 21st FG with the return of Col Ken Powell from convalescence in Hawaii. Powell's deputy would be Lt Col Charles E. Taylor, who was an old "Pineapple" returning to the Pacific after a year of duty Stateside and a temporary assignment in England. Capt Art Bridge, another veteran of the Marshall Islands campaign, moved up to take command of the 45th FS, and Maj Jim Tapp took over the reins of the 78th FS.

Following the fiasco over Kyushu, VII Fighter Command put on another airfield sweep for April 19, with Atsugi Naval Airfield near Tokyo as the primary objective. This time, the planning was better, the target was more lucrative and the results would be excellent. The 21st FG, assigned the attack role with the 15th FG providing top cover, swept across Atsugi on the deck and caught the Japanese by surprise. The base was crowded with an estimated 150 to 200 parked aircraft, and the Mustang pilots tore into them, claiming 14 destroyed and another 53 damaged. Pulling off of the target, the 46th and 72nd FSs came upon a flight of J1N1 "Irving" twin-engined naval fighters and claimed nine destroyed and one damaged. Similarly, the 531st encountered a number of training airplanes flying near Atsugi and shot down several.

Two P-51s were lost in the strafing attack – 1Lt Thomas L. Cole of the 46th FS was hit by ground fire and crashed to his death over Atsugi, while 1Lt Arthur R. Beckington of the 531st FS was last seen with smoke pouring from his engine as he approached the Tama River. Beckington, on his first mission, was later learned to have been taken prisoner, making him the first of nine Iwo Jima-based fighter pilots to become PoWs. After the war ended, he was found by occupying troops in a Yokohama jail in an emaciated condition and flown to San Francisco to recover his health. Not long after that, Beckington had a reunion with fellow 531st FS pilot Dave Scotford, who related their discussion:

I asked Art if he knew how he was shot down. He replied that it was ground flak near Atsugi. He said he noticed his oil pressure was low and decided to try to get to the coast and find the rescue submarine, which would have been located about 20 miles offshore. However, his engine stopped and he bellied into a field before he could even make a turn to get to the sea. The plane ploughed across the field and came to a stop at the end of the field, with the tail up and nose in a ditch. Beckington's head hit the gunsight, but he got the canopy off and tried to get out of the cockpit, but had forgotten to release the seat belt. He fell back, got his seat belt off and rolled out of the cockpit to the ground.

Immediately he was grabbed by some kids. Knowing that the P-51 was soon going to burn, Beckington dragged them away from the airplane. Just as he cleared the wing, the fighter exploded in flame, but he and his captors were not hurt.

After staggering away, they were met by some policemen who took him to a Yokohama jail. Beckington was first faced in the jail by a number of policemen who took turns kicking him in the groin. He was put in a small cell and not given much to eat. He said he could occasionally hear the engines of American airplanes, and worried about us.

After two months a few other American fighter pilots were brought to the jail. Several times Beckington was interrogated about the P-51, which was new to the Japanese. They had no idea what an expert they had – a fighter pilot who was a lifelong model airplane builder and aeronautical engineering student at MIT. The specifications he gave them were plausible, but bogus. Late in the war our intelligence picked up this information and relayed it to us. We found it funny, because it was close, but so wrong.

Although caught by surprise, the Japanese were able to launch a number of fighters in opposition to the marauding Mustangs. The 15th FG encountered mostly J2M "Jacks," a stubby but formidable naval fighter, claiming five destroyed and two damaged for no losses. Maj Jim Tapp, leading the 78th FS, nailed one of them for his aforementioned sixth victory. Also getting a victory that day was Capt F. H. "Herb" Henderson of the 45th FS, a seasoned veteran of the Marshall Islands campaign, who gave this account:

I was the leader of a flight that also consisted of John Kester, Don Statsmann and a fourth pilot who may have aborted on take-off. We were ready to return to Iwo Jima when I spotted two J2M "Jacks" headed toward the mainland. We gave chase, and the three of us took shots at the trailing "Jack." I made a pass on him, scoring hits, but had to break off because I overran him. Kester was next to score hits, but he too overran and had to break off. Statsmann finally finished him off. The "Jack" literally started coming apart and spun into the water. We split the credit three ways.

I still had the lead "Jack" in sight, and went after him. When I got in range I began spraying him. He headed for the deck, making violent turns right and left. I managed to catch him in a steep turn to the right and got fatal hits on him. My gun camera confirmed the kill. We were over land by that time.

As I broke off, I found that I was alone. I had lost both my wingman and element leader in the chase. As a matter of fact, I did not see another Mustang anywhere. The en route weather to Iwo became so bad I was flying on instruments. I broke into a clear space and spotted a B-29. I closed on him and asked if he would drop me off at Iwo. I flew his wing through weather until he let down and pointed to the left, and there was Iwo. What a great group the B-29 guys were.

The next VLR mission was a fighter sweep on April 22 targeting Suzuka airfield at Nagoya – the Mustangs' first visit to this area south of Tokyo. After their success at Atsugi, the Mustang pilots looked forward to another fruitful mission, and that's what they got. The claims were 14 aircraft destroyed on the ground and nine more in the air, for the loss of one pilot. Maj Fred Shirley of the 46th FS took the scoring lead in the 21st FG, shooting down two "Jacks" to bring his total to four confirmed aerial victories. He was not fated to get a fifth kill and make ace, however, as weather conditions hampered operations and precluded any further scoring by VII Fighter Command over the next month, by which time Shirley had completed his tour and returned to the US.

Bad weather would cost VII Fighter Command six pilots on April 26, when the P-51s escorted B-29s to Kanoya, and one more on the April 30 escort against Tachikawa Army Air Arsenal. On the latter mission, 1Lt John Galbraith was leading the submarine cover flight of the 531st FS – normally a boring job, as the rescue submarines were rarely threatened, but not on this day. He filed this report:

At 1200hrs the submarine called our escort "Superdumbo" (a Navy PBY patrol airplane) and said, "Send your chickens against three picket boats ahead of me." I acknowledged his call and started a climb to the cloud base, which was at 2,300ft, and was about 4,000ft thick. A haze hung below the clouds and offered concealment. The three boats were in line abreast, approximately a quarter of a mile apart, heading for the submarine at maximum speed judging from their wakes. I told my element leader, 1Lt Harry DeRieux, to take the boat on the left, while my wingman 1Lt Dale Meyer took the middle one and I went after the one on the extreme right.

We all made a simultaneous attack from bow to stern, clearing the decks of all personnel. We immediately climbed up to 2,000ft and set up another pass. On the second pass, I noticed a long-barrelled gun of probably 20mm size on the boat that I strafed. It was revolving freely on its mount. After observing this gun, I changed all my passes to rear-quarter attacks from "four" or "five o'clock." The stack and pilot house blanked out the possible fire from the gun at this angle, and I observed no return fire. We made from six to seven passes, each man alternating on every boat, leaving two boats dead in the water and burning fiercely. One boat was smoking slightly, but still moving aimlessly.

We returned to the submarine and orbited, from where two large columns of white smoke could be seen rising from the burning ships. Within a few moments the sub told us to hit the third boat again, as he thought it was still coming. We went back and I looked it over – no signs of life were evident and black smoke was rising, but the prop was still churning, so we made two passes apiece on it. After this attack it stopped and began burning about the pilot house. I observed the other two at this time – ammunition was exploding on one, observed by the sub, which asked if a gun were firing. Both the other boats were burning from bow to stern and settling in the water. We returned to the sub, which submerged at 1238hrs.

It was a fitting end to the first month of VLR operations. The next three weeks would be less notable for operations than they were for the arrival of a third P-51 group on Iwo Jima.

MORE MUSTANGS JOIN THE FIGHT

On a sunny morning in early autumn 1944, Col Bryan B. Harper welcomed Maj Malcolm C. Watters into his office at 53rd FG headquarters on Page Field at Fort Myers, Florida. Harper, 33-year-old commander of the training unit, had just received news that he had been waiting for since the war began nearly three years earlier. A new fighter group, the 506th, was being formed for a combat assignment to provide Very Long Range escort in the Pacific theater, and Harper would be its commanding officer. Now he needed a solid core of subordinates to help train and lead the new group, which was why he had summoned Watters to his office.

Harper was well acquainted with Maj Watters, who had served in the 53rd FG during its deployment to the Panama Canal Zone earlier in the war, and now commanded one of its training squadrons. Like Harper, he had been hoping for a combat assignment for a long time, and now the colonel offered him a job as a squadron commander in his 506th FG. Watters was intrigued, and asked Harper who was in the group. "If you say 'yes,' it's you and me!" Harper replied.

Watters readily accepted command of the 457th FS, and the new VLR group was on its way. The 506th was activated on October 21, 1944 and set up shop at Lakeland Army Air Field, Florida. Soon pilots, mechanics, armorers and support personnel began arriving from all over. Harper tapped another of his squadron commanders at Fort Myers, Maj Harrison B. Shipman, to command the 458th FS. Maj Thomas D. DeJarnette, commanding the 462nd FS, was a combat veteran, as were the deputy group CO, Lt Col Harvey J. Scandrett, and the group operations officer, Maj Harley Brown. All three pilots had flown P-39s during 1942–43 in New Guinea, and Scandrett had one confirmed kill to his credit.

Many of the other pilots in the 506th were escapees from Air Training Command, with long flying résumés and great skill, but no combat experience. Typical of these men was 1Lt Wesley A. Murphey Jr, who had a total of 996.20 hours of flying time when he made his first Mustang flight at Lakeland on November 3, 1944:

I was flying P-39s at Venice, Florida, in August 1943. About the end of the month, because of maintenance problems and a lack of flyable aircraft, a group of us were transferred to a P-47 Replacement Training Unit at Fort Myers. After completing the 60-hour training course in this airplane, six of us were selected to remain at Fort Myers as instructors. Several months later I was appointed to the squadron gunnery officer's job. I completed the gunnery officer's course in P-47s at Matagorda, Texas, in April 1944. On May 1 our P-47s were transferred to II Fighter Command, and we received new P-40Ns in their place.

Then in October our group commander, Col Harper, was selected to organize a long-range fighter group for escort duty in the Pacific theater. We were to train in P-51s at Lakeland. Chauncey Newcomb, Jack Folsom, John Benbow, Daun Anthony, Vance Middaugh, myself and several other pilots from Fort Myers went to Lakeland with Col Harper. The 506th FG was formed, and I wound up in the 457th FS as assistant flight commander of "C" or "Blue Flight" under Jack Folsom. Our squadron commander was Malcolm Watters.

We started flying around November 1, and had all models of P-51s – As, Bs, Cs, Ds and Ks. One night we were taking off to fly a group formation – all three squadrons. I had an old A-model, and shortly after take-off it had an engine fire. By the time I got back on the ground and the crash crew had put the fire out, the airplane was damaged beyond repair. We finished training in early February 1945.

The training regime centered on learning cruise control techniques that would produce maximum range from the Mustangs. It also included practice scrambles, assembly and landing procedures, escort formations, aerial gunnery and bombing practice, and an occasional dogfight. A month after the 506th started flying, the USAAF produced document 50-100, which was the training directive for Very Long Range operations. Fortunately, the group had already met many of the requirements by then, two glaring exceptions being instrument flying and rocket firing. The final weeks of training were concentrated on mastering those tasks.

The day that the Marines landed on Iwo Jima – February 19, 1945 – found the air echelon of the 506th FG aboard a train bound for California, where the aircraft carrier USS *Kalinin Bay* was waiting to carry them across the Pacific. On March 6, when VII Fighter Command Mustangs first landed on Iwo Jima, the 506th was enjoying a night of liberty in Honolulu prior to setting sail for Guam the next day.

The ship delivered the 506th to Guam on March 17, and a week later the pilots flew their new P-51D-20s to Tinian. There they would stay for seven weeks, flying combat air patrols and practice missions while the field engineers on Iwo Jima prepared a new base for them at the northern end of the island. At some point, it was decided that the 506th FG would be assigned to the Twentieth Air Force, which would "loan" the unit to "Mickey" Moore's VII Fighter Command.

Meanwhile, the ground echelon of the 506th was proceeding to Iwo Jima aboard the MV *Bloemfontein*, which, incidentally, was the same ship that had carried many of the American Volunteer Group personnel to Burma back in 1941. The ship delivered the men of the 506th FG to Iwo on April 25, and they set to work preparing North Field for the arrival of the group's pilots and airplanes. 1Lt Proctor Thompson, a ground echelon officer assigned to group headquarters, wrote this account of the 506th's first weeks on Iwo:

> The dead Japs, the vegetation, dud shells, mines, rocks and caves had been cleared by the 81st Service Group bulldozers. The night found us cold, uncomfortable, apprehensive. In the next few days, the setting up of our temporary area was nothing but indescribable confusion. Pup tents, wall tents, pyramidal tents went up willy-nilly, helter-skelter, in no semblance of order. But toward the end of the month the confusion diminished. Men were housed in 12-man squad tents, and officers moved up the slope to a cleared area below Bloody Ridge. The more technically minded men scraped out foxholes and slit trenches.
>
> Meals were unadulterated C- and K-rations, mostly C, which was substantial enough, but a trifle high in beans and extremely monotonous after the first few days. The first few nights were hideous, with apprehension and rifle fire squeezed off by trigger-happy guards. Men crept to the latrine only when pangs from their bulging bladders overcame their better judgment. One or two Japs were sighted on Bloody Ridge during the third night, but gradually things quieted down.

From this time forward, the job was organization of the living areas, mess facilities and the line. Construction of our airfield – Strip No 3, or North Field – begun by the Seabees under Jap fire, was near complete by May 5. The strip was dusty, bumpy and, by courtesy of Lucifer, sulfur-steam heated, but it was usable. The air echelon did not arrive on schedule because of dirty weather between Iwo and Tinian, but finally the skies cleared, and the airplanes came in. It was May 11, 1945.

The weather closed back in, and it was not until May 18 that the 506th could fly its first combat mission – an obligatory strike on Chichi Jima by the 462nd FS. The other two squadrons followed shortly with their own missions to Chichi, and then – after several weather delays – the 506th FG was ready to fly its first mission to Japan.

With Col Harper leading, the group set out on May 28 for its first VLR mission – a fighter sweep and strike against Kasumigaura Airfield, northeast of Tokyo. This target was farther north than any of the previous VLR missions had ventured, but the mission went off without a hitch. The 457th FS attacked first, diving and strafing from 8,000ft down to 4,500ft so as to suppress the flak installations. The 462nd FS and then the 458th FS followed, attacking airfield installations in roughly line-abreast formations against moderate and inaccurate ground fire. Following VII Fighter Command policy, the 506th FG made one pass and then withdrew, leaving seven large fires burning on the field. One Mustang reported minor damage from ground fire in return.

As the 458th FS pulled off the target, a radial-engined enemy fighter attempted to make a pass at 1Lt Quarterman Lee of "Yellow Flight." Capt Francis C. Carmody, leading "Blue Flight," shot the airplane down as it broke off at low altitude in a slow chandelle to score the 506th FG's first confirmed aerial victory. Moments later about six Ki-44 "Tojos" made an ineffective run against "Blue" and "Green" flights of the 457th FS, the Mustang pilots claiming hits on two of them – Maj Watters was subsequently credited with one confirmed victory.

As the fighters withdrew southward toward the Rally Point, they strafed several other airfields along the route. The 462nd attacked Iba, and in doing so Capt Kensley M. Miller was hit by ground fire and crashed to his death. This was a big loss to the squadron, as Miller was a combat veteran who had flown 80 missions in the MTO on P-40s. The 506th had lost several pilots previously in crashes, but Miller was the group's first loss due to enemy action.

STRONG END TO A SOGGY MONTH

Bad weather – including a typhoon that blew across Iwo Jima in mid-month – hindered VII Fighter Command operations for much of May. On the 17th of the month, while the

15th FG was bogged down in the mud at Airfield No 1, the 21st FG mounted a fruitful strafing mission against Atsugi Naval Airfield, but lost four pilots in the process. Then two more missions, on May 19 and 24, had to be aborted due to weather. By this time further changes were occurring in the leadership ranks of VII Fighter Command as more veteran pilots earned their tickets home. In the 15th FG, CO DeWitt Spain was replaced by Lt Col Julian E. "Jack" Thomas, who was yet another old "Pineapple" pilot.

Thomas, a survivor of the Pearl Harbor attack, had commanded the 45th FS throughout its highly successful campaign in the Marshall Islands, and was returning to action after a frustrating year in Air Training Command. He was known as an especially aggressive pilot, and as an officer who put great stock in the military philosophy that commanders must lead from the front. In the 47th FS, Maj John Piper handed over command to his operations officer, Capt Ed Markham.

Two squadron commanders in the 21st FG, Maj Fred Shirley in the 46th and Maj Paul Imig in the 72nd, headed for home at this time and turned their units over to Majs Benjamin C. Warren and James C. Van Nada, respectively. In a few weeks, Col Ken Powell would get his orders home as well, turning command of the 21st FG over to Lt Col Charlie Taylor. Another new face with a strong combat résumé was Lt Col John W. Mitchell of VII Fighter Command staff. Already an ace with eight victories scored in the South Pacific during 1942–43, he was best known for having led the P-38 mission that shot down Adm Isoroku Yamamoto, architect of the Pearl Harbor attack. Mitchell wasted no time in getting himself assigned to fly missions with the 15th FG.

Finally, on May 25, the 15th and 21st FGs were able to sortie on a maximum-effort mission against airfields in the Tokyo area. A heavy weather front reduced the force from 128 P-51s taking off, including spares, to just 67 reaching Japan. The 15th FG, led by Lt Col Mitchell at the head of the 47th FS, hit several airfields, starting with Matsudo. The 47th FS arrived over the target at 500ft and made a pass on a line of fighters, believed to be Ki-44s, getting hits on seven of them and leaving one on fire.

Next came the 78th FS, with Capt "Todd" Moore leading. One flight of 78th FS Mustangs carried rockets on this mission – a first for VII Fighter Command – and was trailing. Because of the extra drag imposed by the six 5in high-velocity rockets carried under their wings, the four P-51s were equipped with 165-gallon drop tanks in place of the normal 110-gallon models to give them sufficient range to reach the target. Maj Jim Tapp and his wingman, 1Lt Phil Maher, fired their rockets successfully at two hangers on Matsudo Airfield, setting fire to both targets.

As Capt Moore pulled up from Matsudo, he spotted a formation of enemy fighters to the north and gave chase. Always aggressive, Moore flamed two A6M Zeros in the scrap that ensued, and the other 78th FS pilots claimed six more. Moore's two kills took his tally to six victories (including one scored with the 45th FS during the Marshall Islands campaign), thus making him the second VLR ace. Tempering Moore's success, squadronmate 1Lt Robert W. Williams was shot down and taken prisoner. He later died of his wounds.

The 21st FG, led by Lt Col Taylor, attacked Tokorozawa Airfield west of Tokyo and destroyed eight aircraft, but did not encounter any aerial opposition. However, Taylor's Mustang was subsequently badly hit by return fire when he strafed a tugboat just off the coast. He bailed out close by the rescue submarine USS *Razorback* and was quickly hauled aboard, wet, but unhurt.

Shortly afterwards, the engine in 1Lt Walt Kreimann's P-51 caught fire about 375 miles short of Iwo Jima, and the 78th FS pilot also jumped out. Although his body and his parachute were partially burned, Kreimann survived the jump and was picked up by another submarine, USS *Tigrone*. Both men returned to Iwo Jima when the submarines completed their patrols, but Kreimann spent the next two and a half months in the hospital recovering from his burns.

The XXI Bomber Command mission on May 29 would be the first strike of any kind against Japan's great port on Tokyo Bay, Yokohama. This was to be a daylight incendiary raid on the city's industrial area, with 101 Mustangs of the 15th and 21st FGs returning to the escort role to provide protection for 454 bombers from all four of Gen LeMay's B-29 wings. The stage was set for what would turn out to be one biggest air battles of the entire Pacific War — and the most fruitful day for aerial victories that VII Fighter Command ever had.

The P-51s took off just at 0630hrs and headed north, dropping to 2,000ft at one point to pass under a weather front, before climbing to their escort altitude of 20,000ft for rendezvous with the B-29s. The Mustangs reached the Departure Point, which was landfall, ahead of the B-29s, and made two orbits before the bombers arrived at 1000hrs. Then the fighter flights spread to cover the bombers, and the massive formation headed east from Mount Fuji on a vector toward the target. The Japanese defenses were ready and waiting. Soon the sky was dotted with bursting flak and small formations of intercepting fighters. It was time for the P-51 pilots to get to work, and they did so with a vengeance. Within minutes, Mustangs were engaging Japanese fighters at points all around the B-29 formations.

Capt R. W. "Todd" Moore was leading a 45th FS flight covering the lead section of B-29s, having transferred from the 78th FS just a day or two prior. He spotted three J2M "Jacks" at "ten o'clock high" and gave chase, instructing his second element to attack the No 3 "Jack" while he went after the leader. Moore fired a deflection shot into the lead airplane and saw immediate hits, followed by the pilot bailing out. The No 2 "Jack" peeled off into a steep dive, and Moore followed. His Mustang quickly overtook the Japanese fighter, and he fired a telling burst from a range of 300 yards that sent it crashing to the ground.

Reforming his flight, Moore patrolled along the bomber stream for several minutes before spotting two N1K "Georges" circling over Yokohoma and giving chase. One "George" dove away as Moore attempted to attack, while the other approached his Mustang from behind. The Mustang pilot circled tightly with this fighter and eventually got behind it, allowing him to fire a short burst into its wing. A second burst hit the Japanese fighter squarely, and its pilot bailed out. Sadly, a lone A6M attacked Moore's flight as they were withdrawing toward the Rally Point and shot down his wingman, 2Lt Rufus S. Moore.

"Todd" Moore's three kills were two better than Jim Tapp of the 78th FS scored during the mission, allowing Moore to pass his rival as the leading ace of VII Fighter Command with nine confirmed victories. He never relinquished the title. Overall, the Mustang pilots tallied 28 confirmed victories for the loss of one pilot and three P-51s, making May 29, 1945 the most successful VII Fighter Command mission of them all. The next Empire mission would turn out far differently for the "Sun Setters."

THE SETTING SUN

The end of May 1945 found the "Sun Setters" firmly established on Iwo Jima. After two and a half months on the island, the men were now virtually free of the risk of running afoul of any remaining Japanese soldiers. Rumor had it that one of the few enemy holdouts had sneaked into an outdoor theater area one night and watched part of a movie with his American enemies before someone spotted him and took him prisoner. A continuing hazard was mines, which remained sown about the island despite ongoing efforts to clear them.

Living conditions, though still spartan, were improving at the airfields. Soon, the officers would give up their tents for more sturdy metal Quonset huts, which would also replace kitchen tents and other canvas structures serving all ranks. Sgt Chet Raun, a technician in the Photo Section of the 457th FS, recalled this period in a 2002 letter to the author:

The first supply ship arrived around the middle of May, and we had our first hot meals since arriving. All was great except that the first meat was mutton from Australia. Our cooks tried every way known to them to cook the meat so it tasted like something other than candles. It finally occurred to someone that it would be better if the fat was removed before cooking. That helped, but to this day I do not eat mutton. The water problem was also solved by the arrival of a desalinization unit.

Bathing didn't occur for most of us until we found a hot thermal in the water just off the shore at the north end of the island. This was great until nurses arrived on the island, and such bathing became taboo. By this time, however, the squadron had set up saltwater showers using water pumped in from the ocean.

Aside from a machine to process 16mm (gun camera) film, we had all the necessary equipment to operate the film lab. Our responsibilities included the maintenance of the gun cameras in the P-51s, bore-sighting the cameras so that they were synchronized with the airplane's machine guns, loading film into the cameras prior to a mission and retrieving it after the airplane's return. We had to send the 16mm film to Saipan for processing. We also loaded the 16mm film cassettes, processed still camera film and printed same, took pictures when requested and operated the 16mm projectors. In most cases we had ample time to do our work, as long as we were kept posted on mission times.

457th FS crew chief SSgt Lou Lascola listed his most memorable impressions of life on the island at this time:

> Nuisance air raids by the Japanese, just after bed time; getting into a foxhole with a corrugated tin cover; shooing off the gigantic green flies that fed on some not-yet-buried Japanese soldiers or US Marines; avoiding *sakai* bottles in the caves because they could be booby-trapped; avoiding the ghoul "gold-diggers" that pestered us to see if we had any Jap gold teeth to sell; counting and identifying the airplanes returning from a mission, and saying a silent prayer. I cannot begin to explain the tremendous admiration and respect we felt toward these young fighter pilots.

Finally, here are some recollections of Sgt Irv Howard, an armorer in the 462nd FS:

> Later on we lived in larger tents, which housed four to six men in each. We were really crammed and totally isolated on that hellish island. Some of the guys cracked with the loneliness and isolation, missing their wives, newly born offspring etc.
>
> I remember building our own washing machines – a wooden box containing a couple of boards, with a homemade windmill to move the boards up and back inside the box. In one area they constructed a latrine over a cave. After a few days several Japs came out of the cave and surrendered!

Refinements in aircraft equipment and operational procedures were continuing as well. Experience had shown that the tail-warning radar sets installed in some of the P-51s were of little use in combat, so VII Fighter Command initiated a program to remove them from all aircraft. On the positive side, AN/ARA-8 radio homing units, nicknamed "Uncle Dog," were installed in the Mustangs to help the pilots find their way back to Iwo Jima. Problems with the SCR-522 and SCR-695 radio sets were also being addressed. For instance, the 531st FS Communication Section discovered that Iwo's fine volcanic dust was getting into the microphone relays and causing them to fail, so the technicians learned to keep a close eye on the units and replace them as needed.

New Mustangs arrived regularly to replace aircraft lost in combat or in accidents. Among these were some P-51D-25s, which were equipped with the new K-14 gyroscopic gunsight developed by the British to improve accuracy during deflection shooting. The K-14's gyroscope measured the P-51's rate of turn and adjusted the light projector accordingly to move the graticule on the reflector glass, thus displaying the angle of deflection required to hit the target. It required a little more dexterity on the part of the pilot, because he had to adjust the sight to the target aircraft's wingspan prior to making an attack. But the K-14 greatly improved shooting accuracy, particularly at long range and at deflection angles of 45 degrees or more.

The VLR mission procedures continued to be refined as well. For one thing, a senior "Sun Setter" pilot was assigned to fly in each of the navigator B-29s that were used to lead the P-51 formations to Japan. These command pilots, supposedly well versed in the capabilities of the P-51 and the issues involved in safely completing a VLR mission, would call the shots in case the formation ran into bad weather or other problems while en route to the target.

For all these improvements, there was still no getting around the fact that flying an eight-hour mission in a Mustang, most of it over open sea, was an exhausting ordeal for the "Sun Setter" pilots. One of the best descriptions of this was provided by Phil Alston, who flew eight VLR missions in the 457th FS, in response to a question by aviation historian Tom Ivie:

It would take anywhere from two to three hours to get from Iwo Jima up to Japan. I don't know how anybody else felt, but my personal feelings were that I was awfully nervous, I don't mind admitting. And I was sitting there wondering about if I was going to be able to come through this mission. I mean, if I'd be able to get back to Iwo. They gave us a little lunch and a canteen of water to take with us, since the mission lasted all day. But I couldn't eat or drink anything the whole time going up there.

We'd get up there and spend anywhere from half an hour to an hour over the target. Then we'd come off and rendezvous and start on the way back. Well, then you felt quite different. I mean it was just a really happy feeling that you'd have, and that's when I'd pull out my lunch and start eating it. I'd sometimes just sit there and sing – just really enjoy it – because I was happy to be alive and on my way back to Iwo.

As far as the strain of over-the-water flights, well, we really didn't think too much about that. They gave us all the training on ditching the airplanes and survival in the dinghy out in the water – how to fish, what fish to eat and what not to eat. But it didn't really bother me too much flying over water, and that's what just about all our flying was. If anything went wrong, you go down in the water. But they had these air-sea rescue ships that you could navigate from one to the other.

Extraordinary challenges such as those faced by the "Sun Setters" bring out the best in some people, and one of them was Lt Col Joseph "Smoky" Walther, VII Fighter Command flight surgeon. Here was a man completely devoted to the care and well-being of "Mickey" Moore's pilots – a trait he demonstrated more than once. The most extreme example of this came as the result of Brig Gen Moore's frustration over the loss of several pilots who were seen to bail out of their crippled P-51s successfully, yet who drowned before rescue crews could pick them up. He thought it would help if airborne paramedics were available to parachute to the rescue of downed pilots in the water.

When none of Walther's paramedics volunteered to make a test jump from a PBY to attempt rescuing a dummy, Walther agreed to do it himself. On the appointed day, the brave doctor leaped from the PBY, was temporarily knocked cold when one of the shroud lines of his parachute whacked him in the temple, and then nearly drowned when one of the two CO_2 bottles on his Mae West failed. After a miserable few hours in the water, during which time he did manage to "rescue" the dummy, Walther was pulled aboard a destroyer and delivered back to Iwo.

The flying paramedic idea was abandoned as a result of the test, but two new procedures were identified that would help save pilots in the future. For one thing, all CO_2 bottles were tested, and it was found that half of them were defective. Also, a directive was published warning all pilots to put their hands over their temples after pulling the ripcord if they had to bail out.

Smoky Walther's other great contribution to the pilots was the facility that came to be called "Ye Olde Iwo Jima Spa." The doctor was becoming increasingly concerned about the condition of the Mustang pilots when they returned from the exhausting VLR missions to Japan, many times so stiff and sore that they needed help from the crew chiefs just to climb out of their cockpits and down off the wing. Walther decided that what these boys needed at the end of a tough day in the cockpit was a steam bath and a rubdown.

As keeper of VII Fighter Command's medicinal liquor supply, Walther was able to barter with SeaBees on the island for their help in building the spa in a Quonset hut. Drilling into the ground, they were able to tap the near-boiling water that lay just below the surface and direct it into "catchalls" – large tubs normally used for collecting rain water. Pilots were welcome to drop their tired bodies into the tubs of hot water and enjoy a cold beer while their muscles relaxed. Then they could step across the aisle and lie face down on a table, where Walther's team of corpsmen gave them rubdowns. After a visit to the spa, pilots would begin to feel human again.

Despite all the improvements being made on Iwo Jima, one thing beyond repair was the weather. As had already become apparent in May, the northwest corner of the Pacific acts like a mixing bowl with the approach of the summer solstice, when cold weather blowing down off the Asian land mass runs smack into tropical air moving up from the south. The collision of weather systems creates violent storms, the likes of which no World War II fighter was designed to conquer.

If you asked the "Sun Setter" pilots, most would tell you they considered the massive weather fronts they encountered on some Empire missions to be a more fearsome enemy than the Japanese defenses opposing them on Honshu. The most extreme example of this occurred on June 1, 1945.

BLACK FRIDAY

Imagine you are a World War II American fighter pilot, headed north from Iwo Jima in your P-51D Mustang toward Japan. You're flying at 20,000ft, loaded down with a full load of ammunition, internal fuel tanks filled to the brim and a 110-gallon drop tank hanging from each wing. Your speed is just a tad over 200mph, and the Mustang is wallowing along like a truck. Yeah, you've got that big Merlin engine out front, but it's throttled back as far as you dare in order to save fuel for the long trip. Around you, there are forty-some guys from your fighter group in the same boat.

You peer into the distance ahead of you and see a long band of clouds rising from the horizon. "How far away are those damned clouds?" you wonder. Minutes tick by and the cloudbank grows. Pretty soon you realize this is a major weather front. It rises up and up, topping out a good two miles above your present altitude. And it's spread out so wide that there's no chance of flying around it and still completing your mission. If you attempt to fly through, it's possible you will never come out the other side alive. But the B-29s are big enough to penetrate the front safely, and they're going to need your protection from enemy interceptors when they reach the target area.

This was the dilemma facing 148 "Sun Setter" pilots on June 1 as they set out on VLR Mission No 15 to provide escort for 400 B-29s assigned to attack Osaka. They had taken off in good weather at Iwo, clearing the island by 0710hrs and proceeding to the rendezvous point at Kita Rocks, where they met the navigation B-29s that would lead them to the target. But by the time they reached about 370 miles away from base, everyone could see that a well-formed front, with angry cumulonimbus reaching to 30,000ft, was blocking their path.

The navigator B-29s advised the three group leaders – Lt Col Jack Thomas, 15th FG, Maj Charles Chapin, 21st FG, and Lt Col Harvey Scandrett, 506th FG – to begin a climb over the front. But the call came too late, as the heavily loaded Mustangs were too close to the front to climb over it in the fleeting minutes before they would reach the clouds. Perhaps realizing this, the B-29s continued flying straight and level, leading the P-51s directly into the storm.

Flying behind the formation in a B-29, with a bird's-eye view of the scene, was 462nd FS flight commander Capt John Findley. Just prior to going overseas, he had been pulled off terminal leave and sent through an accelerated weather program at Bryan Field, Texas. On June 1, he was assigned as the VII Fighter Command pilot in a B-29 that was supposed to go out 30 minutes ahead of the formation and scout the weather along the route to Japan. Findley's account of what happened during the fateful mission, compiled from a letter to the author and his mission report, is as follows:

I attended the briefing the night before. The mission was ordered off against the wishes of the weather officer. At scheduled take-off, our B-29 developed engine trouble and we had to delay, so the next B-29 in line took our place. Unfortunately, the fighter pilot in that airplane had never had been on a Japan mission – he was new, and had only been to Chichi Jima. After the P-51s took off, we got the B-29 squared away and departed about 30 minutes behind the mission.

I can still see in my mind's eye that endless line of cumulus clouds that marked the front, visible from about 100 miles away. We were aware of the tremendous build-up and began to climb. We were pushing the B-29, yet it appeared that no matter how fast we climbed, the tops of the clouds stayed with us, and the closer we got the more obvious it was we'd never get over the top. I remember looking at the rate-of-climb indicator, and it was at 1,000ft per minute. Still the clouds boiled up faster.

Not long before we hit the front, the problem was obvious. The radio chatter was incessant and confused. We decided to go into the soup on the chance we might pick up an airplane or two that could fly wing on us until we could get them out. We did so, and by some good chance we ran into a hole among the clouds and saw several P-51s milling about in a circle. We dropped down, got them to tuck in tight, and led them out of the front and headed back toward Iwo.

We decided to try this again, and found either the same hole or another one and circled in it waiting for survivors. We didn't find any. We headed for the deck in search of others. The front went down almost to water level. We searched, but found no one. Clearly the mission was over, and the remaining airplanes headed back to Iwo. We landed and learned quite a number of P-51s had not returned.

The experience was even worse for the "Sun Setter" pilots in the P-51s that penetrated the front. The report filed by the 458th FS after the mission described it this way:

The front was entered between 10,000 and 11,000ft. Visibility was zero, rain heavy, turbulence intense and violent. Groups, squadrons, flights and elements lost contact and scattered. Traffic on all radio channels was so heavy that communication was nearly impossible. Some pilots lost control completely, spun, recovered and spun again. Some recovered in time, some did not. Only 27 P-51s – none from the 458th – passed through the front and arrived over the target area.

The experience of 72nd FS pilot 1Lt Leo Hines was typical. He described what happened to him:

We headed into the soup. The confusion was unbelievable. Our formation dissolved from absolute necessity. I found myself alone, so I tacked onto a B-29 and flew formation with him until he indicated we were at 200ft. I had seen the water a couple of times and figured I would be safer on my own. I picked up a reciprocal heading and broke into the clear on the Iwo side of the front. Maj Crim was in the vicinity, so I tacked onto his wing and returned to Iwo. God, what a mess.

Capt Francis Lee of the 462nd FS was one of the 27 pilots who made it through the front. He described his experience as follows:

Tom DeJarnette was leading the squadron and I was leading the last eight airplanes. Tom called to tell us that in spite of "oranges being sour" (the code term for impassable weather), we were going to penetrate the front. We headed straight into the soup. He was interrupted by screams of pilots on the radio, airplanes bumping into one another, mid-air collisions, shouts of bailouts and pilots in spins. My radio then fell silent. I signaled to my pilots to go into the formation we had practiced at Lakeland – pull to the right ten degrees and make a shallow climb through the front. The cloud cover was so thick I could barely see my wingtips.

After about 15 minutes of slow climbing, the sun was shining and I could see that my gun barrels were covered with ice. Then out of the blue came the call "Flight leader, what is your airspeed?" Startled, I looked to my right and there was my wingman, 1Lt Harley Meyer! He had stuck with me like a flea on a dog. We never saw another P-51 until we landed at Iwo seven hours later. I told Meyer that we would have to go down slowly to melt the ice. Down we went. As we were losing height, I felt the air turbulence of a four-engined aircraft. Sure enough, 15 minutes later I spotted a B-29 with a big "Z" on its tail. I called the B-29 and explained our situation to him. The B-29 pilot said he would make a single pass over the target and then help us with our problem. As he was going into his run, I spotted a Jap "Frank" [Ki-84] preparing to make a pass on the B-29. When the "Frank" spotted us, he took off. The B-29 made his bomb run, then picked us up on the other side of the target. So we tacked onto the bomber and headed for Iwo.

When we landed at Iwo, all our friends climbed onto our wings and seemed genuinely happy to see us. It was great to be home. Then we got the bad news about the mission. The Good Lord really looked after us.

In the 47th FS, the entire "Yellow Flight" and half of "Green Flight" simply disappeared – six pilots gone, which was the worst loss of any squadron in VII Fighter Command that day. But the 47th also had the distinction of scoring the only aerial victory of the mission. 1Lt Robert S. Scamara wrote this account to the author 60 years later:

I thought we would enter the clouds and in a few moments exit on the other side, but that wasn't the case. Imagine taking 65 or so P-51s in tight formation into a weather front with no sight distance, heavy rain and hard buffeting. Very afraid of hitting other airplanes in formation, I was one of the lucky ones and got through it okay. I don't know what happened to my wingman, who was a fill-in from the 45th FS (1Lt Lawrence Lortie, missing in action).

I went on alone toward the target and got there while bombing was under way. I escorted several groups of B-29s over the target, which was one big fire with smoke up to 25,000ft or more. Finally, I saw a two-engined "Nick" heading for the bombers. I dropped my external tanks and gave the P-51 full power to catch up to him. Then my engine stopped. A few terrified moments later, after I realized I hadn't switched to the internal tanks, the engine started up again. I caught the "Nick" easily. He probably never saw me, as he was intent on getting to the B-29s. My first burst, from the left side, knocked out his left engine and set him on fire. I coasted across behind him to his right side, giving him another burst just to get camera coverage of my kill, as I was alone and had no other witnesses. This was a must to get credit for a kill.

After watching him spin down in flames, I looked around and found myself completely alone. I couldn't find the bombers. I tried to find our navigational B-29 that was at the Rally Point. He said he had to head back as he had two other P-51s and they were low on fuel, so he couldn't wait around any longer for me. He gave me his heading for Iwo. I didn't know if I was ahead, behind or parallel to him, but the heading got me home by myself – I hit Iwo on the nose. That's pretty good, finding a three-by-seven-mile island 650 miles away.

The next day I went down to the flightline and asked about my film. The crew chief hesitated a little, then said, "Oh, haven't you heard? Your camera wasn't loaded properly, so no film." Our S-2 officer, Henry Sanders, said he would radio down to Bomber Command to see if any bomber crew had witnessed my kill. This was a long chance, but one crew reported a Jap airplane going down in flames, but didn't see who shot it down. Out of all the airplanes in the air that day, I was the only one to make a claim, so I got credit for my first kill.

Later on, I received the Silver Star medal, pinned on my shirt by Gen "Hap" Arnold. I've never been sure that I earned it after seeing what the Marines had to go through taking Iwo Jima.

The numbers tell the whole lesson of June 1. Of the 24 Mustang pilots lost that day, not one went down as a result of enemy action – Mother Nature took them all. Among the pilots who did not come back were the formation leaders of the 21st FG, Maj Chapin, and the 506th FG, Lt Col Scandrett. John Findley recalled that an inquiry was held immediately after dinner that night, when it was discovered that the P-51 weather pilot in the lead B-29 had no combat experience. As a result, VII Fighter Command adopted a rule that in the future only combat-experienced "Sun Setters" could fly as lead weather pilot.

The 45th FS got good news a week later when the submarine USS *Trutta* reported it had picked up one of the squadron's missing pilots, 1Lt Arthur A. Burry. The engine in Burry's P-51 cut out temporarily while he was battling the storm, and he lost contact with his flight. He managed to restart the engine and headed back to Iwo alone, but then he lost power for good and had to bail out about 275 miles north of home. After hitting the water, Burry had a little trouble getting out of his parachute harness, but within two minutes he was able to inflate his liferaft and climb in. Then he settled down to await rescue.

Burry's first few days in the raft passed uneventfully, but on the night of June 5/6 he was caught in a storm that dumped him out of the raft several times and cost him his food supply, which was washed away. The next day he began having delusions – during one of them Burry believed he was at a party when a friend said he was sending a destroyer to pick him up. A report by the 45th FS intelligence officer finishes the story:

Seventh Day – June 7. The morning was clear and bright, and 1Lt Burry realized no destroyer was coming, and that he had been deluded the night before. Presently, he started hearing music, and distinct voices of people singing songs. Later, when the submarine picked him up, he was not delirious, but was somewhat incoherent. He seemed to expect the submarine, and took it as quite normal that he should be picked up. He was able to climb down the hatch without any help.

1Lt Burry's rescue closed the books on Black Friday – the worst mission in the history of VII Fighter Command.

RUNNING UP THE SCORE

Bad weather hampered VLR operations throughout June, with just seven missions completed by the end of the month. After Black Friday, the "Sun Setters" made another escort foray to Osaka on June 7. Again, they encountered a weather front en route, but this time it did not amount to much, and neither did Japanese opposition over the target area. A flight from the 462nd FS shot down an unidentified single-engined aircraft south of the city, and Maj "Todd" Moore of the 45th FS destroyed a Ki-45 a few minutes later for his tenth victory.

The next scheduled mission was planned as a fighter sweep of Kagamigahara Airfield at Nagoya on June 8, but the formation encountered a huge front about an hour after taking off and turned around to come home. Conditions were better the following day, and the mission was completed, with the 21st FG registering aerial claims of one probable and two damaged, plus seven ground kills. Two P-51s were lost to flak in the target area, and a third went down about ten miles from Iwo Jima, its pilot being quickly rescued.

The weather continued to cooperate on June 10, when 107 Mustangs of the 15th and 506th FGs escorted B-29s to the Tokyo area. This time the Japanese put up an estimated 100 fighters in opposition, but their tactics were ineffective, and succeeded only in giving the P-51 pilots something to do. The result was a lopsided victory for the "Sun Setters" – scores of 24 confirmed destroyed, four probably destroyed and seven damaged for no losses. Perhaps more importantly, no B-29s were lost either.

The top scorer on June 10 was 1Lt Doyle T. Brooks Jr of the 78th FS with two confirmed kills and one damaged. This is how he recalled the mission:

My flight leader had to abort during the VLR, and another pilot took his place. I remember looking down and seeing a Zero, and then calling "Let's go get him" over the radio. I dropped down to 5,000ft, and my airplane started porpoising due to excessive speed. I cut the throttle, reached down and put my pipper on top of the Zero's tail and fired. Smoke came out of his wing roots, and then I saw the Zero's pilot opening his 'chute. I then looked over to my right and saw a second Zero. He was fishtailing in front of me to slow me down. He fell into a lazy barrel roll when I fired, and he too went down.

After the mission, several 47th FS flight leaders reported having momentarily mistaken 506th FG Mustangs for Japanese aircraft because their tails appeared to be red (like the Ki-61s of the 244th Sentai) under certain light conditions, and the striped markings tended to camouflage the distinctive outline of the tail – one of the P-51's best recognition features. It may be that the 457th and 462nd FSs converted their tail markings to solid colors (green and yellow, respectively) as a result of this report.

Meanwhile, 462nd FS commander Maj Tom DeJarnette, who had shot down one Ki-61 that day, critiqued his squadron's performance during the mission as exhibiting "poor air discipline." Speaking with the authority only accorded to someone who had survived a full combat tour flying P-39 Airacobras over New Guinea earlier in the war, DeJarnette told his pilots that they had flown too close together, had been too individualistic and not watchful enough, and that the wingmen had not paid close enough attention to their leaders' flying.

The squadron's pilots would have plenty of time to mull their commander's remarks, because the weather would scrub their next two missions. Although the 21st FG pulled off a successful fighter strike against Tokyo on June 11, the 15th and 506th FGs did not get another crack at the enemy for nearly two weeks.

On June 23 the weather finally improved, and 100 P-51s of the 15th and 506th FGs headed out for a fighter strike against airfields in the Tokyo area. Led by Lt Col Jack Thomas, the 15th FG was assigned to attack Shimodate and Kasumigaura airfields, while the 506th went after Hyakurigahara and Katori, with Maj Harrison Shipman leading. Another field day for the "Sun Setters" was in the works.

The 15th FG took off first and arrived at the Departure Point over Japan at 1300hrs. Turning left, the formation proceeded above a deck of clouds for about four minutes, before the 47th FS was jumped by seven Ki-84 "Franks." The Japanese defenders made some moderately aggressive passes, but Lt Col Thomas and his wingman, Flt Off Fronnie A. Jones Jr, were each able to shoot one down. After three and a half years of war, Jack Thomas' determination to repay the enemy for the destruction he had witnessed during the Pearl Harbor attack had finally paid off.

While this was going on, the 78th FS made a strafing attack on Shimodate that netted three Ki-84s destroyed and three other aircraft damaged on the ground. Lt Col Thomas next led his group southeast toward Kasumigaura, and was jumped again about ten minutes later. This time, 17 Ki-84s hit the 47th FS aggressively with an altitude advantage, breaking up the Americans' formation as a wild dogfight erupted and Japanese naval fighters also joined in.

The battle raged for about ten minutes, during which time the 15th FG pilots claimed an additional seven enemy aircraft destroyed, three probables and 14 damaged. The top scorer was 1Lt Bob Scamara of the 47th FS, with three confirmed kills. That made him the unit's leading scorer with four victories. Scamara would go on to complete 15 VLR missions by the end of the war – one of the few "Sun Setters" to reach that total – but never got the opportunity to notch the fifth kill that would have made him an ace.

On the deficit side of the 15th FG's ledger, three P-51s were lost on June 23. Two of the pilots bailed out over the sea and were rescued, but the third wasn't so lucky. During the fight, 1Lt Scamara's wingman, 1Lt John V. Scanlan, was shot up by a Zero and bailed out over Chiba Peninsula, near Chosi Point. He was taken prisoner, but after the war it was learned that he had been executed while held as a PoW.

The 506th FG had an action-packed mission on June 23 as well. The group's navigator B-29s got slightly off course, and as a result the Mustangs made landfall north of the planned route and over an industrial area, where heavy and accurate flak greeted their arrival. The formation broke up, with the 457th FS proceeding to Mito South Airfield, which the pilots mistook for Naruto. There, the pilots made four strafing passes apiece before turning for home with claims of 11 aircraft destroyed on the ground.

The 458th FS, meanwhile, accompanied the 462nd FS to Hyakurigahara, where the former unit was assigned to hunt flak and provide top cover for the latter. Led by Maj Shipman in a rocket-armed P-51, the 458th pilots made a steep dive to the target and shot it up as best they could, before pulling back up to cover the attack by the 462nd FS. According to the mission report, Shipman's rockets destroyed a twin-engined aircraft on the field. One of the 462nd pilots, 1Lt William G. Ebersole, wrote this account of his squadron's subsequent attack:

I received credit for probably destroying one "Zeke" fighter on the ground (on June 23). When we performed these strafing runs on airfields, four of our 16-airplane squadron would make a vertical dive on the target, firing at random to detract the ground fire, while the other 12 airplanes would dive down to treetop level about 15 miles from the field and spread out in a horizontal line, with about 100ft or so between the Mustangs. By staying in a horizontal line, we would not be in danger of shooting our own airplanes, but each pilot had very little room for maneuvering, and had to take the targets in his particular path of flight.

I still get goose bumps thinking back on the excitement of diving down from about 20,000ft at close to full throttle, leveling out at treetop height as one of a dozen airplanes lined up abreast, and racing across an airfield with guns blazing. We each had six .50cal machine guns. Every fifth round of ammunition was a tracer bullet, with two incendiary and two armor-piercing bullets making up the other four of each five rounds. With the tracers ricocheting in all directions, the incendiary rounds exploding when they hit, explosions on the ground and a mass of return fire from enemy flak gunners, it would put any Fourth of July finale to shame.

After covering the 462nd FS strafing run, the 458th FS headed eastward toward the coast and began to climb, losing Maj Shipman's "Blue Flight" in the process. The squadron's mission report detailed what happened next:

Just west of Inubo Saki light, "Yellow Flight" saw eight bogeys far below, flying a sloppy 3-1, 22 formation in trail, and in a climbing turn to the left. "Yellow Flight" bounced from 13,000ft and drove in from above at "seven o'clock." The four trailing Zekes caught the attack. 1Lt [Harold] Davidson flamed one after a heavy burst in the cockpit. 1Lt [Evan] Stuart burned another. One enemy aircraft pulled up and out in a high roll, above Stuart. 1Lt [Roy] Kempert, "Yellow 2," nosed up, fired and got heavy strikes. The "Zeke" broke down and out, spun and trailed smoke. Kempert followed, firing. Finally he broke off and climbed almost vertically to rejoin. Another "Zeke" was starting down, and Kempert was forced to dive away. The "Zeke" did not follow through.

1Lt [Jack] Kelsey, "Blue 3," with "Blue 4," was proceeding to the Rally Point when he saw the fight. He arrived in time to force a break from the enemy aircraft that had hovered above 1Lt Kempert after chasing 1Lt Davidson. The enemy aircraft dove away from 1Lt Kelsey, then chandelled and was hit hard as he did. He burned. The "Zeke" Kempert had originally fired at was, when last seen by Kelsey, in a tight spin, blazing.

Meanwhile, 1Lt Davidson broke upward after his first pass and made a second run on the lead four enemy aircraft. He got strikes on the left wingman, then turned and looked down the gun barrels of a "Zeke" coming in high at "seven o'clock." Davidson snapped under and broke down and out. This "Zeke" is the same one credited above to 1Lt Kelsey.

1Lt Stuart was, in the interim, making high wingovers into and out of the melee. On his second pass, he made strikes on an enemy aircraft in the first flight of four and then pulled up and knocked pieces off the tail of another diving in from "two o'clock high." He recovered, made another run and got strikes on another enemy aircraft. On his last pass, Stuart hit another "Zeke" in the wing, and then saw an enemy aircraft boring in from "five o'clock," firing, so he broke down and out in a spiral dive.

"Red" and "Green Flights" were meanwhile heading about 270 degrees northwest of Inubo Saki light when four "Jacks" in box-four formation were called in at "ten o'clock low." The enemy aircraft were outnumbered and immediately dived for cloud cover. They did not reach it. "Red 1," Capt [J. B.] Baker, ran a burst into the tail of the fourth enemy aircraft, which chandelled tightly, caught Baker's second burst fairly in the cockpit and center section and began to burn. 1Lt [Vance] Middaugh, "Red 3," shot and smoked the No 3 "Jack," which began to trail a small fire from its engine. 1Lt [Norman] Dostal saw this aircraft hit the ground and explode.

1Lt [Max] Ruble, leading "Green Flight," crossed from the inside of the attack over "Red Flight" and put a burst into the belly of the second enemy aircraft, which broke right. Ruble pulled through to a 20–30 degree deflection, fired and set the "Jack" alight. The pilot jettisoned his canopy and rolled onto the wing while his airplane was still taking strikes. As Ruble ceased firing, the pilot opened his parachute. 1Lt [Wilhelm] Peterson, flying on Ruble's left wing, was unable to dodge and chopped the 'chute to bits with his propeller.

"Green 3," 1Lt [Frank] Wheeler, crossed with his leader and opened fire on the flight leader. The "Jack" caught fire and the pilot bailed out. 1Lt [G. B.] Lambert, forced out of position by the last crossover, swung wide to the right. he turned back and suddenly saw a "Jack" sitting ahead of him. He followed the enemy aircraft up to 1,000–2,000ft, firing, and saw strikes and drew smoke. When last seen, the "Jack" was still smoking and in a split-ess at about 1,000ft.

All told, the 458th FS was credited with a score of ten destroyed, two probables and one damaged for the mission, with no losses. This was the "Sun Setters'" deepest penetration into enemy territory to date. The last Mustang returning to Iwo, flown by 1Lt William T. Moore of the 457th FS, landed after a bottom-numbing eight hours and 20 minutes in the air, setting a new record for VII Fighter Command.

The next mission, on June 26, was an escort by all three VII Fighter Command fighter groups to Nagoya. Flak over the target was typically heavy, but few Japanese fighters rose to intercept the Americans. The "Sun Setters" registered just two confirmed victories, but one of them was notable because it was the first kill in more than two years for Lt Col John Mitchell, who led the 15th FG that day. His wingman, 2Lt Doug Reese of the 45th FS, wrote this account:

An airplane speeding toward us was aimed directly at Lt Col Mitchell. When two airplanes are coming together at speeds of over 200mph, events happen fast. In your mind, however, everything is in slow motion. It was a Japanese airplane we had designated as a "Tony." The "Tony" had an inline engine, as did our Mustangs. The colonel thought it was one of our Mustangs, and he banked his airplane right out of the path of the "Tony." I knew it was not a Mustang because of the dihedral of the wings. The six .50cal machine guns in the wings of my Mustang were adjusted to converge 150 to 300 yards in front of the airplane. When the rounds meet at whatever distance, the fire will tear a hole in any aircraft. I started firing short bursts, counting on this fact to destroy the "Tony" before it got to me. It did not happen.

At the last moment, the "Tony" became vulnerable as it started to pull up, and I saw strikes on his engine and puffs of smoke and flame. On the radio someone said, "He bailed out." We turned right. The pilot was swinging in his parachute. We then turned left in line with the bomber stream, heading north. Ahead of us a few miles away was another lone aircraft – a "Zeke." We closed on the pilot from behind, and I held my fire until I saw the colonel fire. My gun camera film was reviewed the next day. It pictured the whole airplane that quickly exploded as the rounds struck home. For a moment it appeared that I would fly into the flame, but the ruins dropped as I pulled up over it.

Weather intervened again, forcing the June 27 fighter strike on Nagoya airfields to abort, so the Mustangs tried once more on July 1. Bad weather again was a factor, making it impossible for the 15th and 506th FGs to attack their targets. But the 21st FG found the conditions over its target – Hamamatsu Airfield – suitable and bored in, firing rockets and machine guns.

After the attack, the group was returning to the Rally Point when it came across a formation of Japanese twin-engined bombers and pounced. The short fight produced three confirmed victories, including one G4M "Betty" bomber for Maj Harry Crim. This was the fifth kill for the young commander of the 531st FS, making him the newest "Sun Setter" ace.

THE FINAL ASSAULT

By this time, it was becoming obvious to the "Sun Setters" that the frequency and numbers of Japanese fighters attempting to intercept the American raids on Honshu were diminishing. This was due in part to losses suffered by the defenders in three months of combat with VII Fighter Command, plus dwindling supplies of fuel. But another factor was the decision by Japanese military leaders to pull most of their forces out of range of the American raiders to save them for use during the Allies' expected invasion of the home islands.

This would not stop the "Sun Setters" from looking for trouble over Honshu, however. They completed 16 VLR missions in July, which was more than double June's total. But the escort of B-29s, originally planned as VII Fighter Command's primary mission, assumed a lesser role. With aerial opposition drastically reduced except for on a few missions, the eager pilots began attacking targets of opportunity on a much greater scale. Their primary targets continued to be airfields, but they also went after rail transportation, power line installations and shipping. As a result, the Mustangs' exposure to flak rose dramatically.

Short-range strikes against targets in the Bonin Islands, primarily on Chichi Jima, continued as well. Aided in finding targets by the arrival on Iwo of a detachment from a Marine Corps photo-reconnnaissance squadron, VII Fighter Command carried out 45 combat missions, comprising 338 sorties, to the Bonins during July and August 1945. Although missions to the Bonins were by nature less dangerous than VLR operations, they nevertheless cost the lives of two more P-51 pilots before the end of the war.

The first of these was particularly frustrating because of the tremendous, but ultimately unsuccessful, effort made to save the pilot. It occurred on July 3, when eight rocket-equipped P-51s of the 15th FG attacked shipping in Futami Harbor, on Chichi. 1Lt Richard H. Schroeppel of the 78th FS was flying wingman in the last element over the target when his Mustang was hit and set on fire. Low and slow in the burning airplane, Schroeppel barely had time to bail out and land in the water at the entrance to the harbor. He climbed into his liferaft and attempted to paddle out to sea, but the currents carried him north among some rocks close to shore.

While Schroeppel was struggling against the tide, the other airplanes in his flight orbited his position and strafed gun positions along the shore that were firing at the downed pilot. Forty more P-51s were despatched from Iwo to aid in the rescue effort, and shortly afterward a B-17 carrying a lifeboat arrived on the scene and dropped it for Schroeppel. The boat grounded on a reef, and Schroeppel was able to reach it, but he was subsequently killed by machine-gun fire from the shore. A PBY flying boat landed and attempted to recover the body, but it was driven off by heavy mortar and machine-gun fire. Ten days later, 2Lt Albert C. Marklin of the 462nd FS went down over Chichi as well, possibly the result of one of the rockets carried by his airplane exploding while still attached to the wing.

Encounters with Japanese interceptors had diminished, but the Honshu defenders had not given up entirely. As a result, the "Sun Setters" scored at least one aerial victory in 13 of the 25 VLR missions flown in July and August. Flt Off Anthony J. Gance of the 531st FS considered the mission of July 6 – a strafing attack on Atsugi Airfield – his most memorable. This is his recollection:

I knew this was going to be an exciting mission because I was going to be wingman for Maj Crim, who was our squadron commander. Crim took more chances than most leaders. I knew he was out to become a double ace.

We got to Japan in less than three hours and started looking for Atsugi Airfield. Crim spotted the base, and within a short time we were over the target at about 14,000ft. Crim signaled to get into line abreast. He got us into position and signaled for the attack. We headed in a dive toward one end of the airfield. At a short distance above the ground, we approached a speed of near 500mph. There was a lot of machine-gun fire at us. The tracers were all around us, but none of us got hit. I guess they didn't lead us enough.

There were a lot of airplanes on the ground. We started to fire our guns, and I had two airplanes explode as I shot them – all members of our flight shot up airplanes. As we came to the end of the field, Crim started a climbing turn. He made a circle and indicated to us that we were going to make another strafing run – most flight leaders didn't do this because the Japs would be ready for us. We made the run and hit more airplanes.

We made our climb, but the other two airplanes in our flight apparently lost us. So it was just Crim and I as we climbed over Tokyo Bay. At about 15,000ft Crim yelled, "Bogeys at 'five o'clock high!'" They were almost at our level. It happened that there were five of them. We both turned to engage, and in short order Crim shot up two airplanes and I got one. Crim then shot down another Jap, but I couldn't get the last airplane. I knew I was getting low on gas, so I dove and headed for the ocean, where a B-29 was to lead us back to Iwo.

As I was heading toward the ocean, I saw another airplane in the distance. It was coming right at me. I thought I had no recourse but to engage him head-on. Then a voice over the radio said, "Is that you, Gance?" I said, "Yes, sir," to which Crim replied, "Get on my wing and let's go home." The next day, my crew chief said we had expended almost all of our ammo. Also, our gas tanks were just about empty. God and luck had been with us.

Crim was credited with one Zero confirmed destroyed in the air for his sixth, and last, victory of the war, plus two Zeros and a "Jack" damaged. Gance received credit for one "Jack" damaged. Also on July 6, 1Lt Clarence "Bud" Bell of the 72nd FS was shot down and taken prisoner.

The July 7 mission was a weather abort, and on the 8th the 15th and 506th FGs tallied six victories at a cost of four pilots lost, including one PoW. The July 8 mission was also notable because the Sub Cover flight of the 458th FS – 1Lts Jack Kelsey, Dean Jensen, Ralph Coltman and Francis Pilecki – stayed aloft for more than nine hours in assisting the attempted rescue of a downed pilot just off the coast of Japan.

A fighter strike to Osaka on July 9 netted 13 confirmed victories for the 21st FG. As the group's three squadrons approached the target, they unwittingly sandwiched two large formations of Japanese fighters between the 531st FS, flying top cover, and the 46th and 72nd FSs below. The 531st dove on the enemy airplanes, which split-essed into a thin layer of clouds and came out among the two strike squadrons underneath. A wild melee ensued. as 2Lt G. R. "Jerry" Nolin of the 46th FS recalled:

> We had proceeded inland about 50 miles in a generally northern direction in squadron formation when two bogeys appeared on our right, coming toward us at about our altitude. I spotted them and called them out. The bogeys swung around behind us about three miles, without acting aggressive. My flight whirled around in an extremely tight 180-degree turn and headed toward the bogeys. I fired at one of them, starting at too long a range. When he noticed I was firing at him, he made a quick break to the left.
>
> The quick turnaround at the start had reduced my airspeed too much, and I was going in the wrong direction. I solved both problems at once by doing a split-ess. This got me going good again, and in the same direction as the rest of the squadron, which was now somewhat above me.
>
> The Mustangs were chasing one of the bogeys around, and he made a quick dive to escape. He happened to pull out of his dive right in front of me. I just put my gunsight pipper on him and fired. The full force of my guns hit the "Tojo." His engine stopped almost instantly. I cut the throttle to avoid overrunning him and drew up alongside the fighter. The pilot was climbing out of the cockpit and bailed out. The fighter continued down, hit the ground and disintegrated in a large ball of flame.

The 531st FS gained a second ace on July 9 as Capt Willis E. Mathews, squadron operations officer, was credited with two victories. Mathews had flown a previous combat tour in P-38s with the 94th FS/1st FG in the MTO, scoring 3.5 victories against the Luftwaffe. He joined the 531st in May 1945 as a replacement pilot, and became ops officer the following month when Capt Charles Betz rotated to the US. Mathews eventually completed 13 VLR missions, left the service after the war and was recalled to fly F-51s during the Korean conflict.

VLR missions continued as the weather allowed during July. The "Sun Setters" struck Tokyo airfields on July 10, gaining one aerial victory and 15 ground kills for the loss of three P-51s, but no pilots. The July 14 mission was scrubbed by weather, and the following day the 531st FS added four more victories to its scoreboard on a strike in the Nagoya area. An additional nine ground victories were credited, but the 47th FS lost two pilots killed, and one pilot of the 78th FS was shot down and captured.

On July 16, the 21st and 506th FGs sent 96 Mustangs to attack airfields at Nagoya. One P-51 went down on the outbound flight when a fuel leak set fire to the airplane – its pilot bailed out and was rescued. The 21st FG, led by Lt Col Mitchell of VII Fighter Command, was first into the target area and encountered an estimated 60 enemy aircraft before the

Mustangs were able to strafe the airfields as originally planned. The 506th FG Mustangs joined the air battle a few minutes later, led by Maj Malcolm "Muddy" Watters, formerly 457th FS CO, and now serving as group operations officer.

According to VII Fighter Command publication *Fighter Notes*, the Japanese defenders proved more "aggressive and able" during this aerial combat than on any previous mission. "However, they did not use mutual support, and our airplanes always had the advantage except when they became separated and several Japs could attack a stray Mustang."

The group reported four Mustangs damaged in the fight, and Capt John W. Benbow, 457th FS operations officers, was lost. Members of Capt Benbow's flight did not see him get hit in the dogfight, and thought his P-51 may have been damaged by debris flying off a Japanese airplane shot down by the "Green Flight" leader, Capt William B. Lawrence. Subsequent research suggests, however, that Benbow was almost certainly shot down by a Ki-100 flown by one-legged Japanese ace Maj Yohei Hinoki, who was an instructor at the JAAF's Akeno Flying School. Hinoki would survive the war with at least 12 kills to his credit.

For the loss of Capt Benbow, the "Sun Setters" claimed 25 confirmed victories, two probable victories and 18 aircraft damaged on July 16. One of the 506th FG pilots claiming his first kills of the war that day was Capt Abner M. Aust Jr, a flight commander in the 457th FS. This was his report of the action:

I was leading "Blue Flight" in the second section of our squadron in the Nagoya area when six bogeys were called out at "nine o'clock low." I called my section to drop their tanks, and we peeled off low on a flight of six "Franks." I made almost a head-on pass at their "Number One" man, and gave him a two- or three-second squirt around the cockpit before he broke away to his right. As I turned with him, and left, I was almost on top of another Jap fighter. I split-essed with him and got hits with a three-second burst around the engine and cockpit area. After I passed him, my flight saw him bail out.

As I pulled up, another "Frank" was almost in front of me, and when I closed in on him he split-essed and I followed him. I was getting hits all the way through, and I finished up with a burst into the cockpit. I believe that I killed the pilot, because he went straight into the clouds. As I pulled up another was coming at me almost head-on. I fired a burst into his engine, and he split-essed and I followed. I closed in on him and got hits in his right wing root and cockpit. He started smoking and burning in the right wing and fuselage as he went straight into the clouds.

We pulled off this one and I was almost behind another. As I closed in, he split-essed and I followed him as he went into a dive. I got hits in the root of the left wing, and before he went into the clouds I saw smoke coming out of the wing. I fired all my remaining ammunition at him and followed him down into the clouds to about 2,000ft and then pulled up because we were doing about 350–375mph and the elevation of the ground was about 1,000ft. He was going almost straight down, and made no move to shake us. I didn't believe he could have pulled out.

In this, the "Sun Setters'" last big air battle of the war, Aust was top scorer with three Ki-84s confirmed destroyed and three damaged. Three days later, on July 19, VII Fighter Command tallied nine more kills, but their one pilot lost was Lt Col Jack Thomas, 15th FG commander. Ever aggressive, Thomas was diving straight down in his attempt to strafe a bomber on Kagamigahara Airfield when his Mustang entered compressibility and shed its wings, carrying the veteran "Pineapple" pilot to his death.

A few days later, Lt Col John Mitchell was appointed the new CO of the 15th FG. Only one more Japanese aircraft was shot down during the rest of the month, although missions were flown on July 20, 22, 24, 28 and 30. During the course of these missions, seven more "Sun Setter" pilots were killed and one was taken prisoner.

In mid-July, a new fighter type began to appear in the skies around Iwo Jima with the arrival of the P-47N-equipped 414th FG. Sharing Central Field with the 21st FG, the 414th initially flew Combat Air Patrol missions in the Iwo vicinity and graduated to Chichi Jima strikes before mounting its first VLR mission on August 1.

The mission was supposed to be the first four-group strike by VII Fighter Command, but bad weather at Iwo prevented the 15th and 506th FGs from taking off. Following the 21st FG, 21 Thunderbolts of the 414th FG strafed installations on Okazaki and Nagoya East airfields, losing one P-47 and pilot in the process. The 414th FG completed two more VLR missions before the end of the war, and one of its pilots shot down a Ki-46 reconnaissance aircraft while on CAP near Iwo on August 4.

ON TO VICTORY

News of the nuclear explosion that leveled Hiroshima on August 6, 1945 caught everyone by surprise on Iwo Jima. Sure, there were rumors that America was developing a super bomb like that, but no one really knew anything about it. As far as the "Sun Setter" pilots had been concerned prior to then, their overriding wish was to complete the 15 VLR missions that would earn them a ticket home. And if they were smart, they were hoping to finish their tours before the actual invasion of Japan started. Now there was reason to expect the Japanese to throw in the towel at any moment.

But the enemy did not collapse immediately, so the "Sun Setters" continued flying missions to Japan. After hitting airfields in the Tokyo area on August 2, 3, 5 and 6, and losing eight pilots in the process, VII Fighter Command put up an escort mission to Tokogawa on August 7 and struck airfields at Osaka 24 hours later, losing three more pilots and six P-51s to ground fire. In these six missions, just one enemy aircraft had been shot down.

The last encounter with Japanese fighters came on August 10, when the 15th and 506th FGs were assigned to escort B-29s to Tokyo. Among the seven victories credited to the "Sun Setters" was one to Maj "Todd" Moore of the 45th FS, bringing the ace's victory total to 12, and two to Capt Abner Aust of the 457th FS, making him the 506th's only ace, and the last pilot of VII Fighter Command to tally five or more victories.

All four fighter groups headed for Japan on August 14 for what would be their last combat mission of the war. 1Lt J. W. "Bill" Bradbury of the 72nd FS recalled that the mission was postponed for two days while surrender negotiations were underway before VII Fighter Command was finally ordered to fly. He recalled the mission:

> We arrived off the coast of Honshu and joined the bomber stream to escort them over their target. They dropped their bombs, and we went back out over the ocean to join our three (navigator) B-29s. As we joined them and started flying back to Iwo Jima, one of the B-29s had picked up radio transmissions and came on the air saying, "Hey fellows, the war's over." I remember someone punching their mike button and replying, "Well the Japs sure as hell don't know it." He was referring to all the flak that was put up over the target against the bombers. We took about three and a half hours to fly back to Iwo Jima and landed. Sure enough, the war was over.

As best can be determined 60 years after the fact, at the cessation of hostilities VII Fighter Command had run up a score of 452 Japanese aircraft destroyed in the air and on the ground. Countless other ground targets had also been attacked during strafing missions. VII Fighter Command had paid a high price for this success, however, as 130 Mustangs were lost and 121 men killed or captured, including the victims of the March 26 banzai raid. But not a single "Sun Setter" would say the sacrifice was not worth the final reward of victory in the Pacific.

For the next two weeks flying was restricted to the local area around Iwo Jima, as everyone awaited word of the actual signing of the peace agreement. Then on August 31 the "Sun Setters" were assigned a final VLR mission to Japan – a "Display of Power" flight over Japan, led by Col Harper of the 506th FG. Few were eager to risk another long haul over the Pacific, and sure enough one pilot, 1Lt William S. Hetland of the 457th FS, experienced engine trouble over the target area. Fortunately, Hetland made a safe landing at Atsugi Airfield and returned to Iwo aboard a C-46.

On September 2, Brig Gen "Mickey" Moore boarded an LB-30 Liberator transport with orders reassigning him to the Pentagon. Within a week, the most veteran pilots and ground personnel began getting their tickets home as well. VII Fighter Command began shrinking rapidly, and in October pre-separation lectures were instituted for the men.

Late in the year, the headquarters was moved to Guam and redesignated the 20th FW. The 506th FG was deactivated in mid-November and its remaining personnel transferred to the 21st FG, while the 15th FG was transferred to Hawaii for deactivation. The 21st FG finally transferred to Saipan in the final weeks of 1945 and then moved to Guam, where it was redesignated the 23rd FG in October 1946.

Between 1952 and 1955, all three VLR groups were reactivated as USAF fighter wings. The 506th Tactical Fighter Wing was inactivated for good in 1959, however, although the other two – now the 15th Airbase Wing and the 21st Space Wing – at present continue to serve their nation.

And what became of the stinky, depressing and dangerous island of Iwo Jima? American forces continued to serve on Iwo for many years after the armistice. Central Field, formerly home of the 21st FG, was maintained and expanded, while the other two runways were abandoned and allowed to be taken back by nature. American servicemen could still find the bones of Japanese soldiers in Iwo's caves into the early 1950s, and the Marine Corps occasionally used the island to conduct combat exercises. The US Coast Guard established a LORAN (LOng RAnge Navigation) station there as well.

According to recently uncovered information, the US stored nuclear weapons on Iwo Jima (and Chichi Jima) from 1956 until 1966. Then in June 1968 the Bonin and Volcano islands were returned to Japan, becoming part of Ogasawara village in the Tokyo

Metropolitan Prefecture. The Japanese Self-Defense Force has used Iwo Jima as a patrol and rescue base ever since.

In 1995, the Japanese government allowed a small delegation of Americans to visit the island for a remembrance ceremony marking the 50th anniversary of the historic events that took place there during World War II.

APPENDICES

354TH FIGHTER GROUP

APPENDIX 1

354TH FG ACES

Name	Sqn	Score
Lt William Y. Anderson	353	7
Capt Richard W. Asbury	356	5
Capt Don M. Beerbower	353	15.5
Lt Carl G. Bickel	353	5.5
Lt Edward E. Bickford	356	5.5
Lt Col Jack T. Bradley	353, HQ	15
Maj Lowell K. Brueland	355	12.5
Lt Bruce W. Carr	353	15
Capt Kenneth H. Dahlberg	353	14
Maj James B. Dalglish	355, 353	9
Maj Glenn T. Eagleston	353	18.5
Capt Warren S. Emerson	355	6
Capt Wallace N. Emmer	353	14
Capt Harry E. Fisk	356	5
Lt Carl M. Frantz	353	11
Lt Robert E. Goodnight	356	7.25
Capt Clayton K. Gross	355	6
Lt Charles E. Gumm Jr	355	6
Lt Ivan S. Hasek Jr	353	5
Col James H. Howard	356, HQ	8.3*
Lt Edward E. Hunt	353	6.5
Lt William B. King	355	5.5
Lt Charles W. Koenig	353	6.5
Maj George Max Lamb	356	7.5
Capt Charles W. Lasko	355	7.5
Capt Maurice G. Long	355	5.5
Col Kenneth R. Martin	HQ	5
Lt Don McDowell	353	8.5
Lt Thomas F. Miller	356	5.25

Capt Frank Q. O'Connor	356	10.75
Lt Loyd J Overfield	353	11
Lt Robert Reynolds	353	7
Lt Andrew J Ritchey	353	5
Capt Felix M Rogers	353	7
Lt Franklin Rose Jr	353	5
Lt Henry S. Rudolph	353	5
Lt Robert L. Shoup	356	5.5
Lt William J. Simmons	355	6
Maj Robert W. Stephens	355, HQ	13
Maj Gilbert F. Talbot	355	5
Lt Col Richard E. Turner	356	11
Capt Jack A. Warner	356	5
Lt Robert D. Welden	356	6.25
Lt Kenneth Wise	353	5

*includes 3 kills scored with the AVG

APPENDIX 2

354TH FG BASES

Hamilton Field, California	November 25, 1942 to January 18, 1943
Tonopah, Nevada	January 18, 1943 to March 1, 1943
Santa Rosa Field, California	March 1, 1943 to June 2, 1943
Portland, Oregon	June 2, 1943 to October 1943
Greenham Common, England	November 2, 1943 to November 13, 1943
Boxted, England	November 13, 1943 to April 17, 1944
Lashenden, England	April 17, 1944 to June 22, 1944
Criqueville, France (A-2)	June 22, 1944 to August 13, 1944
Gael, France (A-31)	August 13, 1944 to September 18, 1944
Orconte, France (A-66)	September 18, 1944 to November 13, 1944
Perthes, France (A-65)	November 13, 1944 to December 1, 1944
Rosiéres-en-Haye, France (A-98)	December 1, 1944 to April 8, 1945
Ober Olm, Germany (Y-64)	April 8, 1945 to April 30, 1945
Ansbach, Germany (R-45)	April 30, 1945 to May 15, 1945
Herzogenaurach (R-29)	May 15, 1945 to end of war

APPENDIX 3

354TH FG GROUP/SQUADRON COMMANDERS

Group Commanders

Col Kenneth R. Martin	November 26, 1942 to February 12, 1944
Col James H. Howard	February 12, 1944 to April 12, 1944
Col George R. Bickell	April 12, 1944 to May 1945
Lt Col Jack T. Bradley	May 1945 to end of war

Squadron Commanders
353rd FS

Maj Owen M. Seaman	November 26, 1942 to December 26, 1943
Capt Richard A. Priser	December 26, 1943 to January 25, 1944
Capt Jack T. Bradley	January 26, 1944 to June 30, 1944
Capt Don M. Beerbower	June 30, 1944 to August 9, 1944
Capt Wallace N. Emmer	August 9, 1944 to August 9, 1944
Capt Felix M. Rogers	August 9, 1944 to October 1, 1944
Maj Jack T. Bradley	October 1, 1944 to October 26, 1944
Capt Glenn T. Eagleston	October 26, 1944 to end of war

355th FS

Capt George R. Bickell	November 26, 1942 to April 12, 1944
Capt Robert W. Stephens	April 12, 1944 to September 1944
Maj Maurice G. Long	September 1944 to October 19, 1944
Maj Marshall Cloke	October 19, 1944 to February 26, 1945
Maj Gilbert F. Talbot	February 26, 1945 to end of war

356th FS

Capt Charles C. Johnson	November 17, 1942 to February 10, 1943
Capt Richard D. Neece	February 10, 1943 to May 24, 1943
Capt James H. Howard	May 24, 1943 to February 12, 1944
Capt Richard E. Turner	February 12, 1944 to October 7, 1944
Maj Robert Brooks	October 7, 1944 to October 20, 1944
Maj Frank Q. O'Connor	October 20, 1944 to November 7, 1944
Maj Earl G. Depner	November 7, 1944 to end of war

332ND FIGHTER GROUP

APPENDIX 1

AERIAL VICTORIES OF THE 99TH FS AND 332ND FG

	Kills	Probables	Damaged	Types (total)
99th FS	34	5.5	13	Fw 190 (20), Bf 109 (13), C.205 (1)
100th FS	24	0	2	Bf 109 (15), Fw 190 (5), Me 262 (3), Re.2001 (1)
301st FS	32	2	6	Bf 109 (22), Fw 190 (10)
302nd FS	29	1	6	Bf 109 (23), Fw 190 (2), He 111 (3), C.205 (1)
Total	119	8.5	27	Bf 109 (73), Fw 190 (37), Me 262 (3), He 111 (3), C.205 (2), Re.2001 (1)

APPENDIX 2

PILOTS WITH MULTIPLE CONFIRMED AERIAL KILLS

Lee Archer, 302nd	5 (5 Bf 109s)
Edward Toppins, 99th	4 (2 Bf 109s and 2 Fw 190s)
Joseph Elsberry, 301st	4 (3 Fw 109s and 1 Bf 109)
Charles Hall, 99th	3 (2 Fw 190s and 1 Bf 109)
Wendell Pruitt, 302nd	3 (2 Bf 109s and 1 He 111)
Roger Romine, 302nd	3 (3 Bf 109s)
Leonard Jackson, 99th	3 (2 Bf 109s and 1 Fw 190)
Clarence Lester, 100th	3 (3 Bf 109s)
Harry Stewart, 301st	3 (3 Bf 109s)
William Green, 302nd	2.5 (1 C.205, 1 He 111 and 0.5 Bf 109)
Luke Weathers, 302nd	2.5 (2.5 Bf 109s)
Roscoe Brown, 100th	2 (1 Me 262 and 1 Bf 109)
Carl Carey, 301st	2 (2 Bf 109s)
Robert Diez, 99th	2 (2 Fw 190s)
Wilson Eagleson, 99th	2 (2 Fw 190s)
John Edwards, 301st	2 (2 Bf 109s)
Frederick Funderburg, 301st	2 (2 Bf 109s)
Edward Gleed, 302nd	2 (2 Fw 190s)
Alfred Gorham, 301st	2 (2 Fw 190s)
Jack Holsclaw, 100th	2 (2 Bf 109s)
Thomas Jefferson, 301st	2 (2 Bf 109s)
Jimmy Lanham, 301st	2 (2 Bf 109s)
Luther Smith, 302nd	2 (1 Bf 109 and1 He 111)
Charles White, 301st	2 (2 Bf 109s)
Robert Williams, 301st	2 (2 Fw 190s)

475TH FIGHTER GROUP

APPENDIX 1

VICTORIES SCORED BY THE 475TH FG

Headquarters	43
431st Fighter Squadron	221
432nd Fighter Squadron	167
433rd Fighter Squadron	121
Total	**552**

APPENDIX 2

475TH FIGHTER GROUP FIGHTER ACES

Maj Thomas B. McGuire (431st FS and HQ)	38†
Col Charles H. MacDonald (HQ)	27
Capt Daniel T. Roberts (432nd and 433rd FSs)	14(4)†
Capt Francis Lent (431st FS)	11†
Lt Col John S. Loisel (432nd FS and HQ)	11
Capt Elliot Summer (432nd FS)	10
Capt Fredric F. Champlin (431st FS)	9
Capt Perry J. Dahl (432nd FS)	9
Capt Joseph M. Forster (432nd FS)	9
Lt Col Meryl M. Smith (HQ)	9†
1Lt David W. Allen (431st FS)	8(2)
Capt Frederick A. Harris (432nd FS)	8†
Capt Kenneth F. Hart (431st FS)	8
1Lt Zach W. Dean (432nd FS)	7
1Lt Vincent T. Elliott (431st FS)	7
Capt Jack A. Fisk (433rd FS)	7
Capt Verl A. Jett (431st FS)	7(1)
Maj Warren R. Lewis (431st and 433rd FSs)	7
Capt John E. Purdy (433rd FS)	7
Maj Calvin C. Wire (433rd FS)	7
1Lt Edward J. Czarnecki (431st FS)	6
Capt Billy M. Gresham (432nd FS)	6†
Capt James C. Ince (432nd FS)	6(2)
Capt Paul W. Lucas (432nd FS)	6†
2Lt John C. Smith (433rd FS)	6†
Capt Horace B. Reeves (431st FS)	6
Capt Joseph A. McKeon (433rd FS)	6(2)
Capt Arthur E. Wenige (431st FS)	6(1)
Capt Harry W. Brown (431st FS)	6(2)
Capt Henry L. Condon (432nd FS)	5†
Capt Grover D. Gholson (432nd FS)	5(1)
1Lt Marion F. Kirby (431st FS)	5

1Lt Lowell C. Lutton (431st FS)		5†	
Capt Jack C. Mankin (431st FS)		5(1)	
1Lt Frank H. Monk (431st FS)		5	
Capt Paul V. Morriss (431st FS)		5	
Maj Franklin A. Nichols (431st FS)		5(4)	
Capt John A. Tilley (431st FS)		5	

() – indicates victories scored with other units
† – killed in action/flying accident

APPENDIX 3

475TH FIGHTER GROUP CASUALTIES

Name	Unit	Date	Remarks
Lt Richard E. Dotson	431st	July 5, 1943	killed in training crash
Lt Andrew K. Duke	431st	August 9, 1943	killed in flying accident
Lt Ralph E. Schmidt	431st	August 18, 1943	killed in action
Lt Allen Camp	432nd	August 20, 1943	killed in flying accident
Lt Richard Ryrholm	432nd	September 4, 1943	missing in action (later changed to killed in action)
Lt Chester D. Phillips	432nd	September 8, 1943	missing in action
Lt John C. Knox	431st	September 13, 1943	killed in action
Lt Noel R. Lundy	432nd	September 13, 1943	declared killed in action on 18 January 1944
Lt Donald Garrison	432nd	September 22, 1943	killed in action
Lt Raymond Corrigan	433rd	September 24, 1943	killed in action
Lt Kenneth D. Kirshner	433rd	September 24, 1943	PoW, and later died in captivity
Lt Virgil F. Hagan	433rd	October 17, 1943	killed in action
? Edward Hedrick	431st	October 17, 1943	killed in action
Lt Edward Czarnecki	431st	October 23, 1943	shot down and rescued, but died in 1976 after years of illness with tropical disease contracted in North Borneo
Lt Christopher Bartlett	432nd	October 29, 1943	shot down and hidden by local villagers until Japanese informed of his position by German missionary and captured, then executed
Capt Fredrick A. Harris	432nd	October 31, 1943	killed in flying accident
Lt Kenneth M. Richardson	431st	November 2, 1943	killed in action
Lt Lowell C. Lutton	431st	November 2, 1943	killed in action
Lt Leo M. Mayo	432nd	November 2, 1943	missing in action (later changed to killed in action)
Lt Donald Y. King	433rd	November 2, 1943	killed in action
Lt Paul Smith	431st	November 8, 1943	missing in action
Lt John Smith	433rd	November 9, 1943	killed in action
Capt Daniel T. Roberts	433rd	November 9, 1943	killed in action
Lt Dale O. Meyer	433rd	November 9, 1943	killed in action
Lt Theodore Fostakowski	431st	November 15, 1943	killed in flying accident

Lt Robert J. Smith	431st	November 16, 1943	missing in action
Lt Ormand E. Powell	431st	December 28, 1943	missing in action
Lt John E. Fogarty	432nd	January 13, 1944	killed in flying accident
Lt Richard Hancock	433rd	January 16, 1944	missing in action (body subsequently recovered and interred in Fort Bonifacio cemetery in the Philippines)
Lt William Ritter	432nd	January 18, 1944	PoW, then executed
Lt John R. Weldon	431st	January 18, 1944	missing in action
Lt Joseph A. Robertson	431st	January 18, 1944	killed in action
Lt McCleod Jones	431st	January 21, 1944	posted missing whilst co-pilot of B-25 on detached service
Lt Martin J. Hawthorne	431st	January 22, 1944	killed in flying accident
Lt Carl A. Danforth	433rd	January 23, 1944	missing in action
Lt Donald D. Revenaugh	433rd	January 23, 1944	missing in action
Lt Wood D. Clodfelter	431st	February 14, 1944	killed in flying accident
Lt Harold Howard	432nd	February 29, 1944	killed in flying accident
Lt Robert P. Donald	431st	March 31, 1944	killed in action
Flt Off Joe B. Barton	432nd	April 3, 1944	killed in action
Lt Jack F. Luddington	431st	April 16, 1944	missing in action
Lt Milton A. MacDonald	431st	April 16, 1944	missing in action
Lt Robert L. Hubner	432nd	April 16, 1944	missing in action
Lt Louis L. Longman	433rd	April 16, 1944	missing in action
Lt Austin K. Neely	433rd	April 16, 1944	missing in action
Lt Louis M. Yarbrough	433rd	April 16, 1944	missing in action
Lt Troy L. Martin	432nd	June 11, 1944	killed in flying accident
Lt Howard V. Stiles	433rd	June 16, 1944	missing in action
Lt Robert L. Crosswait	431st	June 30, 1944	missing in action
Lt William A. Elliot	432nd	July 28, 1944	missing in action
Capt William S. O'Brien	431st	August 4, 1944	killed in action
Lt Nathaniel V. Landen	431st	September 19. 1944	killed in action
Lt Walter W. Weisfus	432nd	September 24, 1944	killed in flying accident (in P-39)
Lt Charles H. Joseph	433rd	October 1, 1944	killed in flying accident
Capt Billy M. Gresham	432nd	October 2, 1944	killed in flying accident
Lt Donald W. Patterson	431st	October 13, 1944	killed in flying accident
Lt Arnold R. Neilson	431st	November 2, 1944	killed in flying accident
Lt Grady M. Laseter	432nd	November 10, 1944	killed in action
Lt Erland J. Varland	431st	November 24, 1944	missing in action
Lt Morton B. Ryerson	433rd	December 6, 1944	killed in action
Lt Col Meryl M. Smith	HQ	December 7, 1944	killed in action
Lt Robert H. Koeck	431st	December 25, 1944	killed in action
Lt Enrique Provencio	431st	December 25, 1944	killed in action
Lt Clifford L. Ettien	433rd	December 31, 1944	killed in action
Capt Henry L. Condon II	432nd	January 2, 1945	killed in action
Maj Thomas B. McGuire	431st	January 7, 1945	killed in action
Maj Jack B. Rittmayer	431st	January 7, 1945	killed in action
Capt Paul W. Lucas	432nd	January 16, 1945	killed in action
Lt Robert Patterson	431st	January 29, 1945	missing in action
Flt Off Charles C. Nacke	432nd	January 29, 1945	missing in action

Lt Arthur J. Schmidt	431st	February 15, 1945	missing in action
Flt Off Charles R. DeWeese	433rd	March 28, 1945	killed in action
Lt Wesley J. Hulett	433rd	March 28, 1945	killed in action
Lt Laverne P. Busch	433rd	April 2, 1945	recovered, but died from injuries on 5 April 1945
Lt Reed L. Pietscher	432nd	April 15, 1945	killed in action
Lt Millard R. Sherman	431st	May 30, 1945	killed in action
Lt Alvin G. Roth	431st	June 18, 1945	killed in action
Lt Edward Carley	431st	June 18, 1945	killed in action
Lt Herbert S. Finney	431st	June 21, 1945	killed in flying accident
Lt Charles C. Zarling	433rd	July 8, 1945	killed in flying accident
Capt George W. Smith	HQ	July 11, 1945	killed in flying accident

Also, on February 22, 1945 a runaway P-47 careered into the 433rd FS flightline, killing crew chiefs SSgt Charles Huff, Sgt Edward J. Hamilton and Cpl William E. Maddock

15TH, 21ST AND 506TH FIGHTER GROUPS

APPENDIX 1

VLR UNIT COMMANDERS

VII Fighter Command

Brig Gen Ernest M. "Mickey" Moore	1944 to end of war

15th FG

Col James O. Beckwith Jr	March 5, 1943 to April 15, 1945
Lt Col DeWitt Spain	April 15, 1945 to May 15, 1945
Lt Col Julian E. Thomas	May 15, 1945 to July 19, 1945 (killed in action)
Lt Col John W. Mitchell	July 19, 1945 to end of war

45th FS

Maj Gilmer L. Snipes	April 4, 1944 to April 16, 1945
Maj Arthur M. Bridge	April 16, 1945 to June 3, 1945
Capt Harold D. Collins	June 4, 1945 to July 18, 1945
Maj Robert W. "Todd" Moore	July 19, 1945 to end of war

47th FS

Maj John A. Piper	November 7, 1944 to May 26, 1945
Maj Theon E. "Ed" Markham	May 26, 1945 to June 11, 1945
Capt Walter H. Powell	June 11, 1945 to July 30, 1945 (killed in action)
Capt Ernest W. Hostetler	July 30, 1945 to August 4, 1945
Maj Theon E. "Ed" Markham	August 5, 1945 to end of war

78th FS

Maj James M. Vande Hey	April 14, 1944 to April 16, 1945
Maj James B. Tapp	April 16, 1945 to June 16, 1945
Capt Joe Fitzsimmons	June 16, 1945 to August 5, 1945
Maj James B. Tapp	August 6, 1945 to end of war

21st FG

Col Kenneth R. Powell	April 21, 1944 to June 14, 1945
Lt Col Charles E. Taylor	June 14, 1945 to end of war

46th FS

Maj Fred A. Shirley	November 20, 1944 to May 1945
Maj Benjamin C. Warren	May 1945 to June 1945
Maj Robert L. McDonald	July 1945 to end of war

72nd FS

Maj Paul W. Imig	1944 to May 1945
Maj James C. Van Nada	May 1945 to end of war

531st FS

| Maj John S. "Sam" Hudson | April 15, 1944 to March 26, 1945 (wounded in action) |
| Maj Harry C. Crim Jr | March 31, 1945 to end of war |

506th FG

| Col Bryan B. Harper | October 1944 to end of war |

457th FS

| Maj Malcolm C. Watters | October 1944 to June 1, 1945 |
| Maj Daun G. Anthony | June 2, 1945 to end of war |

458th FS

| Maj Harrison Shipman | October 1944 to end of war |

462nd FS

| Maj Thomas D. DeJarnette | October 1944 to end of war |

APPENDIX 2

AERIAL CLAIMS

VII Fighter Command

| Lt Col Robert J. Rodgers | 0-0-0.5 |
| Maj Howard D. Sutterlin | 2.5-0-0 |

15th FG

Lt Col John W. Mitchell	3-0-0 (plus 8 kills with 339th FS in 1942-43 and 4 kills with 39th FIS/51st FIW in 1953)
Lt Col Julian E. "Jack" Thomas	1-0-1
Maj Wayne L. Wells	3-0-1

45th FS

Capt Arthur H. Bridge	0-0.5-0.5
1Lt Wesley E. Brown	2-0-0
2Lt Arthur A. Burry	0-0-0.5
Capt Bruce S. Campbell Jr	2-0-0
Capt Harold D. Collins	1-0-1
1Lt Frederick C. Condon	1-0-0.5
1Lt Ceil A. Dennis	0-0-0.5
1Lt George H. Dunlap	1-0-0.5
1Lt Lloyd C. Edwards	0.5-0-0
Capt Francis L. Ennis	0.5-0-0.5
1Lt William J. Farrell	1-0-0

2Lt Walter Harrigan	0-0.5-0
1Lt Fred H. 'Herb' Henderson Jr	1-0.5-0.333
1Lt William H. Hodgins	1-0-0
Capt George H. Hunter Jr	1.5-1-0
1Lt John E. Kester	1-0-0
Capt William L. Kester	0-0-0.33 (plus 1.5 kills with 44th FS in 1943)
Capt Morton M. Knox	1-0-0 (plus 1 kill on 26/1/44)
Capt Albert E. Maltby	1-0-0 (plus 1 probable on 26/1/44)
Capt Robert W. "Todd" Moore	11-1-1 (also with 78th FS, plus 1 kill in 1/44)
2Lt William W. Redus	0-0.5-0
2Lt C. Douglas Reese	2-0-0
2Lt Vincent V. Reinert	0-0.5-0
1Lt Gerhard C. Rettburg	0-1-0
1Lt Joseph G. Richins	1-0-0
1Lt Alvan E. Roberts	0.5-0-0
Flt Off Billy J. Singleton	0.5-0-0
1Lt Jay W. Slater	1.5-2-0
Maj Gilmer L. Snipes	1-1-0 (plus 1 kill in 10/43)
1Lt William H. Sparks	0.5-0-0
1Lt Donald E. Statsman	3-0.5-0.333
2Lt Robert M. Thornton	0-0-1
1Lt Joe D. Walker	1-1-2
2Lt Leroy E. Yakish	0.5-0-0

47th FS

Maj Truman F. Anderson	1-0-0
1Lt Frank L. Ayres	1-1-0
1Lt Harold L. Baccus	1-0-2
1Lt Bernard P. Bjorseth	0.5-0-0.5
1Lt Eurich L. Bright	3.5-0-0
2Lt Robert C. Burnett	1-0-0
1Lt Charles J. Cameron	2-1-0
1Lt Richard J. Condrick	1-0-1
Capt Robert R. Down	1.5-0-0
2Lt Andrew C. Elliott	0-0-1
Flt Off John W. Googe	0-0-1
1Lt Fred T. Grover	3.5-0-0
1Lt Richard H. Hintermeier	2.5-0-0 (plus 1 kill with 45th FS in 1/44)
Flt Off Fronnie A. Jones Jr	1-0-0
1Lt Roy E. June	0.5-0-0.5
Maj Emmett L. Kearney Jr	2.5-0-0
Capt Theon E. Markham	2.5-0-0
1Lt Joseph A. McCormick	0-0-1.5
1Lt George N. Metcalf	1-0-0
1Lt Jules C. Mitchell	1-0-0
1Lt Stanley A. Moore	0-0-1
2Lt Albert G. Olivier Jr	0-0-1.5
1Lt Oliver E. O'Mara Jr	0.5-0-2
1Lt George C. Petrouleas	0.5-0-0
Maj John A. Piper	0.5-0-0
Flt Off Harold E. Powell	0-0-0.5
Capt Walter H. Powell	1-1-0
1Lt Warren G. Reed Jr	1-1-0
1Lt Henry C. Ryniker	0.5-0-0
1Lt Robert S. Scamara	4-1-6
1Lt ? Stelling	0-0-0.5
1Lt Harry M. Tyler	1-0-0
2Lt Robert A. Worton	4-0-0

78th FS

1Lt Frederick A. Bauman	1-0-0
1Lt Doyle T. Brooks	2-0-1
1Lt Robert Carey	1-0-1
1Lt Robert Carr	0.5-0-0
1Lt Robert C. Coryell	2-0-0
1Lt Richard D. Duerr	1-0-2
Capt Joe Fitzsimmons	1.5-0-0
2Lt James F. Hawkins	0-0.5-0
1Lt Walter W. Kreimann	1-0-0
1Lt Philip J. Maher	1-1-0
1Lt Paul A. Martin	0-1-0
2Lt Daniel Mathis	0.5-0-0
2Lt Thomas L. McCullough	1.5-0-0
Capt Nelson P. Merrill Jr	1-0.5-1

Capt Victor K. Mollan	1.5-0-0
1Lt Richard Schroeppel	0.5-0-1
1Lt Malcolm M. Sedam	0.5-0-1
1Lt Robert F. Sherbundy	0-1-0
Maj James B. Tapp	8-0-2
Maj James M. Vande Hey	1-0-0 (plus 2 kills with 45th FS in 1/44)
1Lt Robert L. Williams	0.5-0-0
1Lt Jerome Yellin	0.5-1-1

21st FG

Lt Col Elmer E. Booth	0.5-0-0
Maj Charles J. Chapin	1-0-0
Capt Howard J. Kendall	1-0-0

46th FS

1Lt John W. Brock	3-0-1
1Lt Joseph D. Coons	1.5-0-1
1Lt John H. Dunn	0-0-1
2Lt Frank Garcia	1-0-0
Capt J. V. Garnett	0-1-0
1Lt Louis C. Gelbrich	1-0-0
1Lt Judd Hoff	0-0-1
2Lt Billy J. Knauff	0-0-1
1Lt Russell L. Mayhew	0-1-0
1Lt Robert V. Merklein	1-0-0
1Lt Eugene A. Naber	1-0-0
2Lt Gervais R. Nolin	1-1-3
Capt Jack K. Ort	1-0-0
1Lt Walter R. Parsley	1.5-0-0
Capt Charles O. Rainwater	3-0-0
2Lt Morgan R. Redwine	0-0-1
2Lt Burdette F. Robinson	0-0-1
Maj Fred A. Shirley	4-0-0
1Lt Richard L. Vroman	1-0-0
1Lt Paul H. Wine	1-1-0

72nd FS

2Lt Albert J. Allard	1.5-0-1
2Lt James Bradbury	0.5-0-0
2Lt Horace R. Brandenberger	1.5-0-0
Capt Adolf J. Bregar	2-0-0
2Lt Howard C. Brown	1-0-0
1Lt Ritchfield J. S. Cameron	0-0-1
Capt James C. Carlyle	1-1-1.5 (plus 2 kills in 12/43)
1Lt Thomas W. Denman	1.5-1-0
2Lt Chester F. Fitzgerald	0-0-1
1Lt Jacob W. Gotwals Jr	1-0-0
2Lt Claude A. Lane	0-0-1
Capt Ernest S. McDonald	1-0-0

1Lt William E. Merritt	3-0-0
1Lt Harry W. Norton	1-0-0
2Lt Harrison V. Parker	0.5-0-0
2Lt Louis A. Pendergrass	1-0-2
1Lt William A. Robinson	1-0-1
Capt Howard L. Russell	1.5-0-0
2Lt John E. Skripek	1.5-0-0
2Lt Robert S. Starr	1-0-0
2Lt Alfred V. Stuart	3-0-0
Capt James C. Van Nada	1-0-0 (plus 1 kill in 12/43)
Capt Harry E. Walmer	2-0-0
1Lt Horace Wallace	0-0-1

531st FS

2Lt Lloyd L. Bosley	1-0-0
2Lt Jack Counts	1-0-0
Capt Edwind R. Crane	0-0-1.25
Maj Harry C. Crim Jr	6-0-4.25
2Lt Earl D. Crutchfield	0-0.5-0
1Lt Albert B. Davis	1-0-0
1Lt Edward H. Dibble	1-0-0
Capt Theodore H. Fox	1-0-0.25
Flt Off Anthony J. Gance	0-0-1
Capt Vincent A. Gaudiani	0-0-1
Capt Frederick J. Gibson	1-0-0
2Lt Henry J. Koke	1-1-0
2Lt William B. Litcher	0-0-1.5
Capt Robert I. Mallin	1-0-0
Capt Floyd L. Manning	1-0-0 (plus 0.25 kill with 72nd FS in 12/43)
1Lt Wade W. Marsh	1-0-0
Capt Willis E. Mathews	2-2-2.5 (plus 3.5 kills with 94th FS in 1943)
1Lt Conrad E. Mattson	1-0-0
1Lt Floyd E. Rice	0-0.5-0
Flt Off Armand G. Rowley	1-0-0
1Lt Frank L. Seymour	0-0-1
2Lt Roy K. Shoemaker	0-0-1
2Lt Irvin P. Skansen	0-0-1
1Lt Fred H. Sickler Jr	0-0-2
2Lt John D. Thompson	2-1-2
2Lt John M. Tomlinson	0-0-1
2Lt John D. Wilson	2-0-0.25

506th FG

Lt Col Harley Brown	0-0-1
Maj Malcolm C. Watters	2-1-1 (plus 1 kill with 457th FS)

457th FS

1Lt Francis C. Albrecht	1-0-0
Maj Daun G. Anthony	0-0-1
Capt Abner M. Aust Jr	5-0-3
1Lt Thomas W. Carroll	1-0-2
2Lt Walter J. Cawley	0-0-1
Capt Francis B. Clark	0-0-2
2Lt George C. Donnelly	0-0-1
2Lt Ralph S. Gardner	1-0-0.5
2Lt William G. Hetlund	0-0-0.5
2Lt Jackie M. Horner	0-0-1
1Lt William B. Lawrence Jr	1-0-0.5
1Lt Wesley A. Murphey Jr	1-0-1
1Lt Chauncey A. Newcomb	2-0-0
2Lt Clement S. Ross	0-0-1
1Lt Omar K. Skiver	0-0-1.5
2Lt Thomas O. Wessell	0-0-1

458th FS

Capt J. B. Baker Jr	1-1-0
Capt Richard W. Barnes	2-0-0
Capt Francis C. Carmody	1-0-0
1Lt Harold G. Davidson	2-0-0
2Lt Raymond Feld	1-0-0
1Lt Jack A. Kelsey	1-0-0
2Lt Roy E. Kempert	1-0-0
2Lt G. B. Lambert	0-1-0
1Lt Quarterman Lee Jr	1-0-0
1Lt Vance A. Middaugh	1-0-0
1Lt Edward H. Mikes Jr	1-0-0
Capt Peter Nowick	2-0-0
1Lt Max E. Ruble	1-0-0
2Lt Henry J. Seegers Jr	1-0-0
1Lt Vaughan E. Sowers	1-0-0
1Lt Myndret S. Starin	1-0-0
1Lt Evan S. Stuart	2-1-1
2Lt Frank H. Wheeler	2-0-1

462nd FS

1Lt Edward F. Balhorn	0-0-1
1Lt Darrell S. Bash	1-0-0
1Lt Frank C. Buzze	1-0-0
2Lt Allen F. Colley	0-0-1.5
Maj Thomas D. DeJarnette	1-0-0
1Lt Gordon C. Dingee	1-0-0
1Lt William J. Jutras Jr	1-0-0
Capt Francis L. Lee	1-0-0
Capt Norman T. Miller	1-0-1
2Lt James E. Rosebrough	1-0-0
Capt Frederick A. Sullivan	1-0-1
Unspecified flight	1-0-0

INDEX

The rank given for an individual is the highest achieved within the text.